Better Homes and Gardens®
Furniture
PROJECTS

Better Homes and Gardens® Books
Des Moines, Iowa

Better Homes and Gardens® Books
An imprint of Meredith® Books

Furniture Projects
Editor: Christopher Cavanaugh
Contributing Editor: Kay Sanders
Associate Art Director: Lynda Haupert
Contributing Designer: Michael Burns
Copy Chief: Angela K. Renkoski
Contributing Copy Editor: Mary Helen Schiltz
Electronic Production Coordinator: Paula Forest
Production Manager: Douglas Johnston
Prepress Coordinator: Marjorie J. Schenkelberg

Meredith Books
Editor-in-Chief: James D. Blume
Director, New Product Development: Ray Wolf
Vice President, Retail Marketing: Jamie L. Martin

Better Homes and Gardens® Magazine
Editor-in-Chief: Jean LemMon

Meredith Publishing Group
President, Publishing Group: Christopher Little
Vice President and Publishing Director: John P. Loughlin

Meredith Corporation
Chairman of the Board and Chief Executive Officer: Jack D. Rehm
President and Chief Operating Officer: William T. Kerr
Chairman of the Executive Committee: E.T. Meredith III

The projects in this book first appeared in the WOOD® Shop Library
Editor: Benjamin W. Allen
Produced by Cy DeCosse, Inc.

On the cover: Country Cabinet, see page 136

All of us at Better Homes and Gardens Books are dedicated to providing you with information and ideas you need to enhance your home. We welcome your comments and suggestions about this book of furniture projects. Write to us at Better Homes and Gardens Books, Do-It-Yourself Department, RW 240, 1716 Locust Street, Des Moines, IA 50309-3023.

Anyone who loves to work with wood will applaud the 41 furniture projects designed specifically for this book. These pieces of fine furniture will give you enjoyment again and again: You'll savor time in the workshop, experiencing the satisfaction of creating something useful; you'll delight in the finished product; and you'll feel a glow of pride when friends and family shower you with well-earned compliments.

You'll discover a wide variety of projects in *Better Homes and Gardens® Furniture Projects*. There's something for every skill level. Detailed project diagrams, step-by-step directions, and how-to photographs guide beginning woodworkers from step one through to the finishing of a project.

Advanced woodworkers can expect to hone their skills and learn a new technique or two from the tips provided by our experts. There are projects for every room in your house and for every style preference, from an Early American coffee table to a Mission bed, from a traditional barrister's bookcase to a country cabinet.

To ensure your success, each project was checked by woodworking experts. A prototype of every piece of furniture was built by the experts to expose any glitches. Our goal at Better Homes and Gardens® Books is to help you produce gracefully designed, masterfully crafted home furnishings, beautiful enough to be passed from one generation to the next. And, we want you to have fun doing it.

Table of Contents

CHAPTER 1

Tables

Solid Performers

We gather around them for boisterous family meals, formal dinners, and fun-in-the-sun picnics. We use them as work surfaces: to prepare food, play games, and pay bills. They hold lamps, books and magazines, alarm clocks, and photos of loved ones.

Versatile and hardworking, tables are indispensable household furnishings. That doesn't mean they need to look utilitarian. As you'll see here, tables can be pretty as well as practical. This is the place to showcase beautiful woods such as white oak, walnut, ash, cherry, and maple. Use wood stock with exquisite grains for the tabletop or embellish with inlays.

Classically simple or beautifully ornate, a handsome table can become a centerpiece, setting the style for your room. In this chapter, you'll find projects for every room in your house: kitchen or dining room, living room, family room, and bedroom—even the patio or deck.

Coffee Table

The rich walnut inlays and distinctive design make this coffee table a pleasing place to rest your favorite mug.

Coffee tables attract attention, whether they stand at the foot of a comfortable loveseat or nestle into a quiet corner between the sofa and the wall. You spot a coffee table the moment you walk into a room, and you see it every time you pick up a mug or set down a magazine. The coffee table shown here, with its alluring inlays and contemporary design, is one piece of furniture you'll be delighted to see.

We used thin strips of oak and walnut to create the inlaid tabletop that's the most distinguishing feature of our coffee table. The ¼"-thick strips are edge-glued together, then bonded to a plywood tabletop base.

We used oak for the table frame and base, but other hardwoods, like ash or maple, can be used with good results. The inlay strips also can be made from just about any hardwoods you choose, but

the overall effect will be most satisfying if you use the same type of wood for the wider inlay strips as you use in the frame and base.

By reducing the dimensions of our coffee table design, you can create matching end tables to add a strong design element to your living room. Make sure, though, that you retain the square shape. The inlay pattern on a tabletop that is even slightly out of square will lose its symmetry.

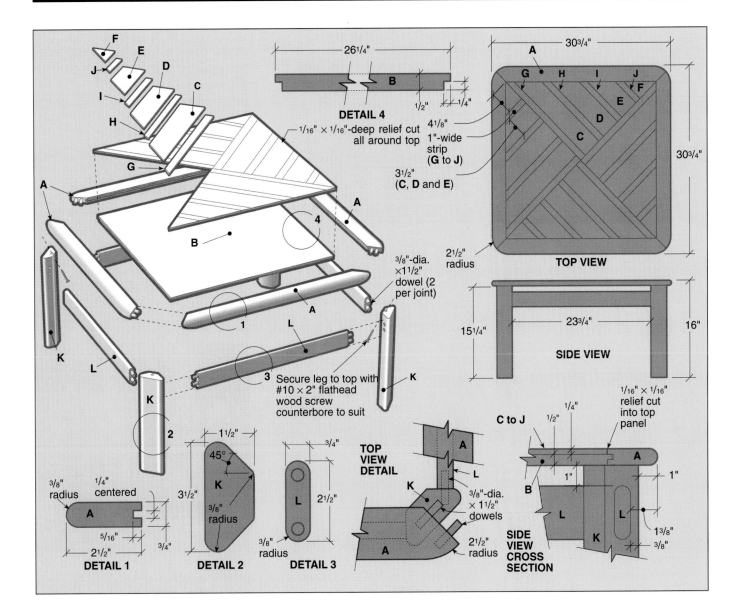

DETAIL 4

1/16" × 1/16"-deep relief cut all around top

4 1/8"
1"-wide strip (**G** to **J**)

3 1/2" (**C**, **D** and **E**)

TOP VIEW

2 1/2" radius

30 3/4"

30 3/4"

SIDE VIEW

15 1/4"   23 3/4"   16"

3/8"-dia. ×1 1/2" dowel (2 per joint)

Secure leg to top with #10 × 2" flathead wood screw counterbore to suit

1/16" × 1/16" relief cut into top panel

C to J

DETAIL 1
3/8" radius   1/4" centered   **A**   5/16"   2 1/2"   3/4"

DETAIL 2
1 1/2"   45°   **K**   3 1/2"   3/8" radius   3/4"

DETAIL 3
3/4"   **L**   2 1/2"   3/8" radius

TOP VIEW DETAIL
A   **K**   **L**   **A**   3/8"-dia. × 1 1/2" dowels   2 1/2" radius

SIDE VIEW CROSS SECTION
1/2"   1/4"   1"   **B**   **L**   **L**   1"   **K**   1 3/8"   3/8"

Making the inlaid tabletop

1 Cut the 1/2"-plywood tabletop base (B). Oversize the panel by about 2" in both dimensions.

Resaw guide

2 Select a piece of oak stock that has consistent color and grain pattern on all sides, then rip it into blocks 3 3/4" in width, using your tablesaw with a combination planer blade (50 teeth). Resaw the blocks to a thickness of 9/32", using a bandsaw with a 1/2" blade.
3 Select a piece of walnut stock and rip it into 1 1/4" strips on your tablesaw. Resaw the walnut strips to a thickness of 9/32".
4 Joint the oak inlays to 3 1/2" width and the walnut inlays to 1" width, then trim the inlays to 1/4" thickness on your planer.
5 Draw diagonal reference lines from corner to corner on the tabletop base to use for arranging the inlay pieces.
6 Miter-cut one end of each inlay strip at a 45° angle. NOTE: The 45° angle allows you to use a 45° clamping jig (see *step 10*) to exert even side-to-side pressure on the inlay pieces after they're edge-glued into quadrants.

CUTTING LIST

Key	Qty.	Description & Size
A	4	**Oak frame,** 3/4 × 2 1/2 × 30 3/4"
B	1	**Plywood tabletop base,** 1/2 × 26 1/4 × 26 1/4"
C	4	**Oak inlay,** 1/4 × 3 1/2 × 17 5/8"
D	4	**Oak inlay,** 1/4 × 3 1/2 × 13 1/8"
E	4	**Oak inlay,** 1/4 × 3 1/2 × 8 5/8"
F	4	**Oak inlay,** 1/4 × 3 1/2 × 4 1/8"
G	4	**Walnut inlay,** 1/4 × 1 × 18 5/8"
H	4	**Walnut inlay,** 1/4 × 1 × 14 1/8"
I	4	**Walnut inlay,** 1/4 × 1 × 9 5/8"
J	4	**Walnut inlay,** 1/4 × 1 × 5 1/8"
K	4	**Oak leg,** 1 1/2 × 3 1/2 × 15 1/4"
L	4	**Oak rail,** 3/4 × 2 1/2 × 23 3/4"

Note: All inlay pieces are oversized in length to allow for waste.

Misc.: Glue, 3/8" dowels, #10 × 2" flathead wood screws.

7 Arrange the long walnut inlays (G) with the square ends fitted into each corner formed by the diagonal lines (see pattern in *Diagram*).

8 Dry-fit all the remaining inlay pieces around the long walnut strips in the sequence G, C, H, D, I, E, J, F. Once the pattern is set, remove the pieces, one at a time, marking the position of each piece as you remove it.

9 Place a sheet of wax paper over the tabletop base, then reassemble the inlay pieces for one quadrant. Apply glue to each mating edge, then edge-glue the inlay pieces together in the proper position. Lightly clamp the square end of the assembly with a small bar clamp and protective wood scraps at each clamp jaw.

10 Make 45° clamping jigs for clamping the mitered end of the quadrants. To make 45° clamping jigs, gather a few wood scraps the same thickness as the workpieces, and trim one edge at a 45° angle. Hot-glue the jigs to the top and the center of the mitered end of the glued section, preferably so the jigs span at least one joint, and apply bar clamps.

11 Arrange, edge-glue, and clamp the remaining three quadrants. Do not remove the clamps until you are ready to glue the pieces to the plywood tabletop base.

WOODWORKER'S TIP

When edge-gluing thin materials or veneer, it's important to put even pressure on the edge-glued pieces as they dry. Rather than using hold-down clamps, try setting a clean sand bag or a sturdy bag of flour on the glued-up sections.

Guard removed for clarity — **Final trim line**

12 Remove the clamps, then carefully cut a straight edge on the square end of each edge-glued section, using your tablesaw and miter gauge or panel cutting jig.

13 Surface-glue one inlay section to the tabletop base using the diagonals as a guide. Apply a thin coat of carpenter's glue to the section and the base, using a brush. After the first inlay section is set, glue down the remaining sections.

14 Weight the surfaces to apply pressure as the glue dries. Let the glue dry completely (at least three days) before you trim and finish the tabletop.

15 After the glue has dried thoroughly, sand the inlaid top until all the joints are smooth, using fine-grit sandpaper.

16 Mark the tabletop to trim to finished size (26¼ × 26¼"). Make sure that the cutting lines create a frame with the center exactly at the point where all four sections meet. Otherwise, the inlaid pattern will not be symmetrical.

17 Once you have made any adjustments and established that the frame is square, cut one edge of the panel on your bandsaw, about ⅛" out from the frame mark.

18 Joint the tabletop edge that you cut on your bandsaw to meet the frame line.

19 Set the fence of your tablesaw to the final cutting width of the top panel. Feed the top panel through the saw with the jointer-trimmed side against the fence.

20 Repeat *steps 18 and 19* for the two opposite sides of the tabletop that haven't been trimmed.

Framing the tabletop

The oak frame gives stability and a finished look to the tabletop. Because it uses double dowel joints at the mitered corners, assembling the frame can be tricky. Carefully follow the assembly sequence given below.

1 On your tablesaw, install a dado-blade set that is adjusted to make a ¼ × ¼" rabbet cut.

2 Create a "tongue" on the edges of the tabletop by cutting a ¼ × ¼" rabbet on the top and bottom edges of all sides of the tabletop.

3 Prepare four pieces of ¾ × 2½ × 30¾" oak for the tabletop frame (A).

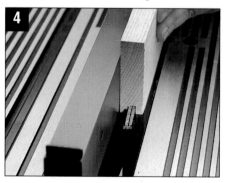

4 In one edge of each frame piece, cut "grooves" to accept the "tongues" on the edges of the tabletop. Use the dado-blade set to cut a ¼ × ⁵⁄₁₆"-deep groove, centered in the inside edge of each frame piece. Test-fit the frame pieces and the tabletop.

Pay close attention to grain patterns when selecting wood. Where possible, use only boards that have been quartersawn, or only boards that have been flat-sawn. Mixing grain patterns can detract from the beauty of a design, especially a very geometric one like you see in the inlaid top of our coffee table.

5 Miter-cut the four frame pieces to frame the tabletop (make sure to allow for the tongue-and-groove joint). Dry-assemble the frame around the tabletop to check your work.

6 Reinstall a combination planer blade in your tablesaw, and set the blade and fences to make a ¹⁄₁₆ × ¹⁄₁₆" relief cut at the outside edges of the tabletop. Make the relief cut on all four top edges of the tabletop for expansion.

7 Mark the mitered ends of the frame pieces with a doweling jig, and drill holes for two ⅜ × 1½" dowels at each joint. Make sure the outside dowel holes are inset at least 1" to allow for the round-over that will be cut into the corners after the frame is assembled.

8 Apply glue to the tongues on two adjacent tabletop edges, and to the grooves and ends of two frame pieces. Join the frame pieces with ⅜ × 1½" dowels and glue, then slip the assembly over the tabletop tongues.

9 Apply glue to the other two frame pieces and the remaining tongues, then join the frame pieces with ⅜" × 1½" dowels and glue. Apply glue to the mitered ends of the frame pieces that are already in position, then slide the second assembly into position on the tabletop tongues, simultaneously completing the dowel joints between the first and second assembly.

10 Use bar clamps to secure the tabletop and frame joint.

11 Once the frame joints have dried, remove the clamps and mark the corners of the frame for trimming. Mark a 2½"-radius curve at each corner, then cut them with a sabersaw.

Cutting rails & legs

1 Trim ¾" oak stock for rails (L) to 2½" width, then shape all edges with a router and roundover bit. Cut the rails to 23¾".

2 Trim 1½" oak stock for the legs (K) to 3½" width. If you don't have lumber that thick, glue two pieces of ¾" stock together. Cut the legs.

3 Set your tablesaw blade to 45°, then bevel-cut the sides of the leg pieces as shown in the *Diagram*.

4 Round the vertical edges of each leg by sanding or using a router and ⅜" roundover bit.

Assembling the table

1 Drill two ⅞"-deep holes for the ⅜" dowels used to make the joints between the legs (K) and the rails (L). Use a right-angle drill guide or jig to make sure the holes are perpendicular, then insert dowel points into the holes on one rail.

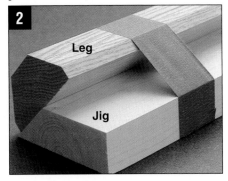

2 Make a simple jig to help you mark and drill holes for dowels in the legs. We found that a scrap of 2 × 4 beveled along one edge at 45° works well. Just place the face of one of the legs against the beveled edge of the 2 × 4, then hold the pieces in place with tape. When you set the jig down on a flat surface, one edge of the leg will be parallel to the flat surface.

3 Make a mark on each leg edge that is centered from side to side and 1½" down from the top. Center the rail with the dowel points just below the 1½" mark on the leg in the jig. Mark holes, and drill, using a right-angle drill guide. Drill holes in both edges of the remaining legs, in the same position.

4 Join a rail between two legs, using glue and ⅜ × 1½" dowels.

5 Install the rest of the rails between the legs. Rap the dowel joints with a wooden mallet to make sure they are tight, then secure the assembly with a band clamp or pipe clamps. Check to make sure assembly is square. Set the leg and rail assembly on a flat surface, then allow the glue joints to dry for several hours.

6 Cover a flat surface with cloth or plastic to protect the tabletop surface, then lay the tabletop upside down on the covered surface. Remove the clamps from the leg and rail assembly, then set the assembly rail-end-down on the underside of the tabletop.

7 Center the leg and rail assembly on the tabletop, leaving an overhang of ¹³⁄₁₆" on all four sides. Mark the outside edges of the legs for reference onto the underside of the tabletop.

8 With a ⅛" bit, drill two angled pilot holes down through the inside face of each leg, extending no more than ½" into the underside of the tabletop.

9 Counterbore the pilot holes for the screws (pocket screw style) using a ⅜" Forstner bit. Make sure the counterbore is deep enough that the entire screwhead will be recessed.

10 Make sure that the legs are still aligned exactly with the marks on the tabletop, then drive a #10 × 2" flathead wood screw through each pocket-screw pilot hole and into the tabletop.

11 Finish-sand the entire table, then apply the stain and finish of your choice. A few coats of polyurethane on the tabletop will create a long-lasting finish.

Occasional Tables

It's easy to enjoy yourself with these multipurpose game tables.

These three ash nesting tables are made with mortise-and-tenon joinery. The smaller two tables have veneered gaming board tops, one for checkers and one for backgammon.

Making the legs & rails

1 Buy or laminate enough ash to make 2"-square ash stock for small legs (B), medium legs (F), and main legs (J).
2 Make stopped taper cuts on two adjacent sides of each leg.

Stop the tapers 3½" from the tops.
3 Cut the small rails (C), medium rails (G), and main rails (K) from ¾"-thick ash.
4 Cut ¾ × ¼" rabbets on the inside and outside faces of each end of the rails to start the tenons.
5 Cut ¾ × ¾" rabbets on the top and bottom edges of each end of the rails to finish the ¼ × ¾ × 2" tenons on the end of each rail.
6 Cut a ¼ × 2 × ⅞"-deep mortise in each tapered side of the legs. Start the mortises ¾" from the top of

each leg and ¼" from the outside edges of each leg.
7 Dry-fit the rails and legs, and adjust joints as necessary.
8 On one main rail, cut a 2⅝ × 21⅛" opening for the drawer.
9 Sand the legs and rails to finished smoothness.
10 Glue and assemble legs and rails to form the framework for the three tables. Clamp with band clamps or pipe clamps, and check for square. Allow to dry.

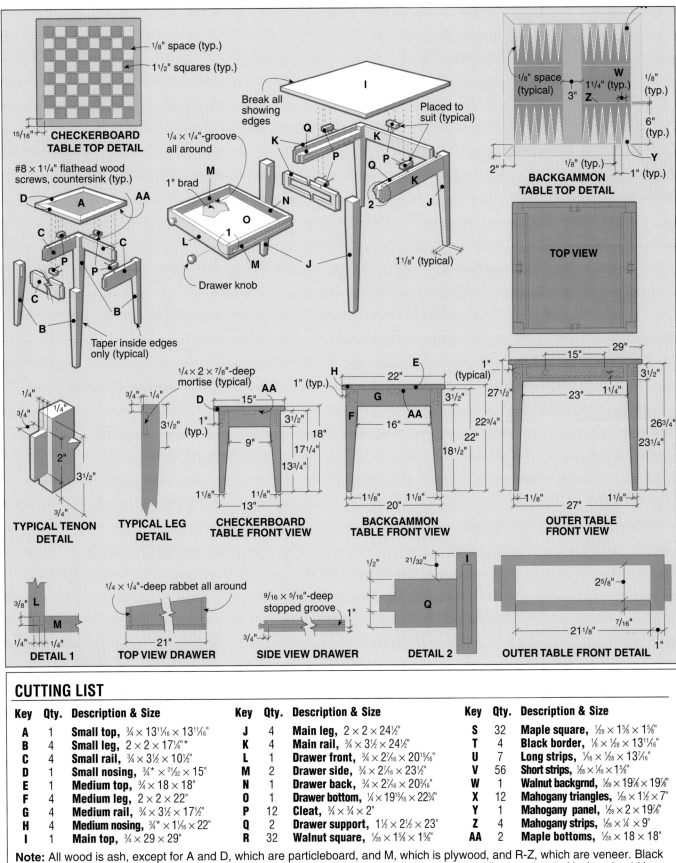

CHECKERBOARD TABLE TOP DETAIL
- 1/8" space (typ.)
- 1 1/2" squares (typ.)
- 15/16"

BACKGAMMON TABLE TOP DETAIL
- 1/8" space (typical)
- 1 1/4" (typ.)
- 3"
- W
- Z
- 1/8" (typ.)
- 6" (typ.)
- Y
- 2"
- 1/8" (typ.)
- 1" (typ.)

Break all showing edges
- I
- Q
- K
- P
- K
- P
- Q
- 2
- J
- J
- 1 1/8" (typical)

Placed to suit (typical)

1/4 × 1/4"-groove all around
- M
- 1" brad
- N
- O
- 1
- L
- M
- J

Drawer knob

#8 × 1 1/4" flathead wood screws, countersink (typ.)
- D
- A
- AA
- C
- C
- C
- P
- P
- B
- C
- B
- B

Taper inside edges only (typical)

TOP VIEW

TYPICAL TENON DETAIL
- 1/4"
- 3/4"
- 1/4"
- 2"
- 3 1/2"
- 3/4"

TYPICAL LEG DETAIL
- 3/4"
- 1/4"
- 1/4 × 2 × 7/8"-deep mortise (typical)
- 3 1/2"
- AA

CHECKERBOARD TABLE FRONT VIEW
- D
- 15"
- 1" (typ.)
- 3 1/2"
- 18"
- 17 1/4"
- 9"
- 13 3/4"
- 1 1/8"
- 1 1/8"
- 13"

BACKGAMMON TABLE FRONT VIEW
- H
- E
- 22"
- 1" (typ.)
- G
- 3 1/2"
- F
- AA
- 16"
- 27 1/2"
- 22 3/4"
- 22"
- 18 1/2"
- 1 1/8"
- 1 1/8"
- 20"

OUTER TABLE FRONT VIEW
- 29"
- 15"
- 1" (typical)
- 3 1/2"
- 23"
- 1 1/4"
- 26 3/4"
- 23 1/4"
- 1 1/8"
- 27"
- 1 1/8"

DETAIL 1
- 3/8"
- L
- M
- 1/4"
- 1/4"

TOP VIEW DRAWER
- 1/4 × 1/4"-deep rabbet all around
- 21"

SIDE VIEW DRAWER
- 9/16 × 5/16"-deep stopped groove
- 1"
- 3/4"

DETAIL 2
- 1/2"
- 21/32"
- I
- Q

OUTER TABLE FRONT DETAIL
- 2 5/8"
- 7/16"
- 21 1/8"
- 1"

CUTTING LIST

Key	Qty.	Description & Size	Key	Qty.	Description & Size	Key	Qty.	Description & Size
A	1	**Small top,** 3/4 × 13 11/16 × 13 11/16"	J	4	**Main leg,** 2 × 2 × 24 1/2"	S	32	**Maple square,** 1/28 × 1 5/8 × 1 5/8"
B	4	**Small leg,** 2 × 2 × 17 1/4"*	K	4	**Main rail,** 3/4 × 3 1/2 × 24 1/2"	T	4	**Black border,** 1/8 × 1/28 × 13 11/16"
C	4	**Small rail,** 3/4 × 3 1/2 × 10 1/2"	L	1	**Drawer front,** 3/4 × 2 7/16 × 20 15/16"	U	7	**Long strips,** 1/16 × 1/28 × 13 11/16"
D	1	**Small nosing,** 3/4* × 21/32 × 15"	M	2	**Drawer side,** 3/4 × 2 7/16 × 23 1/2"	V	56	**Short strips,** 1/28 × 1/16 × 1 5/8"
E	1	**Medium top,** 3/4 × 18 × 18"	N	1	**Drawer back,** 3/4 × 2 7/16 × 20 3/16"	W	1	**Walnut backgrnd,** 1/28 × 19 7/8 × 19 7/8"
F	4	**Medium leg,** 2 × 2 × 22"	O	1	**Drawer bottom,** 1/4 × 19 15/16 × 22 3/4"	X	12	**Mahogany triangles,** 1/28 × 1 1/2 × 7"
G	4	**Medium rail,** 3/4 × 3 1/2 × 17 1/2"	P	12	**Cleat,** 3/4 × 3/4 × 2"	Y	1	**Mahogany panel,** 1/28 × 2 × 19 7/8"
H	4	**Medium nosing,** 3/4* × 1 1/16 × 22"	Q	2	**Drawer support,** 1 1/2 × 2 1/2 × 23"	Z	4	**Mahogany strips,** 1/28 × 1/4 × 9"
I	1	**Main top,** 3/4 × 29 × 29"	R	32	**Walnut square,** 1/28 × 1 5/8 × 1 5/8"	AA	2	**Maple bottoms,** 1/28 × 18 × 18"

Note: All wood is ash, except for A and D, which are particleboard, and M, which is plywood, and R-Z, which are veneer. Black banding and satinwood banding are sold as strips cut for veneering projects. Cut bottoms to fit groundwork. Nosing should be 1/32" thicker than groundwork. *Approximate size.

Misc.: Glue, #8 x 2 1/2" roundhead wood screws, #6 x 1 1/4, #8 x 2, #8 x 2 1/2" flathead wood screws, 3/4"-diameter knobs, veneering tape.

11 Cut the cleats (P) from ¾"-thick ash. Drill shank holes in the cleats for #6 × 1¼" roundhead screws, ½" from each end on the same side for attaching to the rails. Drill one hole through the center of the adjacent side for attaching the tabletop pieces.
12 Mount the cleats on the rails, centering each cleat and placing it flush with the top of each rail.

Making the drawer

1 Cut the drawer front (L), drawer sides (M), and drawer back (N) from ¾"-thick ash.
2 Cut ¼ × ¼" grooves starting ¼" from the bottom, on the inside faces of the drawer front, drawer sides, and drawer back to hold the drawer bottom.
3 In the end edges of the drawer front, cut a ¼ × ⅜"-deep dado, starting ¼" from the front face to make drawer corner joints.
4 In the inside faces of each end of the drawer sides, cut a ¼ × ⅜"-deep dado, starting ¼" from each end for drawer corner joints.
5 In the outside face of each drawer side, cut a 9/16 × 5/16"-deep groove, starting 1" from the bottom edge of each drawer side.
6 Cut a ⅜ × ⅜" rabbet on the inside face of each end of drawer back.
7 Cut the drawer bottom (O) from ¼"-thick plywood.
8 Sand the drawer parts to finished smoothness.
9 Glue and assemble the drawer around the drawer bottom. Do not glue the bottom. Clamp, check for square, and let dry.
10 Cut the drawer supports (Q) from 1½"-thick stock.
11 Cut a ½ × ½" rabbet on the top and bottom of one edge of each drawer support. The resulting ½ × ½" tongue serves as the drawer runner. Slightly round over the edges of the tongue.
12 Drill three evenly spaced countersunk holes in the supports for #8 × 2½" flathead wood screws. Drill two of the holes above the runner, 2" from each end, and drill one hole below the runner in the center. Sand the support to finished smoothness.
13 Measure and mark a line 21/32" from the top on the insides of the two main rails on either side of the rail with the drawer cutout.
14 Clamp the drawer supports to the rails so the tops of the supports meet the lines drawn on the insides of the rails.
15 Temporarily attach the supports to the rails, using #8 × 2" wood screws. Then remove the clamps from the drawer assembly and dry-fit it on the supports. Adjust the supports as necessary so the drawer is centered in the rail.
16 Apply glue to the drawer supports and fasten them to the rails, using #8 × 2½" screws.
17 Drill ⅛"-diameter mounting holes on the drawer front for the knobs. Center the holes on the drawer front, 7½" from each side of the center of the front.

Making the tops

Because the smaller tables receive veneer game tops, they are made from ash-edged particleboard instead of solid ash to provide flat groundwork for the veneer.
1 Glue up enough ¾"-thick ash to cut the main top (I) 1" longer and wider than its final dimensions. Clamp, and let dry for a week.

> BUYER'S TIP
>
> *Ready-made veneer designs for checkerboard and backgammon tops are available from woodworking stores and through mail-order suppliers, such as Constantine's.*

2 When dry, joint one side of the stock for the main top. Then rip and crosscut the main top to finished size.
3 Sand the top of the table to finished smoothness
4 Cut small nosing (D) and medium nosing (H) from ¾"-thick ash. Note: Top of nosing must rise above particleboard by 1/32". Measure particleboard. If necessary, plane nosing to correct thickness from 1"-thick stock.
5 Cut the small top (A) and medium top (E) from ¾"-thick particleboard.
6 Make a 45° miter cut on the ends of each piece of nosing.
7 Cut slots on the inside of each mitered edge of the small nosing to join it together with #0 biscuits. Cut slots on the inside of each mitered edge of medium nosing to join together with #0 biscuits.
8 Cut slots for #0 biscuits to join the small top to the small nosing and the medium top to the medium nosing. Cut slots 4" apart.
9 Apply glue and attach the nosing to the tops and to each other with biscuits. Clamp until dry.
10 Scrape away excess glue. Then sand the nosing to finished smoothness.

Making the checkerboard

1 Cut walnut squares (R) from 1/28"-thick walnut veneer.
2 Cut maple squares (S) from 1/28"-thick maple veneer.

3 Lay out and cut a piece of black border (T) for each side of the gameboard. Miter-cut the corners.
4 Lay the walnut squares and maple squares loosely in the frame, alternating veneers to pro-

duce the checkerboard design.

5 Lay out and cut short strips (V) of black banding to fit horizontally between the squares and vertical banding.

6 Lay out and cut the long strips (U) of black banding to fit vertically between the squares from edge to edge.

7 When the veneer is laid out as desired, apply veneer tape to the design. Remove the taped design and set it aside.

8 Roughen the tabletop with a rasp. Then carefully remove all traces of dust.

9 Apply glue to the tabletop. Then reapply the veneer.

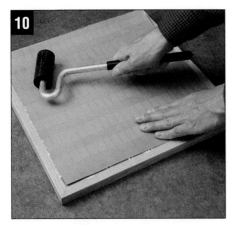

10 Use a J-roller or a veneer-smoothing blade to squeeze air and excess glue from the veneer. Press or weight the veneer until dry. Note: If drying time or clamping are a problem, apply veneers with hot melt adhesive sheets.

11 When dry, remove veneer tape and scrape the veneered tabletop with a cabinet scraper. Work at a diagonal to the veneered components to avoid tearout.

12 At the edges of the tabletop, lightly round the veneer edge to blend into the ash. Scrape with the grain on the borders.

13 Sand the veneered top with 220, then 400-grit sandpaper.

14 Apply several coats of water-based polyurethane, sanding and removing all dust between coats, until the surface is perfectly flat and smooth.

WORKSHOP TIP

When making projects that involve a lot of veneer cutting, set up a cutting corner. The ideal spot includes:

- *A bright light source, such as an architect's lamp, that can be repositioned to eliminate shadows as you cut from different angles.*
- *A small, steady worktable for cutting that is free from vibrations.*
- *A smooth cutting surface, like the self-healing cutting mats sold in art stores that remain smooth after many cutting operations.*
- *A cork assembly board that helps in pinning the pieces in place before taping.*
- *Plenty of ventilation, especially when using contact cement.*

Making the backgammon top

1 Cut the walnut background (W) from ⅛"-thick veneer using a crafts knife and straightedge.

2 Cut the mahogany triangles (X) from ⅛"-thick veneer. Make each triangle 7" long with a 1½" base.

3 Lay the mahogany triangles over the walnut background as shown in the *Diagram*. Fasten the mahogany triangles with tape, then use a crafts knife and straightedge to cut along the sides of the triangles, applying enough pressure to cut through the walnut background. Remove walnut triangles and fit the mahogany in place.

4 Tape the triangles in position with veneer tape.

5 Cut ¼ × 9" horizontal slots in the walnut background, starting ¼" above the points of the triangles (see *Diagram*). Cut mahogany strips (Z) to length to fit the slots.

6 Cut a 2"-wide rectangle from the center of the walnut background (see *Diagram*).

7 Cut a 19⅞ × 2"-wide mahogany panel (Y) to replace the walnut from the center.

8 Dry-fit the backgammon board by placing the background, the triangles, and the center strip into the nosing. Trim any pieces as necessary for a perfect fit. Tape the design in place with veneer tape. Remove the taped design and set it aside.

9 Apply the backgammon game-board veneer to the medium table-top following steps 10 through 14 under *Making the checkerboard*, page 12.

Finishing up

1 Cut and apply a maple (or any other economical veneer) veneer bottom (AA) to each game table to prevent warping. Clamp or press until dry. Sand edges to blend with ash nosing.

2 Apply Danish oil to table legs and rails and to the drawer. Follow the manufacturer's instructions.

3 Apply Danish oil to both sides of the main tabletop.

4 Mount tabletops by centering them over the corresponding table. Allow 1" overhang on each table.

5 Clamp or weight the tops to hold them in place. Then drill pilot holes for #6 × ¼" wood screws through the cleats into tabletops.

6 Drive the screws through the cleats to secure the tops.

7 Attach pull knobs to the drawer front of main table.

8 Topcoat tables as desired with paste wax.

WOODWORKER'S TIP

To cut several pieces of veneer to exactly the same size, make a template for cutting. Lay out the design in full size on a thin piece of plastic, metal, hardboard, or wood. Carefully cut out the shape with an appropriate saw, then plane, sand, or machine to the exact size and shape needed. Roughen the bottom of the template, or coat with latex rubber, to keep the template from slipping as you trace the shape with a knife.

End Table

*The solid cherry base and Corian tabletop join forces
in a beautiful end table that's built to last.*

Don't be fooled by the attractive appearance—this end table is made to be used. The solid-surface tabletop is highly resistant to any dents, dings or stains. We used genuine Corian-brand (Glacier White style), but any cultured marble or similar solid-surface countertop material can be used.

The roomy drawer adds a useful feature to this end table, providing a handy spot for storing coasters,

napkins, magazines, or even the remote control for your television.

Make the legs

The solid cherry legs are turned from square stock. The turning stock may be glued up, but the glue lines probably will be visible.
1 Joint and plane four 23⅛"-long pieces of cherry to 1¾" square for the legs (B). Note: The finished legs will be 21⅛" long, but add 1" at each end to secure to the lathe.

2 Use a soft pencil to lay out lines for the top shoulder and the foot of the leg.
3 Drill a ⅛ × ½"-deep hole centered in each end of the turning stock. Place a drop of machine oil in the hole for the tailstock center. Mount the stock in your lathe.
4 Working at slow speed (600 rpm), use a 1" gouge to rough the turning stock into a cylinder shape between the top shoulder and the bottom foot.

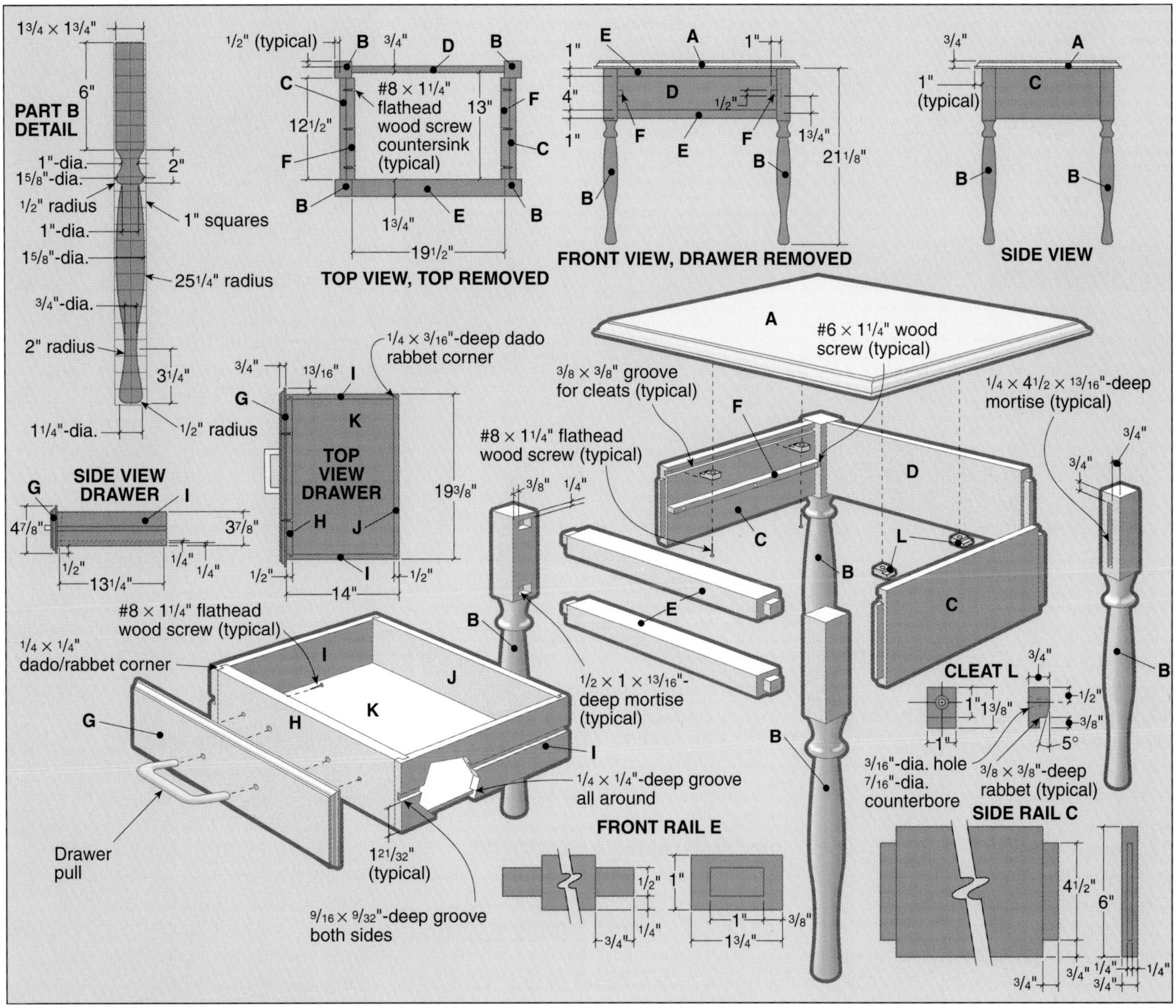

1³/₄ × 1³/₄"
6"
PART B DETAIL
1"-dia.
1⁵/₈"-dia.
2"
¹/₂" radius
1"-dia.
1" squares
1⁵/₈"-dia.
25¹/₄" radius
³/₄"-dia.
2" radius
3¹/₄"
1¹/₄"-dia.
¹/₂" radius
¹/₂" (typical)
B ³/₄" D B
C
#8 × 1¹/₄" flathead wood screw countersink (typical)
12¹/₂"
13"
F
F
C
B
1³/₄"
E
B
19¹/₂"
TOP VIEW, TOP REMOVED
E A 1"
1"
4"
D
¹/₂"
1"
F E F
1³/₄"
B
21¹/₈"
B
FRONT VIEW, DRAWER REMOVED
³/₄" A
1" (typical)
C
B B
SIDE VIEW
¹/₄ × ³/₁₆"-deep dado rabbet corner
³/₄" ¹³/₁₆" I
G
K
TOP VIEW DRAWER
19³/₈"
H J
I
¹/₂" 14" ¹/₂"
G SIDE VIEW DRAWER I
4⁷/₈"
3⁷/₈"
¹/₂"
13¹/₄"
¹/₄" ¹/₄"
A
#6 × 1¹/₄" wood screw (typical)
³/₈ × ³/₈" groove for cleats (typical)
¹/₄ × 4¹/₂ × ¹³/₁₆"-deep mortise (typical)
F
#8 × 1¹/₄" flathead wood screw (typical)
D
³/₄"
³/₄"
³/₈" ¹/₄"
C
L
B
E
C
B
#8 × 1¹/₄" flathead wood screw (typical)
¹/₄ × ¹/₄" dado/rabbet corner
I
J
K
G
H
¹/₂ × 1 × ¹³/₁₆"-deep mortise (typical)
B
CLEAT L
³/₄"
1" 1³/₈"
¹/₂"
³/₈"
5°
1"
³/₁₆"-dia. hole
⁷/₁₆"-dia. counterbore
³/₈ × ³/₈"-deep rabbet (typical)
I
¹/₄ × ¹/₄"-deep groove all around
FRONT RAIL E
SIDE RAIL C
Drawer pull
1²¹/₃₂" (typical)
⁹/₁₆ × ⁹/₃₂"-deep groove both sides
¹/₂" 1"
³/₄" ¹/₄"
1" 1³/₄" ³/₈"
4¹/₂" 6"
³/₄" ³/₄" ¹/₄" ³/₄" ¹/₄"

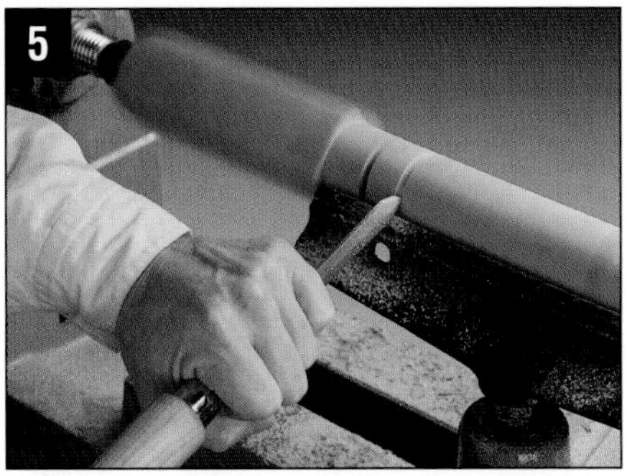
5

5 Stop the lathe, then draw lines around the cylinder to mark the shoulders and valleys in the leg pattern (see *Diagram*). Increase the lathe to medium speed (1,200 rpm), then scribe the shoulder lines to the required depths, using the parting tool. Square off the joint where the curved portion of the leg meets the square top, using a 1" angled skew.

6 Use a ½" gouge to cut the knob shape just below the square leg top (see *Diagram*).

7 Use the gouge to rough-in the main curved section in the center of the leg below the knob, and the smaller curve above the foot of the leg.

DESIGN TIP

When turning several pieces to the same shape, make a full-size template of the cutting profile from ¼" plywood or stiff cardboard. Cut out the profile from the template with a bandsaw. Use the template to check your work as you cut.

CUTTING LIST

Key	Qty.	Description & Size
A	1	**Tabletop,** Corian ¾ × 18 × 25"
B	4	**Leg,** 1¾ × 1¾ × 21⅛"
C	2	**Side apron,** ¾ × 6 × 14"
D	1	**Back apron,** ¾ × 6 × 21"
E	2	**Front stretcher,** 1 × 1¾ × 21"
F	2	**Drawer glide,** ½ × 1 × 12½"
G	1	**False front,** ¾ × 4⅞ × 21"
H	1	**Drawer front,** ½ × 3⅞ × 18¾"
I	2	**Drawer side,** ½ × 3⅞ × 14"
J	1	**Drawer back** ½ × 3⅞ × 18¾"
K	1	**Drawer bottom,** ¼ × 13⁷⁄₁₆ × 18⁵⁄₁₆"
L	4	**Floating cleat,** ¾ × 1 × 1⅜"

Note: All wood is cherry except the birch plywood drawer bottom (K).

Misc.: Glue, flathead wood screws (#6 × 1¼", #8 × 1¼"), #6 × 1" roundhead wood screws, drawer pull, plastic screw anchors, silicone caulk.

8 Use the 1" angled skew to trim the top shoulder of the foot to ¾" diameter. Blend the foot with the main curve, using a roundnose scraper.

9 Check the leg contours (a template is very helpful for this—see *Design Tip*, page 15). With the lathe at highest speed (2,000 rpm), sand the leg with 100-through 220-grit sandpaper.

10 Cut the leg to about ¼" diameter at the waste side of the foot, using a parting tool. Shut off the lathe and remove the leg.

11 Repeat steps 2 to 10 to complete the remaining legs.

12 Trim the legs to finished length at the top and bottom, using a power miter box.

13 Mark ¼ × 4½ × ¾"-deep vertical mortises on two adjacent sides of each rear leg, centered side to side, and beginning ¾" from the top of the leg. Also mark a mortise of the same dimensions on one side of each front leg. These mortises will accept the tenons in the sides (C) and back (D).

14 Mark two ½"-tall × 1"-wide × ¹³⁄₁₆"-deep horizontal mortises on the square part of each front leg, for

---

WOODWORKER'S TIP

Most solid-surface materials require the use of carbide-tipped blades and bits for cutting and routing. When working with solid-surface materials, make sure the temperature of the workshop and the material is at least 60° F. Be sure to wear a dust mask and eye protection, and to provide adequate ventilation—when cut, most solid surface materials release vapors that can irritate the eyes, nose and throat.

---

the drawer stretchers (E). The top of the upper horizontal mortise should be centered ¼" down from the top of each front leg. The lower horizontal mortise should be located ¼" from the bottom of the leg top.

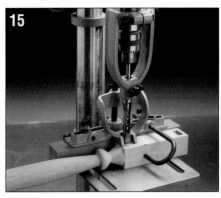

15 Cut the marked vertical and horizontal mortises in the leg tops. We used a drill press and a mortising set with a ½"-diameter bit. If you don't own a mortising set, clean out the waste from the mortise area with a ½"-diameter drill bit, then square off the mortises with a ½" wood chisel.

16 Finish-sand the tops of the legs.

Install the apron & stretchers

The base of our end table includes the side and back aprons, mortised into the legs, and a pair of stretchers that are mortised between the front legs to form an opening for the drawer. Test-fit all mortise-and-tenon joints before assembling them with glue.

1 Cut the side aprons (C), back apron (D), and front stretchers (E).

2 Use your tablesaw and a dado-blade set to cut a ¼"-thick × 4½"-high × ¾"-deep tenon in the center of each apron end, to fit into the vertical mortises in the legs.

3 Cut a ⅜ × ⅜" groove in the inside surface of each apron, starting ⅜" from the top edge. The groove will hold the floating cleats for the tabletop.

4 Use your tablesaw and dado-blade set to cut a 1"-wide × ½"-high × ¾"-deep tenon in the ends of both front stretchers. Tenon shoulders should be ¼" from the top and bottom of the stretcher ends, and ⅜" in from the sides.

5 Dry-fit the aprons and the front stretchers with the legs.

6 Disassemble, then finish-sand the aprons and stretchers.

7 Glue the apron tenons into the mortises in the legs, then glue the front stretcher tenons into the leg mortises. Clamp the assembly with padded pipe clamps, and check to make sure everything is square. Let the glue dry.

8 Scrape away any excess or spilled glue, then finish the assembly (we used burled cherry-tinted Danish oil).

Make & attach the tabletop

Our tabletop is made from Corian-brand solid-surface material. Similar brands include Swanstone and Avonite, and many brands of cultured marble. In most cases, solid-surface materials are purchased to exact sizes from building supply centers. Make sure you bring the required dimension (¾ × 18 × 25") with you when ordering your tabletop.

1 Clamp the tabletop (A) to your worksurface with well-padded clamps and minimal pressure.

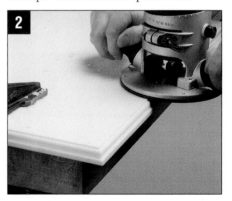

2 Install a carbide-tipped, ¾" cove bit in a router with at least 1½ hp of power. Shape each edge of the tabletop in a single, smooth pass

3 Cut a cherry workpiece at least 8" long to ¾ × 1⅝", from which you will cut the floating cleats (L). Rout a ⅜ × ⅜" rabbet along one long edge of the workpiece, then mark off four 1¼" sections, making sure to allow for the saw kerf between sections.

4 Drill a ³⁄₁₆"-diameter pilot hole in each of the four sections, centered end to end ½" from the edge opposite the rabbet.

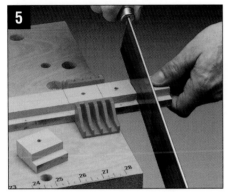

5 Clamp the workpiece to your worksurface, then use a handsaw to trim off the floating cleats. Sand the edges of the cleats.

6 Set the tabletop upside down on your worksurface, with a clean pad underneath. Invert the leg/apron assembly, and center it on the tabletop so there is a 1" overhang around it on all sides.

7 Near each corner, fit the tenon part of a floating cleat (created by the rabbet cut) into the groove at the edges of the aprons.

8 Install a ³⁄₁₆"-diameter, carbide-tipped drill bit into your portable drill, then drill through the hole in each cleat just far enough to score the tabletop. Remove the cleats, and set the leg/apron assembly aside.

9 Check the dimensions of your nylon or plastic screw anchors. Select a drill bit equal in diameter to the widest part of the anchor, then drill a guide hole at each drill mark in the tabletop, equal in depth to the length of the anchor (but not exceeding ½").

10 Insert the anchors snugly into the guide holes, pounding lightly with a rubber mallet if necessary.

11 Apply a light bead of silicone caulk to the edges of the aprons and stretchers that will contact the tabletop. The silicone keeps the tabletop from shifting or rattling, and it still allows room for expansion and contraction of the tabletop and the table base.

12 Fit the cleats back into the grooves, aligning the holes with

the screw anchors. Drive #8 × 1¼" roundhead wood screws through the pilot holes and into the screw anchors. Tighten the screws until the top is secure, but be careful not to overtighten them.

Build & install the drawer

To add storage capacity to our end table, we built a simple overlay drawer with dado rabbet joints. We designed the end table so the drawer runs the full length of the table, but if you want the table to fit into a narrow space, you may want to redesign it so the drawer fits into the narrower side. To accomplish this, make two back aprons, instead of one, and replace one of the side aprons with two stretchers, resized to match the length of the side aprons. Make sure the mortise-and-tenon joints reflect the design change.

1 Cut the drawer front (H), sides (I), and back (J) from ½"-thick cherry.

2 Cut a ¼ × ¼" groove ¼" up from the bottom edges on the inside surfaces of the drawer parts to hold the drawer bottom (K).

3 On the inside surfaces of the drawer sides, cut a ¼ × ¼" dado ¼" from the ends.

4 Cut a centered ⁹⁄₁₆ × ⁹⁄₃₂"-deep groove in the outside surfaces of the drawer sides, to accept the drawer glides.

5 Cut a ¼ × ¼" rabbet on the outside faces at the ends of the drawer front and back.

6 Cut the drawer bottom from ¼"-thick birch plywood. Finish-sand all drawer parts.

7 Dry-fit the drawer assembly, and adjust if necessary. Glue and assemble the sides, front, and back around the bottom (don't glue the bottom into the grooves). Clamp until the glue is dry.

8 Cut the drawer glides (F) from ½"-thick cherry.

9 Drill and counterbore holes for three #6 × 1¼" screws in the middle of each glide (see *Diagram*). Position the glides so they are centered against the side aprons, and extend the pilot holes into the aprons. Attach the glides with glue and #6 × 1¼" flathead wood screws.

10 Cut the drawer false front (G) from ¾"-thick cherry. Rout profiles on all four edges of the face, using a ¾" Roman ogee bit. Finish-sand the false front, then apply finish to match the table base.

11 Center the false front on the drawer front and mark its position by tracing a line along the bottom edge of the drawer front.

12 Attach the false front in position, using #8 × 1¼" counterbored flathead wood screws.

13 Attach the drawer pull to the false front.

14 Apply wax to the drawer glides and the grooves in the drawer sides, then insert the drawer.

MATERIALS TIP

One of the main advantages to using solid-surface countertops, like Corian, is easy maintenance and cleanup. If your solid-surface tabletop becomes stained or discolored, the affected areas can simply be sanded out with fine-grit sandpaper or steel wool. To maintain a glossy finish, burnish the surface with a scrubbing pad attached to your orbital sander.

Butler's Table

This convenient serving cart combines elegance with functionality.

Entertain your guests in style with this practical butler's table. A convenient serving tray sits on the bottom rack and the canted stemware rack and sliding accessory drawer store utensils and glasses with safety and ease. The functional design provides stability when you are serving guests and rolling the table.

Making the side assemblies

1 Use $2 \times 2 \times 26$" maple stock for the legs (A). If these dimensions are not available, glue the maple stock. Laminate the pieces with opposing grains. Clamp and allow them to dry.

2 Cut the legs to size. Use a tablesaw with a taper jig to cut the legs to 1¼" width at the bottom, and 1¾" width at the top on the two inside faces of each leg.

3 Cut a 5° miter on top of each leg with a miter saw. Make sure the untapered faces are flat against the fence and table. To make miter cuts on the legs in directional pairs to accommodate the facing legs, cut two legs from the left side of the blade with an 85° cutting angle. Cut the other two legs from the right side of the blade at a 95° cutting angle.

4 Use a router with a ½"-diameter, 9° dovetail bit to rout a ⅜"-deep × 1"-wide × 3"-long dovetail pin to secure the handle brackets (V) on the side face of all four legs.

5 Use a combination square to

measure a 2½"-deep notch on inside corner of each leg. Measure 1" from inside corner along the sides, and mark the measurements. Draw cutlines. Use a backsaw to cut the notch (see *Photo*).

6 Sand legs to finished smoothness.

7 Drill a ⁷⁄₁₆ × 1⅜" hole on the bottom of each leg for the casters. Turn drill press table to 90°. Make sure one untapered face is against the table, the other perpendicular to the table. Adjust drill until the bit is perpendicular and centered over leg bottom. Clamp the leg to drill press table and drill the hole.

8 Use a tablesaw to cut lower end rails (B) and upper end rails (C) from ¾"-thick maple.

9 Measure and mark biscuit slots for #0 biscuits on the lower end rails, the upper end rails, and both inside leg faces. Center the marks 4" from the bottom of the legs.

10 Use a biscuit joiner to cut the biscuit slots into the legs.

11 Use a tablesaw with a dado blade to cut ⅜ × ⁹⁄₁₆"-wide grooves

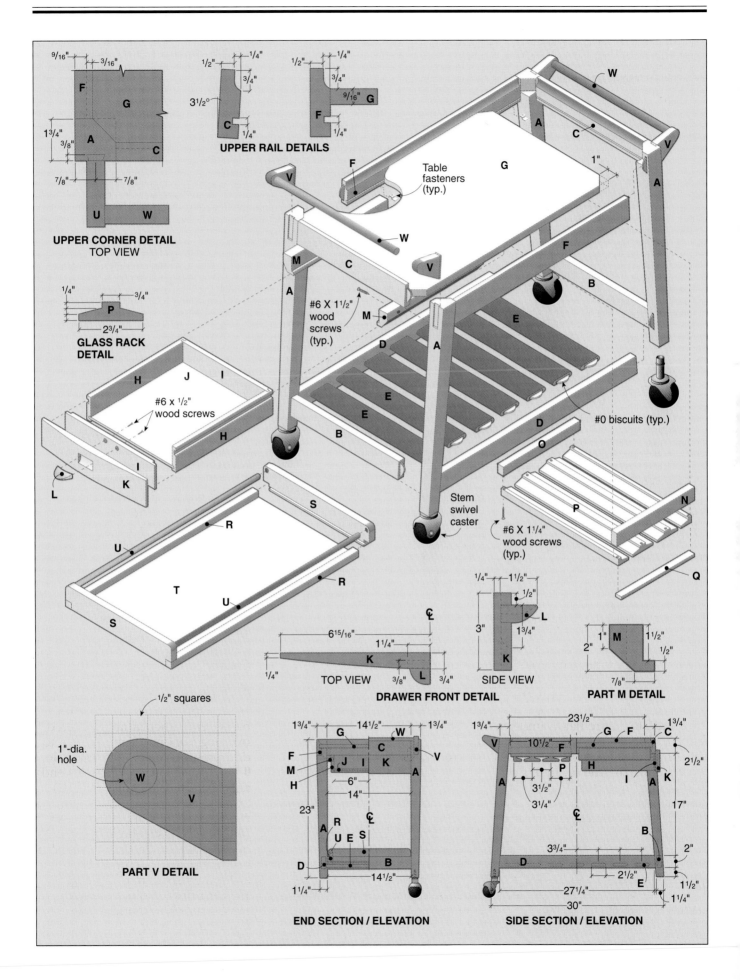

UPPER CORNER DETAIL
TOP VIEW

UPPER RAIL DETAILS

GLASS RACK DETAIL

Table fasteners (typ.)

#6 X 1½" wood screws (typ.)

#6 x ½" wood screws

#0 biscuits (typ.)

Stem swivel caster

#6 X 1¼" wood screws (typ.)

DRAWER FRONT DETAIL
TOP VIEW   SIDE VIEW

PART M DETAIL

PART V DETAIL
½" squares
1"-dia. hole

END SECTION / ELEVATION

SIDE SECTION / ELEVATION

CUTTING LIST

Key	Qty.	Description & Size
A	4	**Legs,** 1¾ × 1¾ × 23"
B	2	**Lower end rail,** ¾ × 2 × 14"
C	2	**Upper end rail,** ¾ × 2½ × 14"
D	2	**Lower rail,** ¾ × 2 × 27¼"
E	7	**Slats,** ¾ × 2½ × 15"
F	2	**Upper rail,** ¾ × 2½ × 24"
G	1	**Tabletop,** ½ × 16⅜ × 26"
H	2	**Drawer sides,** ¾ × 2¾ × 13⅛"
I	2	**Drawer ends,** ¾ × 2¾ × 12⅜"
J	1	**Drawer bottom,** ¼ × 11½ × 12⅜"
K	1	**False front,** ¾ × 3 × 13⅞"
L	1	**Drawer handle,** ¾ × 1½ × 2½"
M	2	**Drawer slides,** 2 × 2 × 13¼"
N	1	**Thick rack spacer,** ¾ × 1½ × 10½"
O	1	**Thin rack spacer,** ¾ × 1 × 10½"
P	4	**Glass rack,** ¾ × 2¾ × 16"
Q	1	**Glass rack stop,** ¼ × ¾ × 11"
R	2	**Tray side,** ¾ × ¾ × 26"
S	2	**Tray end,** ¾ × 2½ × 14¼"
T	1	**Tray top,** ¼ × 13¼ × 10¾"
U	2	**Tray handles,** ½"-dia × 25¼"
V	4	**Handle brackets,** 1¼ × 4 × 4"
W	2	**Table handles,** 1"-dia × 16"

Note: All wood is maple, except for the table top G, tray top T, and drawer bottom J, which are birch plywood. The glass rack P is walnut.

Misc.: Glue; polyurethane, contact cement; disposable foam brushes or rollers; wood putty; #6 × 1½" wood screws; #6 × ½" wood screws; #4 finishing nails; #0 wood biscuits; 3"-dia. stem swivel casters; 1/16"-thick laminate; tabletop fasteners.

on the inside faces of the upper end rails to hold the table top. Start the grooves 13/16" from the top edge of each upper end rail.
12 Use a router table with a ¾"-diameter core-box bit to cut a cove on the inside face on each upper rail. Start the cove 11/16" from the top edge of each upper end rail.
13 Use a tablesaw to cut a ⅜"-deep rabbet along the top of the inside face of each upper end rail. This cut meets the routed cove.
14 Sand the workpieces to finished smoothness.
15 Glue and attach the legs, lower end rails, and upper end rails with #0 biscuits. Clamp and let dry.

Making the bottom assembly
1 Cut lower rails (D) and slats (E) from ¾"-thick maple.
2 Use a power miter box to make a 5° miter cut on each end of lower rails across their faces to accommodate the leg slant.
3 Measure and mark seven evenly spaced slots on the inside faces of the lower rails and the slats for #0 biscuits.
4 Measure and mark slots on the ends of lower rails for #0 biscuits.
5 Use a biscuit joiner to cut biscuit slots into the lower rails and slats.
6 Sand the lower rails and slats to finished smoothness.
7 Glue and attach the lower rails and slats with #0 biscuits. Clamp and let dry.

Making the upper assembly
1 Use a tablesaw to cut upper rails (F) from ¾"-thick maple.
2 Use a power miter box to make a 5° miter cut on each end of upper rails across faces of the workpieces to accommodate leg slant.
3 Cut a ¼× ¼"-deep groove ½" from the bottom of the inside edge on the upper rails and upper end rails. Make each groove the length of the workpieces. (These grooves will hold the tabletop fasteners.)
4 Use a router table with a ¾"-diameter core-box bit to cut a ¼"-deep cove on the inside face of each upper rail. Center the cove ⅜" from the top edge of each upper rail.
5 Use a tablesaw to cut a ¼ × ⅜"-deep rabbet along the top of the inside face of each upper rail. This cut meets the routed cove.
6 Use a tablesaw to cut the table top (G) to size from ½"-thick birch plywood on a tablesaw.
7 Use a power miter box to cut the corners off the table top in order to fit against the legs. Measure and mark 1" on each side of tabletop corners. Connect the points with a diagonal cutline and make the cuts.
8 Cut the table surface from 1/16"-thick plastic laminate and affix it to the tabletop. Use a router with a flush-trim router bit to trim the laminate edges. Be careful to avoid burning the laminate.

Assembling the frame
1 Assemble the frame on its side. Glue and attach bottom assembly and one upper rail to one side assembly with glue and #0 biscuits.
2 Attach the remaining upper end rail to the leg with glue and #0 biscuits.
3 Attach the remaining side assembly with glue and #0 biscuits. Secure assembly with band clamps, and allow it to dry.

Making the drawer
1 Cut drawer sides (H) and drawer ends (I) from ¾"-thick maple.
2 Cut the drawer bottom (J) to size from ¼"-thick birch plywood.
3 Cut a ¼ × 5/16" groove on inside faces of the drawer sides and ends to hold drawer bottom. Make cuts ¼" from the bottom edges.
4 Cut two ⅜ × ⅜"-deep dadoes on each inside face of drawer sides with a tablesaw and a dado blade (see *Diagram*). Make the cuts ⅜" from the front and back edges.
5 Cut ⅜ × ⅜" rabbets on the side edges of the drawer ends.
6 Sand workpieces to finished smoothness.
7 Attach the drawer sides to one drawer end with glue.
8 Slide the drawer bottom into grooves in drawer sides and end.

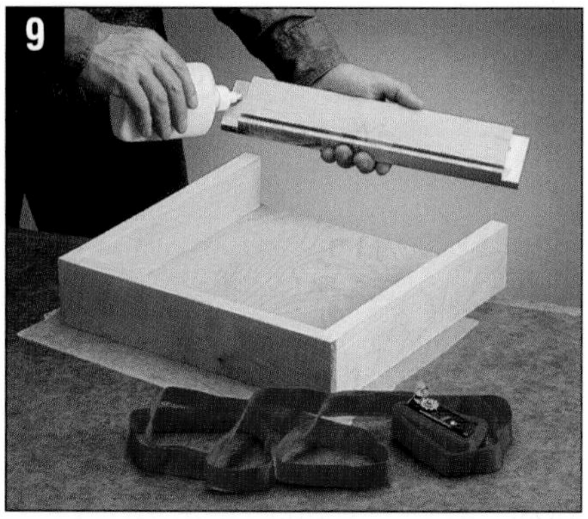

9 Glue the remaining drawer end to the drawer sides. Band-clamp, check for square, and allow to dry.
10 Cut a ½× ½"-deep groove on the outside face of the drawer sides. Use a tablesaw and dado blade to make the cut ½" from top edge of drawer sides.
11 Cut the false front (K) from ¾"-thick maple.
12 Use a router table with a ¾"-

diameter core-box bit to cut outline of a centered, 1¾ × ⅜"-deep recess for the drawer handle. The top of recess should be ½" from top of false front. Use a mortising bit to clear waste. Square corners with a chisel.

13 Use a belt sander to taper the false front from a ¾" width at the middle to a ⅝" width at the ends.

14 Cut drawer handle (L) to ¾ × 1½ × 2½" from walnut.

15 Use a drill press with a 2"-diameter drum sander to shape the drawer handle as desired.

16 Cut drawer slides (M) to size from 2"-thick maple. To accommodate the legs, cut a ¾"-wide × 1⅛"-long rabbet on the front outside edges of drawer slides. Then cut a ¾"-deep, 1½"-wide rabbet along the inside faces of drawer slides with a tablesaw and dado blade.

17 Measure and mark 1" down from the top of drawer slides. Then measure and mark ⅞" in from the inside edge on the bottom of the workpiece. Draw a diagonal cutline connecting these points. Make the cut, putting a bevel on the outside faces of drawer slides (see *Diagram*).

18 Clamp drawer slides under the tabletop. Use a hand drill with adjustable counterbore bit to insert three evenly spaced #6 × 1½" wood screws through long rabbets into upper rails. Insert drawer.

19 Drill two evenly spaced, ⅛"-diameter holes through the handle recess to attach the handle.

20 Insert the drawer into the butler table. Position the false front onto the drawer end. Temporarily attach the false front to the drawer end with wood screws.

21 Remove the drawer. Mark the position of the false front with a pencil. Drill pilot holes through the drawer end for #6 × 1" wood screws. Make each hole 3" from the center of the false front.

22 Remove the false front. Attach the drawer handle to the false front with two countersunk, #6 × ½" screws.

23 Reattach the false front to the drawer front with #6 × 1" screws. Maintain the original positioning.

Making the glass rack

1 Cut the thick rack spacer (N) and the thin rack spacer (O) to size from ¾"-thick maple. Sand to finished smoothness.

2 Crosscut 3 pieces of glass rack (P) to length from ¾"-thick walnut. Ripcut 1 piece to form 2 outside pieces (see *Diagram*).

3 Align thick and thin glass rack spacers under the upper rails and clamp them in place. The spacers' differing widths create a slant, stabilizing the glasses when moving.

4 Use a hand drill and an adjustable counterbore bit to insert three evenly spaced #6 × 1¼" wood screws through the glass rack spacers into the upper rails.

5 Attach glass rack to the spacers with #6 × 1¼" wood screws. Space the rack according to glass size.

6 Cut the glass rack stop (Q) to size from ¾"-thick walnut. Glue it to the lower end of the glass rack to prevent glasses from sliding out.

Building the tray

1 Cut tray sides (R) and tray ends (S) with a tablesaw to size from ¾"-thick maple.

2 Make a ¾"-radius cut on top corners of tray ends, using a bandsaw.

3 Cut ¾ × ¾"-deep rabbets on the bottom corners of tray ends, using a tablesaw with a dado blade.

4 Use a tablesaw to cut a 5⁄16 × ¼"-deep groove on the inside faces of the tray ends and sides. Stop the groove ¼" from the side ends. Start the cut ¼" from the bottom edges.

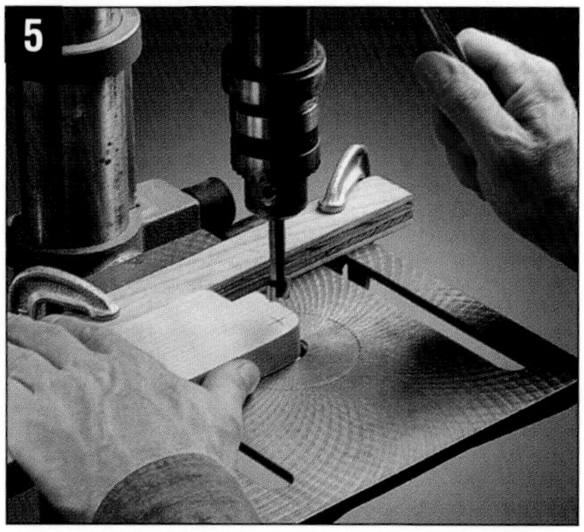

5 Use a ½"-diameter Forstner bit in a drill press to cut ½"-deep mortises on the top inside faces of the tray ends for the dowel handles. Center the mortises ½" from the top and ½" from the side in the left and right corners of tray ends.

6 Cut the tray top (T) to size from ¼"-thick birch plywood. Cut the tray surface from 1⁄16"-thick plastic laminate and affix to the tray top. Trim with a flush-trim router.

7 Cut tray handles (U) to length from ½"-diameter maple dowel rod.

8 Insert tray handles into tray ends with glue. Attach tray sides to tray ends with glue and #4 finishing nails. Set and fill all nail holes.

Completing the butler's table

For best results, assemble the handle brackets and handle as one piece before attaching it to legs.

1 Transfer grid from *Diagram* and draw the profiles for four handle brackets (V) on a side face of a 1¼ × 4 × 12"-long piece of maple.

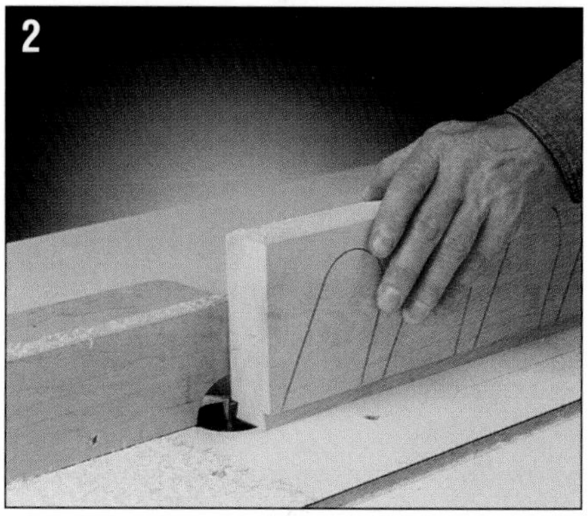

2 Use a router table with a ½"-diameter, 9° dovetail bit to cut a ⅜"-deep × 1"-wide × 3"-long dovetail tenon on one long edge of the maple piece.

3 Use a bandsaw to cut four handles from the drawn profiles.

4 Sand the workpiece to finished smoothness.

5 Use a 1"-diameter Forstner bit on a drill press to make a ¾ × 1"-wide mortise on the inside of the handle brackets to receive the table handles (W).

6 Cut the table handle to length from 1"-diameter maple dowel.

7 Assemble the handle assemblies.

8 Glue and attach the handle assemblies to the legs.

9 Insert the casters into the legs.

10 Finish with tung oil.

11 Attach the table top with tabletop fasteners and screws provided.

A rich, solid maple tabletop and graceful, gloss black legs give this contemporary kitchen table a stunning appearance. The table is designed to complement the kitchen chair design shown in *Seating and Beds,* pages 52 to 55.

Kitchen Table

With the extra leaf, this table will seat eight people comfortably.

The kitchen table is the center of most households—the warm place where families gather to share meals and conversation. But the kitchen table also plays an important role in the design and the overall feel of your home. With its luxurious maple tabletop and a hint of contemporary styling, the kitchen table we've designed will welcome guests to your home and become a valued part of your family life.

Because the maple tabletop is such a prominent design feature in our table, taking care to create a smooth, well-matched, and square glue-up is time well spent. Plan on allowing at least a week of drying time for the tabletop glue-up (and any other glued-up parts).

Make the legs

You may be able to find 3¼"-thick maple stock for the table

legs, but more likely you'll have to glue up enough maple to make four blanks sized at 3¼ × 3¼ × 32". Make sure the edge grain on all the boards in the glue-up runs in the same direction.

1 Make four 3¼ × 3¼ × 32" blanks, and joint one side of each blank to make a straight, even surface. Plane or cut the opposite surface to parallel the jointed side. Run the blanks through your jointer until they're 3" square.

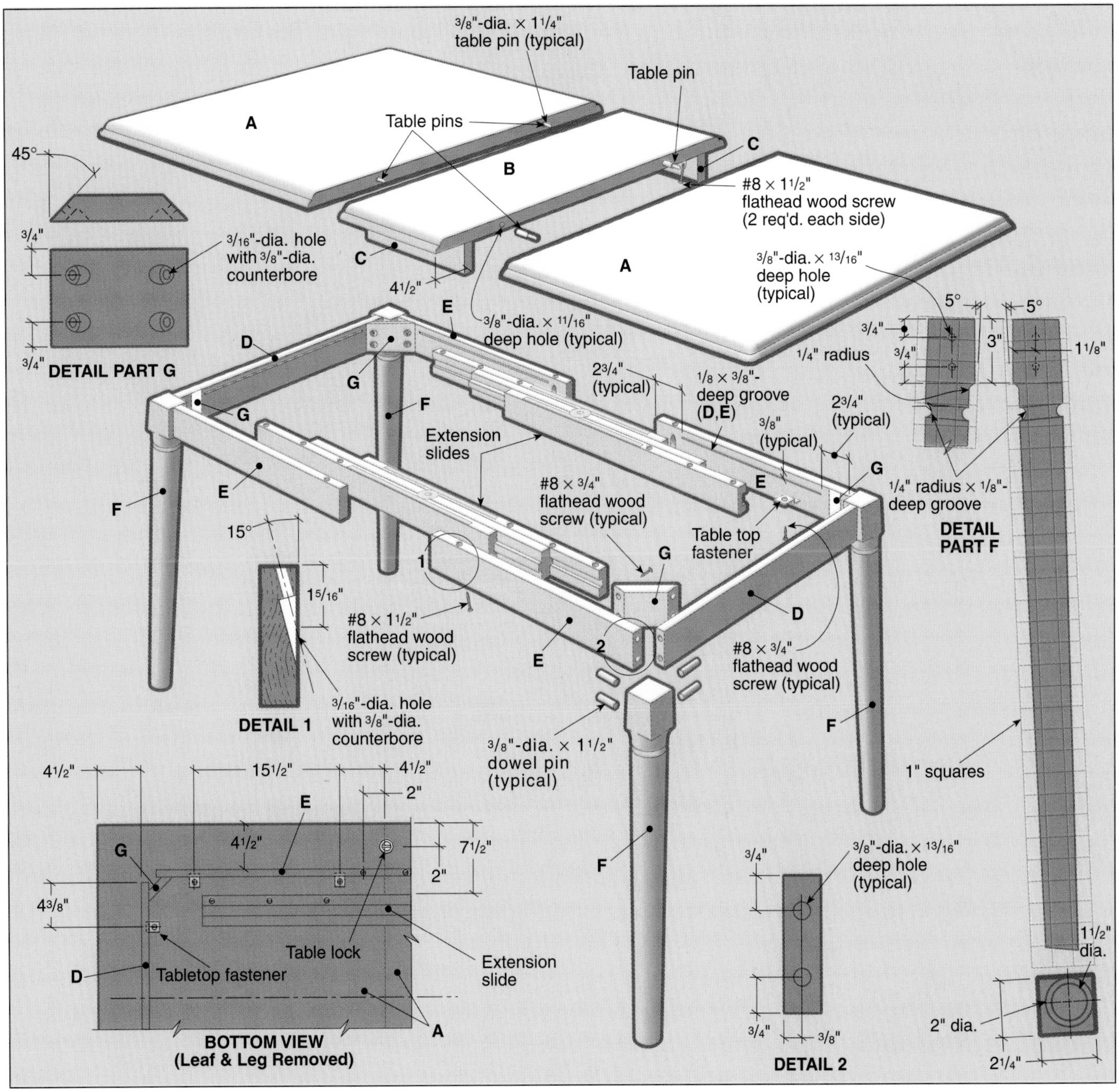
3/8"-dia. × 1 1/4"
table pin (typical)
Table pin
A
Table pins
C
B
#8 × 1 1/2"
flathead wood screw
(2 req'd. each side)
45°
3/4"
3/16"-dia. hole
with 3/8"-dia.
counterbore
C
A
3/8"-dia. × 13/16"
deep hole
(typical)
4 1/2"
E
3/8"-dia. × 11/16"
deep hole (typical)
5°
5°
3/4"
3"
1 1/8"
1/4" radius
3/4"
DETAIL PART G
D
G
F
2 3/4"
(typical)
1/8 × 3/8"-
deep groove
(D,E)
2 3/4"
(typical)
G
3/8"
(typical)
Extension
slides
G
1/4" radius × 1/8"-
deep groove
E
F
E
#8 × 3/4"
flathead wood
screw (typical)
E
DETAIL
PART F
Table top
fastener
15°
G
1
15/16"
#8 × 1 1/2"
flathead wood
screw (typical)
D
2
#8 × 3/4"
flathead wood
screw (typical)
E
3/16"-dia. hole
with 3/8"-dia.
counterbore
DETAIL 1
F
3/8"-dia. × 1 1/2"
dowel pin
(typical)
1" squares
4 1/2"
15 1/2"
4 1/2"
2"
E
G
4 1/2"
7 1/2"
2"
F
3/4"
3/8"-dia. × 13/16"
deep hole
(typical)
4 3/8"
Table lock
1 1/2"
dia.
D
Tabletop fastener
Extension
slide
A
2" dia.
3/4"
3/8"
BOTTOM VIEW
(Leaf & Leg Removed)
DETAIL 2
2 1/4"

2 Draw diagonals, then mark centerpoints on ends of the blanks.
3 Lay out shoulder lines, in pencil, 4¼" from the top of the blank and 1" from the bottom.
4 Drill ⅛ × ½"-deep holes for the lathe centers at the centerpoints. Place a drop of machine oil in the hole at the tail stock end.
5 Mount the blank in your lathe. With the lathe set at low speed (600 rpm), rough the blank to a cylinder shape between the top and bottom shoulder lines, using a 1" gouge.
6 Stop the lathe and pencil in layout marks for the decorative groove and foot of the leg (see *Diagram*).
7 Set the lathe to medium speed (1,200 rpm), and scribe the foot of the leg to 1½" diameter with a parting tool. Also scribe the top shoulder line to 2" diameter.
8 Set the lathe at high speed (2,000 rpm) and use a 1" skew to taper the cylinder evenly from the top shoulder to the foot.

CUTTING LIST

Key	Qty.	Description & Size
A	2	**Top,** 1 × 30 × 40"
B	1	**Leaf,** 1 × 12 × 40"
C	2	**Leaf apron,** ¾ × 3 × 12"
D	2	**End apron,** ¾ × 3 × 27¾"
E	4	**Side apron,** ¾ × 3 × 24"
F	4	**Leg,** 3 × 3 × 29⅜"
G	4	**Corner block,** ¾ × 3 × 4¼"
H	12	**Cleat,** ¾ × 1 × 1⅜"

Note: All wood is maple.
Misc.: Glue, flathead wood screws (#8 × 1½", #8 × ¾"), ⅜ × 1¼" table pins, ⅜ × 1½" dowels, (2) table locks, (2) table extension slides, (12) tabletop fasteners.

9 Use a ½" roundnose scraper to cut the ⅛"-deep decorative groove.
10 At high speed, sand the leg with 100- to 220-grit sandpaper, then finish-sand with 400-grit. Remove the leg from the lathe, then make the remaining legs.
11 Begin trimming the square leg tops to finished size and shape. Place one leg against the fence of your radial-arm saw. Make a square cut across the top of the leg, 3³⁄₁₆" up from the bottom of the shoulder.
12 Use your tablesaw to trim two adjacent sides of the leg top so they're flush with the round portion of the leg.

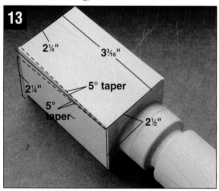

13 Measure and mark points 2¼" out from each of the trimmed sides, at the tops of the legs. Set the miter gauge of your tablesaw at 5°, and make sure the blade is at 0°. Cut a downward taper from each 2¼" mark in each leg, so the bottom is wider than the top.

TOOL TIP

An inexpensive pocket-hole guide will help you drill pocket holes quickly and accurately. Pocket-hole guides are available in a variety of sizes designed for drilling holes at different angles.

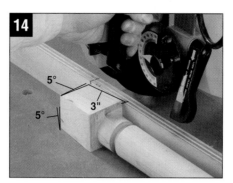

14 Tilt the saw blade on your radial arm saw at a 5° bevel and a 5° miter to make the compound angle cut for the let top. Lay one nontapered edge of a leg on your saw table, and position the other nontapered edge against the fence. Make a compound miter cut at the top of the leg, beginning 3" up from the bottom shoulder of the leg top.

15 With the same fence and saw blade settings, slide the leg along the fence until the sawblade lines up with the marks made in step 6 for the foot of the leg. Cut the leg to a 29⅜" length, making certain that the cut is parallel to the cut at the top of the leg. Cut all legs, then finish-sand the leg tops.

Make the aprons

The aprons fit between the legs, flush with the leg tops, to form the sides and ends of the table. The side aprons are constructed in halves so you can extend the table to accept the leaf.
1 Cut the aprons for the leaf (C), ends (D), and side (E) from ¾"-thick maple.
2 Check the specifications for installing the tabletop fastener hardware, and machine the aprons as needed. We cut a groove for the tabletop fasteners in the inside surfaces of all the apron pieces. The fasteners we used require a

⅛ × ⅜"-deep groove, starting ⅜" down from the top edges of the aprons. In the end and side aprons, the groove is stopped 2¾" from each end and squared off with a wood chisel.

3 Drill ³⁄₁₆"-diameter, 15° pocket holes for securing the tabletop (see *Diagram*) into the inside surface of each side apron. Drill one pocket hole 1⁵⁄₁₆" down from the top of each side apron and 2" in from the ends where the apron pairs will meet. Drill a ⅜"-diameter counterbore at each pocket hole. Also drill pockets and pilots in the inside surfaces of the leaf aprons, 2" in from the ends.
4 Finish-sand the aprons.

Assemble the base

The legs and aprons form the base of our table. Dowel joints and corner blocks hold the components together firmly.
1 Mark and drill ⅜ × ¹³⁄₁₆"-deep holes for dowels in the ends of the side and end apron pieces, where they'll join with the legs (see *Diagram*).
2 Drill two ⅜ × ¹³⁄₁₆"-deep holes for dowels on both inside faces of each leg so the holes line up with the dowel holes in the aprons.
3 Attach the end aprons between the leg pairs, using glue and ⅜ × 1½" dowels.
4 Attach the side aprons to the leg/apron assemblies, using glue and ⅜ × 1½" dowels. Cut two 29½" spacers from scrap wood and set one between each pair of loose ends of the side aprons. Clamp the side aprons together with bar clamps. Let the glue dry.
5 Make the corner blocks (G). For speed and uniformity, we cut all four corner blocks from one block

of ¾ × 4¼ × 14" maple, with the long edges beveled at 45° (see *Diagram*).

6 Drill two ³⁄₁₆"-diameter pilot holes straight through each beveled end, ¾" from the top and bottom of the corners blocks, perpendicular to the bevel. Drill a ⅜"-diameter counterbore at the point where each pilot hole exits through the surface of each corner block. Drill the counterbore just deep enough that the screw head will be flush with the surface.

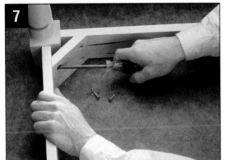

7 Position one corner block in each corner where a leg meets the aprons. Drill ³⁄₃₂" pilot holes through the counterbored holes in the blocks and into the aprons. Fasten the blocks to the aprons with glue and #8 × ¾" flathead wood screws.

8 Tape the decorative grooves in all four legs with masking tape to protect the grooves from paint, then apply sanding sealer to the table base assemblies. When the sealer dries, paint both base assemblies (we used gloss black enamel). Remove the masking tape after the paint dries.

Make the tabletop

Edge-glue pieces of 1¼"-thick maple (usually sold only in widths of 10" or less) to make glue-ups for the two sections of the table-top, and the tabletop leaf. Select your stock carefully, getting the best possible matches in color and grain pattern.

1 Select enough 1¼"-thick maple stock to form two 32 × 42" blanks for the tabletop (A) and one 14 × 42" blank for the leaf (B). These parts are oversized to make it easier to cut them accurately to their finished size after they have dried.

2 Edge-glue the stock to form the blanks, clamp, and let the glue-ups dry for about one week.

3 Unclamp the glue-ups, then sand the surfaces with a belt sander or random-orbit sander until they're perfectly smooth and flat (their finished thickness should be about 1").

4 Use your tablesaw to trim the two top sections and the leaf to finished size (see *Cutting List*).

5 Finish-sand the tabletop with 220-grit sandpaper. Care must be taken to keep the sander level and moving constantly at all times.

6 Shape the outside edges of the top sections and the leaf, using a router and ¾" Roman ogee bit (see *Diagram*).

7 Dry-fit the top sections together, upside down, with the side edges flush. Install table lock hardware 2" in from each outside edge, at the joint. Note: also install table lock hardware on the leaf if you plan to use it on a permanent or semipermanent basis.

8 Insert the leaf between the table-top sections, then draw lines across the leaf and joint, 8" in from each edge, to mark drilling locations for the table pins (available from woodworker's stores, and used to keep the tabletop sections in alignment).

9 Drill ⅜ × ¹¹⁄₁₆"-deep holes for the pins in the joining edges of the top sections and the leaf, centered at the table pin marks (pins are installed after top is attached).

10 Measure the distance between the side aprons and attach the leaf aprons to match, using glue and #8 × 1½" flathead wood screws driven through the pocket holes in the leaf aprons. Don't overtighten.

11 Fasten the tabletop sections together with the table locks, then

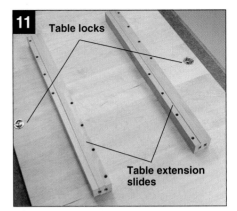

11 Table locks

Table extension slides

attach table extension slides to the tabletop, following the manufacturer's instructions.

12 Finish the top and bottom surfaces of the tabletop and leaf with polyurethane. Wooden extension slides may be left unfinished.

Attach the top

1 Temporarily fasten the two base assemblies together by butting the side aprons, then clamping a piece of scrapwood on each side of the joint between side aprons.

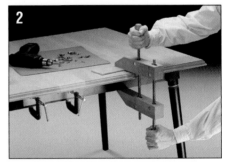

2 Center the tabletop on the base assemblies and clamp the table-top to the side aprons, using handscrews.

3 From underneath the table, drill pilot holes for #8 × 1½" screws into the tabletop, through the pocket holes in the apron. Drive screws to secure the top (don't use glue).

4 Insert tabletop-fastener hardware into the grooves in the top of the aprons. Use a vix bit to drill pilot holes through the fasteners and into the tabletop. Fasten the top with #8 × ¾" wood screws.

5 Pull the top apart, then glue table pins in one top section and one edge of the leaf. Let the glue dry, then slide the top together.

DESIGN TIP

Table hardware is made by many different manufacturers, and not all of it is installed the same way. Buy your table hardware before starting the project, and follow the manufacturer's directions if they conflict with the steps shown here.

Drop-Leaf Tea Table

Made with all-wood moving parts, our drop-leaf table is a real space-saver with quaint styling.

The drop-leaf table has become a fixture in the American home. Drop-leaf tables come in many sizes and shapes, from full-size dining tables, to the scaled-down tea table shown here.

A drop-leaf table gives you the flexibility to accommodate guests, without having to rummage through your closet looking for extra leaves. To increase the usable table surface, simply lift the leaves and slide the wood leaf supports out from inside the table base. For everyday use, our drop-leaf table fits nicely along a wall or in a cozy nook with its leaves down, yet it still offers enough table surface to serve tea.

Most drop-leaf tables are built from solid oak or pine, but we've selected walnut for our tea table. The dark tones of walnut can give a sturdy look to smaller pieces of furniture. If you like to build country-style furniture, however, our design can be built from pine and painted to achieve the country look. The drop-leaf table is a cornerstone of traditional country furniture design.

The most challenging part of building any drop-leaf table is creating the sliding leaf supports and the hinged tabletop. Some woodworkers' stores sell special drop-leaf hardware, but we've created our design to use all wood parts so you can make the leaf supports yourself.

The table also includes a small drawer in each end that's perfect for storing small table linens, candles or silver.

Building the base

As with any table, assembling the base can be a little tricky. To get the best possible glue bond, the legs, aprons, and stretchers must be joined and clamped at the same time. So it's important that you have all your base pieces set to go before starting the assembly.

The legs for our drop-leaf table feature elegant tapers. Cutting tapered legs is a simple task.

1 Plane pieces of walnut stock for the legs (D) down to 2 × 2", then crosscut to length.

2 Cut stopped tapers on the two inside faces of each leg, using a tablesaw and an adjustable taper-cutting jig. The tapers should begin 20⅝" up from the bottoms of the legs, tapering ¾" on each inside face, from 2" at the tops of the tapers to 1¼" at the feet. The finished leg bottoms are 1¼ × 1¼".

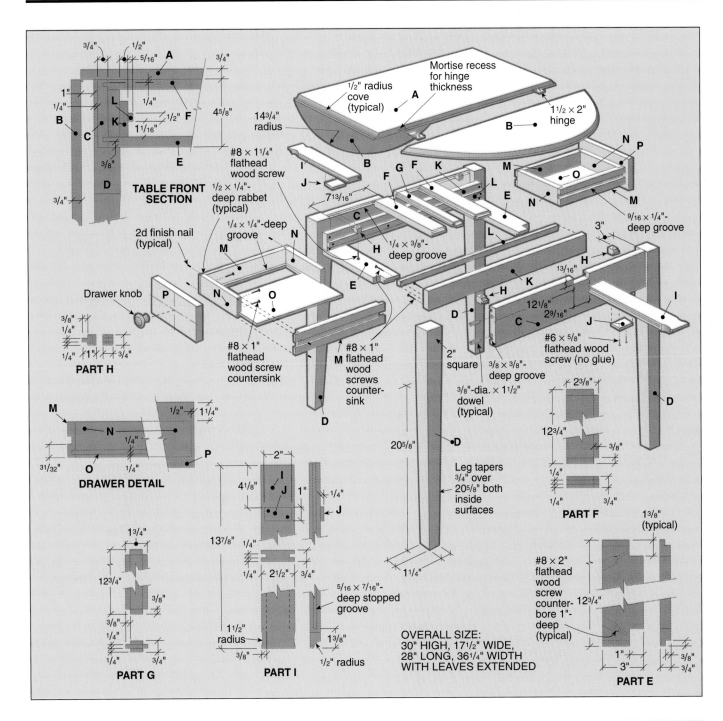

TABLE FRONT SECTION

1/2" radius cove (typical)

Mortise recess for hinge thickness

14 3/4" radius

1 1/2 × 2" hinge

#8 × 1 1/4" flathead wood screw

1/2 × 1/4"-deep rabbet (typical)

1/4 × 1/4"-deep groove

2d finish nail (typical)

Drawer knob

PART H

9/16 × 1/4"-deep groove

1/4 × 3/8"-deep groove

3/8 × 3/8"-deep groove

#8 × 1" flathead wood screw countersink

#8 × 1" flathead wood screws countersink

DRAWER DETAIL

#6 × 5/8" flathead wood screw (no glue)

3/8"-dia. × 1 1/2" dowel (typical)

2" square

20 5/8"

Leg tapers 3/4" over 20 5/8" both inside surfaces

1 1/4"

PART F

12 3/4"

1 3/8" (typical)

#8 × 2" flathead wood screw counterbore 1"-deep (typical)

PART E

PART G

12 3/4"

PART I

13 7/8"

5/16 × 7/16"-deep stopped groove

1 1/2" radius

1 3/8"

1/2" radius

OVERALL SIZE: 30" HIGH, 17 1/2" WIDE, 28" LONG, 36 1/4" WIDTH WITH LEAVES EXTENDED

3 Hand-sand the corners of the legs with 120-grit sandpaper.
4 Cut the two aprons (C) to final width and length, then use a router or a tablesaw with a dado-blade set to cut a 3/8 × 3/8" groove, 3/8" up from the bottom of each apron on each inside face. These grooves will hold the "lips" on the ends of the bottom stretchers. Also cut a 1/4 × 3/8"-deep groove 1/4" down from the top of each apron for the floating cleats (H) that will be used to attach the tabletop.

CUTTING LIST

Key	Qty.	Description & Size
A	1	**Tabletop** (walnut), 3/4 × 16 × 28"
B	2	**Leaf** (walnut), 3/4 × 10 1/8 × 28"
C	2	**Apron** (walnut), 3/4 × 4 5/8 × 22 1/2"
D	4	**Leg** (walnut), 2 × 2 × 29 1/4"
E	2	**Bottom stretcher,** * 3/4 × 3 × 12 3/4"
F	2	**Top stretcher** (outer),* 3/4 × 2 3/8 × 12 3/4"
G	1	**Top stretcher** (mid.),* 3/4 × 1 3/4 × 12 3/4"
H	4	**Floating cleat,** * 3/4 × 1 × 3/4"

Key	Qty.	Description & Size
I	2	**Leaf support** (walnut), 3/4 × 2 1/2 × 13 7/8"
J	2	**Leaf support stop,** * 1/4 × 1 × 2"
K	2	**Glide support,** * 3/4 × 2 1/2 × 24 1/2"
L	2	**Glide,** * 1/4 × 1/2 × 24 1/2"
M	4	**Drawer side,** * 1/2 × 2 1/2 × 12"
N	4	**Drawer end,** * 1/2 × 2 1/2 × 7 7/8"
O	2	**Drawer bottom** (ply.), 1/4 × 7 7/8 × 11 3/8"
P	2	**Drawer face** (walnut), 3/4 × 4 1/2 × 9 7/8"

***Note:** Structural parts made from poplar or any straight hardwood.
Misc.: Glue, #6 × 5/8" flathead wood screws, #8 flathead wood screws (3/4", 1", 1 1/2", 2"), 1" wire nails, 3/8"-dia. × 1 1/2" dowels, 1/2 × 2" butt hinges, drawer knobs.

5 Mark a center point (11¼" from the ends) on the inside face of each apron. On the top of one apron, mark cutout lines for a 2⁹⁄₁₆ × ¹³⁄₁₆"-deep notch (to hold a leaf support). The inside shoulder of the notch should be ⅞" from the centerpoint, with the outside shoulder 7¹³⁄₁₆" from the apron end.
6 Set the other apron next to the first apron, so the centerpoints align. Mark a notch on the second apron, with the inside shoulder ⅞" on the opposite side of the center-point from the first notch, and the outside shoulder 7¹³⁄₁₆" from the apron end. The inside shoulders of the notches should be 1¾" apart.

7 Cut out the notches with a sabersaw. To simplify the sawing, drill ⅜" turning holes for the saw blade just inside the corners of the notch marks. Sand the edges of the notches smooth with 120-grit sandpaper and a sanding block.
8 Cut the bottom stretchers (E), then cut a ⅜ × ⅜" rabbet on each end, forming a lip. Also cut a 1⅜ × 1"-deep notch in the front corners of each stretcher, so the stretcher corners will wrap around the legs when the base is assembled.
9 Cut the three top stretchers, both outer and middle (F, G), to size.
10 Form ¼" tongues along both long edges of the middle top stretcher (G), and on the ends, by cutting ⅜ × ¼"-deep rabbets on the tops and bottoms of all edges. Note: The tongues on the long edges will serve as guides for the grooved leaf support pieces, and the tongues on the ends of the stretchers will be fitted into the grooves in the aprons.
11 Also form ¼" tongues on one long edge and both ends of the outer top stretchers (F).

12 Clamp the stretchers to your workbench, then trim off the ¼ × ¼" corners where the tongues meet, using a backsaw. Notching the tongues makes it easier to in-sert the grooved leaf supports.
13 Finish-sand the parts, then at-tach the aprons to the legs with two ⅜ × 1½" dowels at each joint, 1" from the top and the bottom apron edge. The apron tops should be flush with the tops of the legs, and the outside faces of the aprons should be set back ¼" from the outside faces of the legs. Make sure the ¼ × ⅜" grooves are at the tops of the aprons.
14 Apply glue to the lips on the bottom stretchers, then insert them into the ⅜ × ⅜" groove at the base of each apron, with the notches fitted around the legs. Reinforce each joint with a #8 × 2" screw dri-ven into the leg at a slight angle, through a ⅜ × 1"-deep counterbore (see Part E in *Diagram*).
15 Apply glue to the lips at the ends of the outer top stretchers (F), then insert them into the grooves at the tops of the aprons, flush with the apron tops. The notched tongues on the edges of the stretchers should extend past the shoulders of the notches in the aprons so they'll align with the grooves in the leaf supports.
16 Apply glue to the lips at the ends of the middle top stretcher (G), then insert it into the grooves in the apron, positioned between the notches.
17 Double-check all the joints and make sure the framework is square, then secure it with pipe clamps while the glues dries.
18 Cut the glide supports (K) and drawer glides (L) to finished size.

Attach each glide 1¹⁄₁₆" up from the bottom edge of a glide support, using four evenly spaced #6 × ¾" countersunk flathead wood screws on each glide.
19 Rest the glide support assem-blies on the bottom stretchers with the glides facing in. Overlap each leg by 1". Attach each assembly to the legs with two #8 × 1½" coun-tersunk flathead wood screws at each leg (don't use glue).

Building & installing leaf supports
1 Cut the leaf supports (I) from ¾" walnut, then cut a ⁵⁄₁₆ × ⁷⁄₁₆"-deep groove, centered in the long edges of both workpieces, to fit over the tongues in the stretchers. Stop the grooves 1⅜" from the front edges of the leaf supports, and square them off with a wood chisel.
2 Shape the front edges of the leaf supports, using a router equipped with a ½" cove bit.

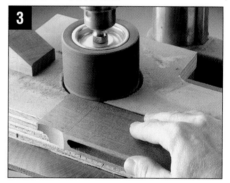

3 Cut a "bite" out of the side edges of the leaf supports, at the fronts, to use as a finger grip. Make the cuts with a 3" drum sander mounted in your drill press. The cuts should be about ³⁄₁₆" deep, with the deepest part 1" from the fronts of the leaf sup-ports. The front edges of the cuts should be at least ³⁄₁₆" from the fronts of the leaf supports.
4 Finish-sand the leaf supports and the table base with 220-grit sandpaper.
5 Insert the leaf supports all the way into the apron notches, then screw a ¼"-thick stop (J) to the bottom of each leaf support, 3" from the end, with #6 × ⅝" flathead wood screws (don't use glue). The stop keeps the leaf supports from being pulled out too far.

Building the drawers

Because our drop-leaf table is relatively small, the drawers are designed to make maximum use of the available space. Grooves for the drawer glides are cut directly into the drawer sides.

1 Cut the drawer sides (M) and ends (N) to finished size, then cut a ¼ × ¼" groove in the inside face of each piece, ¼" up from the bottom edge, to house the drawer bottom (O).

2 Cut a ⅜ × ⅜" rabbet groove in both ends of the drawer sides, on the inside faces.

3 Cut a centered ⁹⁄₁₆ × ¼"-deep groove along the outside face of each drawer side to form a track for the drawer glide.

4 Cut the drawer bottoms (O), then assemble the sides, ends, and bottoms, using 1" wire nails to reinforce the glued rabbet joints. Do not glue the drawer bottoms.

5 Cut the drawer faces (P) and attach each to a drawer end, driving four #8 × 1" counterbored flathead wood screws for each drawer. Drive screws through the drawer ends and into the drawer fronts.

6 Finish-sand the drawers.

Building & attaching the tabletop

When you glue up the stock to make your tabletop, arrange the boards so the grain will run parallel to the aprons when the tabletop is attached. This keeps the amount of end grain showing in the curved leaves to a minimum.

We've chosen a floating cleat method for attaching the tabletop to the base. Small, lipped blocks of wood are inserted into grooves near the tops of the apron, then screwed to the tabletop. The floating cleat method, common in the furniture-making trade, anchors the tabletop solidly, while allowing for expansion and contraction.

1 Select ¾" walnut boards for the tabletop (A) and leaves (B), and use your jointer to create flat edges. Arrange and edge-glue the boards, clamp them together, and allow the glue to dry for at least a day.

2 Trim the panels to finished size (before shaping) on your tablesaw and sand the edges.

3 Dry-fit the tabletop and the leaves on a flat, smooth surface to make it easier to mark the curved edges on the leaves.

4 Mark a point in the center of the outside edge of each leaf, then draw a 14¾" perpendicular line back from the mark. Set two trammel points 14¾" apart on a trammel board, then position the anchor point at the 14¾" mark on one leaf and draw the curve at the edge of the leaf. Draw the curve on the other leaf.

5 Carefully cut the curves you've marked on the leaf pieces, using a bandsaw with a ¼" blade.

6 Sand the edges of the curve smooth, then shape the tops of the curved edges with a router and ½" cove bit. Also shape the 16" side of the tabletop, using the same cove bit.

7 Lay the tabletop and leaves face-down on a flat surface, then position two 1½"-wide butt hinges at each leaf/tabletop joint, 6" in from each end. Trace the outlines of the butt hinges onto the bottoms of the tabletop and leaves, then cut out the mortises with a wood chisel so they're the same thickness as the butt hinges.

8 Join the tabletop and the leaves by attaching the hinges at the mortises. Drill pilot holes, and use screws no longer than ½".

9 Sand the tabletop with 220-grit sandpaper, then apply finish as desired to all parts of the table, including the drawers.

10 Begin making the floating cleats (H) by cutting a ⅜ × ¼"-deep rabbet in the top and bottom of one edge of a piece of ¾"-thick hardwood. Rip the workpiece so the rabbeted section is 1" wide.

11 Mark four ¾"-long cleats to be trimmed from the rabbeted section (don't forget to allow ⅛" between pieces for the saw kerf). Drill a ³⁄₁₆"-diameter guide hole through the center of each marked cleat.

12 Use a sharp handsaw to cut the four ¾" floating cleats from the hardwood stock.

13 For easier access, set the tabletop upside down on a smooth, flat surface, then invert the base and center it on the tabletop. Also unscrew and remove the drawer glide assemblies to allow clear access for attaching the tabletop.

14 Slip the lips of the floating cleats into the ¼ × ¼" grooves at the tops of the aprons (two per side, a few inches from each end).

15 Insert a sharp finish nail into the pilot hole in each floating cleat, and mark the underside of the tabletop for drilling.

16 Remove the base, then drill a ⅜"-deep pilot hole at each mark. Set the base back on the tabletop, so the floating cleats line up with the pilot holes. Attach the top by driving a #8 ×1" flathead wood screw through each floating cleat and into the pilot hole.

17 Reattach the glide assemblies to the aprons, then set the table upright and attach the drawer pulls. Insert the drawers.

Nightstand

Mission styling and solid oak construction make this the nightstand you've been dreaming about.

A Mission-style nightstand looks great in a Southwestern decorating scheme but is also subtle enough to blend well into just about any setting.

Known for simple design and sturdy construction, Mission-style furniture, whether new or antique, is one of the most popular and recognizable furniture styles. Our nightstand borrows from traditional Mission styling to create a look that brings sophistication to any room.

A well-designed nightstand can improve your day at the start and the finish. The large drawer and open shelf included in our nightstand create storage that conserves tabletop space for the few important items you really need to have close at hand.

Typically, Mission-style furniture is made from oak, and our nightstand follows that tradition. The tabletop is made of glued-up oak boards with the joints running parallel to the front of the nightstand. The legs are from 2 × 2" oak stock, trimmed and planed down to a final dimension of 1¾ × 1¾". The rails and slats also are solid oak, but the shelf and the drawer bottom are made from oak-veneer plywood to help save you a little money and to help prevent stress on the joints from expansion.

Although drawers often are made from ½" lumber, we used ¾" oak to strengthen the joints and provide enough material for cutting ⅜" drawer-slide grooves in the sides of the drawer.

The side slats are an important design highlight in our nightstand. We chose to fit them into single routed grooves in the top and bottom side rails, with spacers between the slats. But you may prefer to go the more traditional route for Mission-style furniture, and use mortise-and-tenon techniques to install the slats.

DESIGN TIP

Achieving the distinctive look of Mission-style furniture depends a lot on your wood selection. White oak generally is preferred to red oak, and the subtle figure of quarter-sawn wood will yield better results than face-sawn lumber.

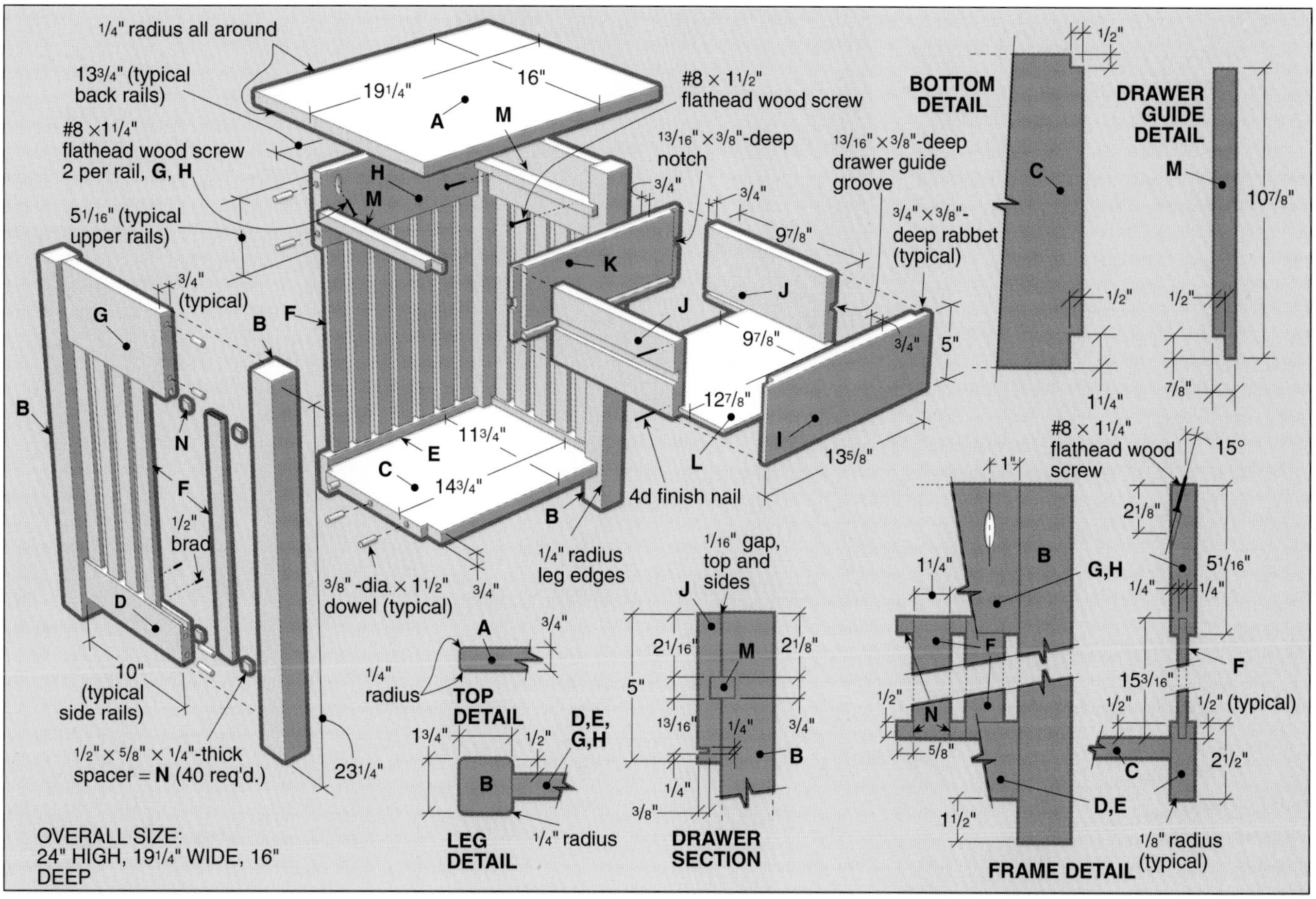

1/4" radius all around
13 3/4" (typical back rails)
#8 x 1 1/4" flathead wood screw 2 per rail, G, H
5 1/16" (typical upper rails)
3/4" (typical)
19 1/4"
16"
A
M
H
M
#8 x 1 1/2" flathead wood screw
13/16" x 3/8"-deep notch
3/4"
3/4"
13/16" x 3/8"-deep drawer guide groove
3/4" x 3/8"-deep rabbet (typical)
9 7/8"
K
J
J
9 7/8"
3/4"
5"
12 7/8"
13 5/8"
I
L
4d finish nail
BOTTOM DETAIL
C
1/2"
1/2"
1 1/4"
DRAWER GUIDE DETAIL
M
10 7/8"
1/2"
7/8"
G
B
F
B
N
F
1/2" brad
D
10" (typical side rails)
1/2" x 5/8" x 1/4"-thick spacer = N (40 req'd.)
23 1/4"
11 3/4"
E
C
14 3/4"
B
3/8"-dia. x 1 1/2" dowel (typical)
3/4"
1/4" radius leg edges
A
3/4"
1/4" radius
TOP DETAIL
1 3/4"
1/2"
D,E, G,H
B
LEG DETAIL
1/4" radius
1/16" gap, top and sides
J
2 1/16"
M
2 1/8"
5"
13/16"
1/4"
3/4"
B
1/4"
3/8"
DRAWER SECTION
#8 x 1 1/4" flathead wood screw
15°
1"
2 1/8"
1 1/4"
B
G,H
5 1/16"
1/4"
1/4"
F
F
15 3/16"
1/2"
1/2" (typical)
1/2"
N
5/8"
C
2 1/2"
D,E
1 1/2"
1/8" radius (typical)
FRAME DETAIL
OVERALL SIZE: 24" HIGH, 19 1/4" WIDE, 16" DEEP

Building the base

The easiest way to build the base for our nightstand design is to cut and assemble the slatted sides and back first, then install them as if they were solid panels.

Once you have built the side panels, the technique for assembling the nightstand becomes very much like cabinetmaking. Because the shelf and the slatted panels are doweled into the legs, it is important to follow the order of assembly as shown.

1 Make the upper side rails (G) and the upper back rail (H) by trimming a ¾"-thick oak board down to 5" in width, then crosscutting the pieces to length.

2 Trim stock for the bottom side rails (D) and the bottom back rail (E) to width, then cut to length.

3 Install a stackable dado blade set in your tablesaw, then cut a ¼" × ½"-deep groove in one edge of all upper and bottom rails.

4 Cut the slats (F) and the spacers (N). If you can't find quartersawn ¼" oak stock, resaw thicker boards to ⅜", then plane them to ¼".

5 Rip the boards for the slats to 1¼" width and rip the boards for the spacers to ⅝" width on your tablesaw. Sand the edges smooth on your stationary sander, creating a slight roundover.

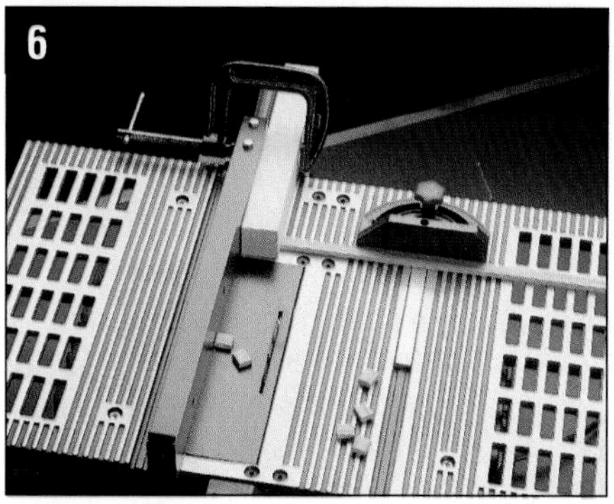
6

6 Use a piece of scrap wood for a tablesaw jig to help you cut the spacers. Clamp the jig to the fence, far enough away from the saw blade to make a ½" cut. The end of the jig should be at least an inch or two in front of the blade. Using the jig as a stop, cut the spacers by feeding the ¼" stock into the blade, using the miter gauge.

7 Adjust the position of the jig and fence so there is 15 13/16" between the jig and the saw blade, then cut the slats.

CUTTING LIST

Key	Qty.	Description & Size
A	1	**Tabletop,** oak ¾ × 16 × 19¼"
B	4	**Leg,** oak 1¾ × 1¾ × 23¼"
C	1	**Shelf,** oak plywood ¾ × 11¾ × 14¾"
D	2	**Lower side rail,** oak ¾ × 2½ × 10"
E	1	**Lower back rail,** oak ¾ × 2½ × 13¾"
F	17	**Slats,** oak ¼ × 1¼ × 15 13/16"
G	2	**Upper side rail,** oak ¾ × 5 1/16 × 10"
H	1	**Upper back rail,** oak ¾ × 5 1/16 × 13¾"
I	1	**Drawer front,** oak ¾ × 5 × 13⅝"
J	2	**Drawer side,** oak ¾ × 5 × 9⅞"
K	1	**Drawer back,** oak ¾ × 5 × 13⅝"
L	1	**Drawer bottom,** oak plywood ¼ × 9⅞ × 12⅞"
M	2	**Drawer slide,** oak ¾ × ⅞ × 10⅞"
N	40	**Spacers,** oak ¼ × ½ × ⅝"

Misc.: Glue, flathead wood screws (#8 × 1¼", #8 × 1½", #8 × 2"), 4d finish nails, ⅜"-dia. dowels (1", 1½"), oak veneer tape.

8 Dry-fit the rails, slats, and spacers to make sure the total finished width of the pieces matches the length of the grooves in the rails. Don't insert the spacers all the way into the slots, or they may become damaged when you try to remove them.

9 Remove the slats and spacers, then lay one bottom side rail on your worksurface. Glue a spacer into each end of the groove, flush with the top edge and the ends of the rail.

10 Attach a stop board to your workbench to keep the workpieces from moving, then draw a line perpendicular to the stop board, near one of the ends, to help you align the end slat with the rail.

11 Run a bead of glue in the bottom of the rail-groove, then lay the top rail against the stop board. Apply glue to the tops of the slats and spacers, one at a time, then insert the slats and spacers. Align one of the outside slats with the perpendicular line to make sure the assembly is square.

12 Run a bead of glue in the groove of a matching bottom rail piece. Dab glue on the ends of the slats, then slip the rail over the slats. Glue the end spacers in place, then add spacers between the slats. Secure the panel assembly with bar clamps, then check the diagonals to make sure the panel is square. Let the glue set.

13 Repeat steps 11 and 12 for the two other slatted panels.

14 Drill an angled pocket screw hole in the inside face of each top rail for attaching the tabletop. Holes should be drilled at a 15° angle, and should be located 1" from the end and 2⅛" from the top edge.

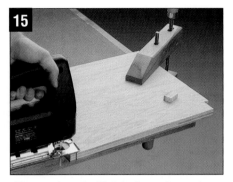

15 Cut the shelf (C) from ¾" oak plywood, then cut a ½"-wide, 1¼"-deep notch in the two front corners to fit around the legs, using a sabersaw with a plywood cutting blade. Cut ½ × ½" notches in the back corners.

16 Sand the surfaces and edges of the shelf (C), then attach a strip of oak veneer tape to the exposed front edge of the shelf.

17 Joint two adjacent faces on a piece of 2 × 2" oak for each leg (B) to create a flat surface, then plane the opposite faces of the leg stock down to a finished dimension of 1¾ × 1¾". Cut the legs to length.

18 Hand-sand all the edges of the leg pieces to eliminate any sharp corners.

19 Mark and drill ⅜" × ⅞"-deep dowel holes for joining the legs to the rails of the side panel assemblies. The legs should be centered side to side on the ends of the top rails, and the top surfaces of the legs and rails should be flush.

20 Mark and drill mating ⅜ × ⅞"-deep dowel holes in the inside faces of the bottom side rails, and in the side edges of the shelf (drill two holes per side).

21 Join the lower and upper side rails of the slatted side panels to a front and a back leg, using glue and ⅜ × 1½"-long dowels.

> ## WOODWORKER'S TIP
>
> *Gluing several pieces together at once to form a carcass, as with our nightstand, can be tricky. To simplify the process and ensure that you've made all of your joints before the glue starts to set, have all of the pieces sanded and ready to go before you start applying glue.*

22 Attach the shelf to the left side panel assembly, using glue and two ⅜ × 1½" dowels inserted in the bottom rail of the assembly.

23 Join the back slatted panel to the left back leg with glue and dowels.

24 Join the right side assembly to the back slatted panel and the shelf, using dowels and glue.

25 Anchor the shelf at the back bottom rail by drilling countersunk pilot holes, then driving #8 × 1½" wood screws through the back rail and into the back edge of the shelf.

26 Check to make sure all elements of the base assembly are squared up, then secure the assembly with bar clamps while the glue dries.

Building the drawer

The drawer glide design we've chosen works like a tongue-and-groove joint. The "tongue" portion of the glide assembly is a ⅞"-wide × ¾"-high strip mounted to the side rail. The "groove" portion of the glide is a ¹³⁄₁₆ × ⅜"-deep groove cut into the drawer. Build the drawer glide pieces along with the rest of the drawer, but don't anchor them permanently to the rails of the base assembly, because they must be removed temporarily when it's time to attach the tabletop.

1 Cut the front (I), back (K), and side pieces (J) for the drawer.

2 Cut a ¹³⁄₁₆ × ⅜"-deep groove in the outside faces of the drawer side pieces using a router or tablesaw. The groove should be centered between the top and bottom edges of the drawer sides.

3 Round over the front edges of the drawer front with a sander.

4 Cut ¾"-wide, ⅜"-deep rabbets in the ends of the front and back drawer pieces, to fit the edges of the side pieces.

5 Cut a ¼" × ⅜"-deep groove ¼" up from the bottom inside edge of the front, back, and side drawer pieces to house the drawer bottom (L).

6 Cut the drawer bottom (L) from ¼" oak plywood.

7 Apply glue to the mating edges of the back piece and the side pieces, then form rabbet joints. Reinforce the joints with 4d finish nails driven through pilot holes, then countersunk with a nail set. Note: Be careful not to get any glue into the grooves for the drawer bottom.

8 Before the glue on the drawer back sets, insert the drawer bottom into the ¼" grooves. To allow for expansion and contraction, don't glue the drawer bottom into the grooves.

9 Attach the drawer front to the drawer sides with ⅜ × 1½" dowels, then clamp the drawer together with bar clamps.

10 Make the "tongues" of the drawer glides (N) by cutting two ¾ × ⅞ × 11⅜" strips of oak. Drill three counterbored pilot holes for #8 × 1" wood screws into one of the ⅞"-wide edges of each strip.

11 Attach the "tongues" to the side rails, 2¼" down from the top edge of the rail, by driving #8 × 1" flathead wood screws through the counterbored pilot holes and into the side rail. Drill three pilot holes, but only drive the two outside screws (the glides will be removed temporarily later).

12 After the glue dries, extend the ¹³⁄₁₆ × ⅜" grooves in the drawer sides all the way through the drawer back. Use a backsaw to cut the shoulders of the grooves, then remove the waste wood with a wood chisel (or use a router and straight bit).

13 Test-fit the drawer in the drawer opening. Sand and finish all parts of the nightstand before attaching the tabletop.

Building the tabletop

Glue up oak boards to make the tabletop. Arrange the glue-up so the glue joints in the tabletop run parallel to the front edge of the nightstand.

1 Cut the boards for the tabletop about 1" longer than finished length. Four pieces of ¾ × 4½" oak will give good results.

2 Joint one edge of each board to create a flat edge, then trim the other edge on your tablesaw (with the jointed edge against the fence) to ensure that the boards are square. Run the sawn edge through the jointer until each workpiece is about 4⅛" wide.

3 Test-fit the pieces to find the best arrangement, then glue and clamp the tabletop together. Remove excess glue. Let the glue dry completely before unclamping.

4 Carefully trim the tabletop to its finished length.

5 Joint the outside edges of the outer boards until the tabletop is the right width. Take an even amount of wood from each side.

6 Shape the edges of the tabletop with a ¼" roundover bit, then sand the top surface to an even, flat finish with a belt sander. Finish-sand the tabletop.

Finishing the nightstand

Most Mission-style furniture has a deep, semi-glossy oak tone when finished. The effect can be achieved easily by carefully applying a medium oak stain and varnish or polyurethane.

Many woodworkers routinely fill the grain of their oak creations with putty before they apply the final finish. With Mission-style furniture, however, you may want to rethink the practice. The quarter-sawn grain pattern is a trademark of Mission furniture, and a slightly raised wood grain accentuates it.

1 Give the base, drawers, and tabletop one last finish-sanding, then apply a medium oak stain to each piece. Reapply the stain until you're happy with the tone, then apply a layer or two of poly-urethane to harden the finish.

2 Set the tabletop on a flat surface with the underside facing up. Mark the position for the base on the underside of the table. The top should overhang the base by 1½" in front and 1" on the sides.

3 Set the base assembly upside down, just inside the outline on the underside of the tabletop. Clamp a spacer (the same length as the back rails) between the front legs so the legs don't shift and throw the base out of square.

4 Remove the drawer glides, then drill a pilot hole into the tabletop, through each pocket-screw hole, using a bit stop.

5 Drive a #8 × 1½" flathead wood screw through each pocket-screw hole and down into the tabletop.

6 Reattach the drawer slides, anchoring them with three screws at each rail. Stand the nightstand upright and insert the drawer.

Early American Coffee Table

The box joints and wedged mortise-and-tenon joints in this maple coffee table add a rustic element to the project.

In the early days of the American Republic, furnituremakers in the New World developed their own style of furniture construction. The earliest American furnituremakers copied and combined different styles of European furniture, usually 50 years or more after a style's tide of popularity had crested in Europe.

American furniture was much more roughly hewn than European furniture. But American furniture's designs and lines were simpler than those of European furniture. This Early American coffee table combines Americanized elements from England's Elizabethan and Jacobean periods of furnituremaking. The overall simplicity of this table's design, however, is quite American.

Making the tabletop

The tabletop is made from glued-up and biscuited stock. To prevent warping, alternate the grain when gluing up the tabletop. Drill the leg holes all the way through the tabletop so the wedged tenons in the legs will be visible.

1 Edge-glue 1¾"-thick maple for the tabletop (A). The glue-up should be slightly oversized (1½" wider and longer and ⅛" thicker than finished size) to allow for sanding, jointing, and cutting the tabletop square and to size. Secure the glue-up with #20 biscuits, placing them every 4-8",

The long tabletop has plenty of room to hold the items you use each day, while the flip-up top of the three-slot compartment keeps stored items out of sight.

CUTTING LIST

Key	Qty.	Description & Size
A	1	**Tabletop,** $1\frac{5}{8} \times 24 \times 49\frac{3}{4}$"
B	1	**Back,** $\frac{3}{4} \times 9 \times 24$"
C	1	**Top,** $\frac{3}{4} \times 10 \times 22\frac{3}{8}$"
D	2	**Divider,** $\frac{3}{4} \times 4 \times 8$"
E	1	**Front,** $\frac{3}{4} \times 4 \times 24$"
F	2	**Side,** $\frac{3}{4} \times 7 \times 27$"
G	4	**Leg,** $2\frac{1}{4} \times 2\frac{1}{4} \times 18$"
H	4	**Large wedges,** $\frac{9}{32} \times 1\frac{1}{8} \times 2$"
I	14	**Small wedges,** $\frac{5}{32} \times \frac{3}{4} \times \frac{3}{4}$"
J	6	**Pegs,** $\frac{3}{4} \times \frac{3}{4} \times 1\frac{1}{2}$"

Note: All wood is maple.

Misc.: Glue, sandpaper, finish materials.

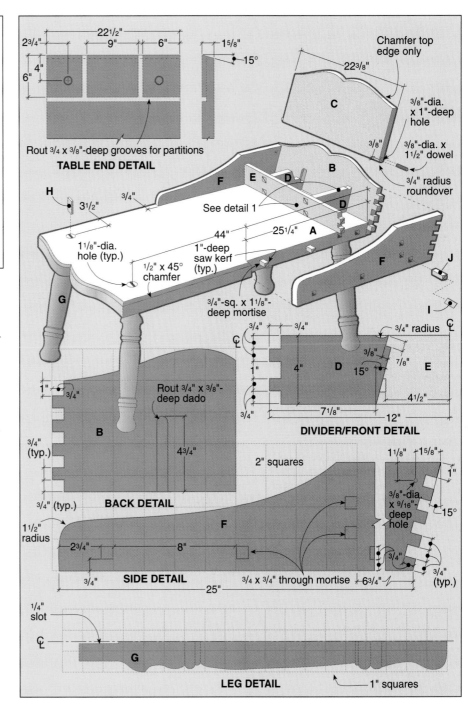

starting 2" from each end. Clamp and let dry for one week. Sanding before the glue is completely dry can cause depressions at glue lines.
2 Joint one edge of the glue-up.
3 Mark and ripcut the tabletop to width.
4 Bevel-cut the back edge of the tabletop at 15°, leaving a longer top face and shorter bottom face on the tabletop.
5 Mark centers for drilling holes for the legs in each corner. All holes should be located 3½" from the nearest side. The back leg holes should be located 4" from back edge. The front leg holes should be located 44" from the back edge (see *Diagram*).
6 Set up the drill press with an auxiliary table or support to hold the tabletop at a 5° slope and 5° tilt (see *Woodworkers Tip,* page 58*).*
7 Drill 1⅛"-diameter holes through the centers using a Forstner bit. Place scrapwood behind the workpiece to prevent tearout.

8 Transfer the pattern shown in the *Diagram* for part B (back) to a

piece of hardboard to make a template for marking the curved profiles of the table. The same template is used on the tabletop, the back, and the top. To mark the front edge profile, place the front of the template 49¾" from the back edge of the tabletop.
9 Cut the front edge profile on the tabletop with a sabersaw and a fine wood-cutting blade.
10 File and sand the tabletop end grain to 220-grit finish with a 10" wood file and sanding blocks.

11 Lay out and cut ¾"-wide notches for the sides (F) in the tabletop (see *Diagram*). Make the short cut with a sabersaw. Ripcut the length of the long notch with a tablesaw, stopping when the blade reaches the short cut on the bottom face of the tabletop. Finish the long notch cut with the sabersaw.
12 Cut ¾ × ⅜"-deep dadoes in the tabletop to hold the front (E) and dividers (D), using a router (see *Diagram*).

13 Chamfer the top edges of the tabletop with a ½" chamfering bit and a router, starting at one edge notch for a side piece and ending at the other. Clean out the V-notch between the curves in the front of the table with a chisel (see *Woodworkers Tip,* below).

14 Sand the tabletop to finished thickness and smoothness with a belt sander. Keep the sander moving at all times, and be careful not to oversand any portion of the top (see *Tables,* pages 22 to 25). If you wish, instead of sanding the tabletop yourself, take it to your local cabinet shop for final sanding on their large belt-sanding machine.

WOODWORKER'S TIP

Router bits do not cut square inside corners. Clean up the profiles of inside corners in routed edges, such as V-notches between chamfered curves. Use a template to mark the correct location for the center of the notch. Then use a chisel to extend the lines of the chamfer and create a sharp V-notch. Clean out the notch with a chisel. Then file and sand the notch smooth.

Making the compartment

The three-slot compartment is made with box joints and wedged mortise-and-tenon joints. The top of the compartment swings open on dowel pivot hinges.

1 Cut the back (B), top (C), dividers (D), front (E), and sides (F), from ¾"-thick maple.

2 Use the template to transfer the curved profile to the top and back. The top is narrower than the template, so center the template

on the top with equal amounts of overhang on either side.

3 Cut the curves in the top and back on the bandsaw.

4 File and sand the end grain to 220-grit finish, using a 10" wood file and sanding blocks.

5 Cut a chamfer on the front edge of the top face of the top. Clean up the chamfer V-notch profile with a chisel.

6 Transfer the curved profile from the grid pattern in the *Diagram* to the sides.

7 Gang-cut the side pieces, using a bandsaw.

8 Mark and cut the 15° angle on the back end of each side (see *Diagram*).

9 Cut a ⅞ × ⅜"-deep notch on each divider top at the angled end.

10 Cut ¾"-radius arc in the dividers to allow the top to open.

11 Lay out and cut ¾ × ¾" tenons on the front and dividers.

12 Lay out and cut ¾ × ¾" box joints on the back and sides where they join.

13 Lay out mortise locations on the side pieces for the pegs and the tenons from the front piece.

portable drill, portable drill guide, and ¾"-diameter brad-point drill bit to start the mortises for the pegs. Drill through the sides into the tabletop.

15 Remove the back and sides. Finish cutting peg mortises in the sides at scribed locations, using a ¾" bevel-edged chisel.

16 Clamp the sides to the tabletop again, lining up the peg mortises in the side with the peg mortise holes drilled into the tabletop. Scribe the outlines of the tabletop peg mortises around the holes drilled in the tabletop, using the squared mortises in the sides as templates. Remove the sides, and finish cutting peg mortises in the tabletop at scribed locations, using a ¾" bevel-edged chisel.

17 Drill ¾"-diameter holes in sides and front for mortises for tenons. Square corners with a chisel.

18 Rout 4¾ × ¾ × ⅜"-deep dadoes in the back to hold the dividers.

19 Dry-fit the mortise-and-tenon joints in the sides, back, front, and dividers to check the fit.

20 Use a backsaw to cut ⅛ × ¾"-deep wedge slots diagonally across all tenons (see *Diagram*).

21 Drill ⅜ × ⁹⁄₁₆"-deep holes in the sides and ⅜ × 1"-deep holes in the top for the dowel pivot hinge.

22 Use a router table with a ¾"-radius roundover bit to round-over both long corners of the bottom edge of the top.

23 Sand sides, dividers, front, back, and top to finished smoothness.

24 Apply glue to the dowel holes in the top, and insert the dowel pins. Allow to dry.

Making the legs

The legs are turned on the lathe, using a template.

1 Buy or glue-up four 3¼"-square, 20"-long blanks for the legs (G).

2 Use the grid in the *Diagram* to make a profile-turning template for the legs. Use ¼"-thick plywood or hardboard for the rigid template.

3 Center a blank between centers on the lathe.

4 Working at slow speed (about 400 rpm), rough the blank to the

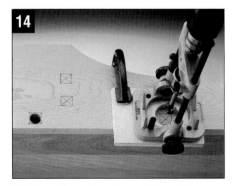

14 Temporarily clamp the sides and back to the tabletop. Use a

largest possible cylinder, using a 1" gouge.

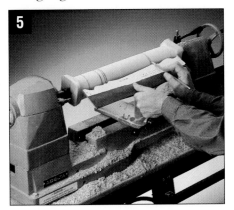

5 Use the template and heavy pencil lines to mark tenon, beads, coves, and fillet lines on the cylinder. The extra-long tenon is cut to length after installation in the table.
6 Working at medium speed (about 800 rpm), use a parting tool mounted on a sizing tool to scribe the drawn lines to the proper depths in the stock.
7 Working at high speed (1000 to 1200 rpm), turn the features into the legs. Form the beads first, using a skew. Check your turnings against the template as you go, to make sure that you produce uniform legs.
8 Shape the large convex curves of the tulip near the top and the long center portion of the leg with the skew.
9 Hollow out the coves in the tulips at top and bottom with a round nose scraper or gouge.
10 Cut the tenon, fillets, and collars at the base of the beads with a skew.
11 Use a skew to shape the foot. Round off the ball, leaving a ½"-diameter stem for parting.
12 At top speed (2000 rpm), sand the legs to finished smoothness. Burnish the legs with the non-abrasive side of the paper, if desired.
13 Cut the waste from the tenon and the stem from the ball, using a handsaw. Leave the tenon about 2" long.

Assembling the table

Wedged tenons and box joints provide strength for this project.

1 Mark tenon wedge alignment lines on the tabletop. Use a square to draw the lines perpendicular to the sides of the tabletop on either side of each hole drilled for the legs. The lines should be centered on the hole to mark the center of the tenon wedge.
2 Dry-fit the legs to the tabletop. Orient the feet on the legs so the table is level when placed on a level surface.
3 Mark center lines on the tops of the leg tenons for slots to hold ¼"-thick wedges. These lines should line up with the alignment marks already on the tabletop. Label each leg and hole for proper reassembly when gluing.
4 Remove the legs and cut ¼ × 2"-deep stopped slots in the tenons, using a bandsaw.
5 Cut $\frac{5}{32}$ × 1⅛ × 2" large wedges (H) from hardwood.
6 Apply glue to the inside of the holes in the tabletop and to the tenons on the legs. Then insert the legs in their proper holes. The ends of the tenons protrude through the mortises. Adjust legs if necessary to match centers of slots with alignment marks on tabletop.

7 Apply glue to the large wedges and drive them into the slots in the legs, using a mallet. Drive them flush with the tops of the tenons. Allow the glue to dry.

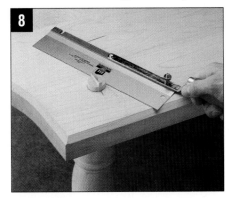

8 Cut wedged leg tenons flush with the tabletop using an offset dovetail saw. Sand the tenon area to finished smoothness.
9 Cut $\frac{5}{32}$ × ¾ × ¾" small wedges (I) from maple.
10 Glue and assemble the front and dividers. Apply glue to the slots in the tenons and drive the small wedges in place to secure them. Sand the wedged areas flush with the surrounding surface when dry.
11 Apply glue to dadoes in the tabletop and back. Attach the front and dividers to the tabletop, and attach the back to the dividers and the tabletop. Clamp and let dry.
12 Cut ¾ × ¾ × 1½" pegs (J) from maple.
13 Cut ⅛ × ¾"-deep slots diagonally across one end of each peg.
14 Attach one side to the tabletop, front, and back, using pegs, wedges, and glue. Sand the wedged areas flush when dry.
15 Apply beeswax to the ends of the dowel pivot hinges.
16 Insert one dowel in the pivot-hinge hole in the attached side. Do not glue the dowel.
17 Attach the remaining side to tabletop, front, and back, using pegs, wedges, and glue. Be sure to insert the remaining dowel pivot hinge in the pivot-hinge hole. Do not glue the dowel. Sand the wedged areas flush when dry.

Finishing the table

You may use any finish you wish, but we used natural Danish oil to finish the table.

Drawing Table

This table draws its appeal from its lyrical lines and classic trestle construction.

A good drawing table should provide more than a sturdy, adjustable worksurface—it should also provide inspiration. With its dynamic design and rich wood tones, our drawing table will bring out the best in any artist or draftsperson.

The double-cross rail trestle that supports our tabletop is based on a building style often used for bridges that was developed thousands of years ago. The pinned mortise-and-tenon joints that secure the trestle absorb changes in structural stress without sacrificing strength—so go ahead and lean into your work without any fear.

Make the tabletop

A drawing surface must be flat and square, as well as resistant to warping, so we used smooth birch plywood framed with solid oak edging to make the tabletop for our drawing table.

1 Cut the tabletop (A) from ¾"-thick birch plywood.

2 Use your tablesaw to resaw a 1"-thick piece of oak into ¼"-wide strips for the edging (E, F, G). Cut each edging strip to length (be careful not to mix them up), then set the front edging strip (G) aside. Plane the back (E) and side (F) strips to ¾" in height.

3 Finish-sand the tabletop and the edging strips with 220-grit sandpaper.

4 Fasten the back edging to the back edge of the tabletop so it's flush with the top of the tabletop and overhangs the sides by ¼" on each side. Use glue and 1" wire brads spaced at 5" intervals to secure the edging.

Because it's made up of two cross rails, the trestle in our drafting table is very sturdy and resistant to the side-to-side wobble that plagues many single-rail trestles.

5 Butt the side edging pieces against the overhanging ends of the back edging (the front ends of the side edging pieces should be flush with the front edge of the tabletop). Attach the side edging with glue and 1" brads. If needed, sand the edging strips so they're flush with the tabletop surface. Set all brads slightly with a nailset.

6 Position the front edging strip (G) against the front edge of the

tabletop so it creates a ¼"-high lip above the tabletop—the lip keeps pens and pencils from rolling off the tabletop. Fasten the edging using glue and #8 × 1" brass flat-head wood screws with cup washers (see *inset photo*), spaced at 10" intervals.

7 Cut the tabletop bearers (I) to 2¾" width. Mark a center line for the length of each bearer, then draw taper lines from full width at the center line to 1" width at each end (see *Diagram*). Cut the tapers on your tablesaw.

DESIGN TIP

Use quartersawn boards for parts that must withstand a lot of directional stress. Quartersawn boards have tight grain that resists warping, swelling, and breaking.

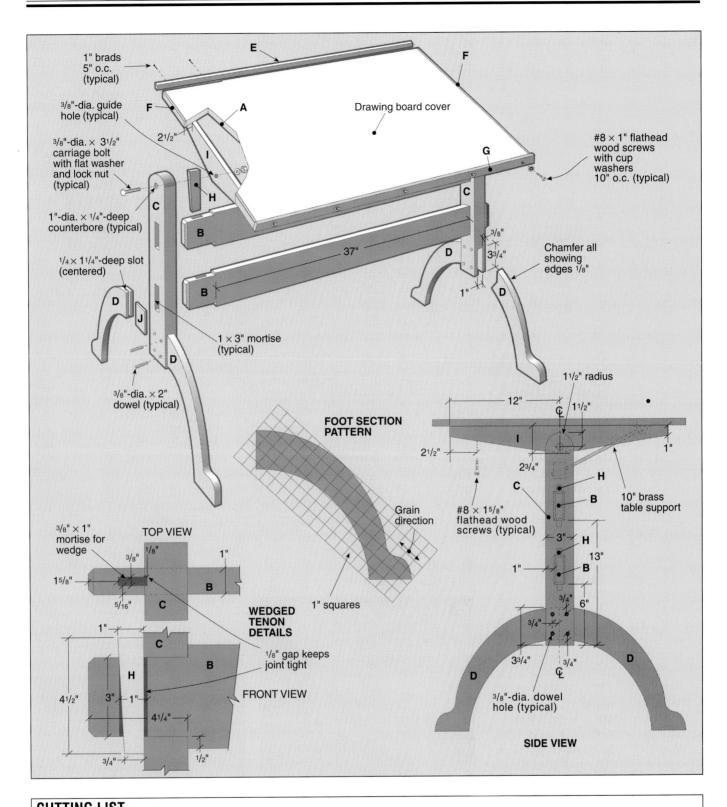

1" brads
5" o.c.
(typical)

3/8"-dia. guide
hole (typical)

3/8"-dia. × 3 1/2"
carriage bolt
with flat washer
and lock nut
(typical)

1"-dia. × 1/4"-deep
counterbore (typical)

1/4 × 1 1/4"-deep slot
(centered)

3/8"-dia. × 2"
dowel (typical)

1 × 3" mortise
(typical)

Drawing board cover

#8 × 1" flathead
wood screws
with cup
washers
10" o.c. (typical)

Chamfer all
showing
edges 1/8"

2 1/2"

37"

3/8"
3 3/4"
1"

1 1/2" radius

12"   1 1/2"

1"

2 1/2"

2 3/4"

#8 × 1 5/8"
flathead wood
screws (typical)

10" brass
table support

3"

1"

3/4"

6"

13"

3/4"

3/4"   3/4"

3 3/4"

3/8"-dia. dowel
hole (typical)

SIDE VIEW

**FOOT SECTION
PATTERN**

Grain
direction

1" squares

**WEDGED
TENON
DETAILS**

1/8" gap keeps
joint tight

3/8" × 1"
mortise for
wedge

TOP VIEW

3/8"   1/8"   1"

1 5/8"   B

5/16"   C

1"

C

B

H   3"   1"

4 1/2"

4 1/4"

3/4"   1/2"

FRONT VIEW

CUTTING LIST

Key	Qty.	Description & Size	Key	Qty.	Description & Size	Key	Qty.	Description & Size
A	1	**Tabletop,** 3/4 × 29 1/2 × 41 1/2"	E	1	**Back edging,** 1/4 × 3/4 × 42"	H	4	**Wedge,** 3/8 × 1 × 4 1/2"
B	2	**Cross rail,** 1 × 4 × 45 1/2"	F	2	**Side edging,** 1/4 × 3/4 × 29 1/2"	I	2	**Tabletop bearer,** 1 × 2 3/4 × 24"
C	2	**Post,** 1 3/4 × 3 × 22"	G	1	**Front edging,** 1/4 × 1 × 42"	J	2	**Spline,** 1/4 × 2 1/2 × 3 1/4"
D	4	**Foot section,** 1 × 6 × 19"						

Note: All wood is oak except A, which is birch plywood.

Misc.: Glue, 1" wire brads, 3/8 × 3 1/2" carriage bolts with lock nuts and washers, 2 × 3/8"-dia. dowels, 10" brass table supports, brass flathead wood screws (#8 × 1", #8 × 1 5/8", 10 × 3/4"), #8 brass cup washers, 30 × 42" drawing board cover.

8 Drill counterbored shank holes for #8 × 1⅝" screws through the centers of the tapered edges of each bearer, 2½" in from each end.
9 Drill a ⅜"-diameter guide hole for the carriage-bolt pivot (see *Diagram*) through each bearer at the center line, ¾" from the point where the tapers meet.
10 Sand the bearers to finished smoothness.

11 Position the bearers on the underside of the tabletop, with the tapered edges facing up, 2½" in from the side edges of the table-top and 3" in from the front and back edges. Drill pilot holes ½" into the tabletop, then attach with glue and #8 × 1⅝" flathead wood screws.

Make the trestle parts

The trestle for our drawing table is made from a pair of matching cross rails connected to two posts by pinned mortise-and-tenon joints. The trestle is supported by two feet, each composed of a pair of curved foot sections joined at the tops with a spline.
1 Prepare four 1 × 6 × 19" pieces of oak, with the grain running lengthwise, to use as blanks for the foot sections. Stack the blanks for gang-cutting, then screw them together in waste areas. Make a foot-section pattern (enlarge the *Diagram* pattern 800%), and attach it to the top board in the stack.
2 Gang-cut the pattern into the blanks, using a bandsaw equipped with a ⅜"-wide, 4 tpi blade. Press down firmly on the stack of blanks as you finish the cut so they don't slip apart.

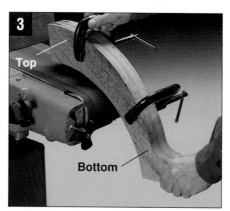

3 Group the 4' sections into two pairs and clamp them together. Smooth out the contours of each pair on your stationary sander, moving the clamps as needed. Label the pairs before unclamping.
4 Use a router and chamfer bit to cut ⅛" chamfers in the edges of the foot sections.
5 Mark centered ¼ × 1¼"-deep slots in the top end of each foot section. Cut the slots with a dado-blade set installed in your tablesaw. The slots hold the splines (J) that form joints between foot-section pairs.
6 Resaw two ¼"-thick splines (J) on your bandsaw, with the wood grain running lengthwise. Trim the splines to size with a handsaw. Dry-fit the splines between foot-section pairs, and trim with a file or sander, if necessary, until the fit is snug.

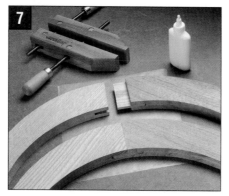

7 Assemble the feet: apply glue to the splines and insert them into the slots in the ends of the foot sections, then press the foot sections together until the joint is flush and the sections form smooth contours on the top and bottom. Carefully tighten a clamp over each joint to keep it from slipping while the glue dries.

8 Cut the posts (C) and cross rails (B) from straight 1"-thick oak, using a tablesaw.
9 On a bandsaw, cut a 1½"-radius semicircle at the top of each post to allow the tabletop to pivot when installed (see *Diagram*). Sand the contour until it's smooth.
10 Cut tenons at the ends of the cross rails. To make the tenons, use your bandsaw to remove a ½ × 4¼" strip of wood (including kerf) from the top and bottom of each cross rail end (see *Diagram*). This will create a 1 × 3 × 4¼"-deep tenon.
11 To hold the wedges (H) that pin the cross rails in place, cut a ⅜"-wide × 1"-long mortise down through the top of each cross rail tenon (see *Diagram*). Start the cut 1⅝" from the end of the tenon, centered side to side.
12 Mark 1"-wide × 3"-high mortises in each post, to hold the cross rail tenons. The bottoms of the mortises should be 6" and 13" up from the bottom of each post, centered side to side. Cut the mortises by removing wood with a drill, then squaring off with a wood chisel; or use a mortising attachment in your drill press.
13 Cut a 3¾"-deep × 1"-wide slot in the bottom of each post, centered side to side, to fit over the spline joints in the feet.
14 Drill a ⅜"-diameter guide hole for the carriage bolt in the center of each post, 1½" down from the apex of the curved contour at the top of each post.

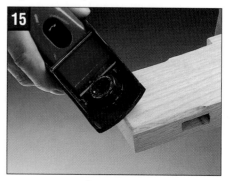

15 Rout ⅛" chamfers on all edges of the cross rails. Use a block plane to chamfer the ends. Sand the cross rails and posts to finished smoothness.

Assemble the trestle

The trestle that forms our drawing table base is pinned together with wedged mortise-and-tenon joints. In addition to combining strength and flexibility, the wedges let you break down the table quickly and easily for convenient transport.

1 On your bandsaw, cut ⅜ × 1 × 4½" blanks for the wedges (H) that pin the mortise-and-tenon joints formed by the posts and the cross rails. Taper one edge of each wedge from 1" at the top to ¾" at the bottom.

2 At the bottom of each post, mark centerpoints for four ⅜"-diameter dowel holes to form the dowel joints between the posts and the feet (see *Diagram*).

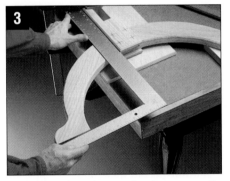

3 Center the slot in the bottom of one post over a foot, and test the fit. Use a framing square to make sure the bottoms of both foot sections are perpendicular to the sides of the post.

4 Drill ⅜"-diameter holes through the post and the feet at dowel-joint locations, using a brad-point bit and a drill press or a portable drill with a drill guide.

5 Disassemble the post-and-foot assembly, then apply glue to the mating surfaces. Reinsert the foot,

and pin it to the post with glue and ⅜"-diameter dowels.

6 When the glue is dry, trim the dowel ends with a flush-cutting saw, then sand to finished smoothness.

7 Make the second post-and-foot assembly, using the same techniques as in steps 3 to 6.

8 Dry-fit the cross rails into the mortises in the posts (don't panic when the the first ⅛" of a wedge mortise is covered by a post—the ⅛" overlap is designed to let you drive the wedge in more securely). Set the straight edge of a wedge against a post, then drive the wedge into the wedge mortise in the top of a tenon. Drive all four wedges, using a piece of scrap wood and a wood mallet (drive the bottom wedges first).

Finish the table

We used medium oak stain and tung oil for a classic finish on our drawing table.

1 Carefully disassemble the mortise-and-tenon joints between the cross rails and posts by driving the wedges back out. Finish-sand any unsanded parts with 220-grit sandpaper.

2 Stain all wood surfaces, following the stain manufacturer's instructions. Be sure to stain the underside of the tabletop.

3 Apply tung oil to all wood surfaces. We used three coats.

> ## WOODWORKER'S TIP
>
> *Use beeswax, paraffin, or paste wax to coat the shanks of bolts or other hardware designed to pivot or move in a guide hole in wood.*

Attach the tabletop

1 Reassemble the mortise-and-tenon joints between the posts and the cross rails. Pin securely with the wedges (see *step 8, Assemble the trestle*).

2 Position the tabletop so the guide holes in the tabletop bearers align with the guide holes in the posts. Slip flat washers onto two ⅜ × 3½" carriage bolts and insert them through the guide holes. Slip washers and lock nuts over the carriage bolts and tighten the lock nuts. Tighten only until secure—the tabletop should pivot with relatively little resistance.

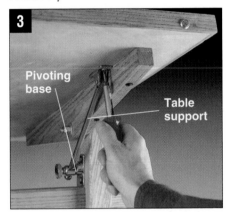

3 Attach 10" brass table supports (available at most woodworkers' stores) to the tabletop just inside the bearer, and to the inside edge of each post, using #10 × ¾" brass flathead wood screws. Make sure the pivoting bases are fastened so the sliding arms clear the top cross rail and extend fully to support the table.

4 You may want to purchase and attach a 30 × 42" drawing-table cover at an artists' supply store to protect the table surface. We used double-sided tape to secure the cover on our drawing table.

Set the table angle

First, find a comfortable chair or stool to use with your new drawing table. Set the chair in front of the table, and loosen the knobs that hold the table supports in position. Lean forward with your back straight and elbows bent and press against the tabletop until your forearms are flat against the surface. Lock down the supports.

Outdoor Folding Trays

Savor the summer breeze and your outdoor cooking on these white oak trays.

White oak, valued for its beauty, is also highly resistant to rot from moisture, which is why we selected it as the material for these outdoor folding trays.

Cutting the tray tops

1 Cut ends (A), free side (B), fixed side (C), and pivots (H) from ¾"-thick white oak.

2 Cut slats (D) and spacers (I) from ¼"-thick white oak (see *Diagram*).

3 Shape the pivots. Transfer the design to the stock (see *Diagram*). Cut the shapes, using a bandsaw. Round over the parts on a sander.

4 Drill ½ × ¾"-diameter holes for the rotohinge on the inner side of the pivots, using a Forstner bit centered ⅝" from the top and 1" from the outside end.

5 Rout ¼ × ½"-deep stopped grooves centered on the inside edges of the free side and the fixed side. Stop the grooves ¼" from each end.

6 On the outside edge of the free side, bevel-cut the top and bottom edges to form a bevel 1" wide, tapering to leave a ¼" shoulder on the outside edge (see *Diagram*).

7 On the ends, cut a ½ × ¼"-deep rabbet on the top face, the bottom face, and the outside edge to form ¼ × 1¼" tenons on each end.

8 Cut one 2 × 2 × 4⅝" piece of white oak for the rests (G).

9 Mark the center on one face of the stock for the rests. Then drill a ¾"-diameter hole through the center mark, using a brad-point bit.

10 Scribe a line 2¼" from the right edge of one undrilled face of the rest stock. Scribe another line 2¼" from the left edge of the other undrilled face of the rest stock.

11 Use a bandsaw to cut into the hole in the center of the rest stock along each of the lines. This forms two blocks, each of which has one long side, one short side, and a ¾"-diameter groove between the long and short sides.

12 Cut a 1 × ¼"-deep rabbet on each rest in the face, opposite the groove yet parallel to the groove, along the side of the piece with the longest edge (see *Diagram*).

13 Sand the ends, free side, fixed side, slats, pivots, rests, and spacers to final smoothness.

14 Dry-fit the tray top with spacers, allowing 1/16" between slats and spacers for expansion. Adjust parts as necessary. Mark locations of spacers on the free side and fixed side to aid in application of glue.

Assembling the tray tops

1 Apply glue to fixed side's end and spacer locations in groove.

2 Glue and insert an end. Then alternate spacers and slats, starting and ending with spacers. Glue the spacers in place, but do not get any glue on the slats. Glue and insert the remaining end last.

3 Apply glue to free side's end and spacer locations in groove.

4 Slide the free side into place over the assembled slats and ends, sliding glued spacers into place between the unglued slats.

5 Clamp the tray with bar clamps, check for square, and wash away excess glue.

6 Clamp the rests and pivots in place. Then drill counterbore, shank, and pilot holes through the top of the fixed and free side to fasten the pivots and rests with #6 × 1¼" wood screws.

7 Plug the holes. Allow all glue to dry before sanding the plugs smooth.

Cutting the tray legs

1 Cut the long legs (E) and short legs (F) from ¾"-thick white oak.

2 Mark hinge points on all the legs 17" from the bottom of each leg.

3 Use a tablesaw to taper-cut legs from 2½" wide at the hinge points to 1¼" wide at top and bottom. Note: The inner legs will have a different taper angle on the top (short) portion of the leg than on the bottom of the leg.

4 Make a 1¼"-radius cut with a bandsaw on the end of each leg.

5 At the center of the radius at the top of the inside legs and 1½" above the hinge point, drill a ⅜ × ⅜"-deep hole to hold the dowels. Use a Forstner bit to create flat-bottomed holes.

6 At the hinge points on the inside of the long legs, drill a ½ × ½"-deep hole with a Forstner bit for the glider hinge.

7 At the hinge point on the short legs, drill a ⁷⁄₁₆ × 1"-diameter counterbore on the inside of each leg. Then drill a ½"-diameter hole through that center, using a brad-point bit.

8 Cut inside dowels (J) from ⅝"-diameter white oak dowel. Cut a ⅛ × ⅜"-wide rabbet on the ends, using a dado-blade set installed on your tablesaw, an auxiliary fence, and a stopblock. Rotate dowel against or through the blade while holding it against the auxiliary fence, creating a ⅜"-diameter tenon.

9 Apply at least two coats of Danish oil to all wooden parts, including the tray.

Assembling the legs

1 At the center of the radius cut

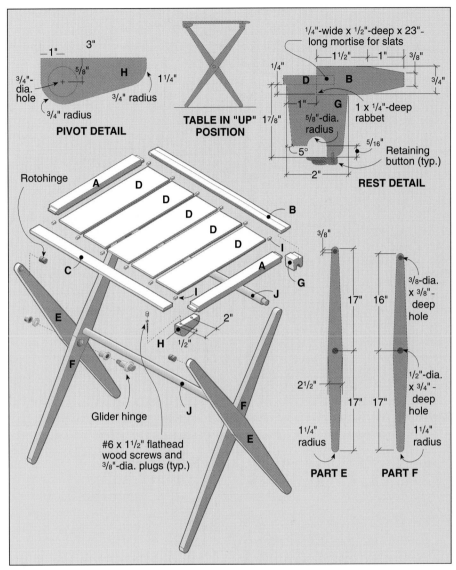

PIVOT DETAIL

TABLE IN "UP" POSITION

¼"-wide x ½"-deep x 23"-long mortise for slats

REST DETAIL

1 x ¼"-deep rabbet

⅝"-dia. radius

Retaining button (typ.)

Rotohinge

Glider hinge

#6 x 1½" flathead wood screws and ⅜"-dia. plugs (typ.)

PART E   **PART F**

on the insides of the tops of the long legs, drill a ½ × ¾"-diameter hole for the rotohinges.

2 Apply glue to the rotohinge holes in the tops of the long legs and in the pivots. Insert the rotohinges in the pivots and press the long legs in place. Allow to dry.

3 Attach the glider hinge (always follow the manufacturer's instructions) to long legs, using glue and the screws provided by the manufacturer.

4 Insert the nylon sleeves in the short legs, and fit the glider hinges into the sleeves in the short legs.

5 Fasten the short legs to the long legs with the nuts and washers provided with the glider hinges.

6 Apply glue to the dowel holes in the legs and insert the dowels. Clamp to dry.

7 Drill pilot holes into the bottoms of the rests and attach the button retainers to the bottoms of the rests, using the screws provided by the manufacturer.

CUTTING LIST

Key	Qty.	Description & Size
A	2	**End,** ¾ × 1½ × 15"
B	1	**Free side,** ¾ × 2½ × 24"
C	1	**Fixed side,** ¾ × 2½ × 24"
D	5	**Slats,** ¼ × 3⅞ × 15"
E	2	**Long legs,** ¾ × 2½ × 34"
F	2	**Short legs,** ¾ × 2½ × 33"
G	2	**Rest,** 2 × 2 × 2⁵⁄₁₆"
H	2	**Pivot,** ¾ × ¾ × 3"
I	12	**Spacers,** ¼ × ¼ × ½"
J	2	**Dowel,** ⅝"-dia. × 20¼"

Note: All wood is white oak.
Misc.: Plastic resin glue; glider hinges; #6 x 1¼", 1½" wood screws; ¾"-diameter rotohinges; plastic button retainers.

This classic cedar picnic table is a pleasant sight in any outdoor setting. The single-unit construction makes this table easy to move so you can enjoy it anywhere in your yard.

Picnic Table

This practical picnic table is easy to make, easy to move and fun to use.

Eating *alfresco* is comfortable and enjoyable on this simple cedar picnic table. The traditional design combines the tabletop and benches as one unit so building the table is easy. To make assembly easier, the entire table is built with the top side down, then it's turned right side up to complete the finishing steps. The table shown here was made out of lightweight cedar, or you can build your table out of pressure-treated lumber. Either one will make a weatherproof picnic table you can enjoy on the deck, on the patio, or out in the yard. Sand and round over the bench slats and tabletop slats before you begin to assemble the tabletop and benches.

Build the tabletop

1 Cut the table slats (A) and lay them side by side on a flat surface, with the ends aligned and ¼" spacers between the slats. Attach a bar clamp across each end.

2 Set your miter box at 30°, and miter-cut the end supports (D) to 60° angles. Lay the supports across the slats, 7½" in from the ends.

3 Counterbore two 1¼"-deep holes in the end supports above each table slat with a ⅜" bit. Attach the supports by driving 3½" galvanized deck screws into the holes.

4 Bevel-cut both ends of the middle support (G) to 60° angles. Lay the middle support across the center of the tabletop. Attach the middle support to the tabletop

slats by driving two 2½" galvanized deck screws into each slat.

Attach the legs and benchtops

1 Miter-cut the ends of the table legs (C) to 60° angles. Trim off 1½" from the bottom outside corner of each leg at a 90° angle from the miter-cut end (see *Diagram*).

2 Clamp the legs to the outside face of the end support, ends flush to the underside of the tabletop and centered between the sides. Using a ⅜" spade bit, drill two holes through each leg and the end support. Use 3" carriage bolts to attach the legs to the end support, securing them with nuts and washers.

3 To mark the position of the bench support on the legs, hold a framing square along the bottom of the tabletop. Measure 13½" up along the vertical arm, then hold a straightedge across the framing square and mark the legs.

4 Miter-cut the bench supports (G) to 60° angles. Clamp the bench supports to the inside face of the legs, centered across the

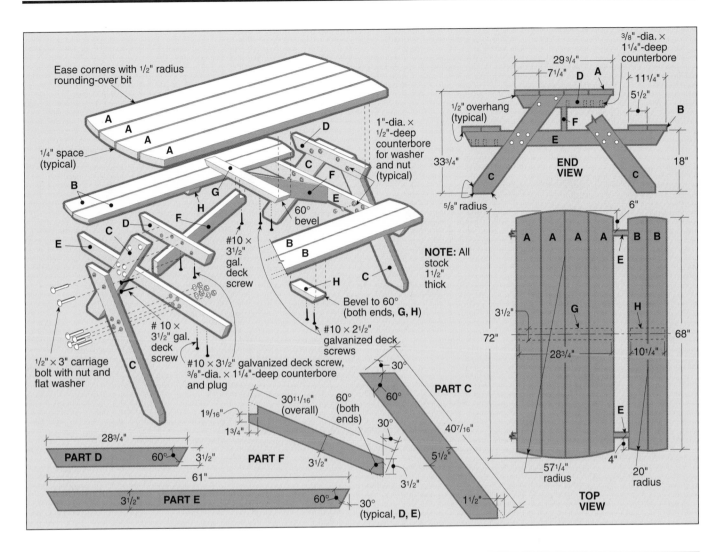

Ease corners with 1/2" radius rounding-over bit

1/4" space (typical)

A A A A

B

C D E F

E

G H

1/2" × 3" carriage bolt with nut and flat washer

10 × 3 1/2" gal. deck screw

#10 × 3 1/2" galvanized deck screw, 3/8"-dia. × 1 1/4"-deep counterbore and plug

D

C F E G

#10 × 3 1/2" gal. deck screw

60° bevel

1"-dia. × 1/2"-deep counterbore for washer and nut (typical)

B

H

C

NOTE: All stock 1 1/2" thick

Bevel to 60° (both ends, G, H)

#10 × 2 1/2" galvanized deck screws

PART D 28 3/4" 60° 3 1/2"

PART E 61" 3 1/2" 60°

PART F 30 11/16" (overall) 1 9/16" 1 3/4" 60° (both ends) 3 1/2" 30° 30° 3 1/2" (typical, D, E)

PART C 30° 60° 60° 30° 40 7/16" 5 1/2" 1 1/2"

3/8"-dia. × 1 1/4"-deep counterbore

29 3/4"
7 1/4" D A 11 1/4"
5 1/2"
1/2" overhang (typical)
B
F
E
33 3/4"
END VIEW
C C
5/8" radius
18"

6"

A A A A B B
E
G H
3 1/2"
72" 28 3/4" 10 1/4" 68"
E
E
57 1/4" radius 4" 20" radius
TOP VIEW

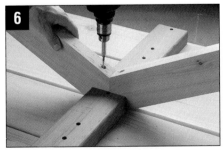

6

6 Center the notched end of the diagonal brace on the middle tabletop support. Drive two 2 1/2" galvanized deck screws through the diagonal brace into the middle support of the tabletop.

table's width. Drill four 1/2" holes on the outside face of each leg, and attach the bench supports with 3" carriage bolts secured with nuts and washers.
5 Miter-cut the ends of the diagonal braces (F) to 60° angles. Cut a 1 3/4 × 1 9/16" rectangular notch in one end of each brace.

7 Center the diagonal braces on the bench supports. Use a 3/8" bit to drill counterbore holes, then drive two 3 1/2" deck screws through the outside face of the bench supports and into the angled braces.
8 Cut bench slats (B) and clamp in pairs, like the tabletop slats.
9 Bevel-cut the ends of the bench cleats to 60° angles. Center the cleats across the bench slats and drive two 2 1/2" galvanized deck screws through the cleats into each benchtop slat.
10 Center bench tops on the bench supports, so the outside edges extend 1/2" past the ends of the supports, clamp them in place.
11 Use a 3/8" bit to drill two 1 1/4"-deep counterbore holes into the bench supports over each slat. Attach the benchtops to the supports by driving 3 1/2" deck screws in each hole.

CUTTING LIST

Key	Qty.	Description & Size
A	4	Table slats, 1 1/2 × 7 1/4 × 72"
B	4	Bench slats, 1 1/2 × 5 1/2 × 68"
C	4	Table legs, 1 1/2 × 5 1/2 × 40 7/16"
D	2	End supports, 1 1/2 × 3 1/2 × 28 3/4"
E	2	Bench supports, 1 1/2 × 3 1/2 × 61"
F	2	Braces, 1 1/2" × 3 1/2 × 30 11/16"
G	1	Middle support, 1 1/2 × 3 1/2 × 28 3/4"
H	2	Bench cleats, 1 1/2 × 3 1/2 × 10 1/4"

Note: All pieces are cedar.
Misc.: Galvanized deck screws (2 1/2", 3 1/2"), 1/2 × 3" carriage bolts with nuts & washers, 3/8" wood plugs, plastic resin glue.

Finishing

1 Glue 1/2" cedar wood plugs in all counterbored screw holes with plastic resin glue.
2 Lay out and cut the curved ends of the tabletop and benches with a sabersaw.
3 Sand all rough edges and apply a waterproof stain or varnish.

Patio Table

Even on the smallest patio or deck, you can experience the pleasure of fine patio furniture with this subtle, compact design.

This cedar patio table, with matching benches, makes a fine addition to any outdoor area. The slatted tabletop pattern provides a touch of originality and interest to a sturdy, functional design that will withstand the forces of the elements.

Although the cedar doesn't need to be treated for weather protection, you can add waterproof stain or varnish for extra protection.

Building the tabletop

Although the tabletop for our patio table is square, we built it in four identical quadrants to achieve

the diagonal pattern. To make sure all four quadrants were the same size and shape, we used a triangular plywood pattern as a guide for trimming the edges with a circular saw. Spacers placed between the individual slats during assembly ensured that the openings in the tabletop are a uniform width.

To cut down on finishing time, select the better face of the stock for the tabletop and run it through your planer.

1 Cut the tabletop slats (parts A to E), oversizing them about 2" in length so they can be trimmed

more easily. Cut the long top support (F), and the short supports (G).

2 Rip four ³⁄₁₆"-wide strips from a scrap piece of ³⁄₄"-thick stock. Cut the strips to the same approximate lengths as the tabletop slats, for use as temporary spacers between the slats.

3 Make the tabletop template. On a piece of ³⁄₄" plywood, draw a right triangle with two 26¼" legs and one 37⅛" side. Use a framing square to draw the triangle. Double check the dimensions of the triangle, then cut it out on your tablesaw, or use a circular saw and a straightedge.

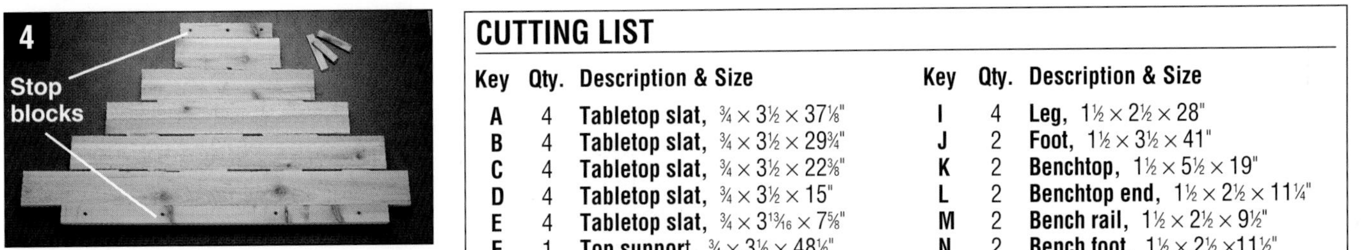

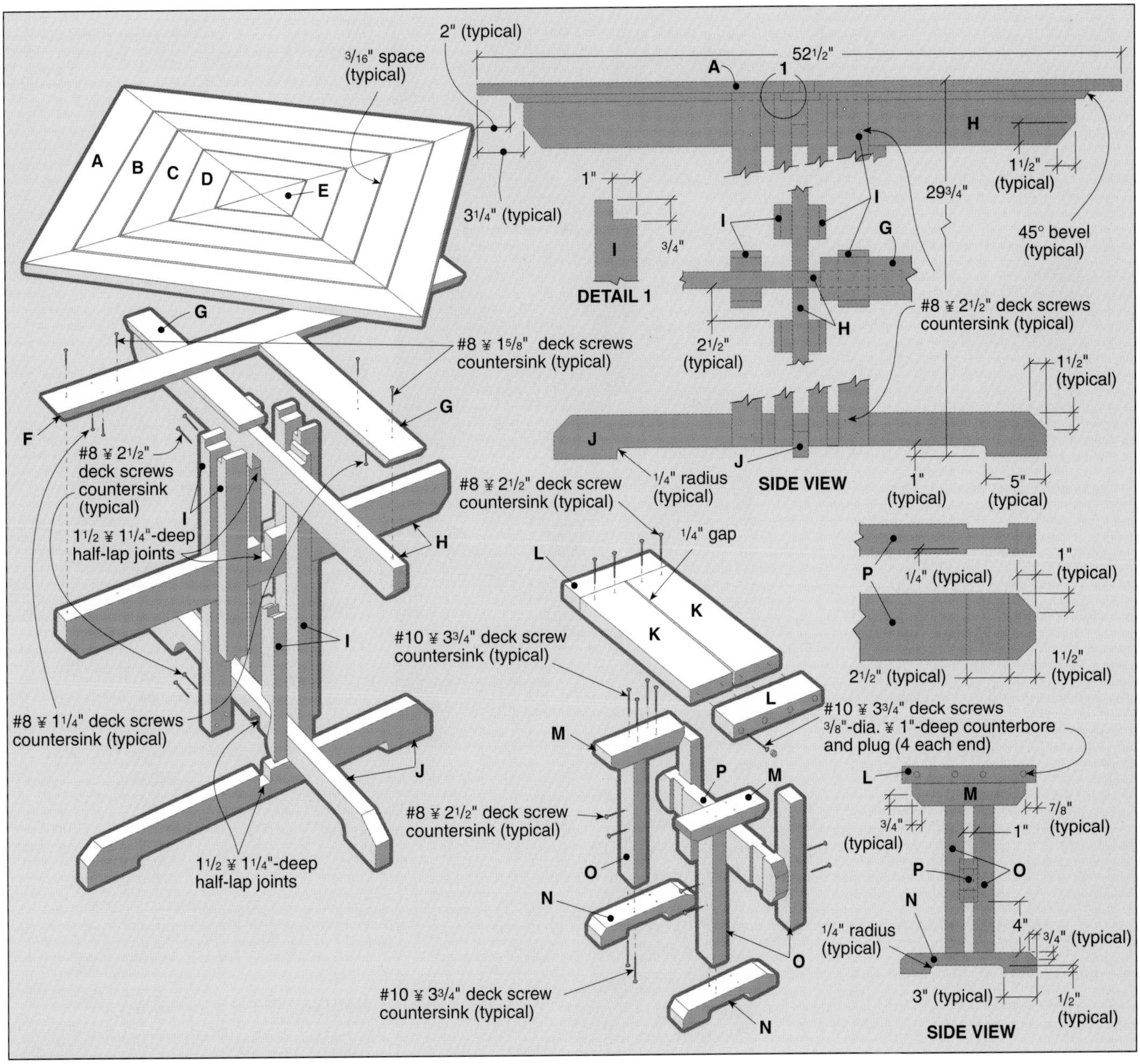
2" (typical)
3/16" space (typical)
52 1/2"
A
1
H
A
B
C
D
E
3 1/4" (typical)
1"
3/4"
I
DETAIL 1
I
I
G
29 3/4"
1 1/2" (typical)
45° bevel (typical)
#8 ¥ 2 1/2" deck screws countersink (typical)
H
2 1/2" (typical)
G
#8 ¥ 1 5/8" deck screws countersink (typical)
G
1 1/2" (typical)
F
#8 ¥ 2 1/2" deck screws countersink (typical)
I
1 1/2 ¥ 1 1/4"-deep half-lap joints
H
#8 ¥ 2 1/2" deck screw countersink (typical)
J
1/4" radius (typical)
J
SIDE VIEW
1" (typical)
5" (typical)
L
1/4" gap
P
1/4" (typical)
1" (typical)
K
K
I
#10 ¥ 3 3/4" deck screw countersink (typical)
2 1/2" (typical)
1 1/2" (typical)
#8 ¥ 1 1/4" deck screws countersink (typical)
L
#10 ¥ 3 3/4" deck screws 3/8"-dia. ¥ 1"-deep counterbore and plug (4 each end)
M
J
P
M
L
M
3/4" (typical)
7/8" (typical)
1"
#8 ¥ 2 1/2" deck screw countersink (typical)
1 1/2 ¥ 1 1/4"-deep half-lap joints
O
P
O
N
N
1/4" radius (typical)
4"
3/4" (typical)
O
#10 ¥ 3 3/4" deck screw countersink (typical)
N
3" (typical)
1/2" (typical)
SIDE VIEW

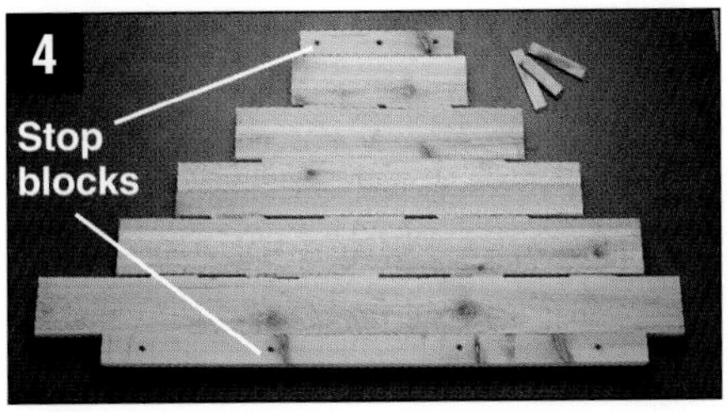
4
Stop blocks

4 Lay the slats for one quadrant of the tabletop in a triangle on a flat surface, good side down. Insert the 3/16" spacer strips between slats, push the slats and spacers together so the edges are tight, then screw stop blocks at both edges to keep the slats from shifting.

5 Measure the setback distance from your circular saw blade to the saw fence, then mark a centerpoint at the outside edge of the short slat (E). Make a mark down from the centerpoint at a distance equal to the saw setback.

CUTTING LIST

Key	Qty.	Description & Size	Key	Qty.	Description & Size
A	4	**Tabletop slat,** ¾ × 3½ × 37⅛"	I	4	**Leg,** 1½ × 2½ × 28"
B	4	**Tabletop slat,** ¾ × 3½ × 29¾"	J	2	**Foot,** 1½ × 3½ × 41"
C	4	**Tabletop slat,** ¾ × 3½ × 22⅜"	K	2	**Benchtop,** 1½ × 5½ × 19"
D	4	**Tabletop slat,** ¾ × 3½ × 15"	L	2	**Benchtop end,** 1½ × 2½ × 11¼"
E	4	**Tabletop slat,** ¾ × 3 13/16 × 7⅝"	M	2	**Bench rail,** 1½ × 2½ × 9½"
F	1	**Top support,** ¾ × 3½ × 48½"	N	2	**Bench foot,** 1½ × 2½ ×11½"
G	2	**Top support,** ¾ × 3½ × 22½"	O	4	**Bench leg,** 1½ × 2½ × 12"
H	2	**Rail,** 1½×3½×46"	P	1	**Bench stretcher,** 1½ × 3½ × 20½"

Notes: All wood is cedar. Bench parts (Qty.) are for one bench only.

Misc.: Waterproof glue, galvanized screws (#8 × 1¼", #8 × 1⅝", #8 × 2½", #10 × 3¾").

6

Saw blade
setback

6 Position the template on the slats, with the point opposite the 37⅛" side touching the setback mark on the short slat (E). Make sure the longest slat (A) is parallel to the edge of the pattern, then secure the template to the slats with 1½" screws. Remove the stop blocks, then clamp the slats and template to your worksurface. Cut the ends off the slats, using the template as a guide for the fence of your circular saw.

7 Cut the remaining three tabletop quadrants using the same template and techniques used for the first quadrant (*steps 4 to 6*).

8 Cut the rails (H) and trim off 1½" corners at the bottom ends of the rails. Also cut 45° on both bottom ends of the long top support (F), and on one bottom end of each short support (G).

9 Cut 1½ × 1¾"-deep notches at the centers of the rails to form half-lap joints (see *Diagram*). Notch the top edge of one support, and the bottom edge of the other.

TOOL TIP

If you're using a template as a guide for a circular saw, as we show here, keep the pressure on the saw as far forward as you can, so the saw doesn't tip back as the waste material falls away. As a general rule, rest the foot of a portable saw on the stock that isn't being cut away, wherever possible.

10

10 Drill pilot holes down through the top rail at the half-lap joint. Drill the holes on opposite corners of the joint. Pull the joint apart, apply glue, then reassemble the pieces. Reinforce with #8 × 2½" galvanized screws driven into the pilot holes.

11

11 Drill pilot holes for #8 × 1¼" screws in the long and the short top supports. Stagger the holes along the centers of the boards, and space them at 4" to 6" intervals.

12 Lay the the rails on-edge, on your worksurface, then center the top supports in position (see *Diagram*) over the rails, with the pilot holes facing up. Extend the pilot holes into the rails, then attach the

top supports to the rails with glue and #8 × 1⅝" galvanized screws.

13 On a flat surface, dry-assemble the tabletop slats for all four quadrants, forming a square. Make sure the finished surface is facing down. Cut each ³⁄₁₆" spacer (*step 2*) into eight sections, and fit one spacer at the end of each slat, near the miter joints. Adjust the slats and spacers until the assembly is exactly square, and the edges of adjoining slats are aligned.

14

14 Carefully place the top support and rail assembly over the tabletop, with the supports centered on the mitered seams. Mark pilot holes for #8 × 1⅝" galvanized screws, located at least 1" from the edges of the top supports. Drill two countersunk pilot holes per slat.

15 Attach the top support and rail assembly to the tabletop with #8 × 1⅝" galvanized screws, driven through the pilot holes. Don't glue the tabletop to the supports.

Building the leg assembly

The leg assembly is relatively easy to build. The top ends of the legs are rabbeted to hold the rails attached to the top supports and tabletop, and the feet fit together with a half-lap joint very similar to the joint used to join the rails. The feet also are trimmed at the corners and shaped on the bottom edge to create a decorative appearance.

1 Cut the legs (I) and the feet (J) to finished length.

2 Cut a 1 × ¾"-deep rabbet in the top end of each leg, to create recesses that will hold the tabletop rails (see *Diagram*).

3 Measure and mark the shaped cutouts on the bottoms of the feet (see *Diagram*).

4 Drill out the corners of the cutout with a ½" Forstner bit, creating a ¼" radius. Make the cutout on your bandsaw, connecting the holes at the corners. Smooth out the cutouts with a ½" drum sander mounted in your drill press.

5 Center and cut a 1½ × 1¼"-deep notch in the top edge of one foot, and in the bottom edge of the other foot, to form the half-lap joint (see *Diagram*).

6 Trim off 1½" corners at the top ends of the feet.

7 Dry-assemble the feet to make sure the half-lap joint fits together properly, then drill two pilot holes at opposite corners above the joint, and complete the joint with glue and #8 × 2½" galvanized screws.

8 Use a piece of plywood and wood scraps to create a spacer the same height as the cutouts in the bottoms of the feet, and slide the spacer into the cutouts.

9 Make a mark 2½" from the half-lap joint on both faces of each foot, to mark position for the inside edges of the legs.

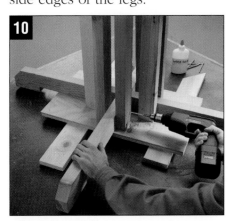

10 Attach the legs to the feet with glue and countersunk #8 × 2½" galvanized screws, making sure the ends of the legs are resting squarely on the spacer, with the inside edges of the legs flush against the 2½" mark.

11 Turn the tabletop upside down, and mark the faces of the rails 2½" from the half-lap joint. Set the leg-and-foot assembly onto the table-top, aligning the inside edge of the legs with the 2½" marks on rails.

12 Attach the legs to the rails with glue and two countersunk #8 × 2½" galvanized screws, driven through pilot holes in each leg.

Building the benches

The construction techniques for the benches are very similar to those used for the patio table. Although the *Cutting List* on page 47 lists enough parts for only one bench, the patio table is designed to accommodate up to four benches, depending on your seating needs.

1 Cut the benchtop slats (K) and the benchtop ends (L). Cut a ¼" spacer to fit between the bench-top slats.

2 On your drill press, drill four evenly spaced pilot holes for #10 × 3½" screws through both bench ends. Drill ⅜ × 1"-deep counterbores at each pilot hole. Dry-fit the benchtop ends and the benchtop slats on a flat surface, inserting a ¼" spacer between the slats. Extend the pilot holes into the slats.

3 Attach the ends to the slats, making sure all edges are flush, using glue and #10 × 3½" galvanized screws. Cut wood plugs with a ⅜"-diameter plug cutter, and insert them in the counterbores.

4 Cut the bench rails (M) and the bench feet (N), then trim a ¾" triangle off the bottom corners of the rails and the top corners of the feet.

5 Mark the cutout section on the bottom edge of the feet (see *Diagram*), then drill out the corners of the cutouts with a ½" Forstner bit, creating a ¼" radius. Make the cutout by cutting between the holes with a bandsaw. Smooth out the cutout with a ½" drum sander installed in your drill press.

6 Cut the bench stretcher (P) and trim a 1" triangle off all four corners of the stretcher.

7 Draw lines on both faces of the stretcher, 1½" from each end. Cut out a 2½ × ¼"-deep dado for each leg, with the outside shoulder of each dado at the 1½" mark.

8 Center the stretcher on the legs, and attach it using glue and two #8 × 2½" galvanized screws at each joint.

9 Center the leg-and-stretcher assembly on the bench feet, then attach the feet with glue and #10 × 3½" galvanized screws driven up through countersunk pilot holes drilled in the cutout, into the legs.

10 Cut the bench rails (M), then trim off a ¾" triangle from both bottom corners on each rail.

11 Center the rails over the legs so they're parallel to the feet, then attach them with glue and #10 × 3½" galvanized screws (two per leg) driven down through the rails and into the top ends of the legs.

12 Center the bench top assembly on the rails, with a ⅞" overhang at the ends of the rails. Attach the bench top with #8 × 2½" galvanized screws, driven into the rails through countersunk pilot holes.

Finishing the patio table set

We used a light, semi-transparent exterior stain for the tabletop and the bench tops, and an opaque green stain for the leg assemblies. The geometric pattern of the table-top lends itself well to the use of contrasting finishes.

1 Sand all exposed surfaces with 120- then 220-grit sandpaper.

2 Apply the stain, as desired. If you're using two shades of stain, apply the lighter stain first.

3 Cedar has naturally high resistance to the elements, but for extra protection, add exterior varnish.

CHAPTER 2

Seating and Beds

Sit. Lay back. Relax.

Who can resist the laid-back attitude of an Adirondack chair, the lazy to-and-fro of a porch swing, the put-your-feet-up comfort of a futon couch? These and four other seating projects in this chapter bid family and guests to sit, settle back, and relax. Several pieces are designed for outdoor use, so you can smell the roses or watch the wildlife in comfort and style.

This chapter also features three beds, guaranteed to turn anyone into a sleepy head. The casual futon couch does double-duty: It folds out to serve as an extra bed. A sturdy trestle cradle gently rocks baby to sleep. The queen-size mission bed establishes a traditional ambience in your bedroom.

We used a variety of woods for these beds and seating pieces. We've suggested durable white oak or cedar for the outdoor swing, benches, and chair. To give the entry bench a country flavor, we selected pine. Oak is the traditional wood for mission-style furniture. Maple gives an heirloom quality to the cradle, futon couch, and kitchen chair.

Kitchen Chairs

Alone or in a set, these lovely chairs combine the classic with the contemporary.

Built from a design that combines the finest features of several styles, these kitchen chairs are as versatile as they come. The Shaker-style spindles and straightforward construction give a casual, breezy quality to our kitchen chairs. At the same time, the elegant, all-maple construction and the custom painting and styling make the chairs right at home in a formal dining setting.

The directions shown here are for a single chair, but if you're building more than one chair, ensure uniform results by making all similar parts at the same time.

This solid maple kitchen chair is designed to complement the kitchen table design shown in *Tables*, pages 22 to 25, but the simple design can adapt to just about any style of table.

WOODWORKER'S TIP

Make an adjustable compound angle jig for your portable drill guide.

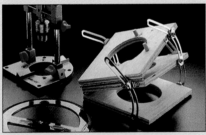

1 *Cut three pieces of ½"-thick plywood at least 1" larger than your drill guide base on all sides.*
2 *Drill a hole in the center of each piece, using a 4" hole saw.*
3 *Join two of the plywood pieces with a continuous hinge, then join the third piece to the top of the assembly with a hinge, so it opens at a right angle to the first two pieces.*
4 *Install a pair of adjustable lid supports between each pair of pieces. Secure the lid supports with wing nuts, allowing you to lock the pieces into position. Use a large protractor to set the angles of the pieces in both directions.*

Build the seat

The seat for our chair design is made of 1½"-thick solid maple for maximum durability and a distinctive look. The trickiest part of the seat construction is creating the seat contours. Drilling the holes for the back spindles is also a challenge, because all the compound angles are different. A jig for drilling at compound angles (see *Woodworker's Tip*, left) is very helpful.

1 Make a 1½ × 18 × 19" glued-up maple blank for the seat. Arrange the boards in the glue-up so the 19" sides, which will be the back and front edges, contain the end grain. Use your jointer and table-saw to square up the blank.

2 Lay out and outline the shape of the seat on the top and the underside of the blank (see *Diagram*). Use the outline as a reference for plotting the position of the spindle holes and leg holes. Draw a center line from front to back on both faces of the seat blank, then mark the centerpoints for the leg holes and the spindle holes, measuring from the center lines.

3 The spindle holes and the leg holes in the seat are drilled at compound angles. The compound angles are different for each hole (see *Diagram*), so write the two angles for each hole on the seat, next to the hole, for easy reference.

4 Turn the seat blank upside down, and clamp it to your worksurface.

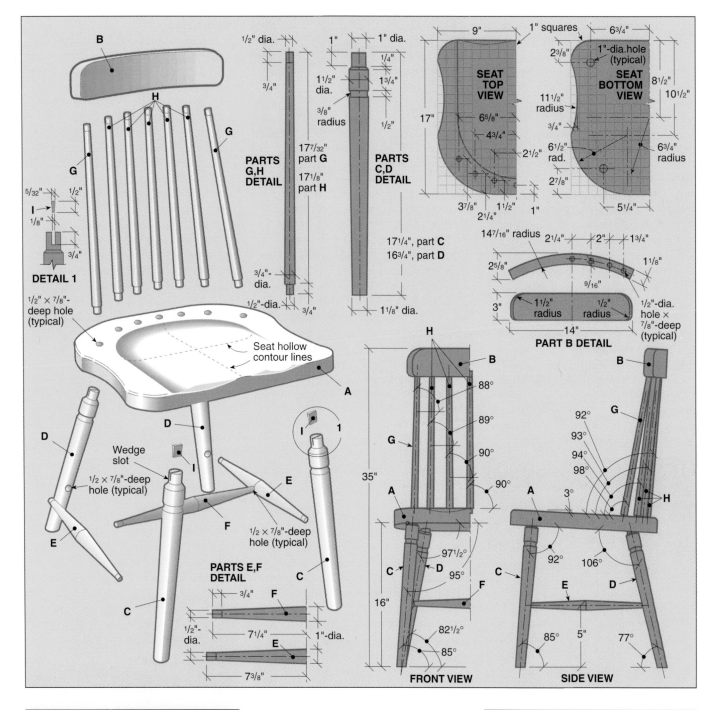

DETAIL 1

$5/32"$ ... $1/2"$

$1/8"$ ... $3/4"$

I

$1/2" \times 7/8"$-deep hole (typical)

B

H

G

G

G

PARTS G,H DETAIL

$1/2"$ dia.

$3/4"$

$17\ 7/32"$ part **G**

$17\ 1/8"$ part **H**

$3/4"$-dia.

$1/2"$-dia.

$1"$

$1"$ dia.

$1/4"$

$1\ 3/4"$

$1\ 1/2"$ dia.

$3/8"$ radius

$1/2"$

PARTS C,D DETAIL

$17\ 1/4"$, part **C**

$16\ 3/4"$, part **D**

$3/4"$

$1\ 1/8"$ dia.

SEAT TOP VIEW

$9"$

$1"$ squares

$17"$

$6\ 5/8"$

$4\ 3/4"$

$2\ 1/2"$

$11\ 1/2"$ radius

$3\ 7/8"$ $1\ 1/2"$

$2\ 1/4"$ $1"$

$6\ 3/4"$

$2\ 3/8"$

$1"$-dia.hole (typical)

SEAT BOTTOM VIEW

$8\ 1/2"$

$10\ 1/2"$

$3/4"$

$6\ 1/2"$ rad.

$2\ 7/8"$

$6\ 3/4"$ radius

$5\ 1/4"$

$14\ 7/16"$ radius

$2\ 1/4"$ $2"$ $1\ 3/4"$

$2\ 5/8"$

$3"$

$9/16"$

$1\ 1/8"$

$1\ 1/2"$ radius

$1/2"$ radius

$1/2"$-dia. hole × $7/8"$-deep (typical)

$14"$

PART B DETAIL

Seat hollow contour lines

A

D

D

C

C

Wedge slot

$1/2 \times 7/8"$-deep hole (typical)

I

E

E

F

$1/2 \times 7/8"$-deep hole (typical)

I   1

E

C

PARTS E,F DETAIL

$3/4"$ F

$1/2"$-dia.

$7\ 1/4"$ $1"$-dia.

E

$7\ 3/8"$

H

B

$88°$

$89°$

$90°$

$90°$

G

A

$35"$

C   D

$97\ 1/2"$

$95°$

$16"$

$82\ 1/2"$

$85°$

F

FRONT VIEW

B

G

$92°$

$93°$

$94°$

$98°$

H

A

$3°$

$92°$

$106°$

C

E   D

$85°$ $5"$ $77°$

SIDE VIEW

5

5 Drill each $1 \times 1"$-deep leg hole at the proper compound angle. We used an adjustable compound

angle jig (see *Woodworker's Tip*, opposite), together with a portable drill and drill guide, to drill our compound holes. Because our drilling jig increases the distance from the drill chuck to the work-piece, we used an extra-long $1"$ brad-point bit.

6 Drill the $1/2 \times 7/8"$-deep spindle holes in the seat at the correct compound angles.

7 Install a $3/8"$ 6-TPI blade in your bandsaw. Check the cutting table to be sure it's square to the blade,

CUTTING LIST

Key	Qty.	Description & Size
A	1	Seat, $1\ 1/2 \times 17 \times 18"$
B	1	Back, $2\ 5/8 \times 3 \times 14"$
C	2	Front leg, $1\ 1/2"$-dia. × $17\ 1/4"$
D	2	Back leg, $1\ 1/2"$-dia. × $16\ 3/4"$
E	2	Side stretcher, $1"$-dia. × $14\ 3/4"$
F	1	Middle stretcher, $1"$-dia. × $14\ 1/2"$
G	2	Outer spindle, $3/4"$-dia. × $17\ 7/32"$
H	5	Inner spindle, $3/4"$-dia. × $17\ 1/8"$
I	4	Tenon wedge, $5/32 \times 1/2 \times 3/4"$

Note: All wood is maple.
Misc.: Glue.

then carefully cut the seat shape out of the blank.

8 Install a 3"-diameter drum sander attachment in your drill press and use it to smooth out the edge contours of the seat.

9 Draw a reference line on the bottom of the seat, connecting the points on the sides where the back curve begins.

10 We shaped the contours in the top surface of the seat by feeding the blank over the tablesaw blade from the side, using an auxiliary fence clamped to the tablesaw as a guide for the seat blank. Clamp a straight board, at least ¾" thick and 24" long, to your tablesaw table for use as the auxiliary fence. Position the fence as if you were about to crosscut it in two, with the edge of the fence 2¼" away from the initial cutting point of the saw blade. Also, mark the center of the blade kerf onto the fence. The kerf mark is used as a pivot point for turning the seat blank as it crosses the blade.

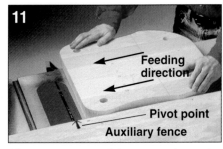

11 Equip your tablesaw with a 10" 40-tooth carbide-tipped blade, and raise it to ³⁄₁₆" above the table. Turn the seat blank upside down and set one side edge against the fence, with the flat front edge of the blank poised an inch or two from the blade.

12 Turn on the saw and begin feeding the seat across the blade, making a ³⁄₁₆"-deep trough in the seat. Carefully feed the seat up to the reference line on the side edges that marks the beginning of the back curve. Feed at an even pace to avoid burning the wood, applying steady downward pressure. Tip: If you've never used a tablesaw in this manner before, practice on a scrap of ¾"-thick wood first.

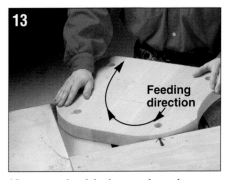

13 Once the blade reaches the mark at the beginning of the curve, start turning the seat 180° to follow the curve of the seat. Make sure the blank stays in constant contact with the pivot point marked on the fence. Turn the blank a full 180°, until the blade meets the other end of the curve reference line (at this point, the other side of the seat should be flush against the auxiliary fence).

14 With the side edge against the fence, feed the blank straight across the blade to finish the trough cut.

15 Move the fence ½" farther away from the blade, and make another pass across the blade. Continue moving the fence and cutting until the inside edges touch, leaving a center ridge.

16 Reset your saw blade to ⁵⁄₁₆" in height, and clamp the fence 2¾" away from the initial cutting point of the blade. Make another cut to deepen the trough in the center. Make additional passes, until the cuts reach a point ½" from the center of the seat on both sides.

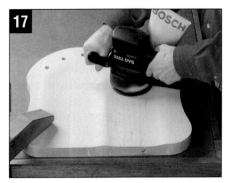

17 Smooth out the seat contours with a random-orbit sander. Sand the contours with 80- through 220-grit sandpaper. Feather the center ridge away from the front, so it disappears 3" from the front edge. Finish-sand the seat edges.

Make the legs

The legs are turned on a lathe from 1¾" square stock. Cut the legs a few inches longer than their finished size so they can be mounted on the lathe. After shaping, the bottoms of the legs will be trimmed at compound angles.

1 Cut the blanks for the legs, then mark the centers on all ends and drill ⅛ × ⅛"-deep holes. Cut ⅛"-deep saw kerfs across the diagonals of the top ends.

2 Dab oil in the hole at the bottom of one piece of leg stock, then mount the stock in the lathe, with the top at the headstock and the bottom at the tailstock.

3 Rough the stock to a 1½" cylinder with a 1" gouge, turning at 800 rpm. Smooth out the cylinder with a skew.

4 Stop the lathe. Mark the tenon shoulder, the end of the leg, and the accent groove (see *Diagram*) on the cylinder with a pencil. Set the lathe at 1,200 rpm and use a parting tool to scribe the tenon depth, groove depth, and the 1⅛" diameter of the leg bottom.

5 Use a 1" skew to taper the leg from the full 1½" diameter at the top to 1⅛" diameter at the bottom.

6 Cut the 1"-diameter tenon on the top end, then trim a ¼" shoulder at the bottom of the tenon, using a ½" skew.

7 Cut the ⅜"-radius accent groove, using a ½" gouge.

8 Finish-sand the leg with the lathe turning at 2,000 rpm.

9 Make the rest of the legs.

10 Mark trim lines on the bottoms of the legs (see *Diagram*). The final length of the front legs at their longest point is 17¼"; the back legs are 16¾".

11 We used a cradle jig to hold the legs for trimming. To make the cradle, cut two ¾ × 2 × 2" pieces of plywood, then drill a 1"-diameter hole through the center of one piece, and a 1³⁄₁₆"-diameter hole through the other. Cut the squares in half, and join one half of each piece with a 15"-long strip of plywood on each side.

12 Set a leg in the cradle, with the shoulder of the tenon pressed tight against the plwood at the 1"-diameter hole. Clamp the cradle to your miter gauge. Make a straight cut at the top end of the leg, leaving a 1"-long tenon.

13 Set up your tablesaw and miter gauge to make the compound cuts (see *Diagram*): The front legs are cut to splay out with a 5° miter and a 5° bevel; the back legs are splayed out with a 7½° miter and a 13° bevel.

14 Set a leg in the cradle, and align the blade with the trim line. Clamp the cradle to your miter gauge, then hold the leg in position in the cradle as you feed the leg through the saw, following the trim line.

15 Set up the saw and miter gauge for the back legs. Make the cuts.

16 Cut a ⅛"-wide, ¾"-deep slot in the center of all leg tenons for the blind wedges (I).

Make the spindles & stretchers

The spindles and stretchers are made using the same basic lathe turning techniques and tools that were used to make the legs.

1 Cut the side stretchers (E) and middle stretcher (F) from 1¼" square stock about 4" longer than the finished length.

2 Secure a stretcher in your lathe, and trim it to a 1"-diameter cylinder shape. Mark the midpoint of the stretcher, which will be the thickest part (1" diameter), and measure from the midpoint to mark the ends (½" diameter).

Scribe depth marks at the ends, then taper the cylinder from the midpoint to the ends

3 Shape ½"-diameter, ¾"-long tenons at both ends, then finish-sand. Shape the remaining stretchers, then make a cradle to hold the parts, and trim them to finished length (note that the side stretchers are ¼" longer than the middle stretcher).

4 Cut the spindles from 1"-square stock. Lay out, shape, taper, and cut spindle tenons using the techniques and tools shown in *Make the legs, steps 1 to 5*. Finish-sand, then trim to finished length.

Make the backrest

1 Outline the shape of the backrest (B) on a 3 × 3 × 15" maple blank (see *Diagram*). Lay out centers for the spindle holes (see *Diagram*) inside the outline, on the bottom edge of the blank.

2 Drill the ½ × ⅞"-deep spindle holes at the compound angles matching the spindle holes in the seat. Use the adjustable compound angle jig, a portable drill guide, and a ½"-diameter brad-point pit mounted in your portable drill.

3 Cut the backrest outline on your bandsaw.

4 Mark 1½"-radius roundovers on the top corners of the backrest, and ½"-radius roundovers on the bottom corners. Round over the corners to rough shape on your bandsaw, then smooth out all bandsaw cuts on your stationary sander. Finish-sand the backrest.

Complete the chair

1 Drill a ½"-diameter, ⅞"-deep hole in each side stretcher, at the midpoint (see *Diagram*). Dry-assemble the stretchers.

2 Dry-assemble the legs, seat, spindles, and backrest. Make sure all four legs rest flush on the floor, then draw a level line on each leg, 5" up from the floor. Position the stretcher assembly at the 5" marks to make sure it fits (see *Diagram*). Adjust the mark up or down, making sure the line is level with the floor. On the level lines, mark centerpoints for drilling stretcher holes.

3 Remove the legs, and use the leg cradle (see *Make the legs,* opposite) to hold each leg. Drill ½ × ⅞"-deep holes for the stretchers in each leg at the center-point mark, following the angle of the level line drawn on the leg.

4 Tape the tenons and leg accent strips, then paint the legs, stretchers, and spindles. We used gloss black enamel paint. Apply clear finish (we used Danish oil) to the seat, backrest, and accent strips.

5 Cut ¾"-wide × ½"-long maple wedges to fit the slots in the leg tenons. Make the wedges ⁵⁄₃₂" thick at one end, and taper them to ⅛" thickness at the other end.

6 Insert the wedges into the slots in the back legs, apply glue inside the leg holes, and insert the back legs. Make sure the legs are oriented correctly, then tap the seat with a rubber mallet until the wedges are fully seated.

7 Glue the stretcher assembly together, then glue the side stretchers into the holes in the back legs. Glue the front legs onto the stretchers while you glue and wedge them into the seat holes. Clamp with a band clamp wrapped around the legs at stretcher height.

8 Glue the spindles into the holes in the seat, then glue the backrest onto the spindles. Clamp and let the glue dry.

Patio Settee

A rough-hewn bench & hand-shaved spindles give this sturdy patio settee rustic appeal.

Frontier styling and white oak give this seating project a distinctly American flavor. The techniques we used also capture that pioneer spirit: We shaped the spindles, legs, and stretchers by hand, using a bench plane and a spokeshave; and the rough texture of the bench edges and the top of the backrest were obtained with a simple spokeshave or drawknife.

Perfect for a three-season porch, our patio settee can also be used inside, where it brings warmth and charm to even the coldest room. If you think your patio settee will undergo some direct exposure to the elements, use plastic resin glue for the joints and finish it with a coat of marine varnish.

Making the bench

The bench for our patio settee is made from glued-up sections of white oak. If you can find it, use 2"-thick stock for the glue-up so you don't end up with a bench that's a maze of glue joints. Or better yet, you may be able to buy a solid piece of stock big enough for the entire bench at a lumber yard or directly from a retail lumber mill.

1 Cut several pieces of stock for the bench (A) to 51", then plane to 1¾" thickness. Joint the stock to create flat edges, then run the pieces through a parallel planer to ensure that they're square.

2 Edge-glue the oak boards for the bench, then clamp with pipe clamps. Remove excess glue, and let the glue-up dry overnight.
3 Remove the clamps and any dried glue, then sand the surfaces smooth with a belt sander and 60- through 120-grit sandpaper.
4 Designate one of the long edges of the glue-up as the back, then

WOODWORKER'S TIP

From a piece of scrap wood, make a drilling guide to help you drill holes for spindles. Adjust a piece of scrap wood on a drill press table so it's square with the table and clamp it in place with a backer board between the scrap and the table. Tilt the table to 10°, and drill a hole through the scrap with a ⅝" Forstner bit. Draw a line on the scrap, 2½" from the center of the hole on the high side of the table, to mark the distance of the spindle holes from the back edge of the bench.

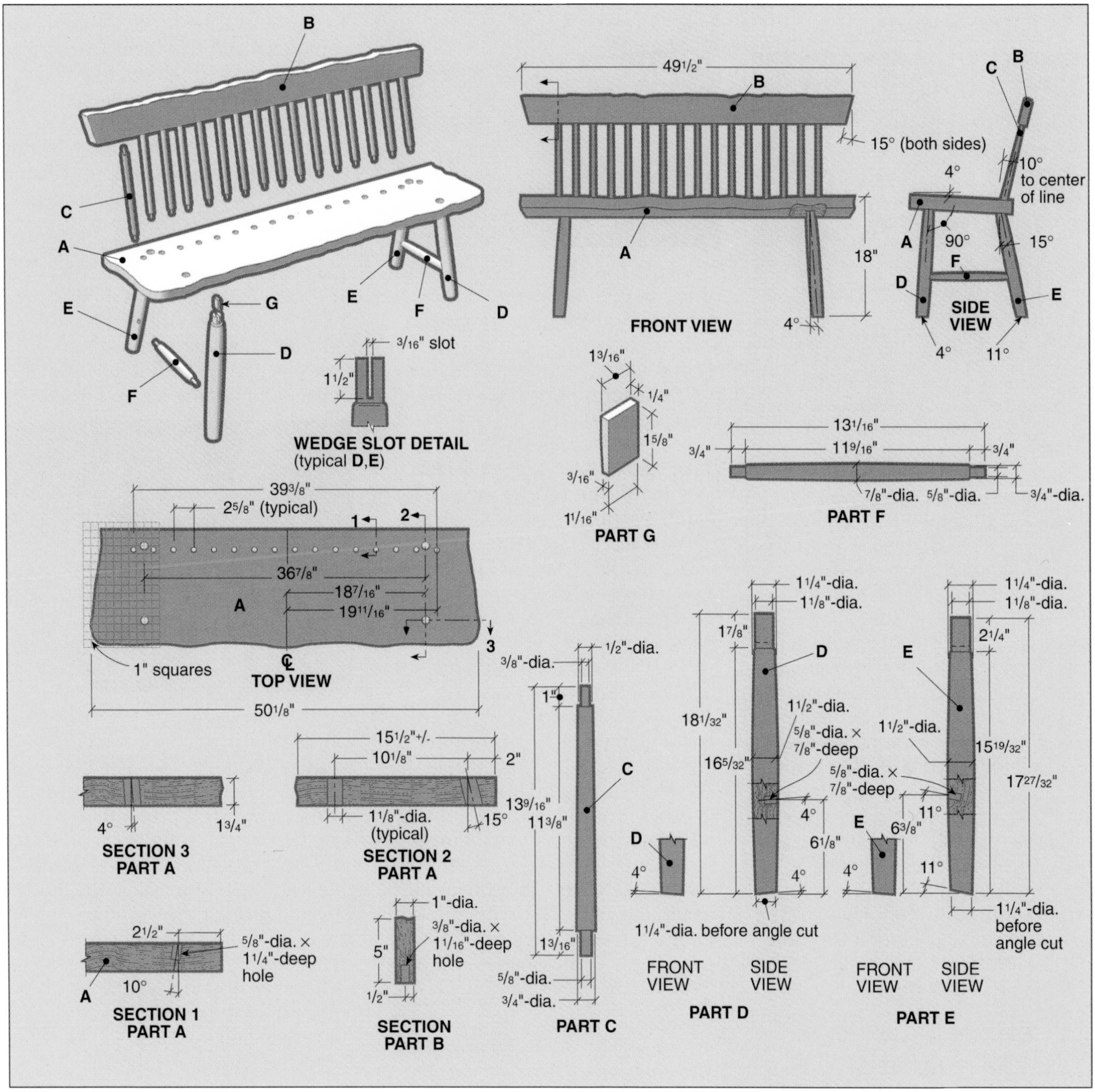

B
C
A
E
G
E
F
D
D
F
49 1/2"
B
15° (both sides)
A
FRONT VIEW
18"
4°
C
B
4°
10° to center of line
A
90°
15°
F
D
SIDE VIEW
E
4°
11°
3/16" slot
1 1/2"
WEDGE SLOT DETAIL (typical D,E)
1 3/16"
1/4"
1 5/8"
3/16"
1 1/16"
PART G
13 1/16"
11 9/16"
3/4"
3/4"
7/8"-dia.
5/8"-dia.
3/4"-dia.
PART F
39 3/8"
2 5/8" (typical)
1
2
36 7/8"
18 7/16"
19 11/16"
A
3
1" squares
TOP VIEW
50 1/8"
1/2"-dia.
3/8"-dia.
1"
C
13 9/16"
11 3/8"
1 3/16"
5/8"-dia.
3/4"-dia.
PART C
1 1/4"-dia.
1 1/8"-dia.
1 7/8"
D
18 1/32"
16 5/32"
1 1/2"-dia.
5/8"-dia. × 7/8"-deep
4°
6 1/8"
D
4°
4°
1 1/4"-dia. before angle cut
FRONT VIEW
SIDE VIEW
PART D
1 1/4"-dia.
1 1/8"-dia.
2 1/4"
E
1 1/2"-dia.
15 19/32"
17 27/32"
5/8"-dia. ×
7/8"-deep
11°
E
6 3/8"
4°
11°
1 1/4"-dia. before angle cut
FRONT VIEW
SIDE VIEW
PART E
15 1/2"+/-
10 1/8"
2"
4°
1 3/4"
SECTION 3 PART A
1 1/8"-dia. (typical)
15°
SECTION 2 PART A
2 1/2"
5/8"-dia. × 1 1/4"-deep hole
A
10°
SECTION 1 PART A
1"-dia.
3/8"-dia. × 1 1/16"-deep hole
5"
1/2"
SECTION PART B

draw a center line across the boards. Lay out the shape of the bench, measuring from the back edge (see *Diagram*) and using the centerline as a reference.

5 Draw a parallel line 2½" from the back edge of the bench to mark the holes for the back rest spindles (C). On the back line, mark centers for the outside spindles, 19¹¹⁄₁₆" from the centerline. Mark points along the line every 2⅝" for the 14 inside spindles.

6 Drill 1¼"-deep holes through the spindle marks, sloping toward the back edge of the bench at 10°, using a portable drill with a ⅝" Forstner bit and a drilling guide (see *Woodworker's Tip,* opposite).

7 Mark centerpoints for the back leg holes on the bench surface, 18⁷⁄₁₆" on each side of the centerline, and 2" from the back edge. Use a square to mark front leg holes, in line with the back leg marks, 12⅛" from the back edge. Centerpoints for the leg holes should be 36⅞" apart.

CUTTING LIST

Key	Qty.	Description & Size
A	1	**Bench,** 1¾ × 15½ × 50⅛"
B	1	**Back rest,** 1 × 5 × 49½"
C	16	**Spindle,** ¾"-dia. × 13⁹⁄₁₆"
D	2	**Front leg,** 1½"-dia. × 18¹⁄₃₂"
E	2	**Back leg,** 1½"-dia. × 17²⁷⁄₃₂"
F	2	**Stretcher,** ⅞"-dia. × 13¹⁄₁₆"
G	4	**Wedge,*** ¼ × 1³⁄₁₆ × 1⅝"

***Note:** All wood is white oak except wedges (G), which are walnut.

Misc.: Glue, sandpaper.

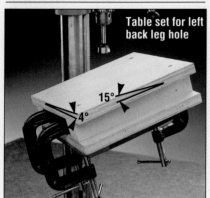

Table set for left
back leg hole

15°

4°

Use your drill press and a drill press table jig to drill holes with compound angles. To make the table jig for this project, bevel-cut two pieces of scrap so they form a 4° slope, and sandwich them between two pieces of plywood that are the same size as your drill press table. Clamp the jig to the drill press table, then tilt the table 15°.

8 Set your drill press table to a 15° tilt, then set a drill press table jig (shown above) with a 4° slope onto the drill press table, making sure the edges of the tables are squarely aligned. With the 4° angle sloping toward the front edge of the table, position the bench on the table, top side up, and support the overhanging edge of the bench from below. Drill one back leg hole through the bench with a 1⅛" Forstner bit, then tilt the drill press table 15° in the opposite direction, and drill the other back leg hole.

9 With the auxiliary drill press table still sloping forward at 4°, set your drill press table at a level position, and drill the front leg holes with a 1⅛" Forstner bit.

10 Secure the bench, then rough-cut the front and side edges, following the layout made in *step 4*. Use a sabersaw and 6"-long, coarse wood-cutting blade.

TOOL TIP

Sharpen spokeshaves, drawknives, and other carving tools frequently (after each five minutes of use with white oak) on your stationary sander, using 220-grit sandpaper.

11 Shape the side and front edges of the bench with a spokeshave or drawknife to create a roundover with a rustic look. The edges should have a carved appearance, but be careful not to leave any sharp edges or splinters exposed.

Make spindles, stretchers & legs

We made the tenons on our spindles, stretchers, and legs first, then used a plane to create the rough shapes, followed by a spokeshave for the final shaping and texturing. The spokeshave creates a rustic look that blends well with the contoured edges of the bench and the back rest.

Woodworkers with a lot of experience using a lathe may prefer to turn the spindles, legs, and spreaders. Using a lathe is probably faster, but the parts will have a much more uniform, machined appearance. If you use a lathe to make these parts, then make the bench and back rest with smooth, sanded edges.

TOOL TIP

Tenon cutters, which are mounted in a drill press, look and work a lot like plug cutters, but they will cut tenons as long as 3", compared to only ¾" with a plug cutter. An easy way to use a tenon cutter is to mount it in your drill press, then turn the drill press table to a vertical position. Make a jig by clamping pieces of scrap wood the same thickness as the workpiece to the table, surrounding the workpiece on all three sides. Add another scrap below to box-in the workpiece. Leave an opening at the bottom of the jig so sawdust doesn't accumulate in the bottom (see photo in step 4 of this section).

1 Cut the blanks for the back rest spindles (C), front legs (D), back legs (E), and stretchers (F).

2 Use a compound miter saw to trim the bottoms of the front and back legs. To cut the back legs, tilt the blade of your compound miter saw to 4°, then set the miter gauge at 11°, and trim one leg bottom. Reset the tilt and the miter gauge 4° and 11° in the opposite directions and cut the second back leg.

3 Keep the blade tilt at 4°, but shift the miter gauge to 4° as well; then cut one front leg. Reverse the angles and cut the second front leg.

4 Tilt your drill press table to vertical, then clamp a tenon-cutting jig to the table (see *Tool Tip,* below left). Install a ⅜"-diameter tenon cutter in the drill press, then cut 1"-long tenons in the tops of all 16 spindles. Install a ⅝" tenon cutter, then cut 1³⁄₁₆"-long tenons in the bottom ends of the spindles.

5 Set the blanks for the stretchers in the tenon-cutting jig on your drill press, and cut ⅝"-diameter, 1³⁄₁₆"-long tenons at the ends of both stretchers.

6 Cut the tenons for the tops of the front and back legs by hand. To cut a front-leg tenon, measure down 1⅞" from the top of the leg and mark a line across all four sides. For a back leg, measure down 2¼" and mark lines. Using a backsaw, make a ⅜"-deep cut at each of the four lines on each leg.

7 Draw diagonals across the end of the workpiece to find the centerpoint, then mark the point. Set a compass to make a ⁹⁄₁₆"-radius circle, then draw the circle on the end of the workpiece. Use a file to trim away the corners until the tenon is round. Drill a 1⅛" hole in a piece of scrap wood, and use it as a guide to check your workpiece as you file.

8 On your bandsaw, cut ³⁄₁₆"-wide, 1½"-deep slots in the top tenons on the front and back legs.

9 Mark points for the holes that hold the stretcher tenons, 6⅛" up from the bottoms of the front legs, and 6⅜" up from the bottoms of the back legs (see *Diagram*).

10 Set the tilt of your drill press table to 4°. Drill ⅝ × ⅞"-deep holes at the marks in the front legs. Reset the drill press table to 11°, then drill ⅝ × ⅞"-deep holes at the marks in the back legs.

11 On each of the spindles, legs, and stretchers, draw a center line lengthwise along each face. Use the center lines as references for drawing cutting profiles on each piece (see *Diagram*).

12 Set one spindle lengthwise between the heads of a bar clamp, and tighten the clamp. Secure the bar in your workbench vise.

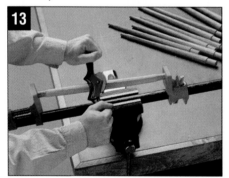

13 Use a bench plane to create the rough shape of the spindle. Start removing wood at a corner next to the top shoulder. Removing a little wood at a time, work toward the bottom shoulder, which has the thickest diameter when finished. Turn the workpiece in the clamp ¼ turn after you round off each corner. When all four corners are rounded, use a spokeshave to smooth out the shape, remembering that the goal is not to get perfectly round parts.

14 Shape all the spindles, then shape the stretchers and legs (see *Diagram*), using the same technique. For the legs and stretchers, work from the middle, toward each end.

Assembling the settee

Dry-fit the legs, stretchers, and bench to make sure all the parts fit together properly. If you've done clean, accurate work, you'll find that the bench is very solid and functional, even without reinforcing the joints with glue. But don't be tempted to leave the joints unglued, since temperature and humidity changes will likely cause some shrinking and swelling of the joints.

1 Cut ¼ × 1³⁄₁₆ × 1⅝" walnut blanks for the wedges (G). Taper the blanks evenly on each side, using your stationary sander. Taper from ¼" to ³⁄₁₆" in thickness, and from 1⅛" to 1¹⁄₁₆", top to bottom.

2 Disassemble the dry-fitted settee, making note of how the stretchers and legs fit together. Glue the stretchers into the holes in the front and back legs.

3 Turn the bench upside down, then glue the legs into the holes in the bench.

4 Flip the assembly onto its legs, and adjust the leg position until the legs rest evenly on a flat surface. Press together the joints between the legs and the bench, and between the stretchers and the legs, to make them as tight as possible.

5 Apply a dab of glue in the slot in the top of each leg, then drive a wedge into each slot with a wood mallet, locking the legs in place. Check the joints between the legs and the stretchers, tightening the fit if needed; then let the glue dry.

6 Sand the exposed tenon-and-wedge parts until they're flush with the surface of the bench, using a belt sander and 120-grit sandpaper.

7 Cut the back rest (B), with 15° angles at the ends (see *Diagram*),

and shape the top edge with your drawknife to the same texture as the edges of the bench.

8 Draw a center line lengthwise along the bottom edge of the back rest, then find and mark the midpoint. Measure out 19¹¹⁄₁₆" from the midpoint in each direction, and mark the centers for the outside spindle. Mark the centers for the interior spindle holes at 2⅝" intervals along the center line.

9 Install a ⅜" Forstner bit in your drill press, and use it to drill ⅜"-diameter × 1⅛"-deep holes in the bottom of the back rest, at the marked intervals.

10 Test-fit the spindles and the back rest, and make minor adjustments, if necessary.

11 Glue the bottom spindle tenons into the holes in the bench. Set each spindle in place by rapping it lightly on top with a wood mallet.

12 Before the glue at the spindle joints dries, apply glue to the top tenons of the spindles, then set the back rest onto the tenons. Press the back rest and spindles together until the joints are tight, then rap lightly all along the top of the backrest, using a wood mallet. Carefully wipe away excess glue around the tenons.

13 Scrape away any dried glue, then sand the entire bench lightly with 220-grit sandpaper. Because of its rustic styling, the patio settee doesn't require extensive sanding and smoothing, but make sure to remove any sharp edges or splinters. Don't oversand the edges of the bench and the back rest.

14 Wipe the patio settee clean; then finish as desired. We used untinted tung oil.

Adirondack Chair

The history of furniture-making would be incomplete without this pioneer of great design—the Adirondack chair.

Adirondack furniture has been a longstanding tradition in the art of fine furniture-making in America. Known for its rustic beauty, sturdy construction and comfortable design, outdoor Adirondack furniture has changed very little over the last hundred years. With its wide, level arms perfect for holding drinks, and its characteristic sloped seat and relined back, this cedar Adirondack chair is a natural for outdoor relaxation.

Construction

1 Lay out the pattern for one of the stringers (A) on ¾" cedar at least 8 × 40", referring to De-tail 1 and Side View (see *Layout Tools*).

2 Use a flexible straightedge to lay out the arch pattern of the stringer.

CUTTING LIST

Key	Qty.	Description & Size
A	2	**Stringer,** ¾ × 5½ × 39¼"
B	1	**Bottom Back Rail,** ¾ × 3½ × 20¾"
C	12	**Slat,** ¾ × 1½ × 20¾"
D	2	**Front Leg,** ¾ × 5½ × 19¼"
E	2	**Back Leg,** ¾ × 2¹³⁄₁₆ × 28⅛"
F	1	**Top Back Rail,** ¾ × 5½ × 20¾"
G	2	**Armrest,** ¾ × 6½ × 31⅞"
H	1	**Stringer Rail,** ¾ × 3½ × 20¾"
I	2	**Brace,** ¾ × 4 × 6"
J-M	7	**Stave,** ¾ × 3½ × 35½"

Note: All material is cedar.

Miscellaneous: 2", 3" galvanized decking screws; ¼ × 3" carriage bolts; waterproof glue.

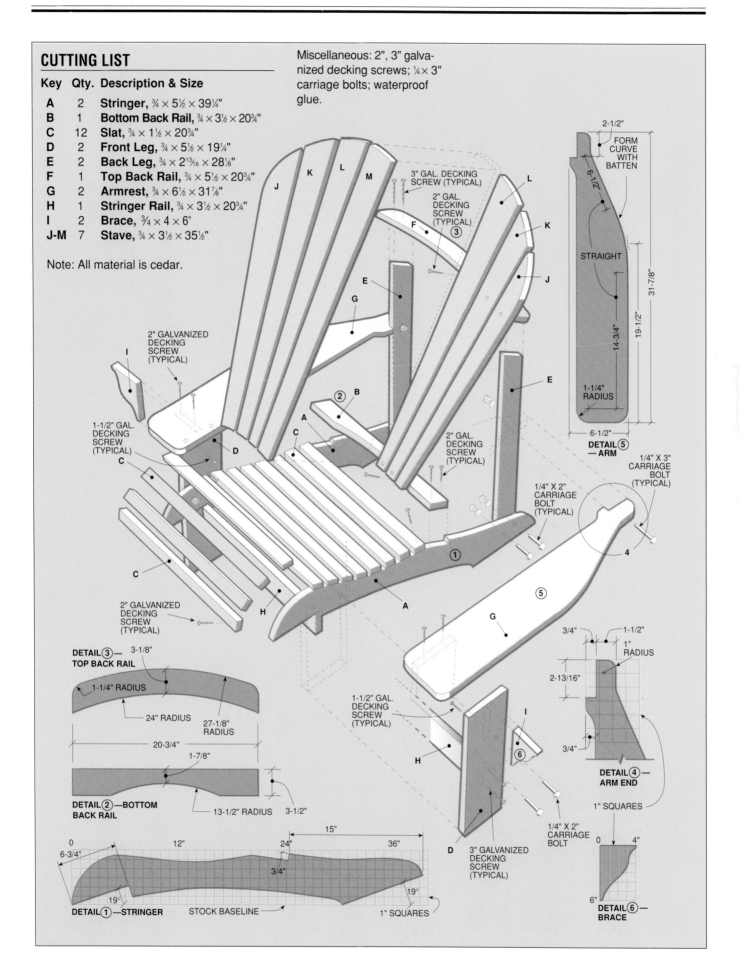

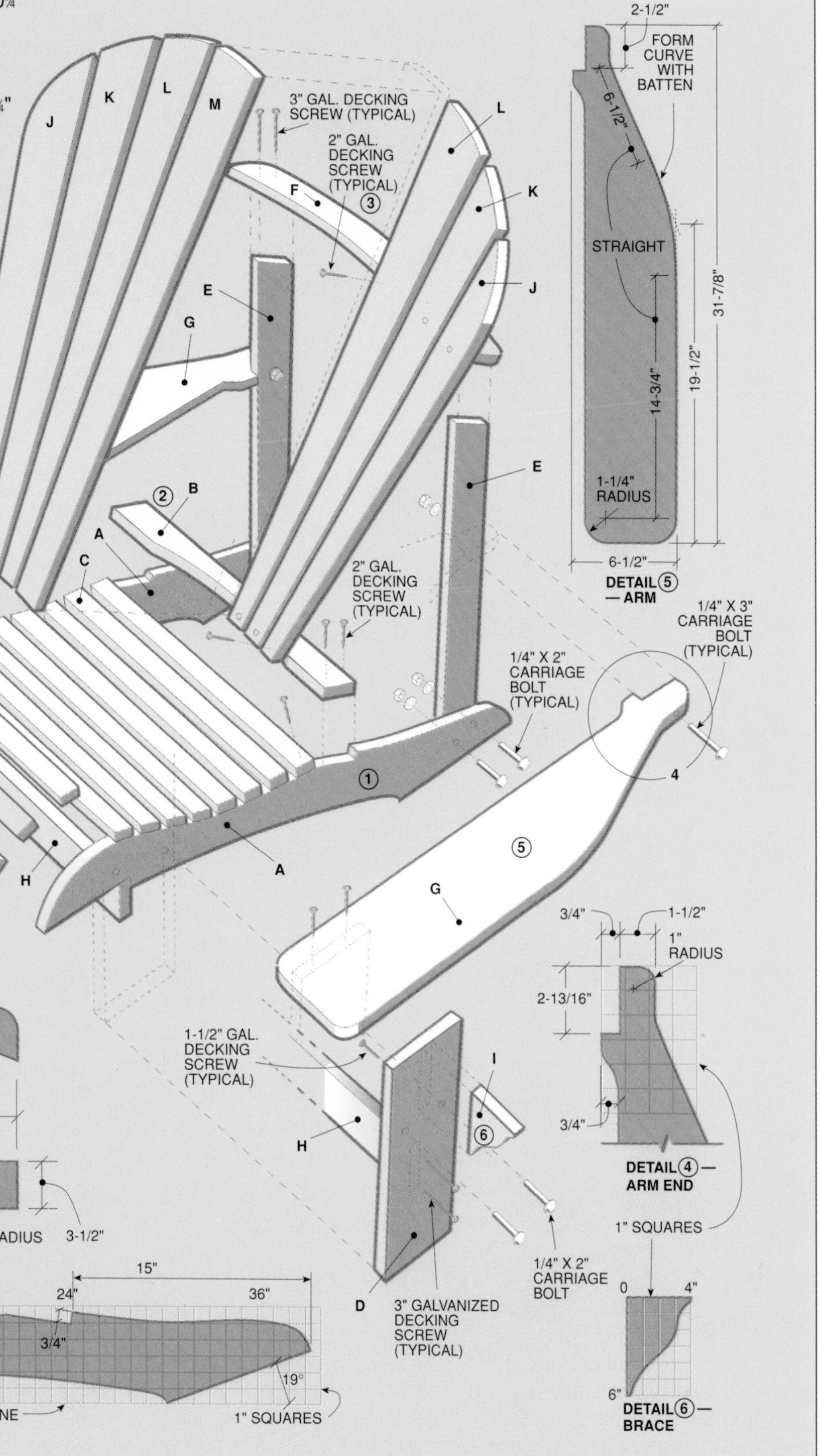
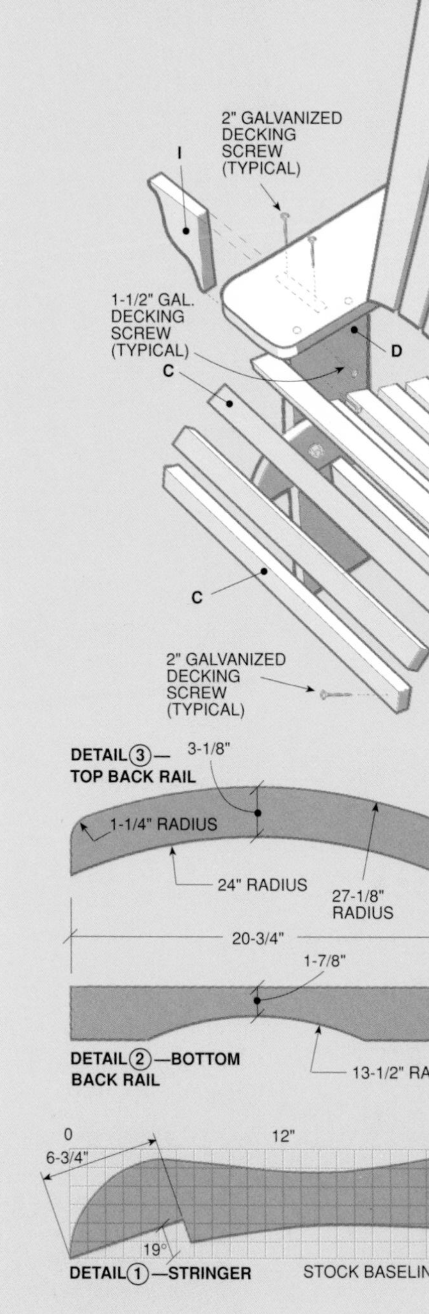
J
K
L
M
3" GAL. DECKING SCREW (TYPICAL)
2" GAL. DECKING SCREW (TYPICAL)
F
E
G
2" GALVANIZED DECKING SCREW (TYPICAL)
I
B
A
C
1-1/2" GAL. DECKING SCREW (TYPICAL)
D
2" GAL. DECKING SCREW (TYPICAL)
1/4" X 2" CARRIAGE BOLT (TYPICAL)
1/4" X 3" CARRIAGE BOLT (TYPICAL)
H
2" GALVANIZED DECKING SCREW (TYPICAL)
1-1/2" GAL. DECKING SCREW (TYPICAL)
1/4" X 2" CARRIAGE BOLT
3" GALVANIZED DECKING SCREW (TYPICAL)
2-1/2"
FORM CURVE WITH BATTEN
6-1/2"
STRAIGHT
14-3/4"
19-1/2"
31-7/8"
1-1/4" RADIUS
6-1/2"
DETAIL 5 — ARM
3/4"
1-1/2"
1" RADIUS
2-13/16"
3/4"
DETAIL 4 — ARM END
1" SQUARES
0
4"
6"
DETAIL 6 — BRACE
DETAIL 3 — TOP BACK RAIL
3-1/8"
1-1/4" RADIUS
24" RADIUS
27-1/8" RADIUS
20-3/4"
1-7/8"
DETAIL 2 — BOTTOM BACK RAIL
13-1/2" RADIUS
3-1/2"
15"
0
6-3/4"
12"
24"
36"
3/4"
19°
19°
DETAIL 1 — STRINGER
STOCK BASELINE
1" SQUARES

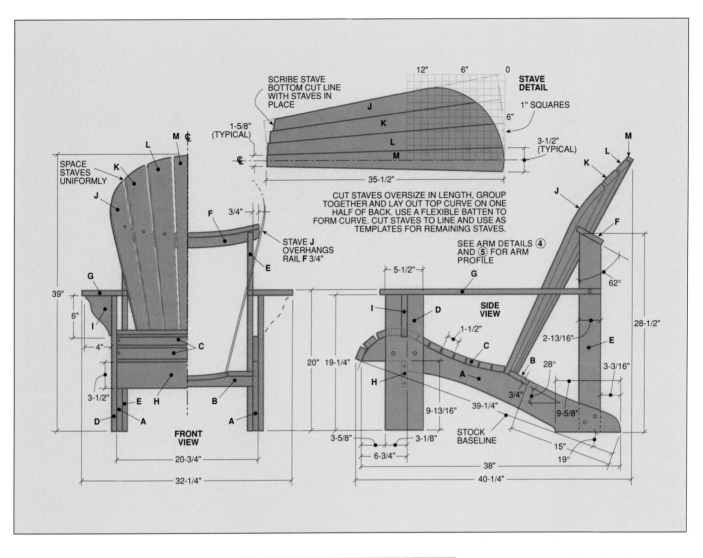

SCRIBE STAVE BOTTOM CUT LINE WITH STAVES IN PLACE

STAVE DETAIL

12"   6"   0

1" SQUARES

6"

3-1/2" (TYPICAL)

J
K
L
M

1-5/8" (TYPICAL)

35-1/2"

CUT STAVES OVERSIZE IN LENGTH, GROUP TOGETHER AND LAY OUT TOP CURVE ON ONE HALF OF BACK. USE A FLEXIBLE BATTEN TO FORM CURVE. CUT STAVES TO LINE AND USE AS TEMPLATES FOR REMAINING STAVES.

SPACE STAVES UNIFORMLY

3/4"

STAVE J OVERHANGS RAIL F 3/4"

SEE ARM DETAILS ④ AND ⑤ FOR ARM PROFILE

39"
6"

FRONT VIEW

20-3/4"
32-1/4"

3-1/2"

5-1/2"

20" 19-1/4"

SIDE VIEW

62°

28-1/2"

1-1/2"

2-13/16"

3-3/16"

28°

3/4"

9-13/16"

39-1/4"

STOCK BASELINE

9-5/8"

15"
19°

3-5/8"   3-1/8"

6-3/4"

38"

40-1/4"

3 Cut out the pattern with a saber saw equipped with a plywood-cutting blade. Using the cut workpiece as a pattern, trace the outline onto another blank workpiece and cut it out as well.
4 Cut the two back rails (B, F), the braces (I) and the armrest (G) to their overall lengths.

5 Draw arcs for top back rail (F) with the aid of a carpenter's square and trammel on a wooden yardstick. This setup is also valuable for laying out the bottom back rail (B).

LAYOUT TOOLS

For this project it is important that you have proper layout tools, such as a protractor, French curves, flexible straightedge, circle template, and a yardstick trammel set.

6 Use layout tools to draw the patterns onto back rails (B, F), one brace (I), and one armrest (G).
7 Cut out the patterns with a band saw equipped with a ¼" fine-tooth blade. Trace the cut brace and the armrest onto blank cedar and cut these out as well.
8 Cut the two back legs (E) to their proper widths and lengths, and then use a power miter box to cut the 62°angle at their tops.
9 Cut the two front legs (D) to size on your table saw.
10 Using your table saw, rip wider stock to a 1½" width to form

enough material for the slats (C). Crosscut slats to proper lengths.
Constructing the Staves
1 Cut seven blanks that are 3½" wide × 35½" long.
2 On one end of a workpiece, keep the measurement at 3½". On the other, center a measurement of 1⅝" (*see Stave Detail*). Draw straight lines connecting these measurements, and cut out the pattern with a saber saw. Transfer this pattern onto the other blank workpieces and cut them out.
3 Lightly joint the edges of the staves on a stationary jointer.

DESIGNER'S NOTEBOOK

The trickiest part of constructing the Adirondack chair is laying out the staves (J, K, L, M). Our method wastes a little bit of material, but it will ensure success.

Assembly

1 Finish-sand all of the project parts. A pad sander is ideal for finishing cedar. Also sand all sharp edges smooth.

2 Clamp one front leg (D) along with one back leg (E) to a stringer (A).(See Side View). Make sure that the stringer rests flat on the ground and that the two legs are vertical. Use a carpenter's square to square this assembly. Secure the legs to the stringer with two ¼ × 2" carriage bolts. The flat washers and the nuts should face toward the assembled chair unit as shown in the diagram. Predrill the holes for the bolts with a ⁵⁄₁₆" bit. Use a backer board to prevent the wood from splitting. Tighten down the carriage bolts.

3 Attach the remaining front and back legs to the other stringer, using carriage bolts with nuts and flat washers, as directed in Step 2.

4 Secure the stringer rail (H) to the two side assemblies with two 3" galvanized decking screws.

5 Secure the bottom back rail (B) by driving 2" galvanized decking screws through the rail and into the stringers (A).

6 Center the top back rail (F) and attach it to the tops of the back legs (E) with 3" galvanized decking screws. The front edge of the back rail should be flush with the front edge (the edge facing the chair) of the back legs. File the exposed tip of the back legs (E) so they are flush with the back edge of part F.

7 Install the two armrests (G) with ¼ × 3" carriage bolts where the armrest contacts the back legs (E). Drill ³⁄₁₆"-diameter holes to accept each of the carriage bolts. Use 2" galvanized decking screws to fasten the armrests to the front legs (D).

8 Attach the braces for the armrests (G) by driving two 2" galvanized decking screws down through the armrests, and driving one 1½" galvanized decking screw through each leg and into each armrest brace (I).

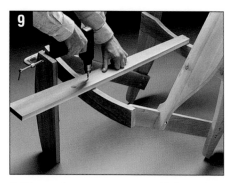

9 Place the center stave (M) so its bottom is flush with the bottom back rail (B) and is centered onto the chair. Secure it with one 2" galvanized decking screw. Tip back the chair so the stave (M) is parallel with the floor. Keep the chair in this position by clamping some scrap wood to prop it into place.

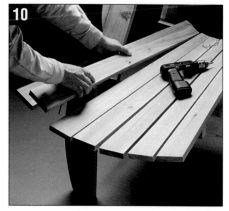

10 Position the remaining staves (J, K, L). Space the staves equally apart and so that the J staves extend about ¾" beyond the top back rail (F)

11 Note: Outside staves (J) extend beyond back rail (F) by ¾". Therefore, with outside staves (J) and center stave (M) in place, fan out the other staves (K, L) equally.

12 Secure each stave to the chair with one decking screw.

13 Use a French curve or flexible straightedge to mark a curved line across the tops of the staves.

14 Scribe the stave lengths by drawing along the lower edge of bottom back rail (B) as shown. Remove all the staves and then carefully cut their patterns on a band saw or with a saber saw.

15 Sand all of the staves and secure them to the top and bottom chair rails with 2" galvanized decking screws.

16 Position the rear slat (C) on the chair so it is against the staves. The rear slat actually contacts only the J slats. If you want to close the gap, file down the outside points of the J slats so that the slat fits more tightly.

17 Install the twelve slats for the seat with 2" galvanized decking screws. Space them equally and make sure that you predrill the screw holes to prevent the wood from splitting.

Finishing

1 Fill in any blemishes with a good exterior wood filler, and then finish sand the entire project.

2 We applied exterior paint with a sprayer. However, spraying or brushing with oil stain or clear oil finish is also suitable.

Entry Bench

Lift up the bench seat to find handy storage for outerwear.

Doubling as a storage center, our pine entry bench is rich with country charm.

Make the seat & backrest

1 Edge-glue pine stock to make a 1 × 14 × 43" piece for the seat (L). Let the glue-up dry for a week, then sand it until it's perfectly flat. Cut the seat to finished size.
2 Round over the top and bottom of the front seat edge with a router and ½" roundover bit.
3 Cut 10 spindles (G) from ⅝"-diameter birch dowels.
4 Cut the backrest rails (F). Mark hole centers every 4" on one long edge of each rail, starting 3" in from each end.
5 Mount a ⅝" Forstner bit in your drill press, and drill ½"-deep spindle holes at each hole center.
6 Glue the spindles into the holes in the rails. Rap the rails together with a mallet until the assembly is square. Clamp the backrest with bar clamps. Unclamp after 1 hour.

Make the sides & front

1 Cut the side stiles (A, B) and the side rails (C, D).
2 Cut ¼ × ⅜"-deep grooves for the panels on the inside edges of the rails, ¼" from the front faces. Also cut ¼ × 10⅞ × ⅜"-deep stopped grooves on the inside edges of the stiles, ¼" from the front faces, beginning 4½" up from the bottoms.
3 Cut a 2"-radius curve at the bottom inside corner of each stile.
4 Measure up 2" from the bottom of each stile to mark the location for the bottom of the bottom side rail, and measure up 18" to mark the top of the top side rail.
5 Lay out and drill holes for dowel

joints between the stiles and rails. Use ⅜ × 2" dowels.
6 Cut and finish-sand all five panels (E), and set three aside.
7 Insert a panel between each set of side rails and stiles, and glue both bench sides together, reinforcing with ⅜ × 2" dowels. Clamp with bar clamps and check the sides to make sure they're square.

8 After the assemblies are dry, mark the curved contours on the side stiles and rails (see *Diagram*). Cut the contours with a sabersaw, then sand the cuts smooth with a drum sander installed in your drill press.

9 Rout a ¼ × ¼"-deep groove in the inside of each side assembly, to hold the bottom panel. Locate the grooves 2½" up from the bottom, and stop them 2¾" from the front and ½" from the back (O). Square off the groove ends with a chisel.
10 Cut the front rails (H, I), stiles (J), and two panel spacers (K).
11 Cut centered, ¼ × ⅜"-deep grooves in the inside edges of the front rails, stiles, and panel spacers to hold the panels (see *Diagram*).
12 Form ¼"-wide × ⅜"-deep tenons on the top and bottom of each front stile and spacer to fit into the grooves in the front rails. To make the tenons, cut a ⅜ × ⅜"-deep rabbet in the front and back of the top and bottom edge of each piece.
13 Assemble the front of the bench by gluing the tenons on the stiles and spacers into the groove in the bottom rail, then sliding unglued panels (E) between the stiles and spacers (see *Diagram*). Glue the top rail to the top tenons, then square-up and clamp the assembly.

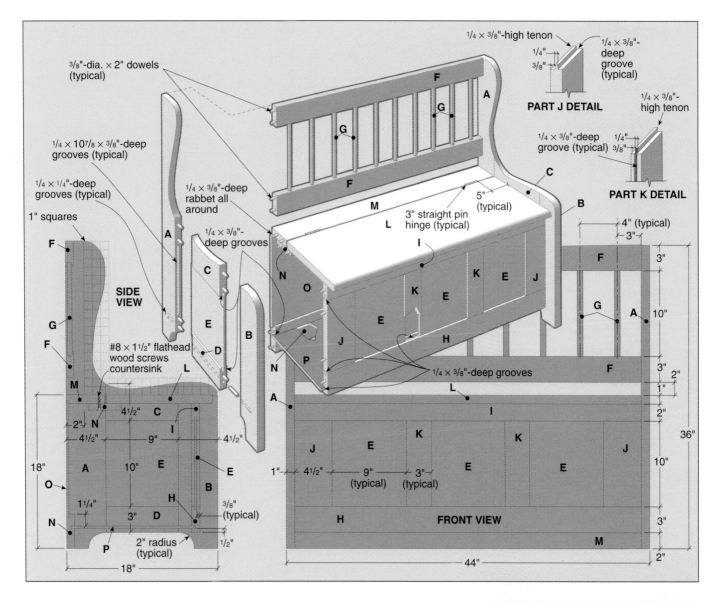

¼ × ⅜"-high tenon

PART J DETAIL

¼ × ⅜"-deep groove (typical)

¼ × ⅜"-high tenon

¼ × ⅜"-deep groove (typical)

PART K DETAIL

⅜"-dia. × 2" dowels (typical)

¼ × 10⅞ × ⅜"-deep grooves (typical)

¼ × ¼"-deep grooves (typical)

1" squares

¼ × ⅜"-deep rabbet all around

¼ × ⅜"-deep grooves

SIDE VIEW

#8 × 1½" flathead wood screws countersink

3" straight pin hinge (typical)

5" (typical)

¼ × ⅜"-deep grooves

4" (typical)

3"

FRONT VIEW

36"

44"

3"

10"

3"

2"

1"

2"

10"

3"

2"

2" radius (typical)

3/8" (typical)

½"

18"

18"

CUTTING LIST

Key	Qty.	Description & Size
A	2	**Side stile** (back), 1 × 4½ × 36"
B	2	**Side stile** (front), 1 × 4½ × 19½"
C	2	**Side rail** (top), 1 × 4½ × 9"
D	2	**Side rail** (bottom), 1 × 3 × 9"
E	5	**Panel**, ¼ × 9⅝ × 10⅝"
F	2	**Backrest rail**, 1 × 3 × 42"
G	10	**Spindle**, ⅝"-dia. × 10⅞"
H	1	**Front rail** (bottom), 1 × 3 × 42"
I	1	**Front rail** (top), 1 × 2 × 42"
J	2	**Front stile**, 1 × 4½ × 10¾"
K	2	**Panel spacer**, 1 × 3 × 10¾"
L	1	**Seat**, 1 × 13 × 41⅞"
M	1	**Seat rail**, 1 × 4½ × 42"
N	2	**Seat cleat/back rail**, ¾ × 4 × 42"
O	1	**Back panel**, ¼ × 13¾ × 42¾"
P	1	**Bottom**, ¼ × 14¾ × 42¾"

Note: All wood is pine except (G), which are birch dowels; and (E, O, and P), which are fir plywood.

Misc.: Glue, #8 × 1½" flathead screws, wire brads, ⅜ × 2" dowels, 3" pin hinges.

Assemble the entry bench

1 Cut the seat rail (M), seat cleat/ back rails (N), back panel (O), and bottom (P).

2 Attach the seat rail onto the seat cleat so the ends are flush and the rail overlaps the cleat by 2" (see *Diagram*). Secure the cleat to the rail with glue and countersunk #8 × 1½" flathead wood screws.

3 Cut a ¼ × ¼" groove in the inside face of the back rail, 2½" up from the bottom, to hold the bottom panel. Also cut a ¼ × ¼" groove in the inside face of the front rail (bottom), ½" from the bottom edge.

4 Lay out and drill ⅜ × 1"-deep dowel holes in the side assemblies to join them to the the front assembly, backrest, seat/rail assembly, and back rail (see *Diagram*).

5 Join the bench parts with glue and ⅜ × 2" dowels (don't glue the bottom). Square up, clamp, and let the glue dry.

6 Rout a ¼ × ⅜"-deep recess in the back, inside edges of the assembly. Square the corners of the recess, and attach the back with wire brads.

7 Finish-sand, then apply a finish (we used stain and tung oil). Join the seat and seat rail with 3" hinges.

Garden Bench

Enjoy the summer hours relaxing on this versatile garden bench.

The garden bench is a durable, comfortable piece of outdoor furniture. If properly maintained, this project will last for many years. Made from cedar, a great outdoor wood, the garden bench should be long-lived and stable. The design is simple and easy to understand, making the garden bench a fine project for a beginning wood-worker or a seasoned professional.

WOODWORKER'S TIP

Western red cedar has always been a versatile resource. Its characteristic spicy scent and reddish-brown color make it easy to identify. It has medium or coarse grain, and lacks messy resin or pitch. As the wood ages, it dulls to a silver-gray tone. Cedar is a lightweight wood and is prized for its stability and durability. It does not hold nails well, but glues and finishes easily.

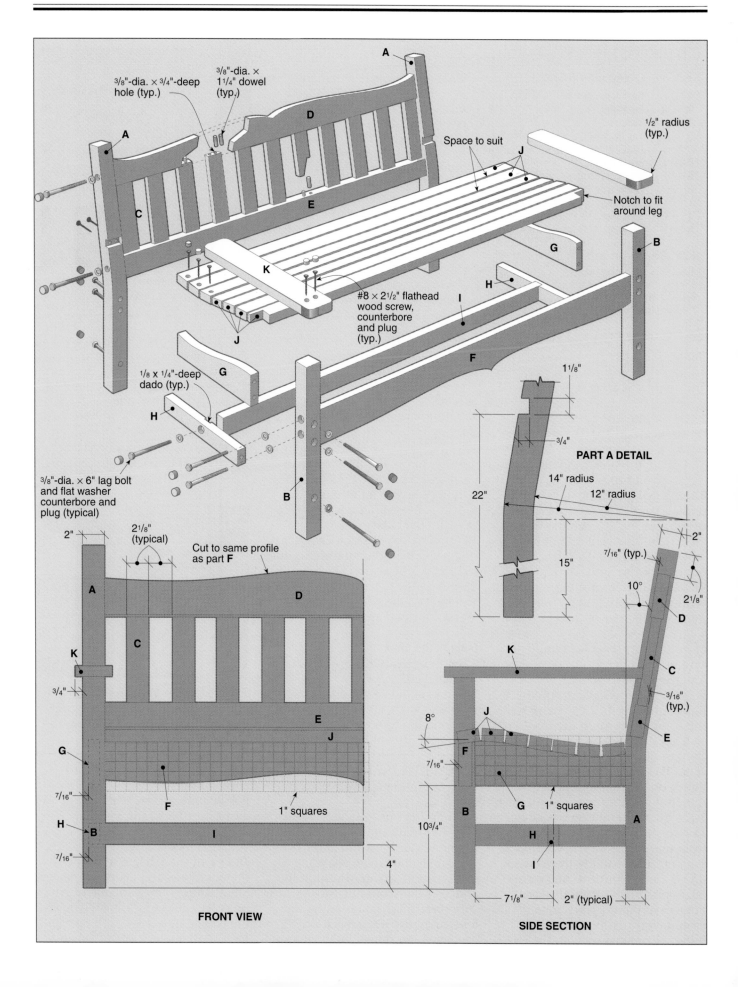

³/₈"-dia. × ³/₄"-deep hole (typ.)

³/₈"-dia. × 1¹/₄" dowel (typ.)

Space to suit

¹/₂" radius (typ.)

Notch to fit around leg

A

D

A

J

C

E

J

K

G

H

B

#8 × 2¹/₂" flathead wood screw, counterbore and plug (typ.)

I

H

F

¹/₈ x ¹/₄"-deep dado (typ.)

G

H

³/₈"-dia. × 6" lag bolt and flat washer counterbore and plug (typical)

B

1¹/₈"

³/₄"

PART A DETAIL

22"

14" radius

12" radius

15"

2"

⁷/₁₆" (typ.)

10°

2¹/₈"

D

C

³/₁₆" (typ.)

E

2"

2¹/₈" (typical)

Cut to same profile as part F

A

D

C

K

³/₄"

E

J

G

F

7/₁₆"

1" squares

H

B

I

7/₁₆"

4"

FRONT VIEW

K

8°

J

F

7/₁₆"

B

G

1" squares

A

H

10³/₄"

I

7¹/₈"

2" (typical)

SIDE SECTION

CUTTING LIST

Key	Qty.	Description & Size
A	2	**Rear leg,** 1½ × 5³⁄₁₆ × 33¹⁄₁₆"
B	2	**Front leg,** 1½ × 2 × 22"
C	11	**Slat,** ¾ × 2⅛ × 9"
D	1	**Top back rail,** 1⅛ × 4½ × 48⅞"
E	1	**Lower back rail,** 1⅛ × 3 × 48⅞"
F	1	**Front rail,** 1⅛ × 4½ × 48⅞"
G	2	**Upper side rail,** 1⅛ × 4½ × 14¼"
H	2	**Lower side rail,** 1⅛ × 2½ × 14¼"
I	1	**Stretcher,** 1⅛ × 2½ × 50¼"
J	7	**Seat slat,** 1⅛ × 2³⁄₁₆ × 52"
K	2	**Armrest,** 1⅛ × 3½ × 19"

Note: All wood is cedar.

Misc.: ⅜ × 1½"-long dowels, ⅜ × 6"-long lag bolts with flat washers, #8 × 2½" flathead wood screws, cedar plugs ⅜", ¾"-diameters, water-resistant wood glue.

Cutting the legs

1 Cut stock for the rear legs (A) to 5³⁄₁₆" wide and front legs (B) to 2" wide from 1½"-thick cedar.

2 Lay out the 10° bend or "dogleg" on the rear legs. Mark the center point of the front of the dogleg 16¼" from the bottom along the front edge of the workpiece.

3 Use a combination square to draw a parallel line for the back of the rear leg 2" from the front edge. Mark the centerpoint for the end of the dogleg 16⅛" from the bottom on that line.

4 Draw a line from the top corner of the back edge to meet the 16⅛" mark on the rear of the leg.

5 The dogleg has a curved bend. Mark radius points for the dogleg on the rear lines 1" above and below the 16⅛" mark.

6 Draw a line parallel to the back line starting at the 16¼" mark on the front edge. Keep the front line 2" from the back line, ending at the top of the stock. Mark radius points on this line and along the front edge 1" above and below the 16¼" mark.

7 Set up a taper jig on the tablesaw to cut a 10° angle. Cut the front line of the dogleg starting at the 16¼" mark on the front edge.

8 Use the rip fence to make parallel stopped cuts along the back lines from the top and bottom. Stop the cuts at the 1" marks.

9 Use a compass to swing a 12"-radius arc connecting the two 1" marks. Swing a similar arc connecting the 1" marks on the front. Use a bandsaw to cut along these curves.

10 Cut the top of each leg square starting at the front top corner.

11 Cut a 1 × 1⅛"-wide dado for the armrest across the front edge of each rear leg starting 22" from the bottom. Use the miter gauge on the tablesaw with a dado blade to make the cuts.

12 From the back side of the leg, drill a shank and counterbore hole for a #8 × 2½" woodscrew centered on the dado.

13 Sand the front legs and rear legs to finished smoothness.

Making the back

1 Cut the slats (C) to size from ¾"-thick cedar.

2 Use a rail jig and a drill press to make two ⅜ × ¾"-deep dowel holes on the end of each slat. Center the dowel holes ½" from each side.

3 Use a tablesaw to cut the top back rail (D) and lower back rail (E) to size.

4 Clamp the rails together. Measure and mark the slat positions on the upper back rail and lower back rail simultaneously using a combination square. Position the end slats 2⅛" from rail ends. Make sure that 2⅛" separates each slat.

5 Separate the rails. Place dowel centers in the dowel holes on one slat and use them to mark the dowel positions on the top back rail and lower back rail. Use your slat position marks and combination square as a guide.

6 Set up a drill press with an auxiliary fence to make ⅜ × ¾"-deep dowel holes in the upper back rail and lower back rail. Center the holes in the points made by the dowel centers.

7 Transfer the *Diagram* grid from front view to the upper back rail and use a bandsaw to cut top radius pattern.

8 Sand the top back rail, lower back rail, and slats to finished smoothness.

9 Assemble top back rail, slats, and lower back rail with glue. Clamp the pieces, check for square, let dry.

10 Dry-fit the back assembly to the back legs and clamp in place. Mark centers for ⅜"-diameter lag bolts 3¼", 5⅛", 15⅝", and 17" from the top centered on each rear leg. Drill ¼"-diameter pilot holes at each mark into the back assembly.

11 Unclamp the assembly and use a drill press and a Forstner bit to drill ¾"-diameter × ¾"-deep counterbore holes into the pilot holes on the rear legs. Drill ⅜"-diameter shank holes through the centers of the counterbore holes.

12 Position the top back assembly against the rear legs with glue. Clamp and secure with lag bolts.

13 Cut ¾"-diameter × ¾"-deep plugs from scrap cedar and insert them into the holes with glue. Note: Lag bolts are used throughout the garden bench project. Refer to the preceding instructions as needed.

Assembling the frame

1 Cut the front rail (F) to size from 2"-thick cedar. Transfer *Diagram* grid from side view to the front rail and use a bandsaw to cut the radius pattern. Sand the workpiece to finished smoothness.

2 Position the front rail so the bottom edge is 10¾" from the bottom of the front legs. Center the front rail on the inside face of front legs.

WOODWORKER'S TIP

Many people prefer the weathered appearance of cedar and choose to avoid finish treatments. In harsh, moist climates, however, cedar will suffer extensive natural damage as it ages. To avoid this, use a water-repellent preservative when allowing western cedar to weather. Water repellents do not change the natural appearance of the wood and are easily applied. Water repellents lessen the initial stage of darkening, but allow ultraviolet bleaching to continue. Western cedar will gradually change from a reddish tone to a lighter shade. Water repellents will also reduce the frequency of watermarks and surface damage on exposed wood. Some repellents even contain fungicidal additives to ward-off decay and discoloration caused by mold and fungal growth. Natural weathering will not always result in a uniform appearance. Individual boards may weather differently, depending on the amount of light and moisture exposure.

---

3 Glue and clamp the workpieces. Secure them with two centered, countersunk ⅜ × 6" lag bolts, located 12¼" and 14⅜" from the bottom of the legs (see *Diagram*).

4 Cut the upper side rails (G), lower side rails (H), and stretcher (I) to size. Transfer the grid pattern from the *Diagram* to make the top profile on the upper side rails. Sand to finished smoothness.

5 Using a tablesaw and dado blade, cut a ¼ × 1⅛"-wide dado at the center of the lower side rails' inside faces.

6 Glue and fit the stretcher into the dadoes on the lower side rails. Clamp and insert centered, countersunk ⅜ × 6" lag bolts through the lower side rails into the stretcher (see *Diagram*).

7 Fill holes with cedar plugs.

8 Position the upper side rails so that their inside faces are flush against the inside faces of the legs. The bottom of the upper side rails should be 10¾" from the bottom of the front legs. Attach the upper side rails with water-resistant glue. Clamp the workpieces and insert two centered, countersunk ⅜ × 6" lag bolts into each side. At the front of the piece, insert these bolts 11½" and 13⅞" from the bottom of the legs. On the back face of the rear legs, insert the bolts 11½" and 13" from the bottom.

9 Fill holes with cedar plugs.

10 Position the two lower side rails and stretcher so that the rails' inside faces are flush against the inside faces of the legs. Attach the lower side rails to front and rear legs with glue and one centered, countersunk ⅜ × 6" lag bolt into each side. Center the lag bolts 5¼" up from the bottom of the legs.

11 Fill holes with cedar plugs.

Making the seat

1 Cut seven seat slats (J) to size from 2"-thick cedar.

2 Round over the front and rear edges of the slats with a router and a ¼" round-over bit.

3 Sand seat slats to finished smoothness.

4 Starting at the rear of the bench, use an adjustable counterbore bit

to drill pilot, shank, and counterbore holes for #8 × 2½"-long flathead wood screws through the slats into the upper side rails (see *Diagram*). Use a portable drill with a drill stand to make these holes. Remember to maintain ⅛" between each seat slat.

5 To enable the front seat slat to fit around the front legs, use a jigsaw to cut a small notch on the front corners (see *Diagram*).

6 Attach slats to the rails with screws. Fill holes with cedar plugs.

Installing the armrests

1 Cut the armrests (K) to size from 1⅛"-thick cedar.

2 Make a ½" radius cut at each corner of the armrests using a bandsaw.

3 Round over the edges with a router and a ¼"-diameter round-over bit.

4 Dry-fit the armrests to the bench. Drill pilot holes for #8 × 2½" wood screws into the armrests.

5 Sand the armrests to finished smoothness.

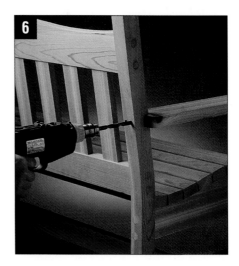

6 Attach the armrests to the bench with glue and countersunk #8 × 2½" wood screws.

7 Fill screw holes with cedar plugs.

8 Finish the garden bench with a clear sealant.

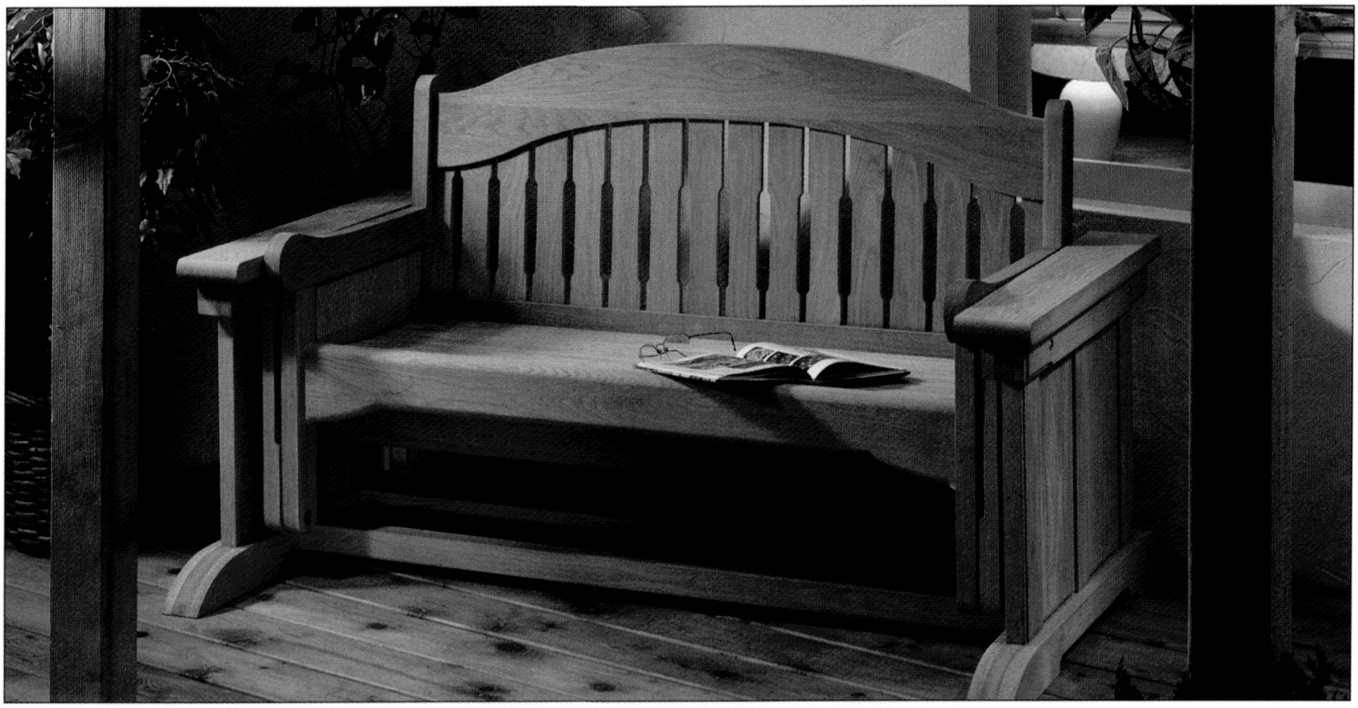

Porch Swing

Build this three-season swing and enjoy the weather in style.

The porch swing is a great winter project. The strength of white oak combines with a smooth glide action and a sturdy mortise-and-tenon design to make this three-season swing impressive and durable. Build it in the winter and unveil it in the spring.

Building the seat back

1 Cut the back arch (A) from 2 × 12" white oak.
2 Cut back rail (B) from 2 × 6" oak.
3 Set up a tablesaw with a dado blade to cut a ⅜ × ¾"-long rabbet on both faces of each end of the arch. Repeat these cuts on faces and edges of the back rail to form tenons for joining to stiles.
4 Transfer the front view grid pattern from the *Diagram* to the back arch. Cut the curve on a bandsaw. Sand with a drum sander and 180-grit sandpaper.
5 Use a backsaw and chisel to cut 5¼ × ¾ × ¾"-wide tenons on arch.
6 Rout a ½ × ½" groove in the center of the inside edge of back arch and back rail to hold slats in place.
7 Cut 1¼ × ⅝ × 13⁄16"-deep mortises in the back rail to accept the four tenons from the seat supports (C). Center the mortises 3" and 17" from the shoulders of the tenons at each end of the rail 13⁄16" above the bottom edge of the rail.
8 Cut the back stiles (D) to size from 2 × 6" white oak.
9 To cut the back stiles to shape, lay out a 5° dogleg on these workpieces. Mark centers for the carriage bolts that will connect the back stiles to the rocker arms (E) as shown in Detail 1 of *Diagram.*
10 Set up a taper jig to make the 5° cut on a tablesaw. (The wide end of the jig will be toward you.) With the waste side of the back stile against the fence, start the taper at the point where the dogleg starts. Continue the cut to the end of the board.
11 Turn the board over and extend the starting point of the dogleg (11⅝" from the bottom on the inside edge) across the face of the piece with a sliding T-bevel. Use a combination square to mark a parallel line 4" from the dogleg cut.
12 Without using the taper jig, make the stopped cut along the second dogleg line. Stop the cut at the extended starting point.
13 Turn the board over and complete the stile by cutting the short end on the tablesaw.
14 Finish the cuts where they meet at the extended starting point and cut the 2" radius at the top and bottom of the back stile.
15 Lay out and cut centered ⅝ × 2 × 13⁄16"-deep mortises on the inside edge of each back stile to form joints with the arm rest (F) and side support (G). The mortise for the arm rest starts 6¾" from the breakpoint of the dogleg. The mortise for side support starts 9¼" from the bottom and extends 2" up.
16 Cut a ⅜ × ⅜" groove centered on the front edge, connecting the mortises made in step 15.
17 Lay out and cut ⅝ × 13⁄16"-deep mortises for joints with the arch and back rail on the inside face of each back stile (see *Diagram*). The distance from the top of the back stile to the top of the arch mortise is 1¼". The distance from the top of the back stile to the top

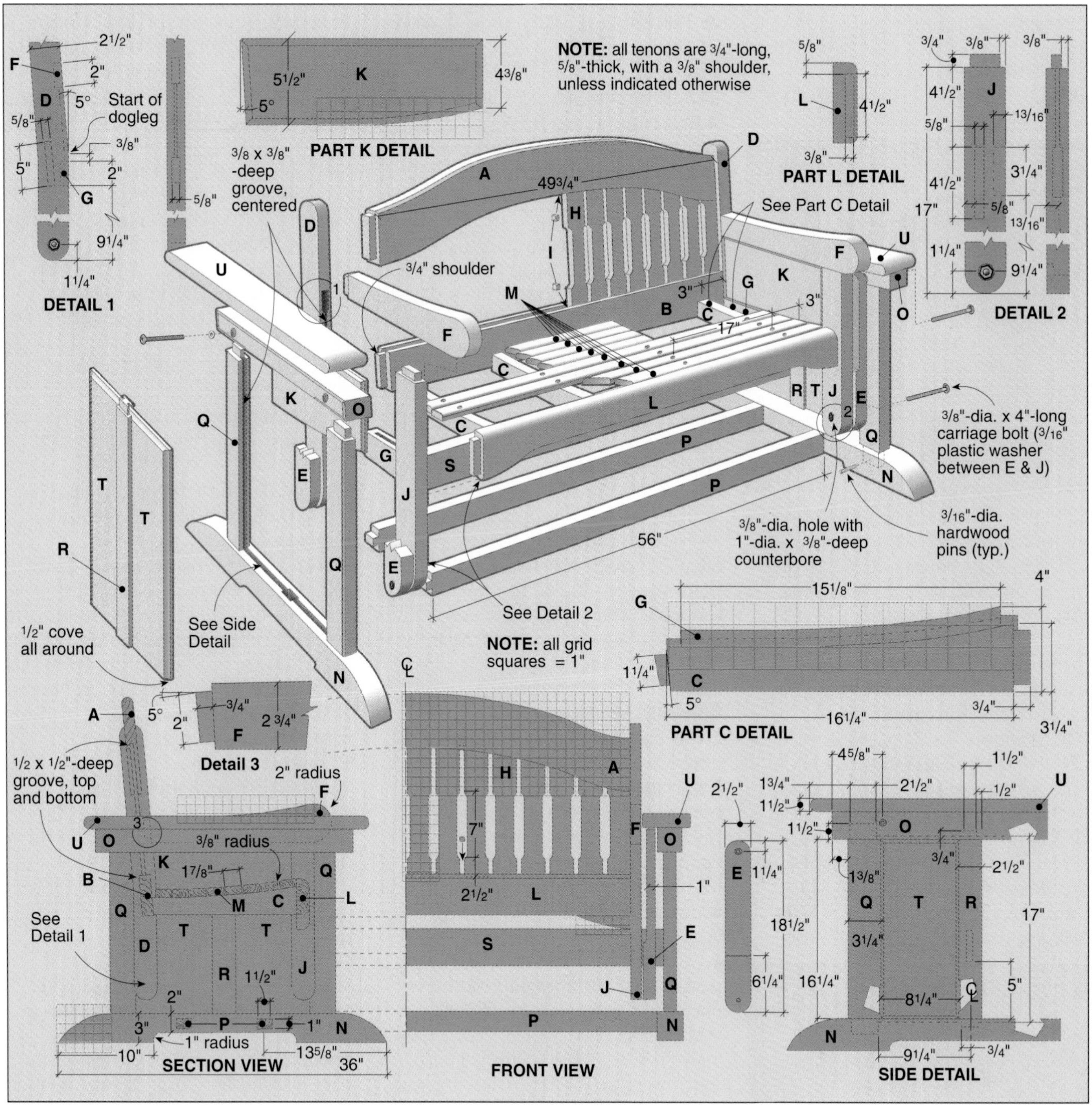
NOTE: all tenons are 3/4"-long, 5/8"-thick, with a 3/8" shoulder, unless indicated otherwise
DETAIL 1
Start of dogleg
PART K DETAIL
PART L DETAIL
DETAIL 2
3/8 x 3/8" -deep groove, centered
3/4" shoulder
See Part C Detail
3/8"-dia. x 4"-long carriage bolt (3/16" plastic washer between E & J)
3/16"-dia. hardwood pins (typ.)
3/8"-dia. hole with 1"-dia. x 3/8"-deep counterbore
See Detail 2
NOTE: all grid squares = 1"
1/2" cove all around
See Side Detail
PART C DETAIL
Detail 3
1/2 x 1/2"-deep groove, top and bottom
2" radius
3/8" radius
See Detail 1
1" radius
SECTION VIEW
FRONT VIEW
SIDE DETAIL

CUTTING LIST

Key	Qty.	Description & Size
A	1	**Back arch,** 1⅜ × 11 × 51¼"
B	1	**Back rail,** 1⅜ × 4¼ × 51¼"
C	4	**Seat support,** 1⅜ × 3¼ × 17¾"
D	2	**Back stile,** 1⅜ × 4 × 30"
E	4	**Rocker arm,** 1⅜ × 2½ × 18½"
F	2	**Arm rest,** 1⅜ × 4 × 21"
G	2	**Side support,** 1⅜ × 4 × 16½"
H	16	**Back slats,** ½ × 2¾ × 15¼"
I	30	**Spacers,** ½ × ½ × 7⁄16"
J	2	**Front stiles,** 1⅜ × 2½ × 17¾"
K	2	**Seat side panel,** ¾ × 5⅜ × 16"
L	1	**Seat front,** 1⅜ × 5½ × 51¼"
M	8	**Seat slats,** ¾ × 1⅞ × 49¾"
N	2	**Foot,** 3 × 3 × 36"
O	2	**Base rails,** 3 × 2½ × 26¾"
P	2	**Stretchers,** 1½ × 2 × 57½"
Q	4	**Base stiles,** 1⅜ × 3¼ × 19¼"
R	2	**Center stile,** 1⅜ × 2½ × 17¾"
S	1	**Middle stretcher,** 1⅜ × 4 × 58¹⁵⁄₃₂"
T	4	**Base panel,** ¾ × 8¼ × 17"
U	2	**Base rail cap,** 1¾ × 5 × 29½"

Note: All wood is white oak.
Misc.: Glue, sandpaper, ⅜"-diameter × 4" carriage bolts (8), ⅜"-diameter × 3" dowels, ¾"-diameter × 1½" dowels, 3⁄16" hardwood pins, ⅜" nylon locking nuts (8), 3⁄16" plastic washers (16).

of the back rail mortise is 20½".
18 Sand arch, back stile, and back rail to finished smoothness.
19 Cut back slats (H) and spacers (I) from ½"-thick white oak.

20
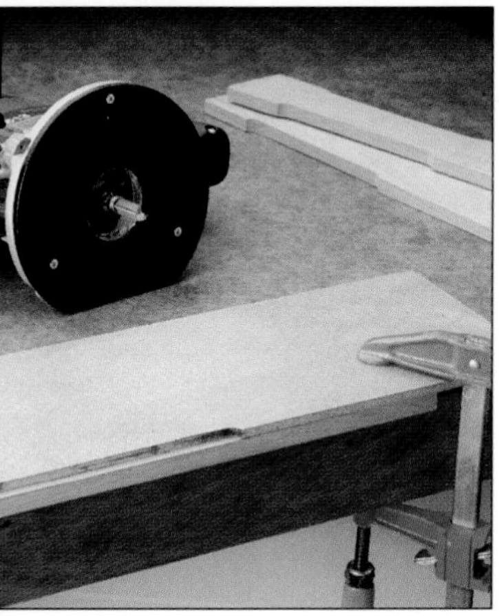

20 Make and use a template to make the decorative router cuts in back slats. The router cuts are made on both sides of the slats. Rip the slats on the far right and left to 1⅞" wide to fit flush with the stiles. These pieces receive router cuts on one side only.
21 Sand the slats to finished smoothness.
22 Dry-fit back stiles to the back arch and back rail. Mark and drill the holes in joints for ³⁄₁₆" pegs.
23 Remove the back arch and insert the back slats and spacers in the back rail. Temporarily place the upper spacers between slats, holding them in place with tape.

24
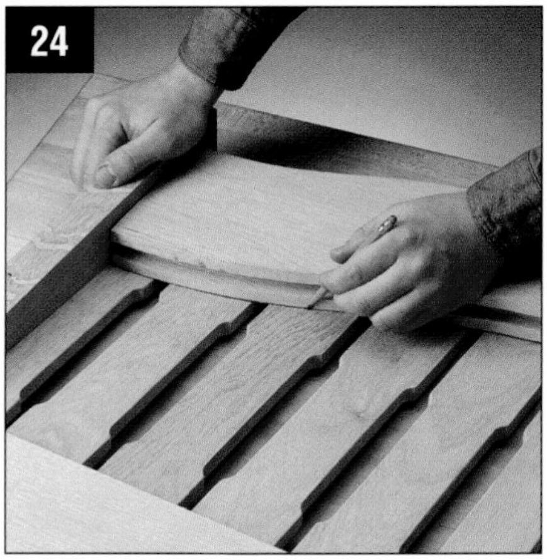

24 Lay the back arch over the back slats in correct alignment with the mortises in the back stiles. Mark the back slats with the curve of the back arch.
25 Remove the back arch, then remark the slats ⁷⁄₁₆" longer than the arch mark.
26 Cut the curves on the back slats, using a bandsaw.
27 Lay the back rail down on a smooth worksurface. Use a 1⁷⁄₁₆" spacer on the underside to support back slats. Place the slats and spacers in the groove in the back rail. Glue in the ½" spacers as you work. Do not glue the back slats.
28 Apply glue to the end of the back arch and one back stile mortise, then assemble the pieces and pin in place with a dowel. Note: Attach both stiles to the back arch before you insert spacers.
29 Insert the back slats and spacers into the groove in the back arch. Glue the spacers as you go. Do not glue the back slats.
30 With back slats and spacers in place, apply glue to the back rail tenons to complete back assembly.
31 Secure the joints with pegs. Clamp and let dry.

Building the seat

1 Cut the front stiles (J) from 2 × 4" white oak.
2 Set up a tablesaw with a dado blade to cut a ¾ × ⅜"-deep rabbet on all four sides of one end of each front stile. The resulting tenon should be ⅝ × 1¾ × ¾" long.
3 Cut a 1⅜" radius on the opposite end of each front stile.
4 Cut the arm rests and side supports from 2 × 6" white oak. Cut the seat supports from 2 × 4" white oak.
5 Cut the seat side panels (K) from 1 × 7" white oak. Transfer the pattern to seat side panels, then cut out the curves on a bandsaw.
6 Miter-cut at 5° one end of each armrest, seat support, and side support to match the angle of the back stiles and rails (see Detail 5).
7 Transfer the grid pattern to the armrests, seat supports, and side supports. Cut the curves on a bandsaw. Clamp all similar pieces together, and gang-sand them to achieve uniform shapes.
8 Set up a tablesaw with a dado blade and cut ¾ × ⅜"-deep rabbets to form tenons on the faces of the armrests, seat, and side supports. Complete tenons on the angled ends with a backsaw and chisel.
9 Cut a ⅝ × 1¾ × ¹³⁄₁₆"-deep mortise in the bottom of each armrest where it will join with front stile. Start the cuts 15⅞" from the back edge of the workpiece.
10 Rout a ⅜ × ⅜" groove centered on the bottom edge of the armrests, the back edges of the front stiles, and the top edges of the side supports to hold the side panels in place.
11 Cut the seat front (L) from 2 × 8" white oak.
12 Lay out and cut ⅝ × ¾"-deep mortises in the front for the seat supports.
13 Transfer the grid pattern to seat front, then cut the curves with a bandsaw.
14 Cut offset tenons on the ends of the seat front to join to the stiles (see *Diagram*). These tenons are 4½" long and are situated ⅝" from the top, ¹⁄₁₆" from the front face, and ¹¹⁄₁₆" from the back face.
15 Use a router to round over the top edge of the seat front with a ¾" roundover bit.
16 Sand the seat front to finished smoothness.
17 Cut ⅜ × ⁷⁄₁₆"-deep rabbet on the outside faces of seat side panels. On a router table, cut a cove into the rabbeted edge using a ½"-radius core-box bit.
18 Dry-fit the front stiles, seat front, side support, seat side panels, seat supports, and armrests to form the seat assembly.
19 Dry-fit the seat assembly to the back assembly. Clamp parts together and drill holes for ³⁄₁₆"-diameter pegs in mortise and tenon joints.
20 Cut the seat slats (M) from ¾"-thick white oak.
21 Round over the top edges of the seat slats with a ⅜"-diameter roundover bit.
22 Drill peg holes for ⅜" dowels through the seat slats, centered 3" and 17" from each end, using a drill press.
23 Sand the seat slats to finished smoothness.

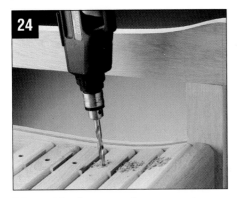

24 Dry-fit the seat slats over the seat frame. Place ³⁄₁₆"-thick spacers temporarily between the slats. Check the seat assembly for square, then drill ³⁄₈ × ³⁄₄"-deep holes into the seat supports through the peg holes in the seat slats, using the peg holes as guides.
25 Remove the seat slats, then reattach them to the seat supports with glue and pegs. Allow the glue to dry.
26 With the seat slats in place, remove the seat assembly from the back assembly.
27 Apply glue to the seat front and seat supports. Reattach them to the back assembly using glue and ³⁄₁₆"-diameter dowels.
28 Apply glue to the front stiles, armrests, and side supports to form armrest assemblies. Slide the side panels into place.
29 Apply glue and attach the armrest assemblies to the back assembly and seat assembly.
30 Secure all mortise-and-tenon joints with ³⁄₁₆"-diameter pins. Clamp and let dry.

Building the base

1 Glue up or buy enough material to cut feet (N) from 3"-square oak.
2 Transfer the pattern from the *Diagram* to the feet for the foot profile. Cut profile with a bandsaw.
3 Clamp the feet together and gang-sand the ends on the stationary sander for a uniform shape.
4 Glue up enough material to cut base rails (O) from 3"-square white oak. Cut around the outside face of the base rails with a ³⁄₈"-diameter cove bit and a router.
5 Cut the stretchers (P), base stiles (Q), and center stiles (R) from 2 × 4" white oak.

6 Cut the middle stretcher (S) from 2 × 6" white oak.
7 Cut the base panels (T) from 1 × 10" white oak.
8 Set up a tablesaw with a dado blade to cut tenons on middle stretcher and base stiles. Tenons for center stiles and middle stretcher should be ³⁄₄" long. Tenons for base stiles should be 1½" long, leaving ³⁄₈" shoulders on all sides.
9 Cut 1 × 1½ × 1½"-deep tenons on each end of the stretchers.
10 Lay out and cut ¹³⁄₁₆"-deep mortises for the center stiles, and 1¹⁄₁₆"-deep mortises for the base stiles, base rails, and feet. Cut the mortises with a router and mortising bit. Use guide strips to stop cut. Note: When mortising components that go together, such as the feet and base rails, lay out the mortises simultaneously. Align and clamp the feet and rails together. Lay out mortises on one piece and transfer the layout to the other pieces by laying a square across the layout and extending the lines to the other pieces. Cut mortises with a router while clamped.
11 Rout a ³⁄₈ × ³⁄₈" groove centered on the inside of both base stiles and on both sides of the center stiles to hold the base panels.
12 Cut stopped ³⁄₈ × ³⁄₈" grooves centered in the inside edges of the feet and base rails. Start and stop grooves in mortises for the stiles.
13 Cut 1 × 1½ × 1¹⁄₁₆"-deep mortises in the feet for the stretchers.
14 Rout a ³⁄₈ × ⁷⁄₁₆"-deep cove using a ³⁄₈" core box bit on all four sides of each base panel.
15 Cut a ¼ × ⁷⁄₁₆"-deep rabbet on the outside of the cove cut just made, to remove the waste and leave a ⁵⁄₁₆" shoulder on the outside of the base panel.
16 Sand the base parts to finished smoothness.
17 Dry-fit the feet, panels, stretcher, and stiles to form the base. Clamp tightly and drill holes for ³⁄₁₆"-diameter dowels in all tenons. Note: Pin tenons on middle stretcher by drilling through groove in the side of the center stile, reaching the tenon.

18 Glue and assemble the feet, middle stretcher, and stiles. To secure the joints, drive pins into the tenons.
19 Glue and attach the middle stretcher to feet and center stiles.
20 Insert the side panels. Glue and attach the base rails. Allow the base assembly to dry. Scrape off excess glue after drying.
21 Cut a ½"-deep cove along the outer edge of the base rails with a router and a cove bit.
22 Cut the base rail caps (U) to size and round over the ends. Drill dowel holes and connect the base rail caps to the base rails with glue and ³⁄₈ × 3"-long wooden dowels.

Assemble the base and swing

1 Cut the rocker arms from 1³⁄₈" white oak. Cut the 1³⁄₈"-radius ends using a bandsaw.
2 Make an 18½"-long relief cut in the inside face of each rocker arm using a bandsaw (see *Diagram*).
3 Drill and counterbore holes for ³⁄₈"-diameter carriage bolts in each end of the rocker arms.
4 Sand the rocker arms to finished smoothness.
5 Dry-fit the rocker arms to the seat and base.

Finishing the swing

1 Stain and seal the work to your own specifications. Use allweather finish if the piece will be outside.
2 Wax rocker arm holes.
3 Attach the seat to the base with the rocker arm. Use ³⁄₈"-diameter carriage bolts with plastic washers and nylon locking nuts to prevent accidental loosening.

Cradle

Pamper your baby in this easy-to-store heirloom cradle.

Safety comes first with this pendant-type, swinging cradle. A baby can't tip this sturdy cradle over–as with rocking chair types–because the pendant action keeps its weight centered.

Whether crafted as a gift to your own child, or with another loved one in mind, it's sure to be treasured by anyone who receives it.

Modern hardware adds a dimension of safety and convenience to the base's classic trestle design. The swinging action is provided by heavy-duty Roto hinges securely fastened in hard maple. Trestle pieces are joined with "knock-down" hardware that, because of threaded components, assembles readily with a single tool.

While you are awaiting that new arrival, the hardware allows you to store the cradle safely and conveniently. Fully assembled, the trestle base can be tightened as needed to provide maximum strength and security.

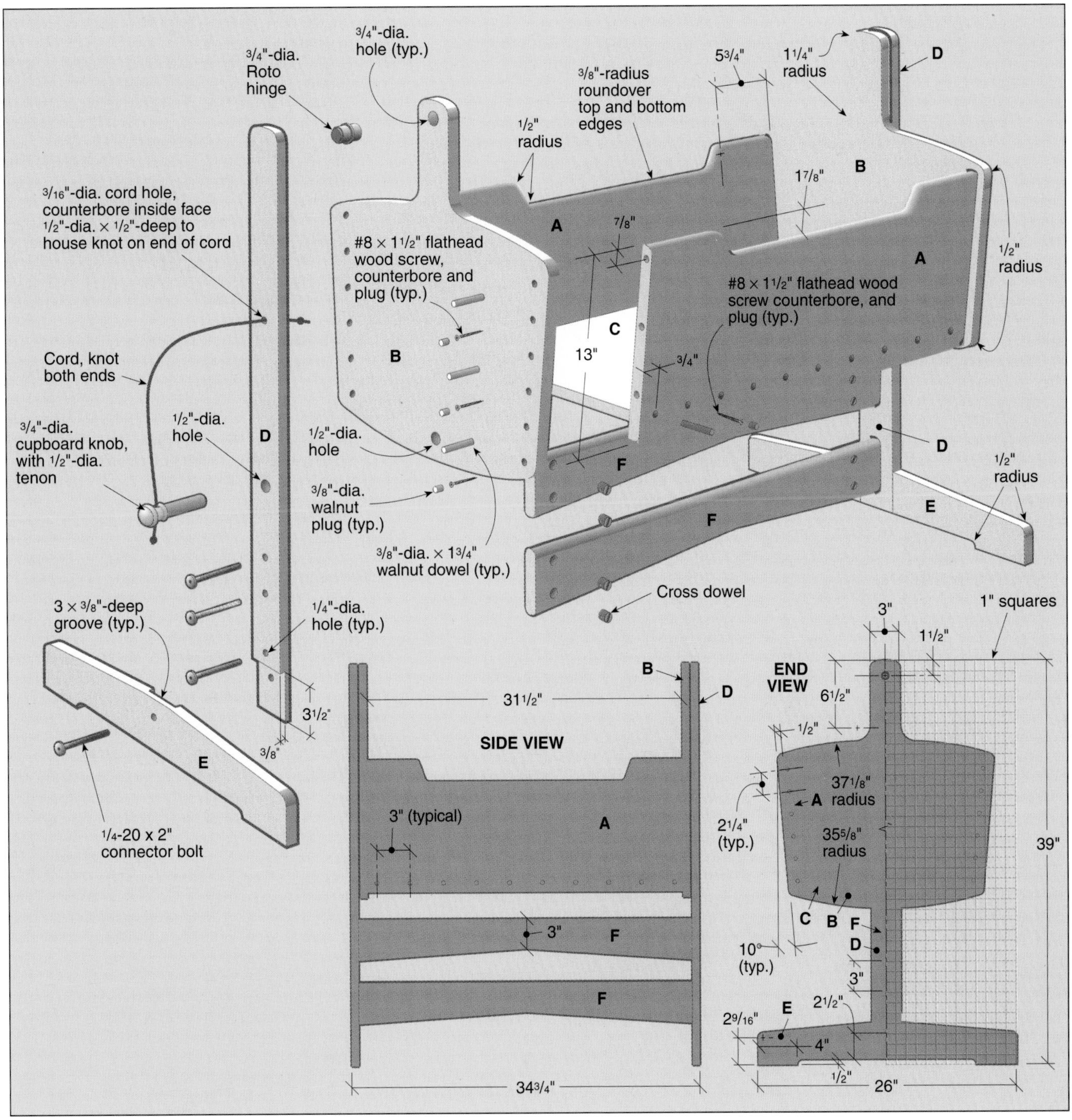

3/4"-dia. Roto hinge
3/4"-dia. hole (typ.)
3/8"-radius roundover top and bottom edges
1/2" radius
5 3/4"
1 1/4" radius
D
B
1 7/8"
3/16"-dia. cord hole, counterbore inside face 1/2"-dia. × 1/2"-deep to house knot on end of cord
A
7/8"
#8 × 1 1/2" flathead wood screw, counterbore and plug (typ.)
1/2" radius
A
#8 × 1 1/2" flathead wood screw counterbore, and plug (typ.)
C
13"
3/4"
Cord, knot both ends
B
3/4"-dia. cupboard knob, with 1/2"-dia. tenon
1/2"-dia. hole
D
1/2"-dia. hole
D
1/2" radius
F
3/8"-dia. walnut plug (typ.)
E
F
3/8"-dia. × 1 3/4" walnut dowel (typ.)
Cross dowel
3 × 3/8"-deep groove (typ.)
1/4"-dia. hole (typ.)
3"
1" squares
1 1/2"
B
D
END VIEW
6 1/2"
31 1/2"
3 1/2"
SIDE VIEW
1/2"
3/8"
E
37 1/8" radius
A
3" (typical)
A
2 1/4" (typ.)
35 5/8" radius
39"
1/4-20 x 2" connector bolt
C
B
F
3"
F
D
10° (typ.)
3"
F
2 9/16"
E
2 1/2"
4"
1/2"
34 3/4"
26"

WORKSHOP TIP

Clearance between the moving parts is essential for the swinging action of the cradle. To maintain clearance (⅛" at each end), keep the wood at a stable temperature and humidity during working and glue-drying times to prevent warping. Seal the wood as soon as possible after sanding to keep moisture out.

CUTTING LIST

Key	Qty.	Description & Size
A	2	**Side,** ¾ × 13 × 31½"
B	2	**End,** ¾ × 22 × 24"
C	1	**Bottom,** ¾ × 16 × 31½"
D	2	**Support,** ¾ × 3 × 38½"
E	2	**Foot,** ¾ × 4 × 26"
F	2	**Stretcher,** ¾ × 4 × 33¼"
G	1	**Maple cupboard knob,** 1⅛"-dia.

Note: All wood is maple.

Misc.: Glue, ¼-20 × 2" connector bolts, 10mm-diameter cross dowels, ⅜ × 1½" dowels, #8 × 1½" flathead wood screws, ⅜"-diameter walnut flat plugs, 1⅛"-diameter maple cupboard knob, ¾"-diameter Roto hinge, ⅛"-diameter cord, stain, salad bowl oil.

Cutting the cradle

Because the cradle is a swinging unit, balance is a prime concern. Keep the ends symmetrical and opposing parts identical in size, shape, and weight by careful layout of designs, gang-cutting, and gang-sanding wherever possible.

1 Edge-glue ¾"-thick maple to produce 13"-wide stock for the sides (A), 16"-wide stock for the bottom (C), and 22"-wide stock for the ends (B). Clamp and check for flatness across the glue-up. Allow the glue to dry about 1 week before cutting or sanding.

2 Scrape away excess glue, then sand the glued panels to flat, smooth stock with a belt sander.

3 Ripcut the sides and ends to width.

4 Bevel-cut the bottom to width. Tilt your blade to 10° to make the cut with a rip blade.

5 Crosscut the sides, ends, and bottom to length.

6 On each rectangle cut for the ends, draw a vertical line through the center of the piece dividing each end into 11"-wide halves.

7 At the bottom of each end, draw a horizontal reference line across the piece 2" from the bottom.

8 Transfer the grid design (see end view of *Diagram*) to one of the cradle ends. Align both end pieces and fasten them in the waste areas at the outside corners of the top and bottom with #6 × 1¼" screws.

9 Gang-cut the ends on the bandsaw. Cut just to the line so the original line will still be visible to preserve symmetry in the size and shape while sanding. Use a 12-tpi blade for smooth cutting.

10 Plane the straight sections on the sides to finished size and smoothness with a jack plane.

11 Gang-sand the curved sections on the ends with a stationary or drum sander.

12 Transfer the grid design to one of the sides. Align the corners and clamp the pieces together along the bottom and ends. Gang-cut the recess in the center of the sides using a bandsaw.

13 Gang-sand the recess with a pad sander.

14 Reclamp the sides at the ends to sand the top and bottom edges with a belt sander.

15 Round over the inside and outside edges of the top and bottom of the sides with a ⅜"-diameter roundover bit.

16 Round over the inside and outside edges of all sides of the ends with a ⅜"-diameter round-over bit.

17 Drill a ⅜ × ½"-diameter hole for the locking pin centered on the vertical line 20" from the top of one end. Use a Forstner bit and drill press to make the hole.

18 Use a combination square to draw a line ⅞" from each side, the full length of each end.

19 Mark six evenly spaced centers for dowels and screws along each line. Mark the first center 1" above the bottom and the last center 1" below the top of each end.

20 Starting at the top mark, drill ⅜"-diameter holes for dowels through the ends at every other center mark using a brad-point bit.

21 At the remaining center marks, drill ¼ × ⅜"-diameter counterbore holes for #8 screws.

22 Drill three evenly spaced holes for ⅜" dowels in each end. Center the holes ⅜" above the horizontal line drawn in step 7 to join the bottom to the ends.

23 Sand the sides, ends, and bottom to finished smoothness.

Assembling the cradle

Hand-tighten screws to avoid stripping holes while dry-fitting.

1 Dry-fit the sides to the ends. Lay ½"-thick spacers on a flat surface to support one side, then clamp the ends to the side with bar clamps.

2 Drill pilot holes for #8 screws into both ends of the side using the counterbore holes in the ends as guides.

3 Separate the sides from the ends and drill shank holes for #8 screws through the pilot holes at both sides of the ends.

4 Temporarily fasten the ends to the side with screws. Lubricate the screw threads with beeswax to prevent breakage.

5 Remove the clamps and temporarily fasten the remaining side to the ends using the techniques described in *steps 1 to 3* above.

6 Remove the clamps and dry-fit the bottom to the ends and sides, making sure the bottom is seated at the horizontal lines drawn on the ends.

7 Drill ⅜"-diameter holes for dowels ¾" deep into the ends of the bottom using the dowel holes drilled in the ends as guides.

8 Drill holes for dowels ¾" deep into the sides using the dowel holes drilled in the ends as guides.

9 Use a pencil to trace the position of the bottom onto the sides.

10 Remove the screws holding the ends to the sides.

11 Use the line traced around the bottom as a reference to mark and drill dowel holes and counterbore and shank holes for #8 screws spaced every 5" along each side. Start with a dowel hole and alternate with screw holes. Start the holes ¾" from each end and drill at a 10° angle through the sides on a drill press using brad-point bits.

12 Refit the sides, bottom, and ends. Use the 10° holes drilled above as guides to drill dowel or pilot holes into the bottom through the sides with a portable drill guide and brad-point bits.

13 Reassemble the cradle using screws, glue, and dowels.

14 Apply glue to the counterbore screw holes and tap walnut flat plugs into the screw holes with a mallet. Allow to dry.

15 Cut the plugs flush and sand to match the surrounding wood.

Make the base

Before cutting all the parts for the base, it is a good idea to measure the length of the assembled cradle. The stretcher length must be ¼" longer than the cradle. Adjust the cutting list, if needed.

1 Cut the support (D), foot (E), and stretchers (F) to length and width from ¾"-thick maple.

2 Taper-cut the undersides of the stretchers from 4" wide at the ends to 3" wide at the center. Cut the tapers on a tablesaw with a taper jig. Finish the cuts with a handsaw at the center.

3 Cut a 3½ × ⅜"-deep rabbet on the bottom of the supports to form half lap joints with the feet.

4 Use a dado blade and tablesaw to cut a 3 × ⅜"-deep dado across the full width of one face of each foot to form a lap joint with the support.

5 Transfer the grid pattern to the feet and cut out the shape on a bandsaw.

6 Clamp the supports to the cradle ends so the edges align with the neck on the ends and the support is centered vertically. Trace the curves at the top onto the supports. Unclamp, then cut the curves on the bandsaw.

7 Sand the supports and feet to 180-grit smoothness.

8 Apply glue to the half lap joints on supports and feet. Assemble the pieces and clamp until dry.

9 Mark the location of the stretchers on the outside faces of each support/foot assembly (see *Diagram*). Be sure to align holes in supports with holes in stretchers.

10 Drill ¼"-diameter holes with a brad-point bit through the supports for connector bolts centered 1¼" from the top and bottom within each stretcher location.

11 Drill 1³⁄₃₂ × ⅝"-deep holes for 10mm cross dowels in the stretchers centered 1¼" from the top and bottom and 1" from the ends.

12 Drill 1½ × ¼"-diameter holes with a brad-point bit into the ends of the stretchers to accommodate the connector bolts. Center the holes so they pass through the centers of the cross dowel holes.

13 Drill a ½"-diameter hole with a brad-point bit through the support 20" from the top to seat the maple cupboard knob (G).

14 Drill a ³⁄₁₆"-diameter cord hole through the support 12" from the top. Counterbore the inside face to ½" deep with a ½"-diameter Forstner bit.

15 Sand the base parts to finished smoothness.

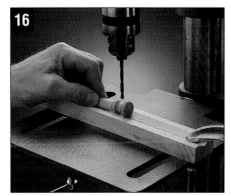

16 Drill a ³⁄₁₆"-diameter cord hole through the cove in the maple cupboard knob to complete the workpiece.

Finishing the cradle

Choose child-safe stains and finishes for any item that children will be in contact with. Most water-based products will be safe, but check the label to be certain.

1 Apply water-based stain to the cradle following manufacturer's instructions.

2 Apply several coats of salad bowl oil to seal the stain and give the cradle a soft, child-safe luster.

3 Drill a ½ × ½"-diameter hole for the Roto hinge centered 1½" from the top of the stem on each end of the cradle. Use a Forstner bit to produce a smooth, flat-bottomed hole in the maple.

4 Drill a ⁷⁄₁₆ × 1"-diameter counterbore hole on the outside of each support for the locking flange nut on the Roto hinge.

5 Drill a ½"-diameter hole through the center of the counterbore for the shaft of the Roto hinge.

6 Apply a few drops of wood glue to the knurled stud on the end of the glider hinge and insert the stud in the hole drilled into the cradle end.

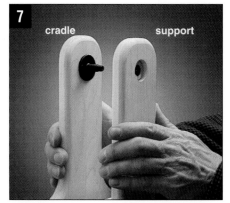

7 Insert the nylon sleeve into the support, and slide the support over the threaded bolt protruding from the hinge on the cradle end. Secure the connection with the locking flange nut provided.

8 Connect the stretchers to the supports with cross dowels and connector bolts. Draw the parts together tightly but avoid over-tightening the joint.

9 Drill a ½ × ⅜"-deep hole for the maple cupboard knob in the cradle end using the hole in the support as a guide. Insert a ⅛ × 18"-long cord through the knob and support. Knot each end to keep the cord in place.

WOODWORKER'S TIP

Knockdown hardware, like the cross dowels and connector bolts used in this project, make it possible to disassemble a project for storage. While the hardware is designed for reassembly many times, it will last longer and hold better if you follow a few easy rules:

- *Never use a stripped or damaged tool to tighten the components.*
- *Never force the threads to turn.*
- *Use wax to lubricate tight threads.*

Futon Couch

Space-saving convenience combines with fashion in this fold-down marvel.

This convenient furniture piece converts easily from couch to bed, saving both space and money. A popular furniture item, this futon couch is a space-saving project with a functional design. Build the frame yourself, then furnish the piece with the comfortable, padded mattress of your choice. The futon couch is great for guests.

Building the seat frame

Frame is built from hard maple.
1 Use a tablesaw and a sliding crosscut table to cut the cross members (F) and seat supports (H) from 1"-thick maple. Cut the slats (K) and braces (L) to size from ¾"-thick maple.
2 Use a tablesaw with a dado set to make a ¾ × ¾ × 1"-long tenon on each end of the braces. Cut ⅞ × ⅛ × 1¹⁄₁₆"-wide slits on the tenons for the wedges (P). Note: The measurements above are for diagonal slits; these slits can be either straight or diagonal.
3 Cut wedges from either matching or contrasting wood. Taper the wedges from ⁵⁄₃₂" to ⅛" at the end. Cut the wedges along the same long grain as the tenons.
4 Use a portable drill stand to make two ¾ × ¾" mortises through the front and back faces of each cross member. Start the mortises 23⁵⁄₁₆" from each end of the workpiece. Start the bottom of the mortise ½" from the bottom edge of the cross member. Finish the cuts with a sharp chisel.
5 Use a tablesaw with a dado blade to make a ⅜ × ⅜" groove along the entire length of the cross members. Make the groove ⅜" from the top edge of the workpiece on the inside face.
6 Use a tablesaw to cut a ⅜ × 1"-wide rabbet at each end of the inside faces of the cross members.

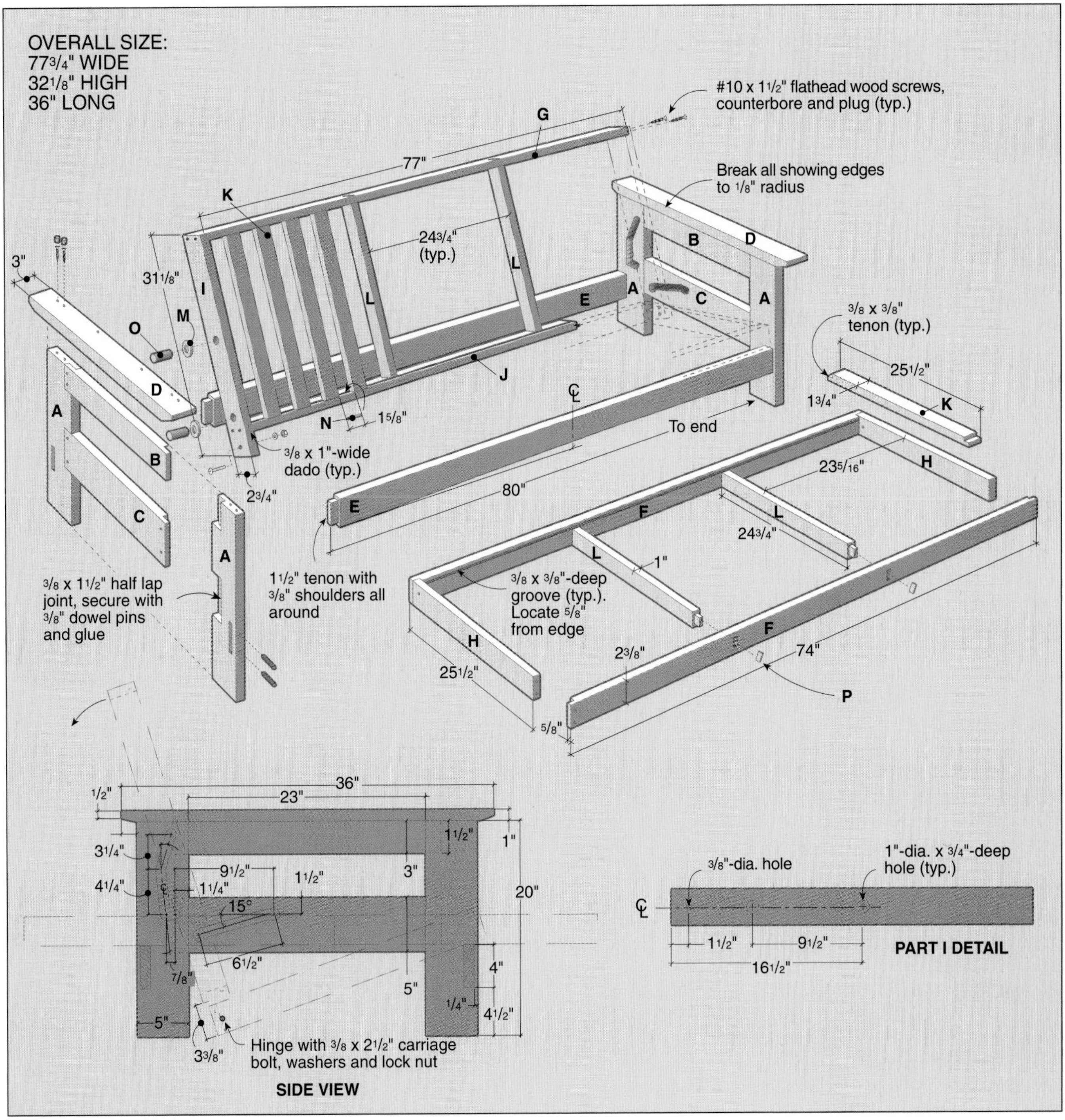
OVERALL SIZE:
77 3/4" WIDE
32 1/8" HIGH
36" LONG
#10 x 1 1/2" flathead wood screws, counterbore and plug (typ.)
G
77"
Break all showing edges to 1/8" radius
K
24 3/4" (typ.)
B
D
3"
31 1/8"
I
L
L
E
A
C
A
O
M
3/8 x 3/8" tenon (typ.)
25 1/2"
D
J
1 3/4"
K
A
N
1 5/8"
To end
B
3/8 x 1"-wide dado (typ.)
23 5/16"
H
2 3/4"
80"
E
F
L
C
24 3/4"
A
L
1"
3/8 x 1 1/2" half lap joint, secure with 3/8" dowel pins and glue
1 1/2" tenon with 3/8" shoulders all around
3/8 x 3/8"-deep groove (typ.). Locate 5/8" from edge
F
H
2 3/8"
74"
25 1/2"
P
5/8"
1/2"
36"
23"
1 1/2"
1"
3 1/4"
4 1/4"
9 1/2"
1 1/2"
3"
1 1/4"
20"
15°
6 1/2"
4"
7/8"
5"
1/4"
4 1/2"
5"
3 3/8"
Hinge with 3/8 x 2 1/2" carriage bolt, washers and lock nut
SIDE VIEW
3/8"-dia. hole
1"-dia. x 3/4"-deep hole (typ.)
1 1/2"
9 1/2"
16 1/2"
PART I DETAIL

CUTTING LIST

Key	Qty.	Description & Size	Key	Qty.	Description & Size	Key	Qty.	Description & Size
A	4	**Posts,** 1⅛ × 5 × 20"	F	2	**Cross member,** 1 × 2¾ × 74¾"	K	46	**Slats,** ¾ × 1¾ × 22¾"
B	2	**Upper stretcher,** 1⅛ × 3 × 27"	G	1	**Back cross beam,** 1 × 2¾ × 77"	L	4	**Brace,** ¾ × 1¾ × 26¾"
C	2	**Lower stretcher,** 1⅛ × 5 × 27"	H	2	**Seat support,** 1 × 2¾ × 25½"	M	4	**Wooden washers,** ¼ × 2"-dia.
D	2	**Arm,** 1 × 3 × 36"	I	2	**Back support,** 1 × 2¾ × 31⅛"	N	88	**Spacers,** ⅜ × ⅜ × 1⅝"
E	2	**Cross stretcher,** 1¼ × 4 × 80¼"	J	1	**Lower cross beam,** 1 × 2¾ × 75¾"	O	4	**Dowels,** 1¾ × 1"-dia.
						P	4	**Wedges,** ⅛ × ¾ × 1 1/16"

Note: All wood is maple.

Misc.: Glue, flathead wood screws (#10 × 1½"), ⅜" carriage bolts, dowels (⅜", ½").

7 Use a tablesaw and miter gauge to cut a ⅜ × ⅜" rabbet on slat ends.
8 Cut 88 slat spacers (N) to ⅜ × ⅜ × 1⅝"-long dimensions.
9 Sand all the workpieces to finished smoothness.
10 Dry-fit and clamp the cross members, seat supports, and braces. Use a portable drill with an adjustable counterbore bit to drill holes at each end of the cross members for attachment to seat supports (see *Diagram*). Disassemble the seat frame.
11 Apply glue to supports, brace tenons, and one cross member. Assemble the pieces with #10 × 1½" flathead wood screws.
12 Glue wedges and drive them into brace tenons with a wooden mallet. Cut off the excess length with an offset dovetail saw.
13 Insert slats; 1⅝" should separate each slat. Place the first slat flush against seat support. Apply glue and insert spacers.
14 Apply glue to the remaining cross member, braces, and seat supports. Attach the pieces with #10 × 1½" flathead wood screws, making sure the slats fit correctly into the cross member groove. Glue and insert spacers and wedges. Insert the plugs into all screw holes.

Building the rear framework

1 Cut back supports (I), back cross beam (G), and lower cross beam (J) to size from 1"-thick maple.
2 Use a portable drill stand to make two ¾ × ¾" mortises through the top face of the back cross beam and lower cross beam. The mortises should start 23⁵⁄₁₆" from

each end of the workpieces. Square corners with a sharp chisel.
3 Use a tablesaw to cut ⅜ × ⅜"-wide grooves along the bottom face of the back cross beam and the top face of the lower cross beam. Start these grooves ⅜" from the front edge of each workpiece.
4 Use a tablesaw to cut a ⅜ × 1" dado on the inside faces of the back supports. Start dadoes 5" from the bottom. Then cut a ⅜ × 1" rabbet on top inside edge of each workpiece.

5 Measure and mark the center-points for the dowel holes on the outside faces of the back supports. These holes hold the groove dowels (see *Diagram*). The top dowel hole should be centered 14½" from the top of the workpiece. The lower dowel hole should be centered 7" from the bottom of the workpiece. Use a drill press with a Forstner bit to drill centered ⅝ × 1"-diameter dowel holes on the outside face of the back supports.

WORKSHOP TIP

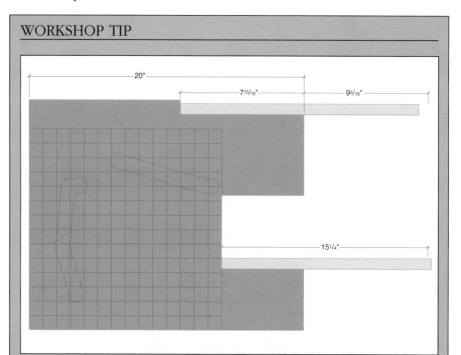

To make the router jig, cut 2 hardwood pieces to ¾ × 2 × 17¼" spacer rails. Then cut a piece of plywood to ½ × 16 × 19¼". Place the lower spacer rail by measuring and marking 4⅛" up, and 5¹⁵⁄₁₆" in from the lower right corner. Draw the cut lines and make the cut with a tablesaw or bandsaw. On the upper right corner, measure and mark 1½" down from the top edge, and 7¹⁵⁄₁₆" from the side. Draw the cut lines and make the cut with a tablesaw or bandsaw. Attach spacer rails as shown with nails or staples.

Transfer the 1" grid pattern (above) onto the plywood to make the routing cuts. Use a drill press with a 1"

Forstner bit to make the initial cuts at both ends of each router cut. Finish each cut with a sabersaw.

Position the jig flat against the leg assembly to rout the dowel grooves. Place the top spacer rail so it sits flush with the upper stretcher. The lower stretcher fits between the posts. Secure the jig with clamps as you rout the cuts with a plunge router. Cut each dowel groove to 1 × 1" diameter. The jig fits snugly into the leg assembly (see opposite) with the upper spacer rail acting as a stop on the upper stretcher and posts.
Note:
Coat dowel grooves and dowels with paste wax before assembly.

6 Dry-fit and clamp lower cross beam, back supports, braces, and back cross beam. Use a portable drill with an adjustable counterbore bit to drill holes through the outside faces of the back supports for attachment to the lower and back cross beams (see *Diagram*). Disassemble the rear framework.

7 Apply glue to lower cross beam, back supports, and braces. Attach with flathead wood screws.

8 Glue wedges and pound them into brace tenons with a wooden mallet. Cut off excess length with an offset dovetail saw.

9 Insert slats, placing the first slats flush against back supports. Glue and insert spacers.

10 Apply glue to the back cross beam, braces, and seat supports. Attach the pieces with #10 × 1½" flathead wood screws, making sure the slats fit correctly into the back cross beam slot. Glue and insert spacers and wedges.

11 Glue and insert plugs into all screw holes. Sand the plugs flush to surfaces.

12 Cut dowels (O) to 1 × 1¾" dimensions, and round the edges on a sander. Glue and insert dowels into holes on back supports.

Building the leg assembly

1 Cut posts (A), upper stretchers (B), lower stretchers (C), arms (D), and cross stretchers (E) to size from 1⅛"-thick maple.

2 Use a router table to cut ⅜ × 1½ × 3"-wide rabbets for half lap joints on outside faces of the posts for upper stretchers (see *Diagram*). Square corners with sharp chisel.

3 Use a router table to cut the ⅝ × 1½ × 5"-wide rabbets for half lap joints on the outside faces of posts for lower stretcher. Square corners with a sharp chisel.

4 Use a drill press with a ½"-diameter mortising bit to cut ½ × 1⅛ × 3¼"-wide mortises on the posts for cross stretchers. Square corners with a sharp chisel.

5 Use a tablesaw with a dado set to make the ⅜ × 1½ × 3"-long rabbets for half lap joints on ends of upper stretchers.

6 Use a tablesaw with a dado set to make the ⅜ × 1½ × 5"-wide half lap joints on both ends of the lower stretchers.

7 Dry-fit posts and stretchers. Use a portable drill with a ½"-diameter brad-point bit to cut two evenly spaced holes through each joint.

8 Assemble the posts, upper stretchers, and lower stretchers with glue. Insert ½"-diameter wooden dowels into the half lap joints with glue to secure the workpieces. Clamp and let dry.

9 To form arc on cross stretcher, cut a narrow strip of flexible plywood, sheet metal, or Plexiglas® 10" longer than the arc to use as a guide. Use finish nails to hold ends of guide. Start arc 8½" from each end. Pull center of guide back to form arc. Trace arc onto cross stretcher. Cut arc with a bandsaw and table extender.

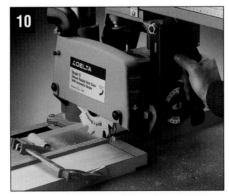

10 Use a radial-arm saw to cut ⅝ × 1⅛ × 3¼"-wide tenons on the ends of the cross stretchers. Make sure that the tenons have ⁵⁄₁₆"-wide shoulders on both sides. Cut slits down the full length of the tenon for wedges.

11 Use a router jig with a ¾"-diameter straight bit with a pattern-following collar to make 1"-deep slots for dowels on the inside face of leg assembly.

12 Use a tablesaw to make a 30° bevel on bottom ends of both arms.

13 Use a router with a ⅛"-diameter round-over bit to round over all exposed edges on the arms.

14 Drill counterbore, shank and pilot holes through arms for five #10 × 1½"-long flathead wood screws. Attach arms to posts and upper stretcher with glue and screws. Space screws evenly.

15 Glue and insert plugs into screw holes. Sand plugs flush.

Assembling the unit

1 Use a drill press with 2"-diameter holesaw to cut wooden washers (M) from ¼"-thick hardwood.

2 Drill and counterbore holes for ⅜"-diameter carriage bolts through back of the seat support and the bottom of the back support. Center these holes 1¾" from the bottom edges of workpieces. Attach seat assembly and back assembly to each other with carriage bolts. Use ⅜"-diameter carriage bolts with washers and nylon locking nuts to prevent loosening.

3 Glue and insert the cross stretchers into one leg assembly. Insert wedges. Remove excess wedge with an offset dovetail saw. Sand wedges flush. Clamp and let dry.

4 With washers in place, insert dowels into grooves on one leg assembly. Glue and insert cross stretchers on opposite side while simultaneously fitting frame dowels in their slots. Glue and insert wedges. Clamp and let dry.

5 Finish the futon with tung oil.

Mission Bed

Mission styling and the strength of oak combine to make this bed a solid choice.

The simplicity of Mission furniture is the first thing you'll notice when you look at our queen-size bed frame. Look more closely and you'll see the detailed joinery that makes Mission furniture last for generations. The pinned mortise-and-tenon joints (here joining the head and foot panels to the bed posts) are a good example of blending sturdy joinery into furniture design. Add modern bed-rail hardware to the project and you'll be rewarded with a lifetime of peaceful sleep.

Prepare the posts

A bed must have sturdy posts. We made the posts for our Mission bed by laminating solid oak stock.
1 Joint and plane stock to produce straight, 3"-square posts for the corners of the bed frame.
2 Cut the posts to length on a radial-arm saw. Use stopblocks so each pair of posts is the same.
3 Lay out and cut a 6½ × ½"-wide through-mortise in each post, starting 7¼" up from the bottom (see *Diagram*). Use a drill press and mortising bit (see *Tool Tip*, opposite) or hand-cut by drilling several ⁷⁄₁₆"-diameter holes to remove waste wood in the mortise area. Square off the edges with a ½" bevel-edge chisel.
4 Cut a 3½ × ½"-wide through-mortise in each post, starting 3¾" from the top, and centered side to side (see *Diagram*).
5 Rout ⅛"-deep × ¹¹⁄₁₆"-wide × 4"-long

mortises for the bed rail fasteners, 6¾" from the bottom and centered side to side in an adjacent face to the through mortises in each post (see *Diagram*).

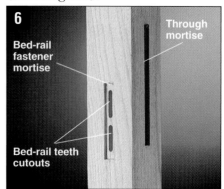

6 Inside the bed-rail fastener mortises, rout two square cutouts, ¼ × 1⅜ × ½"-deep, for the bed-rail teeth. Start the cutouts ½" from the top and bottom of the bed-rail mortises, centered side to side.

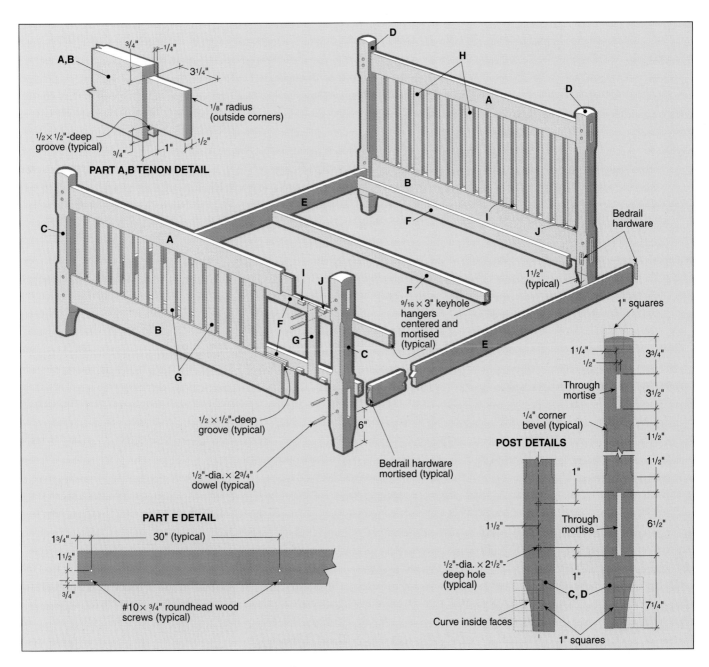

PART A,B TENON DETAIL

3/4"　1/4"

3 1/4"

1/8" radius (outside corners)

1/2 × 1/2"-deep groove (typical)

3/4"　1"　1/2"

A,B

PART E DETAIL

30" (typical)

1 3/4"

1 1/2"

3/4"

#10 × 3/4" roundhead wood screws (typical)

1/2 × 1/2"-deep groove (typical)

1/2"-dia. × 2 3/4" dowel (typical)

Bedrail hardware mortised (typical)

6"

9/16 × 3" keyhole hangers centered and mortised (typical)

Bedrail hardware

1 1/2" (typical)

POST DETAILS

1" squares

1 1/4"

1/2"

3 3/4"

3 1/2"

1 1/2"

1 1/2"

1/4" corner bevel (typical)

Through mortise

1 1/2"

1"

6 1/2"

Through mortise

1"

1/2"-dia. × 2 1/2"-deep hole (typical)

C, D

7 1/4"

Curve inside faces

1" squares

7 Enlarge and transfer the pattern for the curved-profile corner cuts (see *Diagram*) to the two inside faces of each post foot. Cut along the outlines of the curves on your bandsaw. Smooth out the curves with a 2"-diameter, 120-grit drum sander mounted in a drill press.

8 Rout a 1/4"-deep stopped chamfer on all four corners of each post. Start each chamfer 15 1/4" from the post foot, stopping 8 3/4" from the post top (see *Diagram*).

9 Enlarge and transfer the post-top pattern (see *Diagram*) to a 3"-square piece of 1/4"-thick plywood. Cut out the curve on a bandsaw

TOOL TIP

Use a mortising bit mounted in a drill press to cut multiple through-mortises in thick stock. A mortising bit features a chisel-edge bit housing that squares off corners as the drill bit bores into the wood.

and use the piece as a template to mark all four sides of each post top for trimming.

10 Shape the post tops to the profile with a block plane, scraping in toward the center of each post.

11 Smooth the post tops with 120-grit sandpaper, then finish-sand.

CUTTING LIST

Key	Qty.	Description & Size
A	2	**Panel top,** 1 × 5 × 64 1/2"
B	2	**Panel bottom,** 1 × 8 × 64 1/2"
C	2	**Foot post,** 3 × 3 × 38"
D	2	**Head post,** 3 × 3 × 44"
E	2	**Bed rail,** 1 × 5 1/2 × 80"
F	4	**Cross rail,** 1 1/2 × 3 1/2 × 60"
G	16	**Foot slat,** 1/2 × 2 1/2 × 16 1/2"
H	16	**Head slat,** 1/2 × 2 1/2 × 22 1/2"
I	60	**Slat spacer (inner),** 1/2 × 1/2 × 1"
J	8	**Slat spacer (outer),** 1/2 × 1/2 × 1 1/2"

Note: All wood is oak.

Misc.: Glue, 1/2 × 2 3/4" dowels, #10 × 3/4" roundhead and flathead wood screws, keyhole hangers (8), bed-rail fasteners (4).

TOOL TIP

Use a cutting gauge to lay out tenons. Although it looks like a marking gauge, the cutting gauge contains a knife blade instead of a scribing pin. The knife cuts made by the cutting gauge are easier to see on end grain, and they provide a more accurate cutting line than a pencil or scribing tool.

Make the headboard & footboard

The slatted panels that serve as the headboard and footboard on our bed are a distinguishing feature of Mission furniture. They give the bed a solid feel with a look of lightness and simplicity. For best results, test-fit slats and slat spacers before you glue them into the panels.

1 Cut the panel tops (A) and panel bottoms (B) for the headboard and footboard.

2 On the ends of the panel tops and bottoms, use a cutting gauge to mark the ½ × 3¼"-deep tenons that fit into the post mortises. The tenons should start ¾" from the top and bottom edge of each workpiece (see *Diagram*).

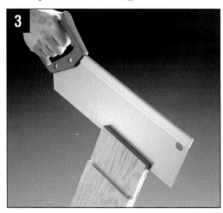

3 Make relief cuts to the tenon shoulders, using a backsaw, then carefully trim off the waste on all four sides of each tenon, cutting just outside the cutting lines.

4 Pare the tenons to finished size with a sharp wood chisel. Dry-fit the tenons in the through-mortises in the posts. Each tenon should fit snugly, protuding slightly through the mortise. Trim the tenons with the chisel, if necessary, until a good fit is achieved.

5 Round over the ends of the tenon, using 180-grit sandpaper and a sanding block.

6 On the top edge of each panel bottom and the bottom edge of each panel top, rout a centered ½ × ½"-deep groove to hold the slats (G, H) and slat spacers (I, J).

7 Rip enough ½"-thick oak stock to 2½" wide to make all the foot slats (G) and head slats (H).

8 Cut the slats to length on your radial-arm saw. Use a stopblock to ensure uniform lengths.

9 Rip enough ½"-thick oak stock to ½" width to make the inner slat spacers (I) and outer slat spacers (J).

10 Crosscut the spacers to length. Note: because the spacers are so small, a power miter saw or radial-arm saw can kick the cut-off pieces up into the blade guard. Your safest bet is to use a handsaw.

11 Finish-sand the panel tops, bottoms, slats, and spacers.

12 Set one panel bottom on your worksurface. Mark the midpoint of the workpiece with a piece of tape, then tape a spacer into the groove, centered on the midpoint.

13 Insert a slat into the groove on each side of the spacer. Position a long scrap piece of ¼"-thick plywood under the slats for support.

14 Mark the midpoint of the matching panel top and center it over the slats. Guide the slats into the groove in the panel top. Press the panel top and bottom together.

15 Slide alternating spacers and slats into the grooves until you reach the final spacer at each end. The end spacers (J) should fit flush with the shoulders of the tenons.

16 Check the panel for square and make sure the distance between the tenons is the same as the distance between the mortises on the head posts. Clamp the panel to the table to hold it in position for fitting the slats.

17 Starting at an end, remove the slats and spacers up to the midpoint. Leave the spacer next to the midpoint slat in place.

18 Carefully brush a small amount of glue into the top and bottom panel grooves for the first slat and spacer in from the midpoint. Insert the slat and spacer.

19 Continue gluing and replacing slats and spacers until the last slat and the end spacer are in place.

20 Remove the loose slats and spacers from the other half of the panel assembly. Beginning at the midpoint, glue and insert the remaining slats and spacers.

21 When all the slats and spacers are in place, draw the top and bottom panels together with a pair of pipe clamps. Tighten the clamps only until the slats are wedged firmly in place. Check the panel for square, making sure the outside spacers are flush with the edges. Let the glue dry.

22 Build the other panel assembly using the same techniques.

Assemble the footboard & headboard

Complete the assembly of the headboard and footboard by attaching the posts to the headboard and footboard panels. We built the footboard first, but feel free to reverse the order if you prefer. To avoid mistakes, dry-fit the pieces and mark them for assembly.

1 Dry-fit the foot posts in the correct position against the footboard panel. Clamp the assembly with pipe clamps to hold it in position while you drill dowel holes.

2 On outside faces of the footboard posts, mark centers for the dowel pins that lock the panel tenons into the post mortises (see *Diagram*). Note: because the dowels are decorative, they are located on the most visible faces of the bed posts, not hidden.

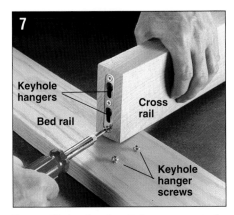

3 Use a drill with a brad-point bit, mounted in a portable drill guide, to bore ½ × 2¾"-deep holes through the posts and tenons. Note: the lowest hole in each post will extend through the post and into the bed-rail fastener mortise.
4 Remove the clamps and disassemble the headboard. Clean all chips and dust from the mortises with a small brush.
5 Purchase or cut 16 ½ × 2¾"-long oak dowels. Trim four of the dowels to 1" in length for the bottom joint on each post, and taper one end of all 16 dowels on the stationary sander to make them easier to drive into the mortise.
6 Brush a light coat of glue on the tenons and inside the mortises, then reassemble the footboard.
7 Insert the dowels into the holes with the end-grain of the dowels running perpendicular to the grain direction in the posts. Tap the dowels into the holes with a wood mallet. Don't drive the 1" dowels so far into the lowest mortises that they extend into the bed-rail fastener mortises. Let the glue dry.
8 Assemble the headboard.

WOODWORKER'S TIP

Coat screw threads with beeswax to make them easier to drive in hardwoods. Unlike soap and other lubricants, beeswax won't leave residue that can discolor wood.

---

9 Position a bedrail fastener in the proper mortise in each post. Use a vix bit to drill pilot and shank holes for #10 × ¾" flathead screws at the screw locations in the fasteners. Drive the screws to secure the fasteners in the mortises.

10 Trim the ends of the dowels flush with the posts, using an offset dovetail saw. Remove saw marks from the dowel ends by sanding them (with the grain).

Make the rails
The mattress and box springs for our queen-size bed are supported by bed rails between the headboard and footboard, and cross rails that span the bed rails.
1 Cut the bed rails (E) and cross rails (F) to width and length.
2 Mark drilling points for the keyhole hanger screws on the inside faces of the bed rails (see *Diagram*). Each bed rail should have four pairs of screws: a pair 1¾" in from each end, and a pair 30" in from each end. The upper screw in each pair should be 1½" from the top of the rail, and the lower should be ¾" from the bottom of the rail. Drill pilot holes, then drive a #10 × ¾" roundhead wood screw at each drilling point, to a depth of ½".
3 In the ends of the bed rails, lay out centered ⅛ × 11⁄16 × 4"-long mortises for the bed-rail hardware (see *Diagram*). Cut the mortises with a ½" bevel-edge chisel.
4 In the ends of the cross rails, lay out centered 9⁄16 × 3 × ⅛"-deep mortises for the keyhole hangers. Cut the mortises.
5 Within each cross-rail mortise, cut two ⅜ × ¾ × ½"-deep mortises for the heads of the keyhole hanger screws that are driven in the bed rails. Cut one mortise ½" from the top of the keyhole-hanger mortise, and cut the other mortise ½" from the bottom.
6 Finish-sand the support rails and bed rails with 220-grit sandpaper.

7 Install the bed-rail fasteners and keyhole hangers. Tape the fastener and hanger parts in place, and drill 5⁄32"-diameter pilot holes and 3⁄16"-diameter shank holes at the screw locations, using a vix bit. Drive #10 × ¾" flathead wood screws into the wood to secure the fasteners.

Finish & assemble the bed
While traditional Mission furniture was colored by exposing it to ammonia fumes (which will darken oak), we used black walnut stain to replicate the traditional dark Mission look.
1 Remove all dust from the wooden bed parts with a vacuum cleaner or a tack rag.
2 Apply stain with a rag or brush, following the manufacturer's instructions. Recoat with stain when dry, as necessary.
3 When the wood color is darkened to your satisfaction, apply two or three coats of clear tung oil to help protect the wood and the finish.
4 For additional protection and a higher gloss, rub on several coats of paste wax.
5 Begin to assemble the bed frame by sliding the keyhole hangers at the ends of the cross rails over the screws in the bed rails. Adjust the screws to achieve a snug fit in the cross rails.
6 Slip the teeth in one of the bed rails into the slots in one of the headboard posts and, while supporting the headboard with one hand, connect the opposite rail into the remaining post.
7 Connect the bed rails to the footboard.

CHAPTER 3

Work Centers

Everything in its place

Organization is the key to efficiency in a work center. The tool you need—be it pen or pliers, computer disc or caliper—should be readily at hand. If you have to track down the proper tool, you waste valuable time. That's why the work centers in this chapter include storage space: drawers, cubbyholes, shelves, or pegboards. There's a place for everything, and everything in its place keeps you efficient.

Adequate work surface is another component to a useful workstation. To keep the work flowing, each of these centers includes a sturdy, flat surface at a comfortable height. You'll relish the elbowroom.

Before you begin building, study all eight designs shown here. You'll find four desks: two writing desks, a computer center, and a pint-size play center for children. If your projects are more workshop-oriented, check out the stations designed for hobbies, woodworking, and the garage.

Don't be afraid to improvise to meet your specific needs. If you want extra storage space in the garage, for example, add the wall-hung cabinet from page 102 to your garage center. Are you shorter or taller than average? Adjust the height on any of these workstations for your personal comfort. Do you have an abundance of computer paraphernalia? Customize the computer workstation to accommodate all your hardware, disks, and books.

Secretary

Organize your paperwork beautifully in this handsomely detailed piece.

The quality stamp of hand-cut dovetails distinguishes this secretary from those found in fine furniture stores. Laminate maple stock for the lid, legs, sides, and desktop in advance to get this project rolling.

Making the upper assembly

1 Edge-glue ¾"-thick maple stock to form the desktop (D), desktop access lid (E), sides (F), top (G), and lid (H). Reinforce the glue joints using #20 biscuits where they will not be exposed by further cutting. Clamp and allow to dry for one week. Remove excess glue. Note: The stock for the access lid should match the grain in the center of the desktop.

2 Cut the desktop to finished size.

3 Use a sabersaw to cut a 9½ × 10½"-long access opening centered on the desktop.

4 Rout a ⅜ × ⅜"-wide rabbet on the top of all four edges of the access opening to hold the access lid.

5 Use a gouge to cut a ⅜ × ⅜ × ¾"-wide tapered finger grip into the front edge of the access opening.

6 Cut the access lid, sides, and top to size.

7 Rout a ⅜ × ⅜"-wide rabbet on the bottom of all four edges of the access lid to fit the access opening. Cut a notch in the front of the access lid to match the finger grip.

8 Lay out and mark ¹¹⁄₁₆"-wide pins

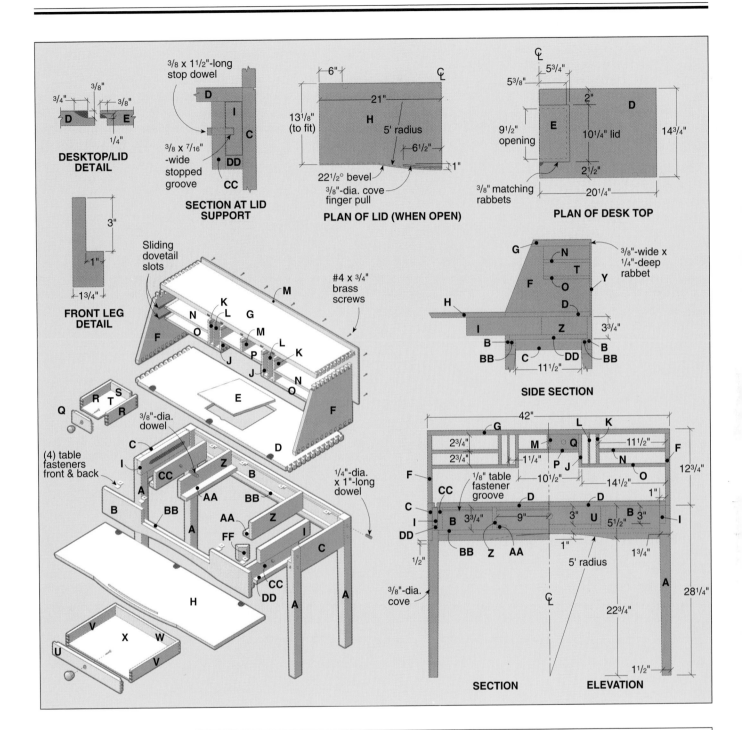

DESKTOP/LID DETAIL — ³/₄", ³/₈", D, ³/₈", E, ¹/₄"

SECTION AT LID SUPPORT — ³/₈ x 1¹/₂"-long stop dowel; ³/₈ x ⁷/₁₆"-wide stopped groove; D, I, C, DD, CC

PLAN OF LID (WHEN OPEN) — 6", 21", 13¹/₈" (to fit), H, 5' radius, 6¹/₂", 1", 22¹/₂° bevel, ³/₈"-dia. cove finger pull

PLAN OF DESK TOP — 5³/₄", 5³/₈", 2", D, E, 9¹/₂" opening, 10¹/₄" lid, 14³/₄", 2¹/₂", ³/₈" matching rabbets, 20¹/₄"

FRONT LEG DETAIL — 3", 1", 1³/₄"

Sliding dovetail slots

#4 x ³/₄" brass screws

³/₈"-dia. dowel

(4) table fasteners front & back

³/₈"-dia. x 1"-long dowel

¹/₄"-dia. x 1"-long dowel

SIDE SECTION — G, N, T, ³/₈"-wide x ¹/₄"-deep rabbet, F, O, Y, H, D, I, Z, 3³/₄", B, BB, C, DD, BB, 11¹/₂"

SECTION / ELEVATION — 42", G, L, K, 2³/₄", M, Q, 11¹/₂", F, 2³/₄", 1¹/₄", N, ¹/₈" table fastener groove, P J, 10¹/₂", 14¹/₂", O, 1", 12³/₄", F, CC, C, I, B, 3³/₄", 9", 3", U, B 3", I, DD, BB Z AA, 1", 1³/₄", ³/₈"-dia. cove, 5' radius, 22³/₄", A, 28¹/₄", 1¹/₂", ¹/₂"

CUTTING LIST

Key	Qty.	Description & Size
A	4	Legs, 1³/₄ × 1³/₄ × 28¹/₄
B	2	Long rails, ³/₄ × 5¹/₂ × 40¹/₂
C	2	Side rails, ³/₄ × 5¹/₂ × 13
D	1	Desktop, ³/₄ × 14³/₄ × 40¹/₂
E	1	Access lid, ³/₄ × 10¹/₄ × 11¹/₄
F	2	Sides, ³/₄ × 15 × 12³/₄
G	1	Top, ³/₄ × 10¹/₂ × 42
H	1	Lid, ³/₄ × 14¹/₈ × 42
I	2	Lid supports, 1 × 2¹⁵/₁₆ × 13¹/₄
J	2	Large dividers, ¹/₂ × 6⁷/₈ × 8³/₄
K	2	Inside dividers, ¹/₂ × 6¹/₂ × 8³/₄
L	2	Middle dividers, ¹/₄ × 6¹/₂ × 8³/₄
M	1	Bin divider, ¹/₄ × 3¹/₄ × 8³/₄
N	2	Middle shelf, ¹/₂ × 12¹/₈ × 8³/₄
O	2	Bottom shelf, ¹/₂ × 15³/₈ × 8³/₄
P	1	Bin shelf, ¹/₂ × 11 × 8³/₄
Q	2	Bin face, ³/₄ × 2³/₈ × 4⁷/₈
R	4	Bin side, ¹/₂ × 2³/₈ × 8⁵/₈
S	2	Bin back, ¹/₂ × 2³/₈ × 4⁷/₈
T	2	Bin bottom, ¹/₄ × 4³/₈ × 8¹/₄
U	1	Drawer face, ³/₄ × 2⁷/₈ × 17⁷/₈
V	2	Drawer side, ¹/₂ × 2⁷/₈ × 13³/₈
W	1	Drawer back, ¹/₂ × 2⁷/₈ × 17⁷/₈
X	1	Drawer bottom, ¹/₄ × 12¹/₂ × 17³/₈
Y	1	Back, ¹/₄ × 41¹/₂ × 12¹/₂
Z	2	Drawer guide, ³/₄ × 3³/₄ × 14
AA	2	Drawer support, ³/₄ × 1¹/₂ × 14
BB	2	Support cleats, ³/₄ × 1 × 38¹/₂
CC	2	Lid support guide, ³/₄ × 3³/₄ × 14
DD	2	Lid support cleat, ³/₄ × 1¹/₁₆ × 14
EE	1	Drawer stop, ³/₄ × ³/₄ × 2
FF	2	Corner blocks, ³/₄ × 2¹/₄ × 3

Note: All wood is maple. Drawer/Bin Bottoms T, X, Back Y are plywood.

Misc.: Glue; ³/₈", ¹/₄" dowels; (3) sewing machine hinges; (2) Shaker drawer pulls, ⁷/₈"-dia.; (1) 1¹/₈"-dia.;#20 biscuits; #6 × 1⁵/₈" flathead screws; self-adhesive felt strips and dots; #4 × ³/₄" brass screws; tabletop fasteners.

for through dovetail joints on the top and bottom edges of the sides. Leave 9/16"-wide spaces for tails.
9 Use the pins marked on the sides as a guide for laying out 7° tails on the top and desktop.
10 Cut the tails with a dovetail saw. Pare the edges with a chisel.
11 Scribe outlines of the tails onto the sides over the pin locations. Cut the pins as you did the tails.
12 Dry-fit the sides, top, and desktop. Adjust joints as needed.
13 Starting at the back inside edge of each side, rout 3/8 × 1/2"-wide sliding dovetail slots for the shelves. Start the upper slot 3 1/2" from the top, and the lower slot 6 3/4" from the top. Make the slots 9" long.
14 Rout 3/8 × 1/2"-wide sliding dovetail slots for large dividers in the inside face of the top 5 1/4" from each side of the center. Rout 1/4 × 1/2"-wide slots for the bin divider and inside dividers in the center of the top and 8 1/2" from each side of the center of the top. Make the slots 9" long.
15 Rout 1/4 × 1/4 × 9"-long dadoes for the middle dividers starting 6 1/2" from each side of the center of the inside face of the top.
16 Sand all upper assembly components to finished smoothness.
17 Reassemble the components using glue. Clamp, check for square, and allow to dry. Remove excess glue when dried.
18 Rout a 1/4 × 1/2"-wide rabbet for the back on the back inside edge of the upper assembly. Square the corners with a chisel.
19 Cut the lid to size.
20 Lay out and mark a 5'-radius arc centered on the top of the lid.
21 Draw a cutline 1 1/2" from the top of the lid. Draw from each end toward the center. Stop the line where it intersects the arc.
22 Cut the arc and top of the lid using a bandsaw with the table tilted at 22 1/2°.
23 Lay out and cut a 3/8 × 1/2"-wide finger groove that matches the arc. Start the 13"-long groove 1/4" from the front edge of the lid.
24 Set the top assembly and lid on a flat worksurface. Align the lid with the desktop and clamp the assembly and the lid to the worksurface. Lay out and mark the desktop and lid for sewing machine hinges (see *Diagram*).
25 Rout mortises for the hinges with a 3/4"-diameter bit. Dry-fit the hinges and adjust as needed.
26 Unclamp the lid and round over the bottom inside edge with a 1/8"-radius round-over bit.
27 Sand lid to finished smoothness.

Building the base

1 Buy or glue up enough maple stock to make four pieces of 2 × 2 × 30" stock for the legs (A).
2 Joint and plane or cut the legs to 1 3/4 × 1 3/4 × 28 1/4".
3 Cut a stopped taper on the two inside surfaces of the legs, using a tapering jig on a tablesaw. Start the taper 5 1/2" from the top of the legs. Taper to 1 1/4" square at the bottom of the legs.
4 Cut a 3 × 1"-deep rabbet on the top inside edges of the front legs to hold the lid supports (I).
5 Cut the long rails (B) and side rails (C) from 3/4"-thick maple.
6 Cut 3/16 × 3/4"-wide rabbets on both faces and 3/8 × 3/4"-wide rabbets on the top and bottom edges of each end of the side rails. These cuts create 3/8 × 3/4 × 4 3/4"-long tenons on each end of the side rails.
7 Cut 3/8 × 3/4 × 4 3/4"-long mortises in the front and rear legs for the side rails. Start the mortises 3/8" from the top of each leg and 3/16" from the outside edge of each leg.
8 Scribe an arc with a 5' radius centered on the front long rail, starting 11" from each side of the center and 1" from the bottom (see *Diagram*). Cut the radius on a bandsaw.
9 Cut a 3 × 18" opening centered in the top of the front long rail for the large drawer (see *Diagram*).
10 On the ends of the front long rails, cut 3/8 × 3/4"-wide rabbets on the bottom edges and 3/16 × 3/4"-wide rabbets on front and back faces to make 5 1/8"-long tenons.
11 Cut a 3/4 × 3"-deep notch in the top of the tenons in the front long rail to hold the lid supports.
12 Cut 3/8 × 1 × 2 1/8"-long mortises in the front legs to join with the front long rails. Start the mortises 3/16" from the front face of the leg at the shoulder of the 1 × 3" notches for the lid supports.
13 Make 3/8 × 4 3/4 × 1"-long tenons on the ends of the back long rails.
14 Cut 3/8 × 4 3/4 × 1"-long mortises in the rear legs to join with the back long rails. Start the mortises 3/8" from the top of the legs and 3/16" from the rear face of the leg.
15 Cut 1/4 × 1/4"-deep grooves 1/2" from the top on the inside of all rails for tabletop fasteners.
16 Cut a stopped cove on the outside corner of each leg, using a 3/8"-diameter cove bit. Stop the cove 1/2" from the top of each leg.

17 Dry-fit the legs and rails and adjust as needed. Drill 1/4× 1"-deep holes for pins in each mortise and tenon joint. Drill holes 1 1/4" from the top and bottom of the rail.
18 Sand the legs and rails to finished smoothness.
19 Use glue to attach the legs and rails, pinning the joints with 1/4× 7/8"-long dowels. Check for square, and let dry.

Making the interior desk supports

1 Cut the drawer guides (Z), drawer supports (AA), support cleats (BB), lid support guides (CC), lid support cleats (DD), drawer stop (EE), and corner blocks (FF) from 3/4"-thick maple.
2 Cut the lid supports (I) from 1"-thick maple.
3 Drill 1/4 × 3/8"-deep holes for knobs centered in the front edge of each support.
4 Rout a 3/8 × 7/16"-wide groove for a stop dowel on the inside face of each support. Start the 7"-long groove 4 3/4" from the front edge of

each lid support. Sand the lid supports to finished smoothness.
5 Drill a ⅜"-diameter through hole for a stop dowel 4" from the front and 1½" from the top of the guide.
6 Fasten the support cleats to the front and back long rails, 1" from the bottom of each, using countersunk #6 × 1¼" wood screws. Be sure the top of the cleat is ¾" below the drawer notch.
7 Fasten the drawer stop to the center of the back rail using countersunk #6 × 1¼" wood screws.
8 Fasten the drawer guides to the outside edge of the drawer supports, using countersunk #6 × 1⅝" wood screws.
9 Attach the drawer guide/support assembly to the desk base assembly, using countersunk #6 × 1⅝" wood screws. Fasten guide/support assembly so it is flush with the drawer opening on the sides and the bottom.
10 Fasten the lid support guides to the outside edge of the lid support cleats, using countersunk #6 × 1⅝" wood screws.
11 Attach the lid support guide/cleat assembly to the support cleats using countersunk #6 × 1⅝" wood screws.
12 Bevel-cut each end of the corner blocks at 45°. Drill holes through the bevels for #6 screws.
13 Attach the corner blocks to the front and back long rails and lid support guides, using four countersunk #6 × 1⅝" wood screws.

Making the bins and drawer

1 Cut bin faces (Q) and drawer face (U) from ¾"-thick maple.
2 Cut bin sides (R), bin backs (S), drawer sides (V), and drawer back (W), from ½"-thick maple.
3 Cut bin bottoms (T) and drawer bottom (X) from ¼"-thick maple.
4 Lay out and mark ½ × ½"-deep tails for lapped dovetail joints in each end of the inside faces of the drawer front and the bin fronts. Cut the tails with a dovetail saw and ⅛"-wide bevel-edged chisel.
5 Lay out and mark ½ × ½"-deep tails for through dovetail joints in each end of the inside faces of the drawer back and the bin backs. Cut the tails as above.
6 Scribe the outlines of the tails on the outside ends of drawer sides and bin sides to lay out pins at each end of the sides. Cut the pins with a dovetail saw.
7 Dry-fit the fronts and backs to the sides. Adjust as needed.
8 Cut a ¼ × ¼"-deep groove to hold the bottoms ¼" up from the inside bottom edges of all drawer and bin fronts, sides, and backs. Stop the grooves ¼" from the ends of the fronts and backs.
9 Sand all parts to finished smoothness.
10 Reassemble the drawer and bins around their bottoms using glue. Do not glue the bottoms in place. Check for square and allow to dry. Remove excess glue.

Making the compartments

1 Cut the large (J), inside (K) and bin (M) dividers and the middle (N), bottom (O), and bin (P) shelves from ½"-thick maple. The grain on the large dividers must run vertically.
2 Cut the middle (L) dividers from ¼"-thick maple.
3 Lay out and mark ½ × ½"-deep tails for dovetail joints along the inside end of the bottom shelves. Be sure the wide ends of the tails are on the top.
4 Lay out and mark ½ × ½"-deep pins for dovetail joints along the bottom edge of the large dividers to match the tails in the shelves.
5 Cut ½ × ⅜"-deep sliding dovetails on the outside ends of the bottom shelves and middle shelves.
6 Cut ½ × ¼"-deep sliding dovetails on the inside ends of the middle shelves, both ends of the inside dividers, bin shelf, and bin divider, and top edge of the large dividers.
7 Cut ½ × ¼"-deep slots for sliding dovetails 3¼" from the top of the dovetails in the outside faces of the inside dividers and the inside faces of the large dividers, and in the center of the top of the bin shelf.
8 Cut ¼ × ¼"-deep dadoes for the middle dividers in the bottom shelves starting 1¼" from the inside ends of the shelves.

9 Dry-fit the shelves and dividers, then dry-fit the resulting compartment assembly to the upper assembly. Adjust joints as needed. Sand the shelves and dividers to finished smoothness.
10 Reassemble the shelves and dividers with glue. Clamp, check for square, and allow to dry. Remove excess glue when dried.
11 Glue and fit the compartment assembly into the upper assembly.
12 Cut the back (Y). Sand to finished smoothness.
13 Fasten the back to the upper assembly with #4 brass screws.

Finishing up

1 Apply several coats of tung oil to the secretary.
2 Attach the upper assembly to the base with tabletop fasteners and the screws provided.
3 Attach knobs to bins, desktop supports, and drawer.
4 Apply ¹⁄₁₆ × ¾ × 8"-long self-adhesive felt strips to the top edge of the lid supports and felt dots to the lid to prevent scratching.

5 Install the lid supports. Apply glue to the middle of the stop dowels. Push them through the support guides into the lid supports so they are seated in the stop-dowel groove.
6 Install the hinges.

Desk

Rich cherry adds depth to this elegant writing desk.

This writing desk, with its plentiful storage drawers and exposed pigeonholes, provides classic style and a comfortable workspace.

Making the legs

1 Joint and plane cherry stock to 1½" square for front legs (A), inside legs (B), and rear legs (C). Cut legs to length.

2 Lay out two adjacent sides of each leg for stopped taper cuts, stopping 17" up from bottom of leg. Legs are 1" square at bottom.

3 Cut stopped tapers on two adjacent sides of each leg.

4 Align and clamp all three leg pairs with opposing tapers facing in, creating upside-down "Vs", and remaining tapers facing up. Set aside inside legs.

5 Mark faceup sides of front and rear legs for ¾ × ⅜"-deep grooves 10¾" long to hold side panels (N) (see *Diagram*) and tenons of side arches (G) and side stretchers (I). Start all grooves ¼" in from outside edges of legs and 17⅜" from the bottom. Use a square to mark all four legs simultaneously.

6 On top portion of rear legs, mark ¾ × ⅜"-deep grooves 7½" long for top side panels (P) and tenons from top rails (M) and top brackets (L). Mark ¾ × ⅜"-deep stopped dadoes for shelves. Start lower dado 7¼" from top, and upper dado 3⅝" from top.

7 Unclamp front and rear leg pairs. Turn front and rear legs until unmarked tapered sides are on top. Clamp pairs of rear legs and front legs separately.

8 Lay out on clamped rear legs ¾ × ⅜"-deep grooves for back panel (O), top back panel (Q), back arch (F), and large stretcher (H) to match grooves on previous face.

9 Clamp inside leg pair with front leg pair whose tapered, unmarked side is up. Line up the bottoms of legs. Lay out ¾ × ⅜ × ⅜"-deep mortises for drawer stretchers (J) and front arches (O) on legs. Lay out ¾ × ⅜ × ⅜"-deep large stretcher (H) mortises on front legs (see *Diagram*). Start front arch mortises 17⅜" from bottom and drawer stretcher mortises 24½" from bottom.

10 Unclamp inside legs and turn top faces inward toward each other until unmarked tapered sides are on top, and clamp.

11 On unmarked tapered sides of inside legs, mark two evenly spaced biscuit slots per leg centered ½" from the outside edge for joints with leg panels.

12 Turn inside legs' top faces inward toward each other again. Mark faceup untapered side of inside legs for ¾ × ⅜ × 1⅛"-long mortises for middle arch (E). Start mortises 2" from top.

13 Rout all dadoes and grooves in legs, using ¾"-diameter bit.

14 Clean up routed dadoes and grooves with a ¾"-wide chisel.

15 Cut slots with biscuit joiner.

16 Sand to finished smoothness.

Making the panels

1 Cut front arches (D) and middle arch (E) from ¾"-thick cherry.

2 Cut back arches (F) and side arches (G) from 1½"-thick cherry.

3 On front arches and middle arches, cut ⅜ × ⅜"-deep rabbets on top and bottom edges of both ends to form ¾"-wide tenons.

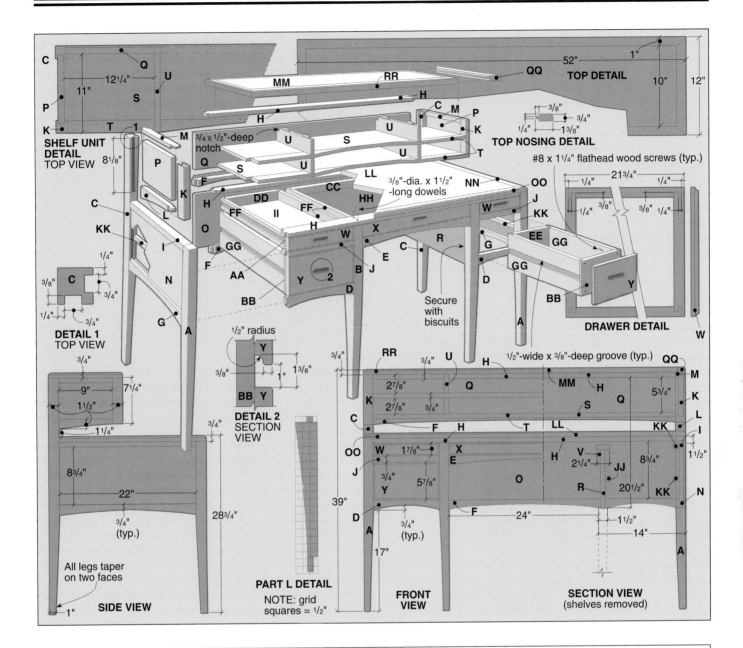

CUTTING LIST

Key	Qty.	Description & Size
A	2	**Front leg,** $1\frac{1}{2} \times 1\frac{1}{2} \times 28$"
B	2	**Inside leg,** $1\frac{1}{2} \times 1\frac{1}{2} \times 27\frac{1}{4}$"
C	2	**Rear leg,** $1\frac{1}{2} \times 1\frac{1}{2} \times 38\frac{1}{4}$"
D	2	**Front arch,** $\frac{3}{4} \times 1\frac{1}{2} \times 11\frac{3}{4}$"
E	1	**Middle arch,** $\frac{3}{4} \times 1\frac{1}{2} \times 24\frac{3}{4}$"
F	2	**Back arch,** $1\frac{1}{2} \times 1\frac{1}{2} \times 49\frac{3}{4}$"
G	2	**Side arch,** $1\frac{1}{2} \times 1\frac{1}{2} \times 22\frac{3}{4}$"
H	3	**Large stretcher,** $\frac{3}{4} \times 1\frac{1}{2} \times 49\frac{3}{4}$"
I	2	**Side stretcher,** $\frac{3}{4} \times 1\frac{1}{2} \times 22\frac{3}{4}$"
J	2	**Drawer stretcher,** $\frac{3}{4} \times 1\frac{1}{2} \times 11\frac{3}{4}$"
K	2	**Top stile,** $1\frac{1}{2} \times 1\frac{1}{2} \times 7\frac{1}{4}$"
L	2	**Top bracket,** $1\frac{1}{2} \times 1\frac{1}{2} \times 10\frac{3}{8}$"
M	2	**Top rail,** $\frac{3}{4} \times 1\frac{1}{2} \times 10\frac{1}{2}$"
N	2	**Side panel*,** $\frac{3}{4} \times 9\frac{1}{2} \times 22\frac{3}{4}$"
O	1	**Back panel*,** $\frac{3}{4} \times 9\frac{1}{2} \times 49\frac{3}{4}$"
P	2	**Top side panel*,** $\frac{3}{4} \times 9\frac{3}{4} \times 6\frac{1}{2}$"
Q	1	**Top back panel*,** $\frac{3}{4} \times 6\frac{1}{2} \times 49\frac{3}{4}$"
R	2	**Leg panels*,** $\frac{3}{4} \times 8\frac{3}{4} \times 22\frac{3}{4}$"
S	2	**Shelf*,** $\frac{3}{4} \times 9\frac{1}{2} \times 50\frac{1}{2}$"
T	2	**Shelf nosing,** $\frac{3}{4} \times 1\frac{7}{8} \times 50\frac{1}{2}$"
U	4	**Top spacer,** $\frac{3}{4} \times 2\frac{7}{8} \times 3$"
V	2	**Double guides,** $\frac{7}{16} \times 2\frac{1}{4} \times 22\frac{3}{4}$"
W	2	**Small false front,** $\frac{3}{4} \times 1\frac{7}{8} \times 10\frac{7}{8}$"
X	1	**Long false front,** $\frac{3}{4} \times 1\frac{7}{8} \times 23\frac{7}{8}$"
Y	2	**Large false front,** $\frac{3}{4} \times 5\frac{7}{8} \times 10\frac{7}{8}$"
Z	1	**Long drawer front,** $\frac{3}{4} \times 1\frac{7}{8} \times 23\frac{7}{8}$"
AA	2	**Small drawer front,** $\frac{3}{4} \times 1\frac{7}{8} \times 10\frac{7}{8}$"
BB	2	**Large drawer front,** $\frac{3}{4} \times 7\frac{7}{8} \times 10\frac{7}{8}$"
CC	1	**Long drawer back,** $\frac{3}{4} \times 1\frac{7}{8} \times 23\frac{1}{8}$"
DD	2	**Small drawer back,** $\frac{3}{4} \times 1\frac{7}{8} \times 10\frac{1}{8}$"
EE	2	**Large drawer back,** $\frac{3}{4} \times 5\frac{7}{8} \times 10\frac{1}{8}$"
FF	6	**Short drawer side,** $\frac{3}{4} \times 1\frac{7}{8} \times 22\frac{3}{4}$"
GG	4	**Tall drawer side,** $\frac{3}{4} \times 5\frac{7}{8} \times 22\frac{3}{4}$"
HH	1	**Middle drawer bottom*,** $\frac{1}{4} \times 22\frac{1}{4} \times 22\frac{7}{8}$"
II	4	**Side drawer bottom*,** $\frac{1}{4} \times 9\frac{7}{8} \times 22\frac{1}{4}$"
JJ	2	**Leg drawer guide,** $\frac{7}{16} \times \frac{3}{4} \times 22$"
KK	4	**Side drawer guide,** $\frac{7}{16} \times \frac{7}{8} \times 22$"
LL	1	**Desktop*,** $\frac{3}{4} \times 22 \times 49$"
MM	1	**Top*,** $\frac{3}{4} \times 10 \times 50$"
NN	2	**Side nosing,** $\frac{3}{4} \times 1\frac{7}{8} \times 23\frac{1}{2}$"
OO	1	**Front nosing,** $\frac{3}{4} \times 1\frac{7}{8} \times 52$"
PP	1	**Rear nosing,** $\frac{3}{4} \times 1\frac{7}{8} \times 49$"
QQ	2	**Top side nosing,** $\frac{3}{4} \times 1\frac{3}{8} \times 12$"
RR	2	**Top nosing,** $\frac{3}{4} \times 1\frac{3}{8} \times 52$"

Note: All wood is cherry, except for * items, which are cherry plywood.
Misc.: Glue, #8 × 1¼" flathead wood screws ,⅜"-diameter x 1½" dowels, #20 biscuits.

4 On back and side arches, cut $\frac{3}{8}$ × $\frac{3}{8}$"-deep rabbets on all sides of each end to form $\frac{3}{4}$"-square tenons.
5 Cut a $\frac{3}{4}$ × $\frac{3}{8}$"-deep groove in top edge of side and back arches to hold their respective panels. Start groove $\frac{1}{4}$" from outside edge.
6 Cut a $\frac{1}{2}$ × $\frac{3}{8}$"-deep rabbet on upper inside edge of top back arch to hold shelf.

7

7 To form curves for each arch (front, middle, back, side), cut a narrow strip of $\frac{1}{4}$"-thick acrylic or plywood, 10" longer than the arch, for a guide. Use finish nails to hold ends of guide. Then pull center of guide back to form arc. Trace arc onto arch with a pencil. Cut arches, gang-cutting identical pieces, using a bandsaw. Note: One of the back arches has three arched cuts to mirror the lines of the front and middle arches. Leave a $1\frac{1}{2}$" flat space on either side of the center cut to hold leg panels.
8 Cut large stretchers from $\frac{3}{4}$"-thick cherry.
9 Cut a $\frac{3}{4}$ × $\frac{3}{8}$"-deep groove $\frac{1}{4}$" from outside edge in one face of two large stretchers for back panels.
10 Cut side stretchers and drawer stretchers from $\frac{3}{4}$"-thick cherry.
11 Cut $\frac{3}{8}$ × $\frac{3}{8}$"-deep rabbets on sides of both ends of large stretchers and side stretchers to make $\frac{3}{4}$ × $\frac{3}{8}$"-deep tenons.
12 Cut $\frac{3}{4}$ × $\frac{3}{8}$"-deep grooves in bottoms of side stretchers, $\frac{1}{4}$" from outside edge, to hold side panels.
13 Cut top stiles (K) and top brackets from $1\frac{1}{2}$"-thick cherry.
14 Cut top rails from $\frac{3}{4}$"-thick cherry.
15 Cut a 1 × $\frac{3}{4}$"-deep rabbet on the bottom of one end of top brackets and 1 × $\frac{3}{8}$"-deep rabbets on the other three sides to create a $\frac{3}{8}$ × $\frac{3}{8}$ × 1"-long tenon on bracket front.
16 Cut $\frac{3}{8}$ × $\frac{3}{8}$"-deep rabbets on all sides of wide end of bracket to form a $\frac{3}{4}$ × $\frac{3}{4}$ × $\frac{3}{8}$"-long tenon.
17 Mark an arc on the bottom of brackets as shown in *Diagram.* Cut arc on a bandsaw and sand it with a drum sander.
18 Cut $\frac{3}{8}$ × $\frac{5}{8}$"-deep rabbets in top inside edge of top brackets and top back arch for shelf and panel.
19 Cut $\frac{3}{8}$ × $\frac{3}{8}$"-deep rabbets on front and back faces of both ends of top rails to create $\frac{3}{4}$"-thick tenons.
20 Cut a $\frac{3}{8}$ × $\frac{3}{4}$ × 1"-long mortise in bottom of top stiles to hold tenon from front of top bracket.
21 Cut $\frac{3}{4}$ × $\frac{3}{8}$"-deep grooves in top rails and top stiles to hold top side panels. Grooves in top stiles also hold tenons from top rails.
22 Cut side panels, back panel, top side panels, top back panel, and leg panels (R) from $\frac{3}{4}$"-thick cherry plywood.
23 Cut $1\frac{1}{2}$ × $\frac{3}{4}$ × $\frac{1}{2}$"-deep notches centered in the flat spaces of the inside of the back arches to hold the leg panels.
24 Sand arches, stiles, brackets, rails, and stretchers to finished smoothness.
25 Cut slots for biscuits in leg panels and back panels where they join and in leg panels where they join inside legs.
26 Dry-fit legs, arches, stiles, rails, brackets, stretchers, and panels.
27 Sand panels to finished smoothness.

Making the shelves

1 Cut shelves (S) from $\frac{3}{4}$"-thick cherry plywood.
2 Cut shelf nosing (T) from $\frac{3}{4}$"-thick cherry.
3 Cut $\frac{3}{8}$ × $\frac{1}{4}$"-deep rabbets on top and bottom of rear edges of shelf nosing and a $\frac{1}{4}$ × $\frac{3}{8}$"-deep groove centered in front edges of shelves to form tongue-and-groove joints.
4 Glue shelf nosing to shelves. Clamp. Scrape away excess glue.
5 Cut $\frac{1}{2}$ × $1\frac{1}{2}$"-long notch in each end of shelf nosing to fit top stile.
6 Use middle arch as a template to mark nosing and shelves for shelf curve arch. Cut curve on a bandsaw. Sand shelves and nosing to finished smoothness.
7 Cut top spacers (U) from $\frac{3}{4}$"-thick cherry. Cut $\frac{3}{4}$ × $\frac{1}{2}$"-deep notches in top back corner of two top spacers to fit large stretcher (H).
8 Cut biscuit slots in top and bottom of each top spacer and in shelves to join them and to join spacers to top (MM).
9 Cut biscuit slots in ends of upper shelf and side panels to join them.
10 Sand spacers to finished smoothness.

Assembling the desk

1 Assemble lower part of desk sides. Glue and join rear legs, side arches, and side stretchers. Insert side panels. Glue and join front legs to assembly. Clamp, check for square, and let dry.

2

2 Assemble upper part of desk sides, completing side assembly. Glue top brackets and top rails to rear legs. Slide top side panels in place. Glue the top stiles to the tenons in top brackets and top rails. Clamp, check for square, and let dry.
3 Join two inside legs by gluing middle arch in place. Clamp front assembly, square, and let dry.
4 Position a large stretcher over the inside legs. Drill $\frac{3}{8}$"-diameter through dowel holes in large stretcher to join to inside legs. Then extend holes $\frac{13}{16}$" into legs.
5 Attach large stretcher to inside legs with $\frac{3}{8}$ × $1\frac{1}{2}$" dowels and glue. Clamp, square, and let dry.
6 Cut double guides (V) from $\frac{7}{16}$"-thick cherry. Sand to finished smoothness.
7 Cut the biscuit slots every 4" in double guides and tops of the leg

panels where they join *(see the Diagram)*

8 Attach double guides to tops of leg panels with biscuits and glue.
9 Unclamp front assembly and place it facedown on a flat worktable. Attach leg panels to inside legs with glue and biscuits. Slide bottom back arch onto bottom of back panel. Slide leg panels into slots on arch. Attach back panel to leg panels with glue and biscuits. Support panels, square, and let dry.
10 Attach spacers to shelves with glue and biscuits. Clamp, square, and let dry.
11 Mark and cut biscuit slots in back edges of shelves and front face of top back panel. Attach top back panel to shelf assembly with glue and biscuits. Clamp, square, and let dry.
12 Turn over front frame assembly so it is faceup. Place ¼" supports of scrap material under back panel. Slide top back arch onto bottom of top panel. Attach one desk side assembly to front frame assembly with glue. Seat back panel in groove in rear leg, but do not glue back panel. Clamp desk side to the front assembly, check for square, and let dry.
13 Apply glue to mortise in rear leg and tenon on a large stretcher. Slide stretcher over back panel to join to desk side.
14 Lay out ¼" spacers of scrap material to support shelf assembly. Then apply glue to rabbet in top bracket. Fasten shelf assembly to desk side, using biscuit joints with middle shelf and top side panel.
15 Glue and join a large stretcher to desk side assembly, over the bottom of top back panel.
16 Apply glue to remaining joints and complete frame assembly by attaching remaining desk side to shelf and desk frame assembly. Clamp, square, and let dry.

Making the drawers

1 Cut the small false fronts (W), long false front (X), large false fronts (Y), long drawer front (Z), small drawer fronts (AA), large drawer fronts (BB), long drawer back (CC), small drawer backs

(DD), large drawer backs (EE), short drawer sides (FF), and tall drawer sides (GG) from ¾" cherry.
2 Cut middle drawer bottom (HH) and side drawer bottoms (II) from ¼"-thick cherry plywood.
3 Cut ¼ × ¼" grooves starting ¼" from the bottom of the inside of each drawer side and front, running the length of each piece.
4 Cut a ¼ × ¾"-deep dado centered in each end of all drawer fronts and backs for drawer corner joints. Place each front and back on the tablesaw with the inside facedown. Then make a ⅜ × ⅜" rabbet cut to form a ¼ × ⅜" tenon.
5 Cut ¼ × ⅜"-deep dadoes ¼" from the inside ends of each drawer side for drawer corner joints.
6 Rout a ⅜₁₆ × ⅛₁₆"-deep groove centered on the outside of the drawer sides to fit over the drawer guides.
7 Sand drawer sides, fronts, backs, bottoms to finished smoothness.
8 Dry-fit the drawers with bottoms in place. Adjust as needed.
9 Glue and assemble drawers around bottoms. Do not glue bottoms. Clamp, square, and let dry.
10 Use a router and router table with a ¾"-diameter box core bit to cut a curved profile around all of the front edges of the false fronts.
11 Cut 1 × 3" through slots centered on false fronts for handles.

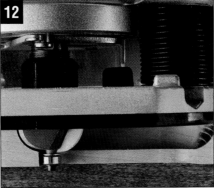

12 Turn the false fronts over so the back sides face up. Rout a ½"-radius cove along the top edge of the handle slot on the back of the false front to make a fingerpull. Use a cove bit with a bearing. Break the edges at the sides of the slot *(see Diagram)*. Sand the false fronts to finished smoothness.
13 Cut the leg panel drawer guides

(JJ), and the side panel drawer guides (KK) from ⁷⁄₁₆" cherry.
14 Cut biscuit slots in the drawer guides and the side and leg panels where they join. Sand the drawer guides to finished smoothness.
15 Attach the drawer guides to the leg panels and side panels with biscuits and glue *(see Diagram)*.
16 Dry-fit the drawers into the assembly. Center the false fronts for the drawers and fasten them to the drawer fronts, using #8 × 1¼" wood screws.

Making the tops

1 Cut desktop (LL) and top (MM) from ¾"-thick cherry plywood.
2 Cut the side nosing (NN), front nosing (OO), and rear nosing (PP) from ¾"-thick cherry.
3 Cut top side nosing (QQ) and top nosing (RR) from ¾" cherry.
4 Cut ¼ × ⅜"-deep rabbets on the nosing to leave ¼ × ⅜" tongues the length of the nosings, starting ¼" from the top.
5 Cut ¼ × ⅜"-deep grooves in the edges of the desktop and top, starting ¼" down from the top face, to fit the tongues.
6 Make 45° miter cuts on both ends of the front nosing, top nosing, and top side nosing. Make 45° miter cuts on the front ends only of the side nosing. Make no miter cuts on the rear nosing.
7 Sand the nosing to finished smoothness.
8 Glue and assemble desktop, top, and nosings. Clamp and let dry.
9 Use a chamfering bit to cut a ¼"-deep chamfer on the front and sides of the desktop nosing and all around the top nosing.
10 Sand the top and desktop to blend the nosing with the top. Sand the top and desktop to finished smoothness.
11 Cut biscuit slots in the top nosing, the desktop nosing, and the assemblies to attach them.
12 Attach the top and desktop with biscuits and glue.

Finish the desk

1 Apply several coats of tung oil, following manufacturer's instructions. Topcoat with paste wax.

Computer Workstation

*Combine the high-tech features your computer demands
with the warm wood tones you desire.*

Today's sleek and powerful home computers can do just about anything, but without an efficient work area, time spent in front of the computer terminal won't be as productive or pleasant as it might be.

The computer workstation we've designed is a striking addition to any home office. The solid oak desktop contains an optional slot for feeding continuous-feed printer paper up to the printer from the storage shelf below. The desktop also provides ample room for spreading out reference materials while you work. A slide-out keyboard shelf pulls out to a convenient typing height and stores your keyboard below the desktop.

With its functional design, our computer workstation boasts a striking appearance. The gleaming oak, the smooth angles, and the sleek lines create a very contemporary, Scandinavian look.

Before building, take a close look at your computer equipment. Use your design skills to add custom features to your workstation, like a platform for stacking components, or a built-in power strip.

Even if you don't own a computer, this workstation design can be modified for use as a standard desk. The printer shelf converts easily to a file drawer, and the keyboard drawer can be replaced with a shallow utility drawer.

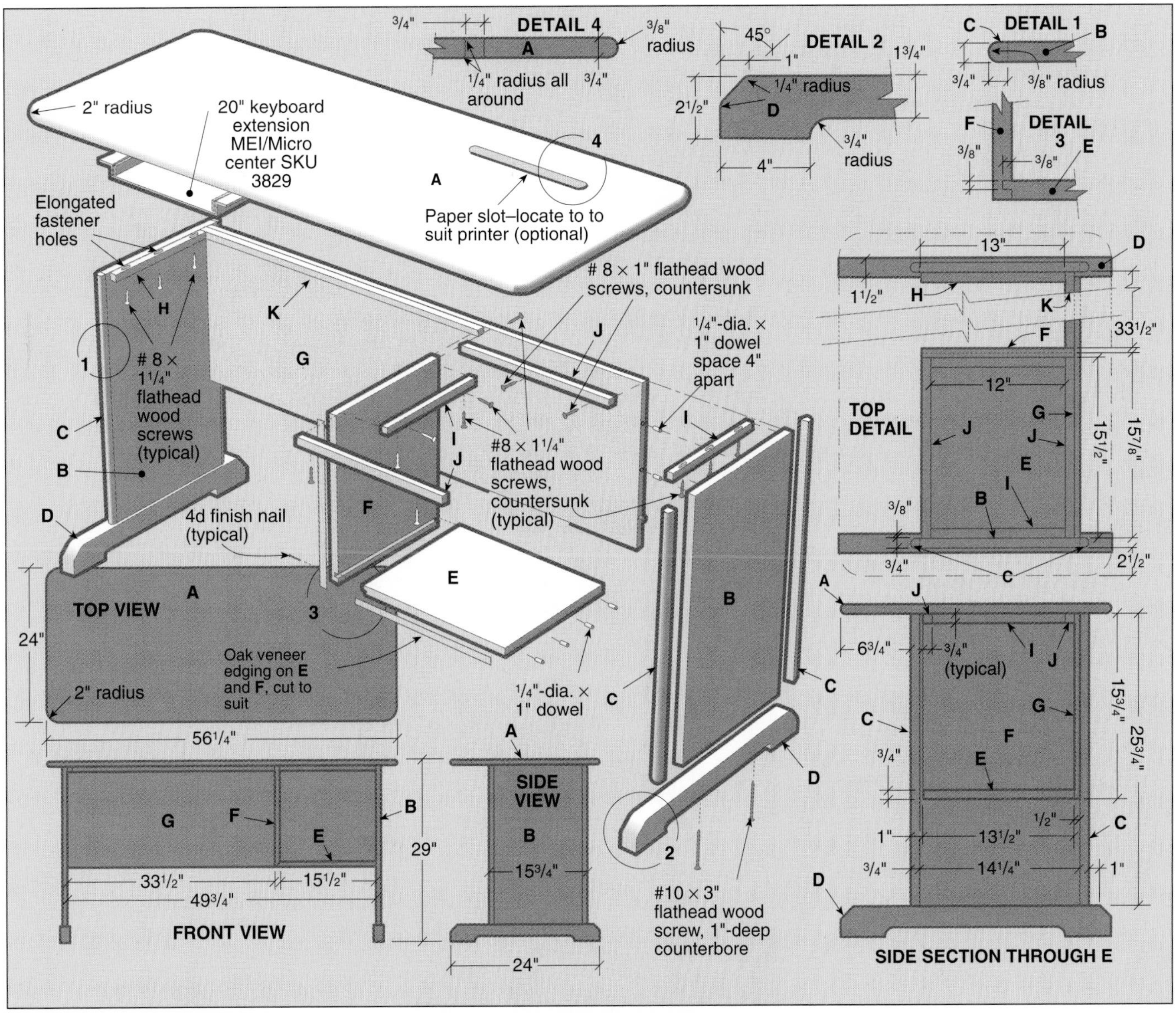

DETAIL 4
A
3/4"
3/8" radius
1/4" radius all around
3/4"
45°
DETAIL 2
1"
1 3/4"
1/4" radius
2 1/2"
D
3/4" radius
4"
DETAIL 1
C
B
3/4"
3/8" radius
DETAIL 3
F
E
3/8"
3/8"
2" radius
20" keyboard extension MEI/Micro center SKU 3829
4
A
Elongated fastener holes
Paper slot–locate to to suit printer (optional)
8 × 1" flathead wood screws, countersunk
H
K
J
1/4"-dia. × 1" dowel space 4" apart
1
8 × 1 1/4" flathead wood screws (typical)
G
C
B
I
J
#8 × 1 1/4" flathead wood screws, countersunk (typical)
I
D
4d finish nail (typical)
F
E
TOP VIEW
A
3
24"
Oak veneer edging on E and F, cut to suit
2" radius
1/4"-dia. × 1" dowel
56 1/4"
A
B
C
C
D
2
#10 × 3" flathead wood screw, 1"-deep counterbore
G
F
E
B
33 1/2"
15 1/2"
49 3/4"
FRONT VIEW
29"
SIDE VIEW
B
15 3/4"
24"
13"
D
1 1/2"
H
K
F
33 1/2"
12"
TOP DETAIL
G
J
J
E
15 1/2"
15 7/8"
3/8"
B
I
3/4"
C
2 1/2"
A
J
6 3/4"
3/4" (typical)
I
J
15 3/4"
25 3/4"
C
G
F
3/4"
E
1/2"
C
1"
13 1/2"
3/4"
14 1/4"
1"
D
SIDE SECTION THROUGH E

Building the desktop

We used five ¾"-thick oak boards to glue up the desktop for our computer workstation. Because this desktop doesn't have a frame to give it rigidity and help prevent warping, it's especially important to use straight, well-dried boards. Match color and grain as closely as you can, cutting boards from the same stock if possible. Alternate the cross grains of the glue-up boards between cupped-up and cupped-down to minimize warp.

1 Cross-cut the oak boards for the desktop so they are about an inch longer than the planned length of the desk (the entire desktop is trimmed to size after glue-up).

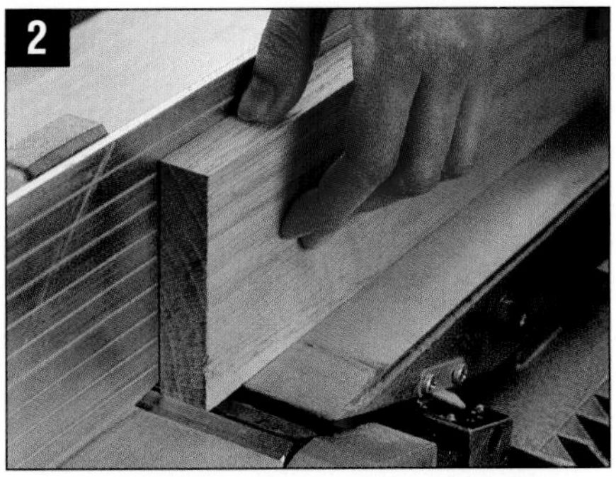

2

2 Joint one edge of each board, then trim the boards to square by pressing each jointed edge against the fence on your tablesaw and ripping the unjointed edge. Make sure the boards are uniform thickness and, when placed edge to edge, they're at least ½" wider than the planned width of the desktop.

CUTTING LIST

Key	Qty.	Description & Size
A	1	**Desktop,** oak ¾ × 24 × 56¼"
B	2	**Upright,** plywood ¾ × 14¼ × 25¾"
C	4	**Edging,** plywood ¾ × ¾ × 25¾"
D	2	**Foot,** oak 1½ × 2½ × 24"
E	1	**Shelf,** plywood ¾ × 13½ × 15⅞"
F	1	**Shelf side,** plywood ¾ × 13½ × 15¾"
G	1	**Back panel,** plywood ½ × 15¾ × 49¾"
H	1	**Upright cleat,** oak ¾ × ¾ × 13"
I	2	**Shelf side cleat,** oak ¾ × ¾ × 12"
J	2	**Top cleat,** oak ¾ × ¾ × 15½"
K	1	**Top cleat,** oak ¾ × ¾ × 33½"

*All plywood is oak-veneer plywood.

Misc.: Glue, flathead wood screws (#8 × 1", #8 × 1¼", #10 × 3"), ¼ × 1"- dia. dowels, 4d finish nails, keyboard shelf, oak veneer edging.

3 Dry-fit the boards on a flat surface with the good side facing up. If there are any visible gaps, run the adjoining edges of the boards through your jointer. Once you've arranged and trimmed the boards to eliminate any gaps, draw a large triangle over all the boards as a reference for repositioning them during the glue-up.

4 Glue up the desktop by applying a light coat of glue to the mating board edges at each joint, then pressing them together with the ends aligned and the top surfaces flush. Clamp the boards together with bar clamps, then remove any excess glue.

5 After the glue has dried, unclamp the desktop and rip it to the finished width on your tablesaw. When trimming off more than ¼", take an equal amount from each edge board to preserve the symmetrical look.

> **WOODWORKER'S TIP**
>
> *When making finish cuts with a circular saw, set the lumber on your workbench with the good side down to avoid tear-out from the saw-blade teeth.*

6 Trim the desktop to the finished length, using a circular saw and a straightedge.

7 Mark a 2"-radius curve at each corner of the desktop, using a compass. Trim the curve, using a sabersaw equipped with a fine wood-cutting blade.

8 Shape the top and bottom edges of the desktop, using a router and ⅜" roundover bit.

Building the base parts

For economy, the uprights, shelf bottom and side, and the back panel of our computer workstation are made of oak-veneer plywood. In addition to saving you money, using plywood instead of glued-up hardwood boards helps stabilize the project by minimizing stress caused by shrinking and swelling.

The feet for the computer workstation are made from 1½" oak stock and shaped using a router

with a roundover bit, and a power sander. If you can't find 1½"-thick oak stock, laminate two ¾"-thick boards together.

1 Cut ¾" oak plywood panels to size for the uprights (B), the shelf (E), and the shelf side (F). Also cut the back panel (G) from ½" oak plywood.

2 Run a ¾"-thick oak board through your jointer to create a flat edge, then rip a ¾"-wide strip on your tablesaw. Cut enough strips to make four 25¾" edging strips (C) and the cleats (H to K). Cut the oak strips to finished length for the cleats and edging strips, using a power miter box.

3 Glue the edging strips to the vertical, outside edges of each upright. Secure the edging with bar clamps, and allow glue to dry.

4 Remove the clamps, then shape both edges on the outside faces of the edging strips, using a router and a ⅜" roundover bit.

5 Cut a ⅜"-wide, ⅜"-deep groove in one 13½" side of the shelf side panel (F), ⅜" up from the bottom edge. Cut a ⅜" rabbet in one bottom edge of the shelf bottom (E). The rabbeted edge of the bottom should fit into the groove near the bottom of the shelf side panel, forming a rabbet-and-dado joint.

6 Rip 1½" oak stock to 2¾" width to create two blanks for making the feet (D).

7 Cut the blanks to length, then trim away the outside corners. Make the trim cut 1" from the corner on the top and end of each foot, using a power miter saw.

8 Round over the edges of the corner cuts, using a sander.

9 Mark the feet along the bottom edge, 4" in from each end, then mark a cutout between the marks, ¾" up from the bottom edge.

10 Create smooth, curved corners for the cutout by drilling holes at the corners with a drill and ¾" bit.

11 Make the cutouts in the feet with a sabersaw or on a bandsaw with a ¼" blade.

12 Sand the edges of the cutout area smooth, using a sanding block or a 1½" drum sander mounted in a drill press.

13 Shape all edges of the feet, except the bottom edges, with a router and ⅜" roundover bit.

14 Finish-sand all project pieces.

Assembling the workstation

Assembling large panels into a carcass or cabinet is always clumsy, so to simplify the task we used a system of stops and shims to apply side pressure to the uprights (see *step 5*).

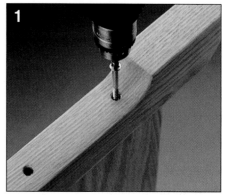

1 Attach the feet to the uprights by drilling ³⁄₁₆"-diameter pilot holes with a 1"-deep counterbore into the cutout section of the feet. Apply glue to the joints, center the feet over the bottom edges of the uprights, then drive #10 × 3" flathead wood screws through the counterbored pilot holes and into the uprights.

2 Mark the side edges of the back panel (G) for three ¼"-diameter dowel holes spaced at 4" intervals. Drill ⅝" deep at the marks, with a brad-point bit, then insert ¼" dowel centers into the holes.

3 Set the back panel on your worksurface with the inside face up, and insert ¾" spacers beneath it (to create a setback for the back panel edging strips). Clamp the panel to the edge of your worksurface. Position the uprights against the side edges of the back panel to mark the dowel hole position, then remove the dowel centers from the back panel.

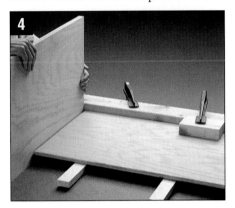

4 Drill ⅜"-deep, ¼"-diamter holes at the dowel positions in the uprights, then glue and insert ¼ × 1" dowels. Apply glue in the dowel holes in the back panel, then join the uprights and the back panel.

5 Create "clamps" for the uprights by pressing stop boards against the edges of the uprights, then clamping or screwing the stop boards to your worksurface. For added pressure, drive shims carefully between the uprights and the stop boards.

6 Join the shelf bottom and the shelf side by applying a bead of glue to each workpiece, then reinforcing the rabbet-and-dado joint with 4d finish nails driven up through the shelf side. Secure with bar clamps while the glue dries.

7 Unclamp the shelf bottom and side, then drill four ¼" × ¾"-deep holes for dowels in the exposed edge of the shelf bottom. Insert dowel centers.

8 Draw a line perpendicular to the top edge of the back panel to mark the position for the outside edge of the shelf side. Butt the shelf assembly against the back panel, flush with the tops of the uprights and the back panel. Mark the upright for dowel holes.

9 Drill ¾"-dia. × ¾"-deep dowel holes, then join the shelf bottom to the upright with dowels and glue. Unclamp the uprights and back, then drive 4d finish nails through the back panel and into the shelf and shelf side.

> ### WOODWORKER'S TIP
>
> *Screw holes in cleats should be drilled slightly larger than the diameter of the screw shank. The goal of cleating is to draw the part attached to the cleat down to the proper position. Also ream out the top of the screw hole in the cleat to allow for expansion and contraction of the attached part.*

10 Drill counterbored shank holes in each cleat (H to K) to provide guide for the screws that will be driven up into the desktop.

11 Attach the long top cleat (K) to the back panel, between the left upright and the shelf side, flush with the top edge of the back panel. Use glue and countersunk #8 × 1" flathead wood screws.

12 Screw and glue the upright cleat (H) to the left upright, then attach one short top cleat (J) and the shelf side cleats (I) inside the shelf box.

13 Apply glue to the second short top cleat, then set it against the ends of the shelf side cleats. Drive 4d finish nails through the short top cleat, into the side shelf cleats.

14 Test-fit the desktop on the assembly by centering it over the feet of the table, with a 2½" overhang on each end.

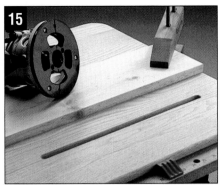

15 (OPTIONAL) Mark the underside of the desktop for a ½"-wide slot at the back of the shelf area to be used for continuous-feed printer paper. Avoid the cleats when marking the slot, and make sure the slot is parallel to the back edge of the desktop. Remove the desktop, and use a ½" straight bit in a portable router to cut the slot. Use a ½" roundover bit to shape the inside edges of the slot on the top and bottom of the desktop.

16 Apply heat-activated oak tape to the edges of the shelf.

17 Sand and finish the desktop and the table assembly separately.

18 When the finish is dry, set the desktop on the assembly and attach the top by driving #8 × 1¼" flathead wood screws up through the guide holes in the cleats.

19 Attach a keyboard slide below the desktop, following the manufacturer's directions.

> ### DESIGN TIP
>
> *Most woodworking stores carry a wide range of desk accessories designed specifically for use with a computer: built-in surge protectors and outlet strips, ventilation enhancers, grommets, and cable organizers are just a few.*

Kid's Desk

Children love this play center.

This desk is made of birch plywood for sturdiness. The angled top allows your child to write or draw in comfort.

Making the desk

1 Cut the left and right sides (A), middle (R), desktop (B), top (C), front (D), back (E), shelves (F), and pencil shelf (G) from ¾"-thick plywood.
2 Cut the pencil lip (H), desk lip (Q), bin bottom (O), and desk bottom (P) from ¼"-thick plywood.
3 Miter-cut the top ends of the sides (see *Diagram*).
4 Make a 20° bevel cut on the top edge of the desk top.
5 Cut a ¾ × 2" notch in the front of the middle to accept the top.
6 Rout ¼ × ¼" stopped dadoes 18" from the bottom of each side for the bin bottom and desk bottom. Stop the dadoes ½" from front and rear edges of the sides and middle. Dado the middle on both sides. Square the stopped ends of the dadoes with a chisel.
7 Rout ¼ × ¼" grooves the full length of the front and the back to hold the bottom pieces. Cut the groove 18" from the bottom of the back and ¼" from the bottom edge of the front.
8 Cut accessory tray (I), like the brush and cup holder shown, from ¾"-thick plywood. Drill holes for cups or other articles as desired.

9 Rout ½"-diameter grooves in the bottom of the accessory tray with

a core-box bit. Center the grooves 1" from the front and back edges.
10 Drill two ¼ × ⅜"-deep holes in the inside face of the left side and middle for dowels to hold the accessory tray. Center the holes 2¼" from the bin bottom, and 5" and 10" from the front edges of the left side and middle pieces.

11 Apply heat-activated edge veneer tape to all the exposed plywood edges. Trim and sand the edges flush with the plywood (see *Woodworker's Tip,* opposite).
12 Lay out and cut #0 biscuit slots in the sides and middle to secure the back, front, and top.
13 Lay out and cut slots in the left side and middle to secure the shelves (F, G) with #10 biscuits.

14 Sand all parts to finished smoothness.

Making the drawers

1 Cut the drawer ends (J, K) from ¾"-thick plywood.
2 Cut the drawer bottoms (N, O) from ¼"-thick plywood.
3 Cut the drawer sides (L, M) from ½"-thick plywood.
4 Apply edge veneer tape to all the exposed plywood edges. Trim and sand the excess until flush with the plywood.
5 Cut a ¼ × ¼" dado ¼" from the ends on the inside face of each drawer side.
6 Cut a ¼ × ½"-deep dado in each outside edge of both drawer ends. Start the dado ¼" from the inside face of each drawer end.
7 Cut a ¼ × ¼" rabbet at both ends of the inside face on the drawer ends.
8 Cut a ¼ × ¼" groove ¼" above the bottom edges of the drawer ends and sides to hold the bottoms.
9 Cut 3½ × 1⅛"-deep handles in the top of the front drawer end, using a bandsaw.
10 Sand the drawer parts to finished smoothness.

WOODWORKER'S TIP

When applying heat-activated edge veneer tape, follow these guidelines:

- *Tape applied to opposite edges of the same piece adds ¹⁄₁₆" to the overall dimension of the piece. Plan for this dimension when cutting parts.*
- *Apply the tape before assembly.*
- *Heat the tape with a household iron on highest heat without steam.*
- *Follow the iron with a smooth wooden block or roller to smooth the tape and set the adhesive.*
- *Trim excess with a crafts knife or utility knife. Cut with the grain along the sides, taking care not to cut into the plywood. Sand the edge with a block and fine sandpaper.*

Painting the desk parts

Painting is easier while the piece is unassembled. Set up and paint multiple pieces at once.

1 Set up 2 × 4 stringers on sawhorses to lay out parts for painting. Two pairs of 8' lengths should hold all parts.

2 Apply masking tape to the edges of all parts where they will receive glue. Cover the corresponding areas on the dividers that will receive glue.

3 Using latex primer, paint the edges, then one face of all the parts using a ¼" nap roller. Let dry.

4 Apply primer to the remaining sides of all the pieces. Let dry.

5 Sand the primed parts with 220-grit sandpaper and a pad sander.

6 Remove all paint dust by vacuuming and wiping with a tack rag.

7 Apply semigloss or washable flat latex paint with a roller using the sequence described in *steps 3 and 4,* above. Let dry.

Assembling the desk

1 Remove masking tape from the edges to be glued.

2 Attach the lips to the pencil shelf and desk top with evenly spaced #6 × 1" screws and cup washers.

3 Reassemble the desk using glue and biscuits.

4 Clamp, check for square, and allow to dry.

5 Use a hacksaw to cut a length of

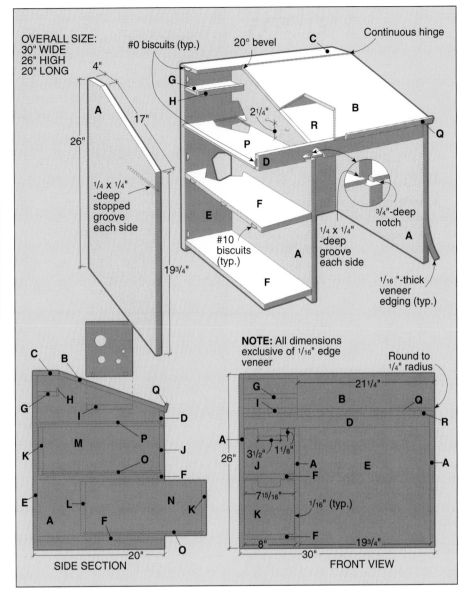

CUTTING LIST

Key	Qty.	Description & Size	Key	Qty.	Description & Size
A	2	**Side,** ¾ × 20 × 25¼"	J	2	**Top drawer end,** ¾ × 6⅝ × 7⅞"
B	1	**Desktop,** ¾ × 17 × 21¼"	K	2	**Bottom drawer end,** ¾ × 8⅛ × 7⅞"
C	1	**Top,** ¾ × 4 × 30"	L	2	**Top drawer side,** ½ × 6¹¹⁄₁₆ × 18¾"
D	1	**Rail,** ¾ × 2 × 28½"	M	2	**Bottom drawer side,** ½ × 8³⁄₁₆ × 18¾"
E	1	**Back,** ¾ × 25¼ × 28½"	N	2	**Drawer bottom,** ¼ × 7⁷⁄₁₆ × 18¼"
F	2	**Shelf,** ¾ × 8 × 19¼"	O	1	**Bin bottom,** ¼ × 8½ × 19"
G	1	**Pencil shelf,** ¾ × 3 × 8"	P	1	**Desk bottom,** ¼ × 19 × 20¼"
H	1	**Pencil lip,** ¼ × 1¼ × 8"	Q	1	**Desk lip,** ¼ × 1¼ × 21¼"
I	1	**Accessory tray,** ¾ × 7 × 8"	R	1	**Middle,** ¾ × 19¼ × 25¼"

Note: All wood is birch plywood.
Misc.: Glue, ¼"-diameter dowel, sandpaper, #0 & #10 biscuits, heat-activated birch edge tape, #6 × 1" wood screws, #6 cup washers, continuous hinge, soft-close lid support.

continuous hinge to 21" long. Tape the hinge in place and drill screw holes with a vix bit. Attach the hinge to the beveled edge of the desk top with the screws provided with the hinge.

6 Attach the soft-close lid support to the desktop and right side. Always follow the manufacturer's instructions.

Hobby Center

A place for everything and everything in its place.

This hobby center, rich with versatile storage space, is essentially composed of two base cabinets that support a countertop and drawer, and a top cabinet that hangs on the wall over the base. Made of birch plywood, it's both strong and attractive.

Make the cubby cabinet

This side of the base unit is compartmentalized into storage cubbies designed to hold a wide variety of sizes and shapes.

1 Cut one cabinet side (J), then rout a ¾ × ⅜"-deep rabbet in the inside, top edge to hold the cubby top panel (E). Also rout a ¾ × ⅜"-deep dado whose bottom shoulder is 3½" up from the inside, bottom edge to hold the cubby bottom panel (E).

2 Cut a 2"-deep × 3½"-high notch in the bottom front corner of the cabinet side for the kick space. Cut a ¾ × ⅜"-deep stopped dado 4⅛" down from the top, outside edge to hold the stretcher (U). Start the dado at the back edge of the cabinet side, and stop it 2½" from the front edge. Square off the end of the dado with a chisel.

3 Cut the section divider (H), the cubby top and bottom panels (E), and the cubby side dividers (G).

4 Rout two ¾ × ⅜"-deep stopped dadoes into the bottom of the top panel, and two matching dadoes into the top of the bottom panel (see *Diagram*), to hold the cubby side dividers (G). Begin cutting the dadoes at the outside edges of the panels, and make them 6" long. Square off the ends of the dadoes with a chisel.

5 Cut a 6"-high × ¹¹⁄₁₆"-deep notch in both outside ends of the top and bottom panels to hold the cubby face panels (D).

Our hobby center is composed of three basic cabinets: the cubby cabinet, the vertical cabinet, and the top cabinet. The cubby and vertical cabinets support the countertop and the drawer.

CUTTING LIST

Key	Qty.	Description & Size	Key	Qty.	Description & Size
BASE UNIT			Q	2	**Drawer side**, ½ × 2¾ × 20¾"
A	1	**Countertop**, ¾ × 30⅛ × 62"	R	1	**Drawer back**, ½ × 2¾ × 28½"
B	1	**Countertop trim** (front), 1 × 2 × 64"	S	1	**Drawer bottom**, ¼ × 20 × 28½"
C	2	**Countertop trim** (side), 1 × 2 × 31"	T	1	**Cabinet back**, ¼ × 29 × 62"
D	2	**Cubby face panel**, ¾ × 6 × 25½"	U	1	**Stretcher**, ¾ × 27½ × 30¾"
E	2	**Cubby top, bottom**, ¾ × 19⅝ × 30"	V	1	**Base trim** (cubby), ½ × 3½ × 19⅞"
F	2	**Cubby side shelf**, ¾ × 5¼ × 29¼"	W	1	**Base trim** (side), ¾ × 3½ × 28"
G*	6	**Cubby side divider**, ¾ × 5¼ × 8¹⁄₁₆"	X	1	**Base trim** (vert. cab.), ½ × 3½ × 11¹⁵⁄₁₆"
H	1	**Section divider**, ¾ × 24¾ × 28½"	**TOP CABINET**		
I	2	**Cubby front shelf**, ¾ × 13⅛ × 29¾"	Y	2	**Hanging cleat**, ¾ × 2⅝ × 60½"
J	3	**Cabinet side**, ¾ × 29 × 30"	Z	2	**Main divider**, ¾ × 9 × 30"
K	2	**Vert. cab. divider**, ¼ × 24¾ × 30"	AA	2	**Top, bottom panel**, ¾ × 10 × 61¼"
L	2	**Vert. cab. top, bottom**, ¾ × 11¼ × 30"	BB	2	**Cabinet side**, ¾ × 10 × 30¾"
M	2	**Cubby pedestal**, 1½ × 3½ × 18⁹⁄₁₆"	CC	2	**Center shelf**, ¾ × 9 × 29¾"
N	2	**Vert. cab. pedestal**, 1½ × 3½ × 10½"	DD	9	**Center divider**, ¼ × 9 × 9¾"
O	1	**Drawer false front**, ¾ × 3¾ × 30"	EE	2	**Adjustable shelf**, ¾ × 8⅞ × 14⅞"
P	1	**Drawer front**, ¾ × 2¾ × 28½"	FF	1	**Back panel**, ¼ × 29¾ × 61"

Note: All parts are birch plywood except: M and N, which are 2 × 4 fir; Y, which is cut from 1 × 6 pine; B and C, which are solid birch; and A, which is particle board.
*Two cubby side dividers (G) will be trimmed to ¾ × 5¼ × 7⅞".
Misc.: Glue, #0 biscuits, flathead screws (#8 × 1¼", #10 × 3½"), ⅝" wire brads, finish nails (4d, 6d), shelf pins, drawer slides, veneer tape, ¹⁄₁₆ × 32 × 64" plastic laminate.

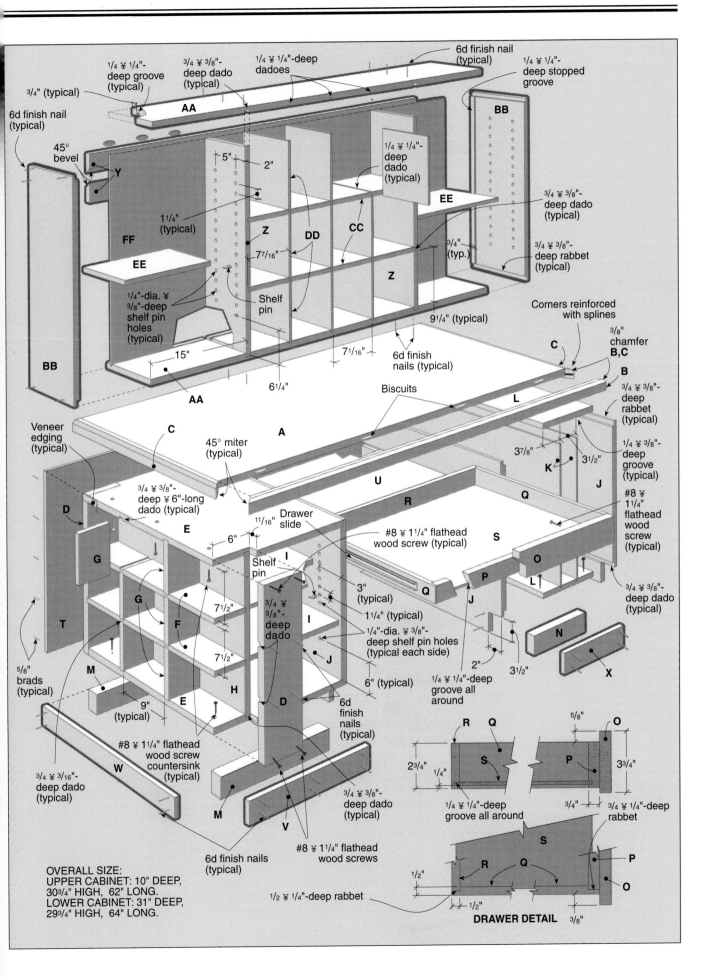

1/4 ¥ 1/4"-deep groove (typical)

3/4 ¥ 3/8"-deep dado (typical)

1/4 ¥ 1/4"-deep dadoes

6d finish nail (typical)

1/4 ¥ 1/4"-deep stopped groove

3/4" (typical)

6d finish nail (typical)

45° bevel

Y

BB

1/4 ¥ 1/4"-deep dado (typical)

AA

EE

3/4 ¥ 3/8"-deep dado (typical)

5"

2"

FF

1 1/4" (typical)

Z

DD

CC

EE

7 7/16"

Shelf pin

Z

3/4" (typ.)

3/4 ¥ 3/8"-deep rabbet (typical)

1/4"-dia. ¥ 3/8"-deep shelf pin holes (typical)

BB

15"

6 1/4"

AA

9 1/4" (typical)

7 1/16"

6d finish nails (typical)

Biscuits

L

Corners reinforced with splines

C

B

3/8" chamfer B,C

3/4 ¥ 3/8"-deep rabbet (typical)

Veneer edging (typical)

C

45° miter (typical)

A

3/4 ¥ 3/8"-deep ¥ 6"-long dado (typical)

U

R

Q

3 7/8"

K

3 1/2"

J

1/4 ¥ 3/8"-deep groove (typical)

D

E

11/16"

6"

Drawer slide

Shelf pin

I

#8 ¥ 1 1/4" flathead wood screw (typical)

S

O

#8 ¥ 1 1/4" flathead wood screw (typical)

G

G

F

7 1/2"

3/4 ¥ 3/8"-deep dado

I

3" (typical)

P

L

3/4 ¥ 3/8"-deep dado (typical)

T

7 1/2"

H

D

J

1 1/4" (typical)

1/4"-dia. ¥ 3/8"-deep shelf pin holes (typical each side)

6" (typical)

Q

J

2"

3 1/2"

N

X

1/4 ¥ 1/4"-deep groove all around

5/8" brads (typical)

M

9" (typical)

E

6d finish nails (typical)

3/4 ¥ 3/16"-deep dado (typical)

W

#8 ¥ 1 1/4" flathead wood screw countersink (typical)

M

V

3/4 ¥ 3/8"-deep dado (typical)

6d finish nails (typical)

#8 ¥ 1 1/4" flathead wood screws

R

Q

5/8"

O

2 3/4"

1/4"

S

P

3 3/4"

1/4 ¥ 1/4"-deep groove all around

3/4"

3/4 ¥ 1/4"-deep rabbet

1/2"

S

1/2"

R

Q

P

O

1/2 ¥ 1/4"-deep rabbet

1/2"

3/8"

DRAWER DETAIL

OVERALL SIZE:
UPPER CABINET: 10" DEEP, 30 3/4" HIGH, 62" LONG.
LOWER CABINET: 31" DEEP, 29 3/4" HIGH, 64" LONG.

6 Cut the cubby face panels (D), then rout ¾ × ⅜"-deep dadoes into the inside faces of the panels (see *Diagram*), for the side shelves (F).
7 Cut the side shelves (F), then cut ¾ × 3⁄16"-deep dadoes in both faces of both shelves (see *Diagram*), to hold the side dividers (G).
8 Assemble the carcass of the cabinet by gluing the joints between the top and bottom panels, the cabinet side, and the section divider. Clamp the assembly with bar clamps, check to make sure it's square, and let the glue dry.

9 Position the cubby face panels into the notches, and attach them with glue and #8 × 1¼" flathead wood screws (two per joint) driven into counterbored pilot holes. Finish-sand the carcass and the rest of the cubby parts with 220-grit sandpaper.
10 Cut the cubby pedestals (M) from 2 × 4" stock, and position them beneath the cabinet. The right ends of the pedestals are flush with the inside face of the cabinet side panel. The outside face of the back pedestal is flush with the back edges of the cabinet, and the outside face of the front pedestal is flush with the toe-space notches. Attach the pedestals with glue and #8 × 1¼" flathead wood screws driven through counterbored pilot holes in the bottom panel of the cubby.
11 Cut the base trim for the front of the cubby (V) from ½"-wide birch plywood, and cut the side trim (W) from ¾"-thick plywood. Cover the exposed ends of the front trim piece with ½"-thick birch veneer tape. Trim the tape edges, then finish-sand both trim pieces.

12 Attach the front trim piece to the pedestal face, and attach the side trim piece to the pedestal ends, using glue and 6d finish nails driven through pilot holes.
13 Drill rows of ¼ × ⅜"-deep shelf pin holes in one face of the divider, and in the inside face of the cabinet side panel, 3" in from the front and back edges. Space the holes 1¼" apart, on center, beginning 6" up from the bottom panel.
14 Cut the adjustable cubby front shelves (I), and apply veneer tape to the front edges. Trim tape, then sand to finished smoothness.
15 Glue the cubby side shelves into the dadoes in the face panels, and reinforce with 6d finish nails driven through pilot holes in the face panels into the shelf edges.
16 Trim 1⁄16" from the height of two of the cubby side dividers (G), and glue them into the dadoes between the two side shelves. Glue the untrimmed side dividers into the dadoes between the bottom shelf and the bottom, and between the top shelf and the top.
17 Cover all exposed plywood edges with veneer tape and plug the counterbores. Set nail heads, fill with putty and sand smooth.

Build the vertical cabinet

The tall storage areas created in the vertical cabinet are perfect spots for blueprints, drawings, and any other oversize documents.
1 Cut two cabinet side panels (J) and machine as shown in *steps 1 and 2* of *Make the cubby cabinet.* Note: Cut the stopped dado 4⅛" down from the top edge on the inside cabinet panel only.
2 Cut the vertical cabinet top and bottom panels (L), and cut ¼ × ⅜"-deep grooves (see *Diagram*) for the vertical cabinet dividers (K).

3 Cut the vertical cabinet dividers (K), and finish-sand both surfaces of each divider. Finish-sand the other parts of the vertical cabinet.
4 Assemble the carcass of the vertical cabinet by gluing the top and bottom panels into the grooves in the side panels. Clamp the assembly, make sure it's square; then let the glue dry.
5 Glue the divider panels into the grooves in the top and bottom, then trim out the front edges of the cabinet with veneer tape.
6 Cut the vertical cabinet pedestals (N) from 2 × 4" stock, then attach them between the cabinet sides, flush with the cabinet back and the toe-space notches. Attach the pedestals with glue and #8 × 1¼" flathead screws, driven from above into counterbored pilot holes.
7 Cut the base trim for the vertical cabinet (X) from ½"-thick plywood. Tape the ends with veneer tape, trim tape, finish-sand, then attach the piece to the pedestal with 6d finish nails. Set the nails heads, fill nail holes, and sand when dry.

Make & attach the countertop

1 Cut the countertop (A) from cabinet-grade particleboard or sanded plywood.
2 Cut the birch countertop trim (B, C). Miter-cut the ends to fit around the countertop.
3 Cut several splines from scrap wood and cut matching slots in the mitered ends of the trim to make the spline joints.
4 Lay out and cut slots in the front and side edges of the countertop and in the inside faces of the trim to form biscuit joints.
5 Glue the trim to the countertop, forming the spline and biscuit joints. Clamp and let the glue dry.
6 Sand the joint between the trim and the countertop, then cut a piece of plastic laminate slightly larger than the countertop and trim.
7 Protect the trim faces with masking tape, then apply contact cement to the laminate and the countertop/trim. Attach the laminate, rolling the surface with a seam roller. Remove the masking tape.
8 After the contact cement sets,

cut the laminate flush with the countertop trim, using a router and a straight laminate-trimming bit. Install a ⅜" chamfering bit in your router, and cut a chamfer on the front and sides of the countertop.
9 Stand the cabinet sections on a flat surface. Cut a scrap piece of ¾"-thick plywood to 30" in width, and use it to set the distance between the cabinets. Lay a long straightedge across the cabinets to make sure they're exactly level. If not, shim under the pedestals. Also make sure the backs and fronts of the cabinets are in alignment.
10 Cut and finish-sand the stretcher (U), and glue it into the dadoes on the facing edges of the two cabinets, flush with the backs.
11 Set the countertop on the cabinets, flush with the back, and centered side-to-side. Fasten the top by driving #8 × 1¼" flathead wood screws up through counterbored pilot holes in the cabinet tops.
12 Cut the cabinet back (T), and finish-sand the inside surface. Attach the back to the cabinet backs and pedestals, using ⅝" wire brads.

Make the drawer
1 Cut the drawer front (P), sides (Q), back (R), and bottom (S). Also cut the drawer false front (O), apply birch veneer tape, then finish-sand the false front.
2 Cut a ¼ × ¼" groove ¼" up from the bottom edges of the sides, front, and back, to hold the bottom.
3 Cut a ¾ × ¼"-deep rabbet in the front end of both drawer sides, and cut a ½ × ¼"-deep rabbet in the back end of both sides.
4 Glue the sides, front, and back together, arranged around the bottom panel (don't glue the bottom in place). Reinforce the corners with 4d finish nails. Clamp, check for square, and let the glue dry.
5 Attach drawer slide tracks to the cabinet sides, between the countertop and the stretcher (see manufacturer's directions), then attach the slides to the drawer sides.
6 Center the false front side to side on the drawer, and attach it with countersunk #8 × 1¼" flathead wood screws. There should be ⅛"

clearance between the top of the false front and the countertop.

Make the top cabinet
1 Cut the side panels (BB), then cut ¾ × ⅜"-deep rabbets in the top and bottom inside faces.
2 Cut ¼ × ¼" grooves in the inside faces of the side panels, ¾" from the back edge, between the rabbets at the top and bottom.
3 Cut the top and bottom panels (AA) to finished size.
4 Cut ¾ × ⅜"-deep dadoes in the inside faces of the top and bottom, to hold the main dividers, and cut ¼ × ¼" dadoes for the center dividers (see *Diagram*). Cut a ¼ × ¼" groove ¾" from the back edge of each panel, to hold the back panel.
5 Cut the main dividers (Z), the center dividers (DD), and the center shelves (CC). Cut ¼ × ¼" dadoes in both the top and bottom faces of the center shelves to hold the center dividers (see *Diagram*).
6 Cut the top cabinet back (FF), and finish-sand the front surface. Finish-sand all cabinet parts.
7 Drill rows of ¼ × ⅜"-deep pin holes at 1¼" intervals (on center) in the main dividers and the side panels (see *Diagram*).
8 Glue the center shelves into the dadoes in the main dividers, then glue the center dividers into the dadoes in the shelves.
9 Lay the assembly on a flat work-surface, facedown, then attach the top panel to the dividers by gluing the dado joints. Make sure the groove for the back is clear.

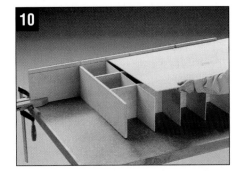

10 Working quickly, slide the back panel into the groove in the back of the top panel. Do not glue the back panel in place.

11 Glue the bottom panel to the divider ends, then glue the side panels to the top and bottom panels. Reinforce the joints with 6d finish nails. Check to make sure the cabinet is square, then clamp with bar clamps and allow the glue to dry.
12 Apply birch veneer tape to the exposed front edges of the cabinet, trim the excess tape, and finish-sand the cabinet.
13 Cut, tape the edges, and finish-sand the adjustable shelves (EE).
14 Cut the hanging cleats (Y) by ripping a piece of 1 × 6 pine down the middle, at a 45° bevel.

15 Attach a hanging cleat (beveled edge facing down and away) to the back edge of the top panel, using glue and biscuits. Reinforce the joints at the side panels with 6d finish nails driven into the hanging cleat. Let the glue dry.

Finishing touches
1 Wipe the top and bottom cabinets clean with a lint-free cloth, then apply a finish (we used Danish oil).
2 Locate the studs in the wall where the hanging cabinet will be mounted, and mark them clearly.
3 Position the second hanging cleat (Y) against the wall, about 78" from the floor, with the high side of the beveled edge facing up and out. Make sure the cleat is level, then attach it to the wall studs with countersunk #10 × 3½" flathead wood screws.
4 Hang the cabinet on the cleat, and center the base unit below.

All-Purpose Workbench

The maple workbench is the hub of your workshop.
Here is a design for a sturdy bench that's simple to make.

A workbench is the focal point of most of your woodworking activities. This basic bench, with its good work surface and neat, streamlined appearance, is the perfect starting point for your shop. You can add any features you need to meet your needs: a bench-mounted vise, a toolholder, a bottom shelf, or bench stops.

The bench itself is designed for easy construction. Its no-nonsense design, with a hard maple surface and sturdy legs, provides the stability you need in a worktable. Yet, the warm tones of the maple and the clean lines of the top and legs, along with the grooves and bevel cuts added as design features to the rails and stretchers, make this an attractive piece of furniture.

Use straight, warp-free material, particularly for the top of the workbench. Beech and hard maple are popular woods for workbenches because they are hard enough to stand up to heavy-duty work. Birch is a good alternative, provided you can find enough wood of a consistent color, though the grain may not be as attractive as maple.

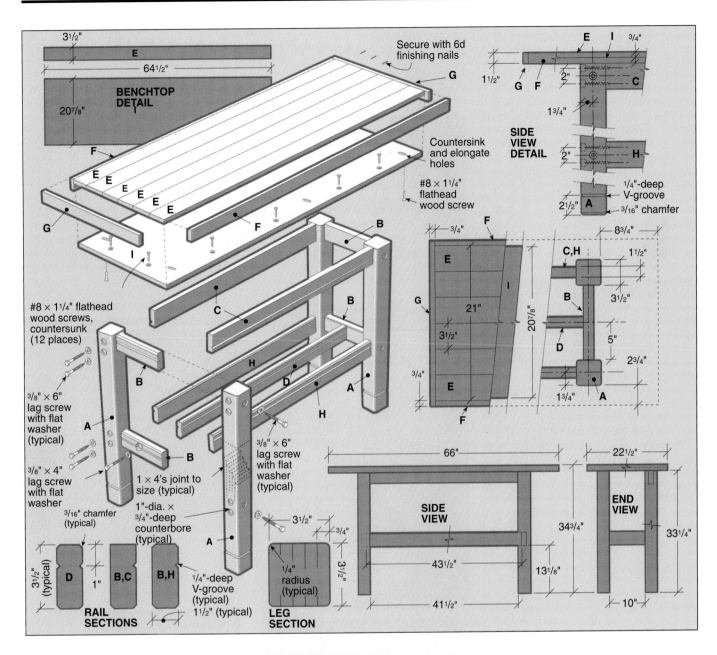

Building the legs

The sturdiness of the legs is a critical part of building a good, solid workbench. We've chosen to make the legs from laminated 1" hard maple stock cut to 4" widths. While 4 × 4 pieces of stock maple simplify building the legs, they are generally hard to find and will be much more expensive than the thinner stock.

1 To make the legs (A), cut twenty 1 × 4 pieces to a rough length of 34". Run all the pieces through a jointer, then face-glue five pieces together to form each leg. Repeat for the remaining three groups of 1 × 4 pieces.

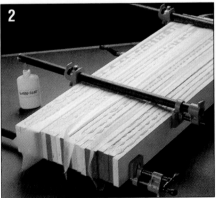

2 Place wax paper between each of the four glued-up leg assemblies, then clamp all of the leg assemblies together and set them aside to dry overnight.

CUTTING LIST

Key	Qty.	Description & Size
A	4	**Leg,** 3½ × 3½ × 33¼"
B	4	**End rail,** 1½ × 3½ × 10"
C	2	**Side rail,** 1½ × 3½ × 41½"
D	1	**Middle stretcher,** 1½ × 3½ × 43½"
E	6	**Benchtop,** ¾ × 3½ × 64½"
F	2	**Edge trim,** ¾ × 1½ × 64½"
G	2	**Edge trim,** ¾ × 1½ × 22½"
H	2	**Stretcher,** 1½ × 3½ × 41½"
I	1	**Underlayment,** ¾ × 20⅞ × 64½"

Note: All materials are maple, except for part I, which is AC plywood.

Misc.: lag screws (⅜ × 4", ⅜ × 6"), ½"-diameter flat washers, #8 × 1¼" flathead wood screws, 6d finish nails, wood glue.

3 Remove excess dried glue with a sharp paint scraper.

4 Feed each glued-up leg through a jointer or a planer to achieve a final width and thickness of 3½ × 3½" square. To ensure evenness, plane an equal amount from each outside leg face, instead of planing only one side.

5 Cut the legs to finished length.

6 Bevel the bottom edges of the legs with a router and a chamfering or V-groove bit.

7 Round over the lengthwise edges of the leg, using a router with a ⅜" roundover bit.

8 Cut a groove around each leg 2½" from the bottom, using a router and a V-groove bit.

Building the bench top

When you choose wood for the bench top, try to match both color and grain, so your bench top will look like it has a continuous grain pattern across its width. Pay attention to the characteristics of the grains, and experiment with the arrangement of the bench top pieces as you dry-fit to get the best look.

For our bench top, we used 1" stock cut to 4" widths.

1 Measure, mark, and cut six 1 × 4s to a rough length of 65", to be glued up for the bench top (E).

2 Joint all edges to be glued and check for any gaps. Rejoint the boards as needed.

3 Dry-fit the pieces on a flat surface. Mark the arrangement with a large triangle that crosses the entire width of the pieces, so you can easily reconstruct your arrange-

ment. The dry-fitted bench top should be about 24" wide. Cut an equal amount from both outside edge pieces to arrive at the desired finished bench top width (21").

4 Apply a light coat of glue to both edges of each joint, and carefully join the six 1 × 4 workpieces edge-to-edge to form the bench top.

5 Clamp the boards together with clamps above and below the workpieces, spaced every 12". Alternating the clamps this way keeps the workpiece flat and prevents buckling. Keep the boards as flush as possible, and don't overtighten.

6 After the bench top workpiece has dried, remove excess glue with a sharp paint scraper.

7 Cut the glued-up bench top to the finished length (64½").

8 Check the bench top surface with a straightedge and belt-sand any minor irregularities out of the surface, sanding diagonally with 60-grit sandpaper. Switch to sanding with the grain using 80-grit sandpaper and work your way up to a final grit of 220.

Building the rails

These 2 × 4 rails have been created by laminating 1" stock cut to a finished 3½" width. Like the legs, the rails can be made of either 2" stock or laminated 1" stock.

1 Cut completed rail stock to length for all the rails (B, C) and all the stretchers (D, H).

Guard removed for clarity.

2 Cut a ³⁄₁₆"-deep chamfer on the lengthwise edges of all rails (B, C) and stretchers (D, H), using a router and a V-groove bit.

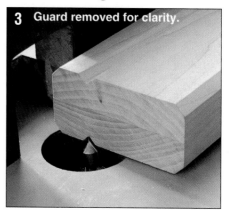

Guard removed for clarity.

3 Cut a ¼" groove on the outside face of each rail (B, C) 1" from the edge, using a router and V-groove bit. The groove should run the entire length of each rail. Cut identical ¼" grooves lengthwise on both sides of the middle stretcher, 1" down from the top edge.

Assembling the workbench

We assembled our workbench by gluing the joints and reinforcing them with lag screws, but if you wish, you can choose other means of joinery.

1 Mark the locations of the lag screws on the outside leg faces (see *Diagram*), then counterbore a 1"-diameter hole, ¾" deep in the outside face of each leg (A) where it will be lag-screwed to the end rails (B).

2 Measure, mark, and counterbore two 1"-diameter holes ¾" deep in the end face of each leg where it will join the side rail (C) and the stretcher (H). Also, counterbore two 1"-diameter holes ¾" deep in the middle of the lower end rail (B) where it secures the middle stretcher (D). Be careful when marking lag holes so no lag screw interferes with another.

3 Drill ⅜" pilot holes for the lag screws through the center of each counterbored hole.

4 Insert dowel points in the pilot holes and dry-fit each joining leg, side rail, and stretcher. Press the joining workpieces together so the dowel points mark the pilots for the lag screws. Make sure you

align the upper rails so the decorative groove faces out and is on the bottom part of the rail. For the lower rails and all stretchers, the groove is closer to the top edge.

5 Drill ¼" pilot holes for the lag screws at each point where the rails and stretchers will join the legs.

6 Apply a light, even coat of carpenter's glue to the joining parts of one leg and two end rails. Align the end rails so that the decorative groove faces outward and is closer to the bottom edge. Glue the leg and the end rails, and secure with lag screws. Glue, then screw another leg to this piece to form an end leg section. Repeat this assembly process for the remaining end leg section.

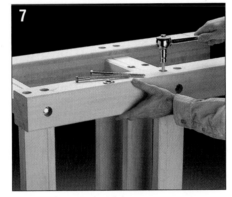

7 Attach one end leg section to the side rails and stretchers with glue and lag screws, making sure the decorative grooves are properly positioned (see *Diagram*). Attach the other end leg section with glue and lag screws.

8 Center the plywood underlayment (I) on the table, with "A" faceup, and attach to the leg and rail assembly with #8 × 1¼" flathead wood screws down through the plywood and into the rails.

9 On the underside of the underlayment (I), mark locations for eight pilot holes just inside the lines formed by the upper rails, placing the marks near each corner and next to the centerpoint of each rail.

10 Drill ⅜"-diameter pilot holes through the plywood at the pilot marks, and rock the bit slightly from side to side. This creates an enlarged, oblong hole for the screw head that allows the table-

top to expand and contract while still secured to the underlayment.

11 Center the bench top on the table. From the underside, mark pilots on the bench top with a pencil through the center of the pilot holes.

12 Cut the edge trim pieces (F, G) to length. Nail the edge trim to the bench top with 6d finish nails. Because the bench top will expand and contract somewhat, nail the edge trim pieces to the bench only, not to each other. Countersink the nails with a nail set.

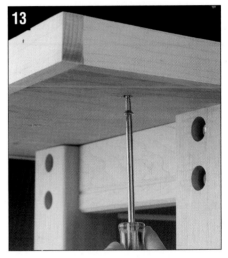

13 Drill ¼" pilot holes into the bench top through the center of the pilot holes on the underside of the plywood. Use a bit stop set for 1¼" depth to prevent piercing the top surface of the bench top. Secure the bench top by driving #8 × 1¼" wood screws through the pilot holes and into the bench top.

14 Sand the bench top surface and the edge trim so they are flush. Repair any surface defects with wood putty, then sand the entire piece (lightly). Apply a finish of your choice.

Workshop Center

Add storage and function to your workshop with these stylish cabinets.

You don't have to sacrifice the look of finely crafted furniture to add storage to your workshop. This workshop center consists of a wall-mounted upper cabinet and a versatile, rolling base cabinet with a slide-out tray, providing permanent storage space as well as a generous amount of worksurface.

Build the wall cabinet

1 Cut the side panels (B), then cut ½ × ⅜"-deep grooves in each panel, inset ¾" from the back edges, to hold the back panel.
2 Cut the top panel (A) and the shelves (D). (One shelf serves as the cabinet bottom.) Cut a ½ × ⅜"-deep groove in the underside of the top panel, ¾" in from the back edge, to hold the back panel.
3 Cut three ½ × ⅜"-deep dadoes for the upper dividers in the top face of the upper shelf. Space the dadoes 7⅜" apart. Cut two ½ × ⅜"-deep dadoes for the bottom dividers in the top face of the bottom shelf, spaced 10" apart (see *Diagram*).

CUTTING LIST: WALL CABINET

Key	Qty.	Description & Size
A	1	**Top panel,** ¾ × 17½ × 31"
B	2	**Side panel,** ¾ × 17½ × 27⅜"
C	3	**Divider** (upper), ½ × 10 × 15"
D	2	**Shelf,** ¾ × 15½ × 31"
E	2	**Divider** (lower), ½ × 12 × 15"
F	1	**Back panel,** ½ × 27 × 31¾"
G	1	**Door** (upper), ¾ × 12⅜ × 30¾"
H	1	**Door** (lower), ¾ × 14 × 30¾"
I	2	**Follower strip,** ¾ × 4 × 23"
J	1	**Spacer,** ¾ × 1½ × 31"
K	2	**Cleat,** ¾ × 3½ × 31"

Note: All parts are birch plywood, except cleats (K), which are 1 × 4 pine.
Misc.: Glue, #0 biscuits, flathead wood screws (#6 × 1", #8 × 1¼", #8 × 1½", #10 × 3"), 4d finish nails, veneer tape, 18" flipper door slides (2 pr.), wire pulls (2).

CUTTING LIST: ROLLING BASE CABINET

Key	Qty.	Description & Size	Key	Qty.	Description & Size
L	2	**Top, bottom panel,** ¾ × 19⅝ × 31¾"	Y	2	**Drawer side,** ¾ × 8⅜ × 18¾"
M	2	**Side panel,** ¾ × 20 × 34"	Z	2	**Drawer side,** ¾ × 9⅜ × 18¾"
N	1	**Facing,** ¾ × 3 × 32½"	AA	4	**Drawer bottom,** ¼ × 18¼ × 29¼"
O	1	**Slide-out tray,** ¾ × 17⅞ × 31¾"	BB	1	**Drawer false front,** ¾ × 4 9/16 × 32½"
P	1	**Stop block,** ¾ × 2 × 14⅛"	CC	1	**Drawer false front,** ¾ × 6 9/16 × 32½"
Q	1	**Cleat,** ¾ × 2 × 17⅞"	DD	1	**Drawer false front,** ¾ × 8 9/16 × 32½"
R	2	**Stretcher,** ¾ × 2½ × 31"	EE	1	**Drawer false front,** ¾ × 10 9/16 × 32½"
S	1	**Drawer front,** ¾ × 4⅜ × 30"	FF	1	**Drawer back,** ¾ × 4⅜ × 29¼"
T	1	**Drawer front,** ¾ × 6⅜ × 30"	GG	1	**Drawer back,** ¾ × 6⅜ × 29¼"
U	1	**Drawer front,** ¾ × 8⅜ × 30"	HH	1	**Drawer back,** ¾ × 8⅜ × 29¼"
V	1	**Drawer front,** ¾ × 9⅜ × 30"	II	1	**Drawer back,** ¾ × 9⅜ × 29¼"
W	2	**Drawer side,** ¾ × 4⅜ × 18¾"	JJ	1	**Back panel,** ¾ × 33¼ × 31"
X	2	**Drawer side,** ¾ × 6⅜ × 18¾"			

Note: All parts are birch plywood.
Misc.: Glue; #0 biscuits; flathead wood screws (#6 × 1¼", #10 × 1¼", #12 × 1¼"); 6d finish nails; veneer tape; drawer slides (4 pr.); 3"-dia. locking casters (4); 1/16"-thick plastic laminate (12 sq. ft.); contact cement; ¾"-dia. knob; wire pulls (4); sandpaper.

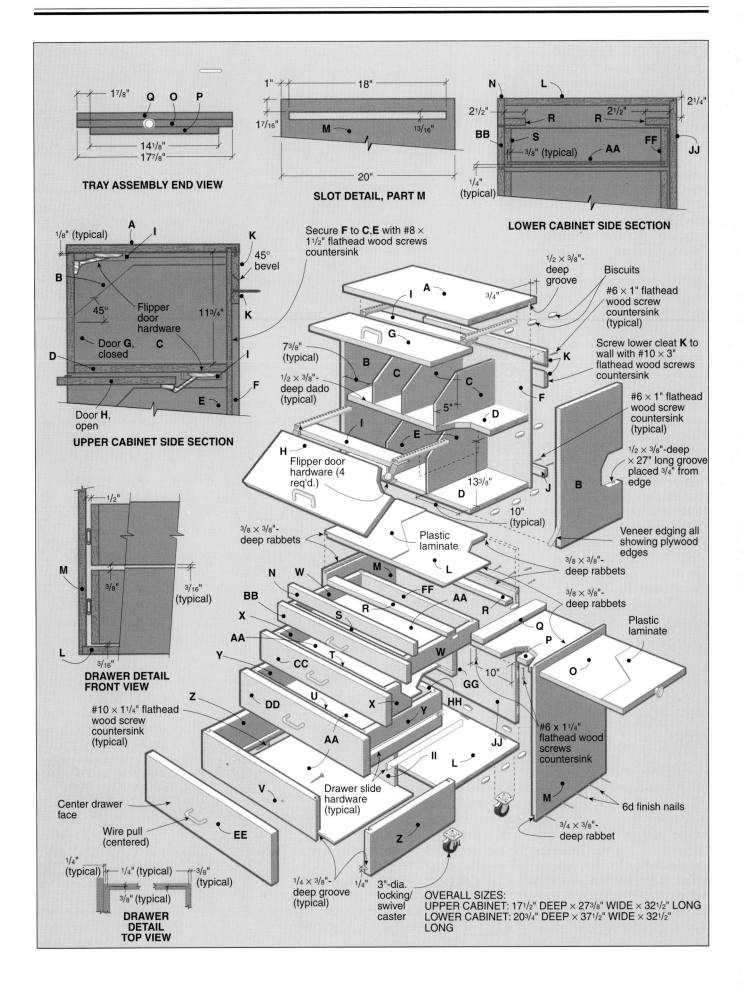

TRAY ASSEMBLY END VIEW

SLOT DETAIL, PART M

LOWER CABINET SIDE SECTION

Secure **F** to **C**,**E** with #8 × 1¹⁄₂" flathead wood screws countersink

UPPER CABINET SIDE SECTION

Door **G**, closed

Door **H**, open

Flipper door hardware

45° bevel

45°

11³⁄₄"

½" (typical)

³⁄₈" (typical)

³⁄₁₆" (typical)

³⁄₁₆"

DRAWER DETAIL FRONT VIEW

¾"

½ × ³⁄₈"-deep groove

Biscuits

#6 × 1" flathead wood screw countersink (typical)

Screw lower cleat **K** to wall with #10 × 3" flathead wood screws countersink

#6 × 1" flathead wood screw countersink (typical)

½ × ³⁄₈"-deep × 27" long groove placed ¾" from edge

Veneer edging all showing plywood edges

7³⁄₈" (typical)

½ × ³⁄₈"-deep dado (typical)

Flipper door hardware (4 req'd.)

5"

13³⁄₈"

10" (typical)

Plastic laminate

³⁄₈ × ³⁄₈"-deep rabbets

³⁄₈ × ³⁄₈"-deep rabbets

³⁄₈ × ³⁄₈"-deep rabbets

Plastic laminate

10"

#10 × 1¼" flathead wood screws countersink (typical)

Center drawer face

Wire pull (centered)

Drawer slide hardware (typical)

#6 x 1¼" flathead wood screws countersink

6d finish nails

¾ × ³⁄₈"-deep rabbet

¼" (typical)

¼" (typical)

³⁄₈" (typical)

³⁄₈" (typical)

DRAWER DETAIL TOP VIEW

¼ × ³⁄₈"-deep groove (typical)

¼"

3"-dia. locking/ swivel caster

OVERALL SIZES:
UPPER CABINET: 17½" DEEP × 27³⁄₈" WIDE × 32½" LONG
LOWER CABINET: 20¾" DEEP × 37½" WIDE × 32½" LONG

4 Cut the three upper dividers (C) and the two lower dividers (E). Trim off the top, front corners of the dividers at 45° angles, 5" from the corners on each edge.

5 Cut the back panel (F).

6 Apply heat-activated veneer tape to the exposed front edges of the top and side panels, and to the tops and the angled edges of the upper dividers. (If necessary, use a razor knife to trim off any overhanging edges of veneer tape.)

7 Mark the locations of the shelves on the inside faces of the side panels (see *Diagram*). Make sure to allow for the ¾" setback from the front edges of the side panels. Using a biscuit jointer, cut slots for #0 biscuits at 4" intervals, at the marks in the side panels and in the top panel and shelves.

8 Assemble the carcass by joining the shelves and top to the side panels with #0 biscuits and glue.

9 Before the glue sets, put the carcass on your worksurface, top side down, then slide the back panel into the grooves in the side panels and the top panel.

10 Square up the cabinet carcass, then drive 4d finish nails through the back panel and into the edges of the shelves and side panels. Set the finish nails with a nail set, then clamp the assembly together, and let the glue dry.

11 Glue the dividers into the shelf dadoes, using a try square to make sure they are perpendicular to the shelves. Secure the dividers with #6 × 1" flathead wood screws, driven through counterbored pilot holes in the back, and into the edges of the dividers.

12 Apply veneer tape to the remaining exposed front edges of the dividers and the shelves.

13 Cut two cleats (K) from 1 × 4 pine, beveling one edge of each cleat at 45°.

14 Attach one of the cleats (K) to the back panel, flush with the bottom of the top panel. Make sure to install the cleat so the beveled bottom edge slopes away from the back panel. Secure the cleat with glue and countersunk #6 × 1" wood screws driven through the cleat and into the back panel. Also drive two countersunk #8 × 1¼" wood screws through each side panel and into the ends of the cleat.

15 Cut a spacer (J) and mount it to the back of the cabinet, flush with the bottom edge, using glue and countersunk #6 × 1" wood screws.

16 Cut the upper and lower door panels, and apply ¾" veneer tape to all four edges of each door.

17 Finish-sand the carcass and doors with 220-grit sandpaper.

Mount the doors & hang the cabinet

We used 18" pivoting door slides (sometimes called "flipper" slides) to mount the doors for our wall cabinet. The flipper slides have tracks that attach to the shelf above each door and pivoting hinges that attach to the back of the door, at the top. A follower strip (I) is secured between each set of hinges to add stability. When opened, the doors pivot up, then slide back on the tracks and into the cabinet.

1 Cut the follower strips (I) for the flipper door hardware, and attach one strip between each pair of flipper door slides.

2 Lay out the position, then mount the tracks for the flipper door hardware on the undersides of the top panel and the center shelf (see manufacturer's directions).

3 Attach the doors to the hinge assemblies, then slip the flipper guides into the tracks and make any necessary adjustments.

4 Mark the planned position for the top of the wall cabinet on the wall. Find the wall studs behind the mark and adjust the location of the cabinet, if necessary. Draw a line parallel to, but 4½" below, cabinet top mark. Be sure to mark the position for the cabinet sides.

5 Attach the second cleat (K) to the wall at stud locations, using #10 × 3" screws. Make sure the beveled edge of the cleat faces up, with the bevel pointing up and away from the wall.

6 Hang the cabinet by setting the cabinet cleat over the beveled edge of the wall-mounted cleat, so the two cleats interlock.

Building the rolling base cabinet

1 Cut the side panels (M), bottom and top panels (L), back panel (JJ), and slide-out tray (O). Cut ⅜ × ⅜" rabbets, stopped ⅜" from the back edge of the side panels, in the tops of the side panels and the back panel to hold the top panel. Also cut ¾ × ⅜"-deep rabbets in the bottoms of the side panels, to hold the bottom panel, and cut a ⅜ × ⅜" rabbet on the side and back edges of the top panel.

2 On the right side panel, cut an 18"-long, ¹³⁄₁₆"-high slot for the sliding tray, using a router and straight bit. The ends of the slot should be 1" from the front and back edges of the side panel, and the top of the slot should be 1⁷⁄₁₆" down from the top edge. Square off the ends of the slot with a wood chisel, then round over the edges with 80-grit sandpaper.

3 Cut the stretchers (R), then lay out and cut slots for #0 biscuits in the side panels, the back panel, and the ends of the stretchers. The ends of the stretchers should be flush with the front and back edges of the side panels, and the tops should be 2¼" down from the top edges of the side panels.

4 Cut biscuit slots, spaced 4" apart, for joining the side panels to the back panel, and for joining the back panel to the bottom panel.

5 Lay the back panel across a pair of sawhorses, then attach the back panel to the bottom panel with biscuit joints.

6 Use glue and biscuits to join one side panel to the back panel. Also glue the bottom panel into the rabbet in the bottom edge of the side panel. Reinforce the rabbet joint with 6d finish nails, then set nails.

7 Use glue and biscuits to join the rear stretcher to the back panel and the attached side panel.

8 Use glue and biscuits to join the other side panel to the back panel and the back stretcher. Glue the bottom panel into the rabbet in the side panel. Reinforce both sides with 6d finish nails, then set nails.

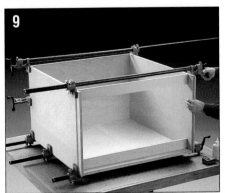

9 Use glue and biscuits to join the front stretcher to the side panels. Clamp the carcass and let the glue dry. Sand dried glue from the joints with 120-grit sandpaper.

10 Apply ¾" veneer tape to the front edges of the carcass.

11 Finish-sand the carcass with 220-grit sandpaper. Apply your finish of choice (we used tung oil).

12 Using a razor knife, cut ¹⁄₁₆"-thick plastic laminate for the top panel (L) and the slide-out tray (O), about ¼" longer on each side than the finished size. Affix the laminate to the plywood, using contact cement.

13 Trim the overhanging edges of the plywood, using a router and flush-cutting bit.

14 Apply veneer tape to the edges. Slightly round the edges and sand the bottom with 120-grit sandpaper.

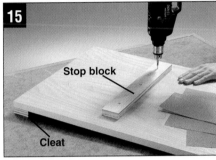

Stop block

Cleat

15 Cut a stop block (P) and cleat (Q). Attach the stop block to the bottom of the tray, 10" from the back end, and attach the cleat to the top of the tray, 2" from the back end. Use glue and countersunk #6 × 1¼" screws. Mask the laminate and apply finish to the edges and bottom of the tray.

16 Stand the carcass upright, then insert the front end of the tray from inside the carcass and out through the slot in the right side panel. Rest the tray on the front and back stretchers.

17 Check the sliding action of the tray on the stretchers and wax the stretchers, if necessary. Attach the knob to the front end of the tray.

18 Glue the top panel into the recess at the top of the carcass and clamp the top in place.

19 Cut the facing (N), then cut biscuit slots for attaching it to the top and side panels, so it covers the edges of the top panel and the front stretcher. Apply veneer tape to the bottom and side edges of the facing, then sand and finish it. Attach it to the cabinet.

20 Turn the cabinet upside down, then attach the locking casters at the corners of the cabinet, following the manufacturer's directions.

Build the drawers

The drawers for the base cabinet get progressively larger from top to bottom, to maximize the storage possibilities.

1 Cut the drawer sides (W, X, Y, Z). Cut a ⅜ × ⅜"-deep dado ⅜" from the back of each piece to hold the drawer backs. Cut a ¼ × ⅜"-deep dado, ¼" from the front of each piece to hold the drawer fronts.

2 Cut the drawer backs (FF, GG, HH, II). On the outside ends of the backs, cut a ⅜ × ⅜"-deep rabbet to create a ⅜ × ⅜" lip to fit into the dadoes in the drawer sides.

3 Cut the drawer fronts (S, T, U, V). Cut a ¼ × ¾"-deep dado in the center of each end. Trim ⅜" from each inside end, on the inside shoulder of the dado only (see *Diagram*).

4 Cut a ¼ × ⅜"-deep dado for the drawer bottom, ¼" up from the bottom of each drawer part.

5 Cut the drawer bottom (AA), then sand all drawer parts with 120-grit sandpaper.

6 Glue the joints, slide the bottom in place, then fit and clamp the drawer parts around the bottom.

7 Attach the drawer guides, centered, to the drawer sides (see manufacturer's directions).

8 Mount the bottom drawer slide tracks on the cabinet side, so the bottom of the drawer will be ¹⁄₁₆" above the bottom panel (L) when the drawer is installed. Mount the tracks for the remaining drawers so there will be a ⅜" gap between drawers (see *Diagram*).

9 Cut the drawer false fronts (BB, CC, DD, EE). Apply ¾" veneer tape to the edges, trim off excess tape, then finish-sand the false fronts.

10 Attach the false fronts so there is a ¹⁄₁₆" gap between fronts. Use two countersunk #10 × 1¼" wood screws for each false front. Apply finish to the drawers.

11 Install the wire drawer pulls.

Garage Work Center

Organize and store your tools in this compact, sturdy garage work center.

Even when you don't have much spare space in your garage, you can create an efficient work area for yourself with room for plenty of tools and materials when you build this garage work center.

The adjustable upper and lower shelves and the perforated hardboard hangerboard above the worksurface allow you to organize your tools and space according to your needs. The fold-down work shelf is supported with special hardware, making it a good light-duty worksurface.

An electric outlet strip and an under-cabinet-style fluorescent light give you convenient access to power and light while working on the fold-down work shelf. And the locks on the doors keep your tools out of children's hands.

The cabinet is made with carcass construction, using biscuit joinery. Its doors and worksurfaces are strengthened with nosing.

Making the carcass

Carcass construction is simple because the side, top, bottom, and back panels are also the framework. Birch nosing on the shelves and doors provides extra strength in areas where screws are located.
1 Cut the sides (A), top (B), cabinet bottoms (C), and work shelf (D) from ¾"-thick cabinet-grade birch plywood.
2 Cut ¼ × ⅜"-wide rabbets on the back inside edges of the top and

sides to hold the back. Stop the rabbets on the sides ⅜" from the top. Square the corners of these rabbets with a chisel.
3 Cut the upper cabinet divider (E) and lower cabinet divider (F) from the ¾"-thick birch plywood.
4 Cut a ⅜ × ⅝"-deep notch in the top front edge of the lower cabinet divider (see *Diagram*) to fit around the bottom door stop (U).
5 Cut the work shelf nosings (G) from ¾" birch.
6 Cut #0 biscuit slots to join two of the work shelf nosings to the work shelf with biscuit joints.
7 Glue and assemble the two

work shelf nosings and work shelf. Clamp and let dry.
8 Cut stretchers (H) from ¾"-thick plywood.
9 Cut slots for biscuits in sides, top, cabinet bottoms, work shelf, stretchers, upper cabinet divider, and lower cabinet divider.
10 Apply veneer tape to remaining exposed edges.
11 Sand the parts to finished smoothness.
12 Dry-fit the carcass assembly to check the fit.
13 Glue and attach the upper cabinet divider to the top and to one cabinet bottom. Glue and attach the

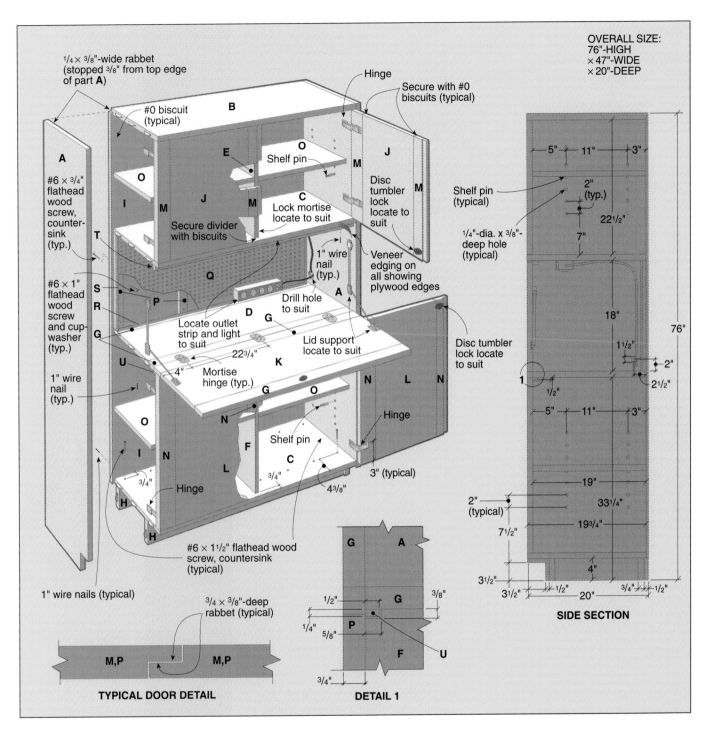

1/4 × 3/8"-wide rabbet (stopped 3/8" from top edge of part **A**)

#0 biscuit (typical)

Hinge

Secure with #0 biscuits (typical)

OVERALL SIZE: 76"-HIGH × 47"-WIDE × 20"-DEEP

A

#6 × 3/4" flathead wood screw, counter-sink (typ.)

B

E

O

Shelf pin

J

O

I

J

M

M

Disc tumbler lock locate to suit

Shelf pin (typical)

1/4"-dia. x 3/8"-deep hole (typical)

Secure divider with biscuits

C

Lock mortise locate to suit

M

T

1" wire nail (typ.)

Veneer edging on all showing plywood edges

#6 × 1" flathead wood screw and cup-washer (typ.)

S

R

R

G

P

Q

Drill hole to suit

A

Locate outlet strip and light to suit

D

G

Lid support locate to suit

Disc tumbler lock locate to suit

1" wire nail (typ.)

U

22 3/4"

K

4"

Mortise hinge (typ.)

G

O

N

L

N

O

N

Hinge

I

N

Shelf pin

F

C

3/4"

4 3/8"

3" (typical)

L

3/4"

Hinge

H

H

1" wire nails (typical)

#6 × 1 1/2" flathead wood screw, countersink (typical)

3/4 × 3/8"-deep rabbet (typical)

M,P   **M,P**

TYPICAL DOOR DETAIL

G   **A**

1/2"   **G**   3/8"

1/4"   5/8"   **P**

F   **U**

3/4"

DETAIL 1

5"   11"   3"

2" (typ.)

22 1/2"

7"

18"

1 1/2"

76"

1

1/2"   2"   2 1/2"

5"   11"   3"

19"

2" (typical)   33 1/4"

7 1/2"   19 3/4"

4"

3 1/2"   1/2"   3/4"   1/2"

3 1/2"   20"

SIDE SECTION

lower cabinet divider to the work shelf and to one cabinet bottom. Then glue and attach the sides to the top, upper cabinet bottom, work shelf, and lower cabinet bottom. Clamp, check for square, and let the assembly dry.
14 Measure and drill countersunk shank holes through the lower cabinet bottom into the stretchers. Drill pilot holes through the shank holes into the stretchers. Drive #6 × 1 1/2" wood screws into stretchers

flush with cabinet bottom.
15 Cut the back (I) from 1/4"-thick plywood. Sand lightly.
16 Install the back on the carcass with 1" wire nails, checking for square as you go.
17 Drill a 1 1/2" hole through one of the sides to hold the cord for the electric outlet strip and the exit grommet. Use a holesaw to drill the hole, which should be centered 2" above the work shelf and 2 1/2" in from the back.

Making the doors
The upper and lower doors have lapped inner nosing so that one door closes over the other. The doors also have nosing at all hinge attachment locations to strengthen them.
1 Cut the upper doors (J), middle door (K), and lower doors (L) from 3/4"-thick plywood.
2 Cut the upper door nosings (M) and lower door nosings (N) from 3/4"-thick birch.

CUTTING LIST

Key	Qty	Description & Size
A	2	**Side,** ¾ × 20 × 76"
B	1	**Top,** ¾ × 20 × 45½"
C	2	**Cabinet bottom,** ¾ × 19¾ × 45½"
D	1	**Work shelf,** ¾ × 13 × 45½"
E	1	**Upper cabinet divider,** ¾ × 19 × 22½"
F	1	**Lower cabinet divider,** ¾ × 19 × 28½"
G	4	**Work shelf nosing,** ¾ × 3 × 45½"
H	2	**Stretcher,** ¾ × 4 × 45½"
I	1	**Back,** ¼ × 46¼ × 76"
J	1	**Upper door,** ¾ × 17 × 22¼"
K	1	**Middle door,** ¾ × 12⅛ × 45¼"
L	2	**Lower door,** ¾ × 17 × 28¼"
M	4	**Upper door nosing,** ¾ × 3 × 22¼"
N	2	**Lower door nosing,** ¾ × 3 × 28¼"
O	4	**Adjustable shelf,** ¾ × 19 × 22⅛"
P	4	**Furring strips,** ¾ × 1½ × 17¾"
Q	1	**Hangerboard,** ¼ × 17¾ × 45½"
R	2	**Top and bottom molding,** ¼ × ¼ × 45½"
S	2	**Side molding,** ¼ × ¼ × 18"
T	1	**Middle door stop,** ¾ × 1 × 45½"
U	1	**Bottom door stop,** ¼ × ½ × 45½"

Note: Back (I) is ¼" plywood; nosing (G, M, N) is ¾" birch; furring strips (P) and middle door stop (T) are ¾" birch; bottom door stop (U) is ¼" birch; hangerboard (Q) and shelf hole template are ¼" perforated hardboard; top and bottom molding (R) and side molding (S) are ¼"-thick pine quarter rounds; all other parts are ¾" cabinet-grade birch plywood.

Misc.: Waterproof wood glue, flathead wood screws (#6 × ¾", #6 × 1", #6 × 1½"), ¾"-wide veneer edging (birch), ¼"-diameter shelf support pins, under-counter fluorescent work light, electric outlet strip, 3 disc tumbler locks, 1 pair of lid support hinges, 3 butler tray table hinges, 4 pairs of fully concealed hinges, #0 biscuits, cup washers, 1½" exit grommet, double-faced carpet tape, 1" wire nails, 1" finish nails.

WOODWORKER'S TIP

Use a squared piece of perforated hardboard as a template for marking locations of vertical rows of holes, such as for cabinet shelf pin holes. When the rows of holes must align horizontally, make sure the hardboard is wide enough to cover the space between the vertical rows. The template sides should be parallel to the workpiece sides. Mark the hole locations through the holes in the hardboard. Then remove the template and drill the holes.

3 Cut a ¾ × ⅜"-deep rabbet on one long edge of two of the upper door nosings and two of the lower door nosings to form the door overlaps (see *Diagram*).

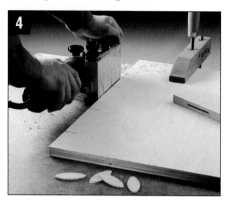

4 Cut slots with a biscuit joiner for #0 biscuits to join the upper door nosings and lower door nosings to their respective doors. The nosings on the inside edges of the upper and lower doors create an overlap when the doors are closed. Place the top lap of the overlapping nosings on the same side of the work center for both the upper and lower doors.
5 Cut slots for #0 biscuits to join the remaining two work shelf nosings and the middle door.
6 Dry-fit the nosings and doors. Then glue and assemble them. Clamp and let dry.
7 Apply veneer tape to the top and bottom edges of the upper and lower doors and to the side edges of the middle door.
8 Sand the doors and nosings to finished smoothness.

Making the adjustable shelves
Use a scrap of perforated hardboard as a template for drilling the holes for the shelf pins.
1 Cut the adjustable shelves (O) from ¾"-thick plywood.
2 Apply veneer tape to the front edges of the adjustable shelves.
3 Sand the shelves to finished smoothness.
4 Mark and drill holes inside the upper and lower cabinets for the shelf pins, using a ¼" brad-point drill bit with a stop collar set to cut ⅜"-deep holes. The front vertical row of holes should be

5" from the cabinet front and back row of vertical holes should be 3" from the cabinet back. Each hole should be approximately 2" from the holes above and below it. Drill the holes into the sides and cabinet dividers (see *Diagram*).

Making the hangerboard
The furring strips between the hangerboard and the back create space for the hanger hooks.
1 Mark and drill two vertical rows of three ⅛"-diameter shank holes through the back, each row centered 1½" from each edge of the back. Then drill two more vertical rows of three shank holes, one row centered 15" from each edge of the back. Use a perforated hardboard scrap as a template for marking the holes.
2 Cut the furring strips (P) from ¾"-thick pine.

3 Use double-faced carpet tape to attach the furring strips to the inside of the back. Each furring strip covers one row of vertical holes.
4 Drill through the shank holes in the back to drill pilot holes in the furring strips for #6 × ¾" round-head wood screws. Drive the screws through the back and into the furring strips. Do not over-tighten the screws.
5 Cut the hangerboard (Q) from ¼"-thick perforated hardboard.
6 Place the hangerboard against the furring strips. Drill shank holes in the hangerboard and pilot holes in the furring strips for #6 × 1" wood screws. Stagger these holes so that these screws will not meet the screws from the back. Drive the screws, along with cup washers, through the hangerboard and into

the furring strips.

7 Cut the top and bottom molding (R) and side molding (S) from ¼"-thick pine quarter rounds.

8 Attach the top, bottom, and side molding around the hangerboard, using 1" brads. Press the brads into the birch surrounding the hangerboard, not into the hangerboard itself.

9 Cut the middle door stop (T) from ¾"-thick birch.

10 Align the front of the middle door stop ¾" from the front edge of the bottom of the upper cabinet. Attach the middle door stop, using glue and 1" finish nails.

11 Cut the bottom door stop (U) from ¼"-thick birch.

12 Align the front of the bottom door stop ¾" from the front edge of the bottom of the work shelf nosing on the front of the work shelf. Attach the lower door stop, using glue and 1" finish nails.

Painting the workcenter

Set up sawhorses to hold the doors and shelves for painting. Always seal and paint wood projects intended for use in garages, basements, or any other place where temperatures and humidity vary greatly. Otherwise, the project will deteriorate quickly.

1 Apply two coats of sealer to fill the grain. Wait for the first coat to dry completely before applying the second coat.

2 Sand the surfaces lightly with 320-grit sandpaper after the sealer has dried. Then clean all sanding dust from the surfaces.

3 Apply two coats of paint to the unit. The first coat should be a light undercoat. After the undercoat has dried completely, sand with 320-grit sandpaper and use a tack rag to remove the dust. Then apply the final coat of paint.

Completing the workcenter

Once the paint is dry, install the hardware and shelves.

1 Put the cord of the electric outlet strip through the hole cut in the side. Affix the outlet strip to the workshelf with screws.

2 Install the exit grommet in the

electric outlet strip cord hole.

3 Install the under-cabinet-style fluorescent light using screws. Plug the light into the electric outlet strip after installation.

4 Mark the mortises for three butler table hinges on the work-shelf nosing (see *Diagram*). Use a chisel to cut the hinge mortises. Attach the hinges with screws.

5 Mark the locations for the upper door concealed cabinet hinges and screws on the sides and the upper door nosing. Then attach the hinges with screws.

6 Mark the locations for the lower door concealed cabinet hinges and screws on the sides and the lower door nosing. Then attach the hinges with screws.

7 Mark the locations for the lid support hinges and screws on the middle door and the sides. Then attach the hinges with screws.

8 Install the locks in the upper and lower top-lap cabinet doors. Locate the upper door lock in the lower inside corner of the top-lap door, and the lower door lock in the upper inside corner of the top lap door. See *Diagram* for examples of lock placement. Exact location of the locks will vary according to the type you buy. Choose locations that are easily accessible and near where it will be easy to cut lock arm mortises. Install the locks according to manufacturer's directions.

9 Cut ¼ × ¼ × 1"-long mortises in the upper and lower cabinet dividers for the lock arms. Cut the mortises in the same side of the upper and lower cabinet dividers as the doors in which the locks are installed. Use a chisel to cut

the lock arm mortises.

10 Install the lock centered in the top of the middle door. See *Diagram* for example. Exact location will vary according to the type of lock. Choose a location that is easily accessible and near where it will be easy to cut a lock arm mortise. Install the lock according to manufacturer's directions.

11 Cut a ¼ × ¼ × 1"-long mortise for the middle door lock arm in the upper cabinet bottom. Use a chisel to cut the mortise.

12 Install the shelf pins in the holes in the upper and lower cabinets. Then install the adjustable shelves on the shelf pins.

WORKSHOP TIP

For safety and stability, fasten the garage workcenter to the wall of your garage.

•Place the garage workcenter against the garage wall to which it will be permanently affixed.

•Cut a 47"-long installation cleat from a pine 2×4.

•Lay the installation cleat across the top of the workcenter, placing the width of the lumber against the wall and the thickness of the lumber firmly against the top of the unit.

•Attach the installation cleat to the wall by driving 3"-long #8 or #10 screws through the installation cleat into the wall.

•Then attach the workcenter to the installation cleat by driving 2"-long #8 or #10 screws up through the underside of the top of the workcenter and into the installation cleat.

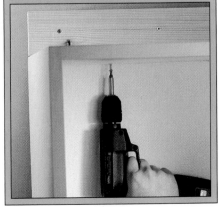

CHAPTER 4

Storage Projects

Stash your stuff!

Whether you've got a bounty of books or an overflow of socks, or you just need space to display your treasures, there's a storage solution in this chapter. Twelve projects offer stylish strategies for every room in the house.

Stow spices, coffee mugs, or fine china in the Scandinavian-style corner cabinet or in the handsome pierced-tin cabinet. Tout your treasures on the wall-hung display cabinet on page 128 or in the heirloom-quality curio cabinet. Tuck away your television, VCR, and other entertainment electronics in the media center. Crafted of pine, the tall cabinet is elegant enough to grace the living room.

Are books stacked in every nook and cranny of your home? Two bookcases in this chapter provide sturdy caches. Build the simple knotty-pine bookcase in a weekend. Want a more elegant repository? The glass-front barrister's bookcase is a true showpiece. For your clothing, there's bedroom furniture too: a practical and pretty maple dresser and a high-style armoire.

Fashion the hope chest for your own prized possessions or as a gift for a loved one. The construction may seem basic, like building a box, but there's nothing basic about its function. A hope chest stores dreams of the future.

Corner Cabinet

This birch cabinet delivers convenient corner storage in a compact design.

This gracefully curved corner cabinet boasts a proud Scandinavian heritage. We built our cabinet from honey-colored birch to accentuate that tradition while providing strength, workability, and a fine-grained surface suitable for staining or decorative painting. Mounted to your wall with sturdy hanging strips, our corner cabinet is sophisticated enough for storing fine family treasures and strong enough to hold a set of your best china.

Make the rails & stiles

The rails for the face frame are cut from 3 × 6 × 32" birch blanks. If you need to laminate smaller stock to achieve this size, as we did, allow plenty of time for the glue-up to dry. Because the doors are set into the face frame, the curved profiles in the doors and face frame must match exactly.

1 Lay out the cabinet rails (D) on birch blanks so the outside face has a 20" radius and the inside face has a 19¼" radius (see *Diagram*). Cut out the profiles on your bandsaw, using a 6-tpi blade. Cut just outside the lines, and save the waste pieces of the blanks to use for cutting and routing jigs.

2 Use the same tools and methods used in *step 1* to cut the door rails (E) from 1½ × 2½ × 8" birch stock.

3 Smooth the curved faces of the rails to final shape on the cylinders at the ends of your stationary sander belt.

4 Use an outer waste piece from a cabinet rail blank as a jig for cutting the door and cabinet rails to length. Cut the waste piece in half and fasten it to a ¾ × 13 × 13" plywood jig base (see photo, *step 5*). Cut a ¾"-thick plywood guide fence with a 20"-radius curve and attach the guide fence to one side of the outer waste piece jig.

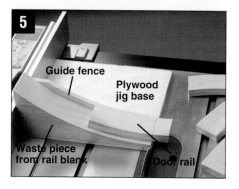

Guide fence

Plywood jig base

Waste piece from rail blank

Door rail

5 Mark the length of each rail on the inside of the curve, then set a rail in the jig against the guide fence, and butt the jig against your tablesaw fence. Carefully align the cutting mark with the blade and cut each rail to length.

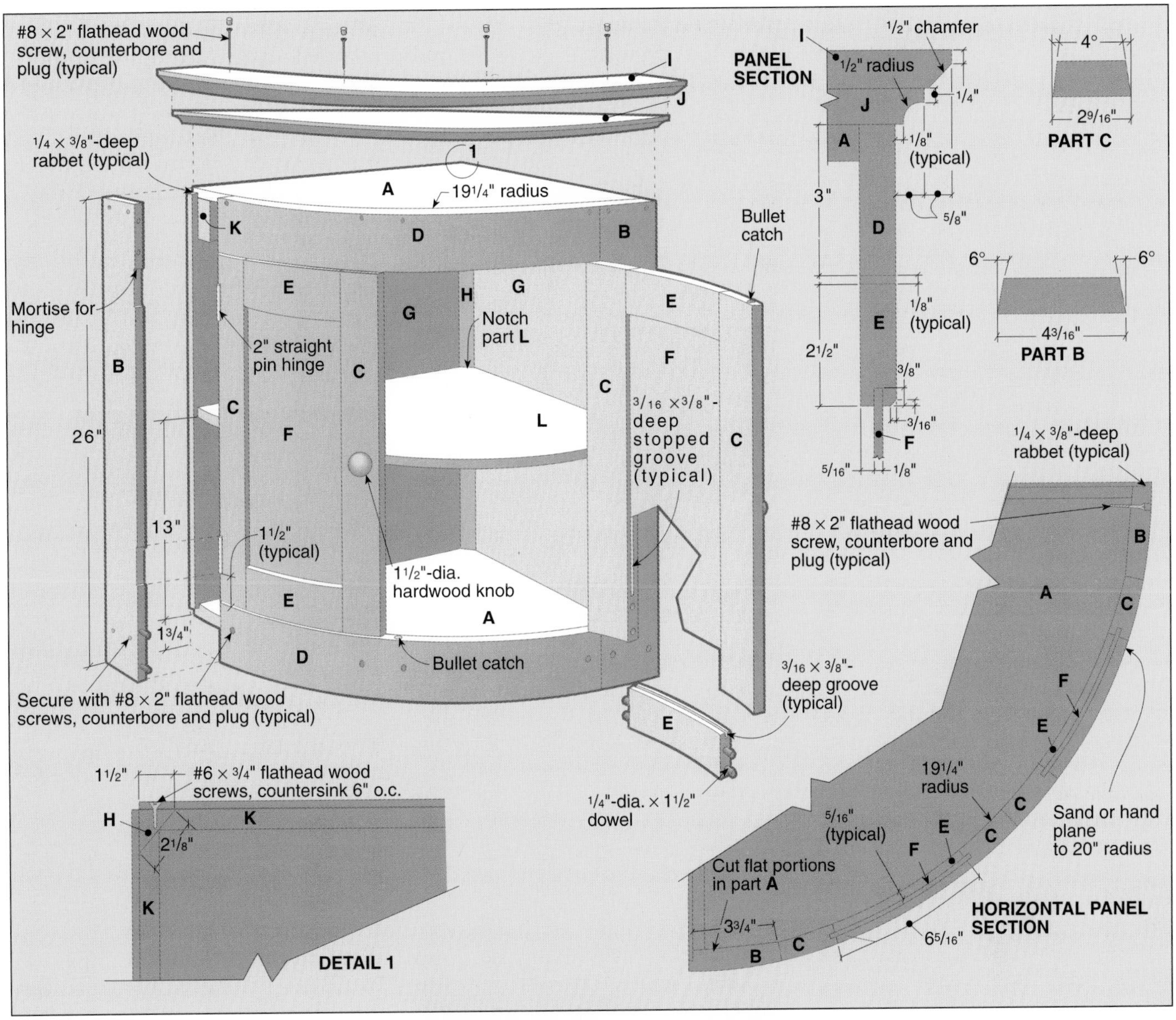
#8 × 2" flathead wood screw, counterbore and plug (typical)
I
J
1/4 × 3/8"-deep rabbet (typical)
1
A
19 1/4" radius
K
D
B
Bullet catch
E
G
H
G
Notch part L
E
Mortise for hinge
2" straight pin hinge
F
B
C
G
C
C
3/16 × 3/8"-deep stopped groove (typical)
C
26"
F
L
13"
1 1/2" (typical)
1 1/2"-dia. hardwood knob
E
A
1 3/4"
D
Bullet catch
Secure with #8 × 2" flathead wood screws, counterbore and plug (typical)
3/16 × 3/8"-deep groove (typical)
E
1/4"-dia. × 1 1/2" dowel
PANEL SECTION
1/2" chamfer
1/2" radius
1/4"
J
A
1/8" (typical)
3"
5/8"
D
E
1/8" (typical)
2 1/2"
3/8"
3/16"
F
5/16"
1/8"
4°
2 9/16"
PART C
6°
6°
4 3/16"
PART B
1/4 × 3/8"-deep rabbet (typical)
#8 × 2" flathead wood screw, counterbore and plug (typical)
B
A
C
F
E
19 1/4" radius
C
Sand or hand plane to 20" radius
5/16" (typical)
E
C
F
Cut flat portions in part A
3 3/4"
B
C
6 5/16"
HORIZONTAL PANEL SECTION
1 1/2"
#6 × 3/4" flathead wood screws, countersink 6" o.c.
H
K
2 1/8"
K
DETAIL 1

6 Cut the cabinet stiles (B) and door stiles (C) to finished length from 1"-thick stock.

7 Bevel-rip both edges of the cabinet stiles (B) at 6° angles (see *Diagram*) so the workpieces are 4 3/16" wide on the outside faces. Bevel-rip both edges of the door stiles (C) at 4° angles so the workpieces are 2 9/16" wide on the outside faces.

8 Cut a ¼ × ⅜"-deep rabbet on the back inside edge of each cabinet stile, using a dado-blade set.

9 Butt a beveled cabinet stile edge to its mating door stile and clamp the pieces together. Draw an arc with a 20" radius on both ends of each pair of cabinet and door stiles, to mark the curves of the outside faces (see *Diagram*).

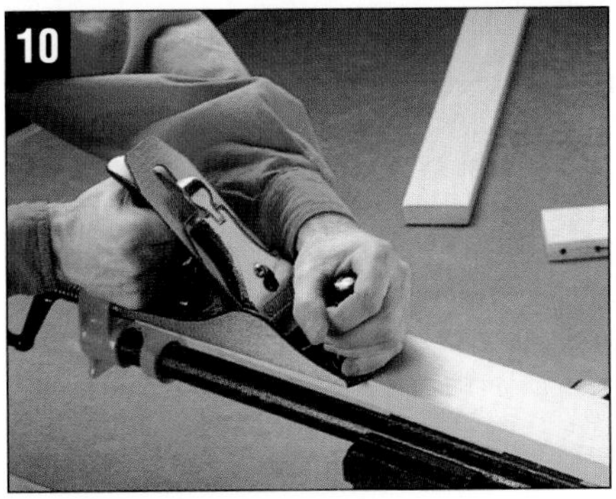
10

10 Secure each stile between the jaws of a clamp or vise, with the inside face down. Shape the curves on the outside face of each stile with a bench plane, using straight, shallow cuts the full length of the board. Refine the curves with a cabinet scraper or sander.

CUTTING LIST

Key	Qty.	Description & Size
A	2	**Top/bottom,** ¾ × 19¼ × 19¼"
B	2	**Stile,** ⅞ × 4 3/16 × 26"
C	4	**Door stile,** 13/16 × 2 9/16 × 19¾"
D	2	**Cabinet rail,** ¾ × 3 × 30"
E	4	**Door rail,** ¾ × 2½ × 6 5/16"
F	2	**Door panel,** ⅛ × 7⅛ × 15½"
G	2	**Back panel,** ¼ × 19⅝ × 23½"
H	1	**Corner strip,** 1½ × 1½ × 22¾"
I	1	**Upper crown,** ¾ × 10 × 33"
J	1	**Lower crown,** ¾ × 10 × 33"
K	2	**Hanging strip,** ¾ × 2 × 18¼"
L	1	**Shelf,** ¾ × 19⅛ × 19⅛"

Note: All wood is birch except parts A, F, and G, which are birch plywood.

Misc.: Glue, flathead wood screws (#6 × ¾", #8 × 1¼"), ¼ × 1½" dowels, 2" pin hinges (4), ¼" bullet catches (4), 1½"-dia. knobs (2), ⅜"-dia. birch plugs, birch veneer tape.

11 Use your router table and $\frac{3}{16}$"-diameter bit to cut a $\frac{3}{16} \times \frac{3}{8} \times 15\frac{5}{8}$"-long stopped groove centered in the inside edge of each door stile, to hold the panels (F).

12 Install a $\frac{3}{16}$" straight router bit in your router table and set it at $\frac{3}{8}$" cutting height. Use an inner wood scrap from a door rail blank as a guide fence for cutting grooves in the rails on your router table. Clamp the guide fence to your router table, $\frac{9}{32}$" from the router bit.

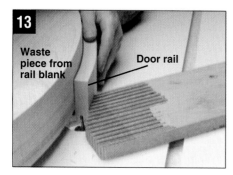

Waste piece from rail blank

Door rail

13 Clamp a featherboard to your router table, $\frac{9}{32}$" from the router bit, on the opposite side from the guide fence (this should leave a $\frac{3}{4}$"-wide gap between the featherboard and the guide fence). Feed each door rail between the guide fence and the featherboard, and over the router bit. This will create a $\frac{3}{16} \times \frac{3}{8}$"-deep groove in the center of each inside rail edge for the door panel.

14 Sand the faces and edges of the rails to finished smoothness. Don't sand the ends of the rails.

Assemble the doors

The frames for our curved frame-and-panel doors are made with dowel joints. The $\frac{1}{8}$"-thick door panels conform to the cabinet-door curves when they're dry-fitted into the grooves in the rails and stiles.

1 Mark center points to drill holes for $\frac{1}{4} \times 1\frac{1}{2}$" dowels for joining the stiles and rails (see *Diagram*).

2 Sandwich a door rail between the slats of a clamping worksurface or in a bench vise, so the end of the rail is flush with the surface of the clamp. Use a drill and portable drill guide to bore two $\frac{1}{4} \times \frac{3}{4}$"-deep holes in each rail end. Drill matching holes in the door stiles.

3 Cut the door panels (F), and sand both panels to finished smoothness. Stain and finish the panels before assembling the doors to keep the finish from sealing the panels into the door frames (see *Complete the cabinet,* opposite).

4 Insert the panels into the grooves in the door rails. Don't use glue.

5 Glue and assemble the dowel joints between the rails and stiles. Bevel-rip two strips of $\frac{3}{4} \times 1 \times 52$" material at 4°, to use as clamping blocks. Set a block on each side of one door assembly, then press the blocks together until glue squeeze-out appears. Clamp the blocks to your worksurface, maintaining the tension with the door. Also weight the rails with light sandbags until the joint is dry.

Make & assemble the carcass

Assemble the face frame of the cabinet first, then use the assembly as a guide for adjusting the size and shape of the carcass pieces, where needed, to match the profiles of the face frame and doors.

1 Join the cabinet stiles and rails, using the same techniques shown in *steps 1, 2 and 5* in *Assemble the doors,* at left. Let the glue dry.

2 Cut three $19\frac{1}{4}$"-square pieces of $\frac{3}{4}$"-thick plywood for the cabinet top and bottom (A) and shelf (L).

3 Set the face frame assembly onto one of the plywood squares so the inside ends of the face frame are flush with opposite corners of the plywood. Trace the curve of the face-frame rail onto the plywood.

4 Gang-cut the curve into the three plywood pieces, using a bandsaw. Test-fit the pieces against the cabinet frame.

5 Cut $\frac{1}{4} \times \frac{3}{8}$"-deep rabbets on the straight edges of the top and bottom to hold the back panels (G).

6 Trim $\frac{1}{4}$" from each straight edge of the shelf. Trim a $1\frac{1}{2}$" triangle from the shelf corner where the straight edges meet to make room for the corner strip (H).

7 Apply birch veneer tape to the front of the shelf. Trim the tape.

8 Cut the back panels (G).

9 Sand the top, bottom, shelf, face frame, back and doors to finished smoothness.

10 Drill $\frac{3}{8}$"-diameter counterbored holes with $\frac{3}{16}$"-diameter shank holes in the face frame, $\frac{3}{8}$" down from the top edge and $2\frac{1}{8}$" up from the bottom edge (see *Diagram* for spacing).

11 Clamp the top to your workbench, with the top surface facing down. Position the face frame against the curved edge of the top, and extend the pilot holes through the face frame and into the edge of the top. Attach the top to the face frame with glue and #8 × 2" flathead wood screws.
12 Insert a 1¾" spacer between the bottom and the worksurface, then secure with a clamp. Attach the bottom to the face frame, using the same method as in *step 11*. Note: Be sure to support the back edge of the top while attaching the bottom.
13 Attach the back to the rabbeted edges of the top and bottom, using #8 × 2" flathead wood screws driven through countersunk pilot holes.
14 Bevel-rip 1½"-square stock at 45° to make the corner strip (H). Finish-sand the strip, then attach it in the back corner of the carcass with glue and #6 × ¾" wood screws driven through the back and into the strip.
15 On the inside faces of the back panels, mark straight lines 13" up from the cabinet bottom to mark the shelf position. Drill ³⁄₁₆" shank holes through the back panels, 6" apart, ⅜" up from the shelf line.
16 Cut three 13" spacers from 2 × 4 scrap, and set them on-end on the cabinet bottom. Slip the shelf into the door opening and rest it on the 2 × 4 spacers.
17 Extend the pilot holes through the back panels and into the edges of the shelf. Attach the shelf with #8 × 1¼" flathead wood screws.
18 Sand the cabinet carcass and the door frames to finished smoothness.

Build & attach crown molding

Make custom crown trim for the cabinet from two glued-up pieces of ¾ × 10 × 33" birch stock.
1 To mark the stock for the upper crown (I), set your bar compass to draw a circle with a 21¼" radius, then draw an arc on one of the ¾ × 10 × 33" pieces of glued-up birch. The tip of the arc should just touch the front edge of the

glue-up. Reset the bar compass and draw a concentric arc with an 18½" radius from the same center.
2 Mark the stock for the lower crown (J) by drawing concentric arcs with radii of 20⅝" and 18½" onto the other glued-up board.

3 Cut out the crown pieces on your bandsaw, then smooth the edges on your stationary sander.
4 Secure the upper crown to your workbench, top down, then use a ½" piloted chamfer bit and a router to chamfer the bottom, front edge of the workpiece (see *Diagram*).
5 Clamp the lower crown to your worksurface, bottom down, then use a ½" piloted cove bit and router to shape the bottom, front edge of the workpiece.
6 Face-glue the top and bottom crown pieces together so the top edge of the top crown overhangs the bottom crown by ⅝". Clamp them until the glue is dry.
7 Place the molding assembly on top of the cabinet, with the bottom of the assembly overhanging the front of the cabinet frame by ⅛". Draw cutting lines on the molding where it meets the front edges of the back panels.

8 Use a handsaw to trim the molding along the cutting lines.

9 Attach the molding assembly to the top panel with counterbored #8 × 2" screws, driven at 10" intervals. Make sure the ends of the molding are flush with the cabinet sides, and the front overhang is ⅛".

Complete the cabinet

1 Cut mortises in the edges of the door panel frames for 2" pin hinges (see *Diagram*), then mount the hinges in the door frame.
2 Set the doors into the face frame, centered top to bottom. Mark hinge mortise locations on the cabinet stiles (don't hang the doors until you've applied the finish).
3 Cut the hanging strips (K) from ¾"-thick birch, bevel the ends that butt against (H), and finish-sand.
4 Attach the hanging strips inside the cabinet at the top of each back panel, using glue and #6 × ¾" wood screws driven through the back.
5 Apply the finish. We sealed the entire cabinet with a 1:1 mixture of oil-based polyurethane and mineral spirits, followed by an undiluted coat of polyurethane. We also hired a Scandinavian folk artist to paint the decorative design on the doors. Finally, we applied a coat of paste wax.
6 Attach the hinges in the face frame mortises.
7 Install a bullet catch at the top and bottom of each door according to the manufacturer's directions and attach the doorknobs.
8 Plug all screw counterbores with ⅜"-diameter plugs.

Hang the cabinet

1 Locate and mark the first wall stud out from the corner where the cabinet will hang. Use a carpenter's level as a guide for drawing level lines at the desired cabinet height (about 72" at the top is an average height).
2 With an assistant, position the cabinet at the level lines, then attach it to the walls by driving #10 × 2" flathead wood screws through counterbored shank holes in the hanging strips, at stud locations. Tighten the screws gradually, alternating from side to side. Plug the holes when you're done.

Library Cabinet

This handy cabinet doubles as an end table and storage space for magazines.

Classic detailing and functional design are combined in this design for a multiuse library cabinet. Newspapers and magazines fit neatly in the slanted shelves underneath, and pencils and reading glasses can be tucked away in the drawer at the top.

We chose mahogany for its rich color and attractive grain, and used a hand-rubbed oil finish to showcase the wood.

Preparing the parts

1 Cut the ¾" top (A) and use a router with a Roman ogee bit to shape the front and side edges.
2 Cut the sides (B) to size, then cut ¾ × ⅜"-deep dadoes in each piece, 2½" up from the bottom edge, for the bottom panel (C).
3 Cut another dado (¾ × ⅜"-deep) in each side piece, 1¾" below the top edges, for the drawer slides.

4 Cut ¼ × ⅜"-deep stopped dadoes in the side pieces to hold the shelves at a 7° angle. There should be 4" between the bottom panel and the front edge of the lowest shelf, and 4" between all other shelves (see *Diagram*). The

dadoes should stop 1" in from the front edges.
5 Rabbet the back edge of each side piece (¼ × ⅜"-deep) and the back edge of the bottom panel to hold the back panel.
6 Cut the ¼" back (E) to size.
7 Cut the ¼" shelves (D) to size, then cut ¾ × ⅜"-deep notches at the front corners of each shelf (see *Diagram*).
8 Hand-sand the shelves to remove rough edges.

Putting it all together

1 Attach the bottom into the lowest dado in the sides with glue and 1" countersunk finish nails spaced every 3".
2 Attach the top panel to the sides with three equally spaced ⅜ × 1" dowels. Leave ¾" overhang on the sides and front.

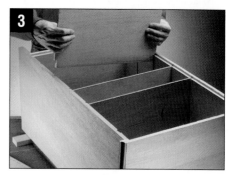

3 Slide the shelves into the dadoes, with the notches going in first.
4 On a router table, cut a ¼" rabbet along one edge of a strip of ½ × ½" mahogany to make shelf edging. Measure, cut, and attach edging to shelves with glue as shown (see *Diagram*).
5 Attach the back panel with ¾" brads driven into the sides, top, and bottom pieces.

6 Measure and miter-cut molding to wrap around the base. Leave a ¼" reveal below the bottom shelf surface—molding should be flush at floor. Attach with glue and 1¼" countersunk brads.

Build the drawer

1 Cut the drawer front (N), sides (I), back (J) and bottom (K).
2 Cut a ¾ × ⅜"-deep rabbet at both ends of the drawer back. Cut a ¼ × ⅜"-deep groove in the drawer sides and the back, ½" up from the bottom edge.
3 Glue and clamp the sides into the rabbeted drawer back and fit the drawer front between the sides. Reinforce with #6 × 1¼" flathead wood screws driven every 3".
4 Slide the drawer bottom into the groove in the drawer sides and back. Glue the false front in place.
5 Cut the false front (H) and use a router with a Roman ogee bit to shape all of the edges.
6 Attach the false front to the drawer with #8 × 1¼" wood screws.
7 Cut drawer slides (L) and attach them to the sides of the drawer with finish nails driven every 3". The top edges of the glides should be 1¾" below the top edge of the drawer.
8 Finish-sand the cabinet, apply linseed oil, and install the drawer and hardware.

CUTTING LIST

Key	Qty.	Description & Size
A	1	**Top,** ¾ × 13¾ × 18½"
B	2	**Sides,** ¾ × 13 × 28⅜"
C	1	**Bottom,** ¾ × 13 × 16¼"
D	4	**Shelf,*** ¼ × 12¼ × 16¼"
E	1	**Back,*** ¼ × 16¼ × 25⅞"
F	1	**Front molding,** ¾ × 3 × 18½"
G	2	**Side molding,** ¾ × 3 × 13¾"
H	1	**False front,** ¾ × 4 × 16¾"
I	2	**Drawer sides,** ¾ × 4 × 12"
J	1	**Drawer back,** ¾ × 4 × 15⅜"
K	1	**Drawer bottom,*** ¼ × 11½ × 4⅝"
L	2	**Drawer slides,** ⅜ × 11⁄16 × 11⅝"
M	4	**Shelf edging,** ½ × ½ × 15½"
N	1	**Drawer front,** ¾ × 3½ × 13⅞"

Note: All pieces are mahogany except D, E, and K, which are plywood.

Misc.: ⅜ × 1" dowels, #8 × 1¼" wood screws, ¾" and 1¼" brads, finish nails.

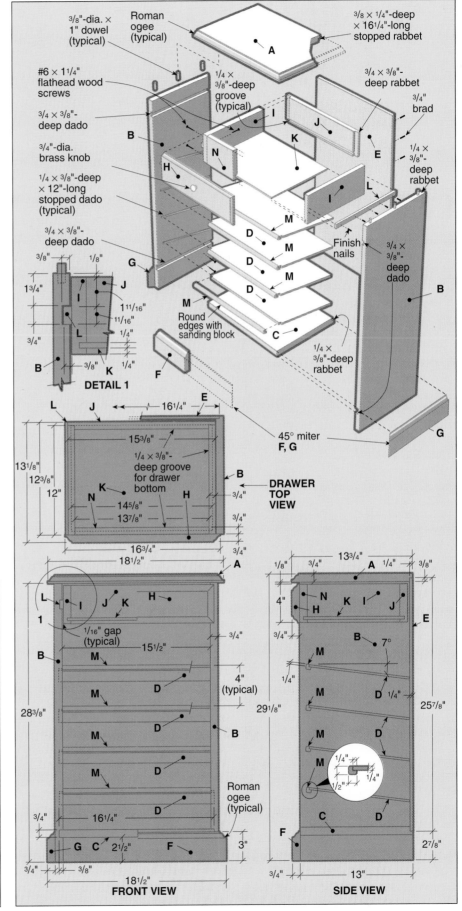

Pierced-Tin Cabinet

This hanging cabinet will bring back memories of days gone by.

Cabinetmakers of earlier days frequently added decorative tin panels to their work. They were especially popular for making pie safes because the small holes punched in the tin allowed the air to circulate freely, filling the house with the tantalizing aroma of baked goods, while keeping the pies safely stowed.

Continue the tradition by building this simple hanging cabinet and learning the technique to create a pierced-tin panel, using our floral pattern or your own personalized design.

Build the carcass

1 Cut the sides (B) from 1 × 12 pine. Transfer the pattern for the curved bottom cut to the pieces (see *Diagram*) and cut them using a bandsaw.

2 Mark the location and cut ¾ × ⅜"-deep dadoes for the shelves (see *Diagram*) in the sides.

3 On the inside back edges of the sides, cut ¼ × ⅜"-deep × 17"-long stopped rabbets where the back will fit (see *Diagram*). Start the rabbet cut 5¼" below the top edge.

4 Cut a ¾"-diameter maple dowel to make the towel rod (F). Check the diameter of your dowel–it may be slightly smaller.

5 Drill ¾ × ⅜"-deep holes (adjust if the dowel is smaller than ¾") in the sides to hold the towel rod.

6 Cut the hanger (C) from 1 × 6 pine. Cut a ¼ × ⅜"-deep rabbet on the bottom back edge.

7 Drill the ends of the hanger for ⅜ × 1½" dowels, and use dowel centers to transfer the center marks to their matching locations on the sides. Drill ½"-deep holes

in the sides for the dowels.

8 Cut the three interior shelves (D) from 1 × 12 pine.

9 Cut the bottom shelf (G), then cut ⅜ × ⅜"-deep notches in the front corners so the shelf will extend past the dado in the sides.

10 Cut the back (E) from ¼"-thick plywood.

11 Finish-sand the shelves, the towel rod, and the back.

12 Assemble the cabinet by laying one side piece on a flat surface and attaching one end of the hanger to it, using dowels. Attach one end of the shelves into the dadoes with glue—brace the shelves in position. Fit one end of the towel rod in the hole at the bottom of the side—do not glue.

13 Glue and fit the other side piece in place (do not glue the rod). Clamp the assembly, check for square, and allow glue to dry. Scrape away any excess glue.

14 Fit the plywood back into the

rabbets in the sides and in the hanger. Fasten one side of the back with ⅝" brads. Check for square, then fasten the other side in place. Do not glue.

15 Cut the face frame stiles (H) and rails (I). Lay out and drill ¼ × 1½" holes for dowel joints in the stiles and rails.

16 Glue and clamp the stiles and rails together, using dowels. Check for square.

17 When dry, scrape away excess glue and sand the back of the face frame. Cut a ¼" stopped cove on the front outside edge of the stiles, leaving 1" uncut at the top and bottom (*see Diagram*).

18 Attach the face frame to the cabinet with glue and 4d finish nails driven every 4". Set the nails, and fill the nail holes.

19 Joint two pieces of pine for the top, and edge-glue and clamp them together. When dry, cut the top (A), and shape the front and

CUTTING LIST

Key	Qty.	Description & Size
A	1	**Top,** ¾ × 12⅞ × 25¾"
B	2	**Side,** ¾ × 11¼ × 35⅜"
C	1	**Hanger,** ¾ × 5½ × 22½"
D	3	**Interior shelf,** ¾ × 11 × 23¼"
E	1	**Back,** ¼ × 17⅜ × 23¼"
F	1	**Towel rod,** ¾"-dia. × 23¼"
G	1	**Bottom shelf,** ¾ × 5½ × 23¼"
H	2	**Face frame stile,** ¾ × 2½ × 24"
I	2	**Face frame rail,** ¾ × 2½ × 19"
J	2	**Door stile,** ¾ × 2 × 19½"
K	2	**Door rail,** ¾ × 2 × 15½"
L	4	**Retainer strip,** ¼ × ⅜ × 16¼"
M	1	**Tin inset,** 28 GA. × 16¼ × 16¼"

Note: All material is pine, except for the back (E), which is plywood, and the towel rod (F), which is maple.

Misc.: #8 × 1¼" flathead wood screws; 4d finish nails; semiconcealed hinges, ⅜" inset; ¼ × 1½" dowels; ⅝" brads; 1"-diameter knob; wood glue.

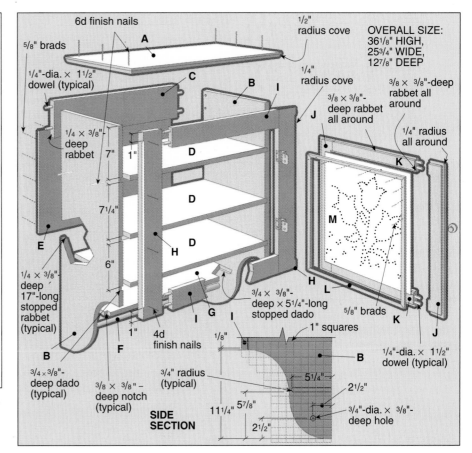

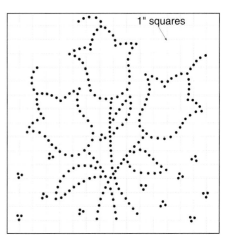

side edges using a router with a ½" cove bit.

20 Attach the top to the cabinet, using 4d finish nails. Fill the holes and let them dry. Finish-sand the entire cabinet.

Build the door

1 Cut the door stiles (J) and door rails (K). Drill ¼ × 1½" holes for dowels (see *Diagram*).

2 Assemble the door frame by gluing and clamping the stiles and rails with dowel joints. Check for square and let dry.

3 Set the door frame facedown, and cut a ⅜ × ⅜"-deep rabbet on the back inside edge.

4 Measure and miter-cut the ends of the ¼ × ⅜" retainer strips to fit inside the rabbeted edge of the frame and hold the tin panel in place when it is installed.

5 Cut a ⅜ × ⅜"-deep rabbet on the back outside edge of the frame, to make a lipped edge that will fit over the face frame.

6 Finish-sand the door frame.

7 Enlarge the tin pattern on a photocopier (we enlarged it 200% twice, then at 145%).

8 Cut a piece of 28 GA. × 16¼ × 16¼" tin for the inset (M) and buff it lightly, using a random orbital

sander with 180-grit steel wool (use lightweight oil as a lubricant). The circular motion of the orbital sander will give the metal a soft, burnished look. Rinse and dry the tin.

9 Tape the tin to a scrap of ¾" plywood. Lay the pattern over the tin and tape it in place.

10 Punch holes in the tin by lightly tapping a #10 common nail with a hammer.

11 When the design is completely punched, coat both sides with spray varnish.

Finish the cabinet

1 Paint the cabinet and door, using several coats of paint.

2 Let the paint dry at least a day, then apply a few coats of clear acrylic medium with a coarse brush to add texture to the surface. Let it dry.

3 Set the door frame facedown, and fit the tin panel into the rabbeted inside edges.

4 Fit the retaining strips against the tin panel and fasten them to the door frame with ½" brads.

5 Install the knob, catch, and hinges according to manufacturer's instructions.

Wall Display

A timely place to display prized dishware and favorite knickknacks.

This practical country-style wall display is an ideal place to safely exhibit your collectibles. It features a 6" clock face with quartz-battery movement, which you can buy at most wood-working stores or hobby shops.

Preparing the pieces

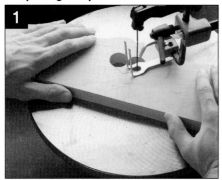

1 Cut the ¾" cherry top and bottom rails (A, B). Trace the curved patterns (see *Diagram*) onto the rails, then drill starter holes and cut the curves on a scroll saw.
2 Drill ¼"-deep peg holes in the bottom rail, using a ¼" Forstner bit.
3 Drill ³⁄₁₆" holes for mounting screws in the top rail and bottom rail, then counterbore each hole to a depth of ⅜", using a ⅜" bit.
4 Cut the ¾" cherry side panels (C). Trace the curved patterns (see *Diagram*) onto the side panels, then cut them with a scroll saw.
5 Cut ¾ × ⅜"-deep rabbets along the bottom of each side panel.

> ### WOODWORKER'S TIP
> *Space the mounting holes to match the on-center stud spacing in your walls, to ensure the wall display can be mounted to framing members. In most homes, studs are spaced 16" or 24" apart on-center.*

6 Cut a ¾ × ⅜"-deep stopped rabbet 2⅛" long along the top back edge of each side panel, where the top rail will fit.

7 Cut a ¼ × ½"-deep rabbet along the back edge of each side panel, from the stopped rabbet to the end of the panel.
8 Cut a ¾ × ⅜"-deep dado across the inside face of each side panel, where the top panel will fit. The top of the dado should be 2½" from the top of the side panel.
9 Cut ½ × ⅜"-deep dadoes across the inside face of the side panels, where the shelves will fit. The tops of the dadoes should be 10¼" from the bottom of the side panels.

10 Cut the ¾" cherry top and bottom panels (D). Cut a ¼ × ½"-deep rabbet along the back edge of each piece, where the back panel will fit.
11 Cut ½ × ⅜"-deep dadoes where the vertical dividers (E) will fit, 13¾" from sides.
12 Cut the ½" cherry dividers (E). Cut ½ × ⅜"-deep dadoes where the shelves will fit.
13 Cut the ½" cherry shelves (F, G). Trim ¼ × ¼" corners off the front edges of the shelves, where the shelves will meet the dividers and side panels.
14 Use a ⅜" veining bit to cut a ⅛"-deep slot along each shelf, 1½" from the back edges. These slots will hold decorative plates upright for display.
15 Cut the ¼" cherry clock frame (H), then drill a ⅜" hole in the center of the frame. Glue the clock face to the frame, then attach the hands and clock movement mechanism.
16 Sand all pieces smooth.

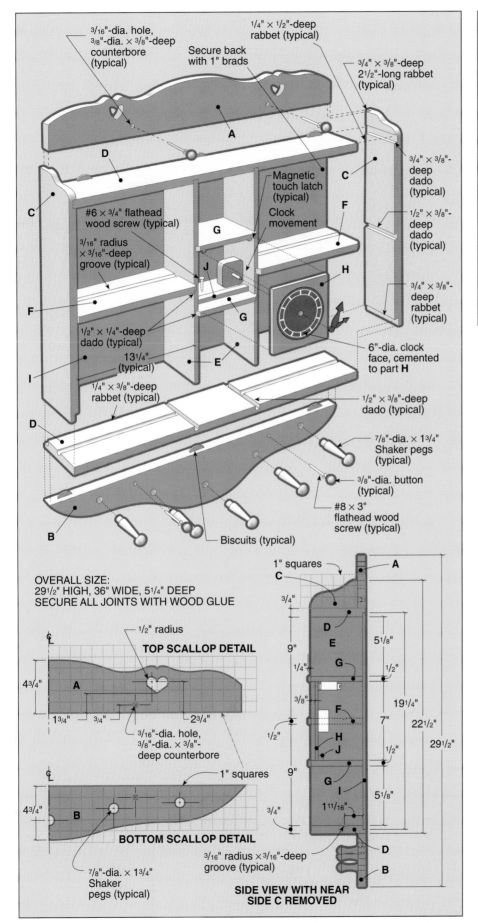

³/₁₆"-dia. hole,
³/₈"-dia. × ³/₈"-deep
counterbore
(typical)

¹/₄" × ¹/₂"-deep
rabbet (typical)

Secure back
with 1" brads

³/₄" × ³/₈"-deep
2¹/₂"-long rabbet
(typical)

A

D

C

³/₄" × ³/₈"-
deep
dado
(typical)

F

Magnetic touch latch
(typical)

Clock
movement

G

#6 × ³/₄" flathead
wood screw (typical)

³/₁₆" radius
× ³/₁₆"-deep
groove (typical)

¹/₂" × ³/₈"-
deep
dado
(typical)

J

C

H

³/₄" × ³/₈"-
deep
rabbet
(typical)

F

G

¹/₂" × ¹/₄"-deep
dado (typical)

13¹/₄"
(typical)

E

6"-dia. clock
face, cemented
to part **H**

I

¹/₄" × ³/₈"-deep
rabbet (typical)

¹/₂" × ³/₈"-deep
dado (typical)

D

⁷/₈"-dia. × 1³/₄"
Shaker pegs
(typical)

³/₈"-dia. button
(typical)

#8 × 3"
flathead wood
screw (typical)

B

Biscuits (typical)

OVERALL SIZE:
29¹/₂" HIGH, 36" WIDE, 5¹/₄" DEEP
SECURE ALL JOINTS WITH WOOD GLUE

TOP SCALLOP DETAIL

¹/₂" radius

4³/₄"

A

1³/₄"   ³/₄"   2³/₄"

³/₁₆"-dia. hole,
³/₈"-dia. × ³/₈"-
deep counterbore

1" squares

BOTTOM SCALLOP DETAIL

4³/₄"

B

⁷/₈"-dia. × 1³/₄"
Shaker
pegs (typical)

³/₁₆" radius × ³/₁₆"-deep
groove (typical)

1" squares

C

A

³/₄"

D

9"

E

G

1/4"

F

H

J

9"

G

I

1¹¹/₁₆"

³/₄"

5¹/₈"

¹/₂"

¹/₂"

19¹/₄"

7"

22¹/₂"

¹/₂"

29¹/₂"

5¹/₈"

³/₄"

D

B

**SIDE VIEW WITH NEAR
SIDE C REMOVED**

CUTTING LIST

Key	Qty.	Description & Size
A	1	**Top rail,** ³/₄ × 4³/₄ × 36"
B	1	**Bottom rail,** ³/₄ × 4³/₄ × 36"
C	2	**Side panel,** ³/₄ × 5 × 22¹/₂"
D	2	**Top, bottom panel,** ³/₄ × 5 × 35¹/₄"
E	2	**Dividers,** ¹/₂ × 4³/₄ × 19¹/₄"
F	2	**Long shelf,** ¹/₂ × 5 × 13⅛"
G	2	**Short shelf,** ¹/₂ × 5 × 7¹/₂"
H	1	**Clock frame,** ¹/₄ × 6¹⁵/₁₆ × 6¹⁵/₁₆"
I	1	**Back,** ¹/₄ × 19¹/₄ × 35¹/₄"
J	1	**Cleat,** ¹/₂ × ¹/₂ × 7"

Note: All material is cherry, except for the back (I), which is cherry plywood.

Misc.: glue; sandpaper; ⁷/₈ × 1³/₄" shaker pegs; 6"-dia. clock face with movement, magnetic latches; ³/₈" buttons; wood screws (#6 × ³/₄", #8 × 3"); wire brads.

Assembling the project

1 On a flat surface, glue, assemble, and clamp the dividers around the short shelves. Measure the diagonals to make sure the assembly is square, then set it aside.
2 Glue, assemble, and clamp the top and bottom panels between the side panels.
3 Apply glue, and insert the divider assembly between the top and bottom panels.
4 Apply glue, and insert the long shelves between the side panels and dividers.
5 Attach the top rail between the side panels with glue and biscuits.
6 Attach the bottom rail to the bottom panel with glue and biscuits or dowels.
7 Cut the ¹/₄" cherry plywood back panel, then fit it into the rabbets on the back of the wall display, and attach it with wire brads (don't glue it).
8 Cut the ¹/₂" cherry cleat and attach it to the lower center shelf ¹/₂" from the front edge, using #6 × ¹/₄" screws.
9 Attach two magnetic latches to the underside of the top shelf and attach the metal strike plates to the back side of the clock frame. Insert the clock frame into the wall display.
10 Attach the pegs to the lower rail, then apply the finish you want. Our wall display was finished with burled-cherry stain.

Bookcase

Store a wealth of written lore and more on this knotty-pine bookshelf.

For inexpensive book storage, consider this attractive pine bookcase you can build in one weekend. Remarkable for its simplicity of design and structural strength, this sharp-looking piece looks great in a bedroom, den, or library. When buying the material for this project, choose knotty pine, but avoid lumber with broken or loose knots. The strips of precut, tongue-and-groove wainscoting used for the back add character and can usually be purchased at home building centers.

Preparing the parts

This bookcase is made primarily with mortise-and-tenon and biscuit joinery.

1 Glue up enough wainscoting to make a sheet at least 74 × 42"-high for the back (A). Clamp the pieces and let dry.
2 Cut the back to its finished height and width, using a tablesaw. For the width, cut equal amounts from each end of the back so that there is a wainscoting piece of equal width on each end. The ends should be flat, without a tongue or groove.
3 Cut the top (B), sides (C), shelves (D), partitions (E), apron (F), top and bottom rails (G, H), and cleat (I) from ¾"-thick pine. You can glue up the top from multiple pieces, alternating the grain to avoid warping.
4 Measure and mark biscuit slots for joining the shelves to the

partitions, and the sides to the top, rails and cleats.
5 Cut the biscuit slots in the shelves, sides, rail, partitions, and cleat using a biscuit jointer.
6 Measure and mark two ½ × 2 × 1"-long tenons centered in the shelf ends using a marking gauge (see *Diagram*).
7 Set up your tablesaw and dado-blade set at ⅛"-deep to cut the tenons on the ends of each shelf. Using a miter gauge and a stop block, make the first cut along the shoulder lines. Make repeated passes until one tenon face is cut. Then turn the board over and cut the other tenon face. Repeat this procedure at the other end of shelf, and for the other shelves.

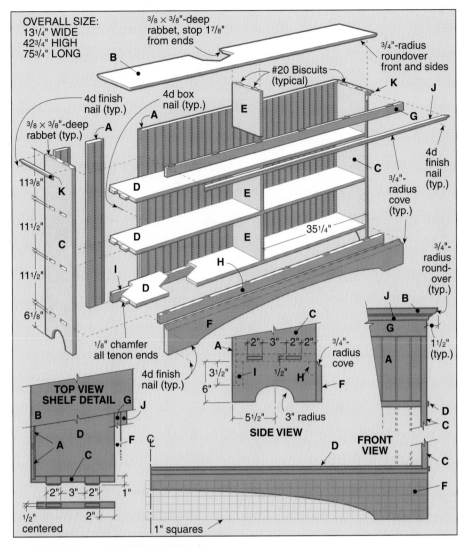

OVERALL SIZE:
13¼" WIDE
42¾" HIGH
75¾" LONG

⅜ × ⅜"-deep rabbet, stop 1⅞" from ends

¾"-radius roundover front and sides

#20 Biscuits (typical)

4d finish nail (typ.)

4d box nail (typ.)

⅜ × ⅜"-deep rabbet (typ.)

11⅜"

11½"

11½"

6⅛"

⅛" chamfer all tenon ends

4d finish nail (typ.)

4d finish nail (typ.)

4d finish nail (typ.)

¾"-radius cove (typ.)

35¼"

¾"-radius round-over (typ.)

1½" (typ.)

¾"-radius cove

TOP VIEW
SHELF DETAIL

SIDE VIEW

3½"
6"
5½" 3" radius
2" 3" 2" 2"
½"
3" radius

FRONT VIEW

2" 3" 2"
½"
2"
1"
centered

1" squares

CUTTING LIST

Key	Qty.	Description & Size
A	1	**Back,** ⅜ × 72 × 39⅞"
B	1	**Top,** ¾ × 13¼ × 75¾"
C	2	**Side,** ¾ × 11 × 41"
D	3	**Shelf,** ¾ × 10⅝ × 73¼"
E	3	**Partition,** ¾ × 10⅝ × 11¼"
F	1	**Apron,** ¾ × 6 × 72¾"
G	1	**Top rail,** ¾ × 2½ × 72¾"
H	1	**Bottom rail,** ¾ × 2 × 71¼"
I	1	**Cleat,** ¾ × 3½ × 71¼"
J	1	**Front trim,** ¾ × ¾ × 74½"
K	2	**Side trim,** ¾ × ¾ × 11¾"

Note: All wood is pine stock, except for the back A, which is tongue-and-groove wainscoting, and the front trim J and side trim K, which are ¾" cove molding.

Misc.: Glue, 4d finish nails, 4d box nails, #20 biscuits.

portable drill and drum sander.
18 Round over the bottom edge of the front and sides of the top using router and a ¾" round-over bit.

Assembling the bookcase

Before assembling the bookcase, make sure you have enough bar clamps to secure the glued pieces.
1 Dry-fit apron and rails to check assembly.
2 Attach cleat and bottom rail to bottom shelf with glue and biscuits.
3 Connect the remaining shelves and partitions, using glue and biscuits. Clamp and let dry.
4 Attach sides to the shelves with glue. Clean excess glue off tenons.
5 Attach the back to the shelves, using 4d box nails. Check for square as you nail.
6 Attach the top to the sides, upper partition, and back using glue and biscuits. Clamp, and let dry.
7 Miter cut the front trim (J) and side trim (K) from ¾" pine cove molding. Before cutting, measure to make sure these pieces will fit actual dimensions.
8 Attach the front and side trim pieces using glue and 4d finish nails. Cross-nail the miter joints on the trim pieces.
9 Use glue and 4d finish nails to attach apron to bottom rail and sides.
10 Set all nails and fill the holes with wood putty.
11 Finish bookcase with tung oil.

8 Cut out remaining waste between the tenons with a coping saw. Square the cuts with a 1" chisel.
9 File a ⅛" chamfer all around the edges of the tenons with a cabinet file. Sand the tenons smooth.
10 Measure and mark ½ × 2"-wide mortises on the side pieces to hold the shelf tenons. Cut the mortises, using a hand drill and a ½"-diameter straight bit. Using a portable drill guide, drill holes through the workpiece, clearing waste until the mortises can be

squared with a mortise chisel.
11 Rout a ⅜ × ⅜"-deep stopped rabbet in the top for the back, using a router and a ⅜" rabbet bit. Rabbet should stop 1⅞" from each end of the workpiece. Square the ends of rabbet with a 10" cabinet chisel.
12 Rout a ⅜ × ⅜"-deep rabbet on the inside back edge of the side pieces to hold the back, using a router and a ⅜" rabbet bit.
13 Measure and mark a 3"-radius arc on the bottom ends of the side pieces using a compass.
14 Cut out the 3"-radius arcs on the sides using a sabersaw.
15 Transfer the apron pattern (see *Diagram*) to the apron, then cut out the pattern contour on the bottom of apron using a sabersaw.
16 Rout a ¾"-radius cove on the top outside edge of the apron.
17 Sand inside edges of the arcs on side pieces and apron using a

Media Center

A roomy storage cabinet for all your electronics.

Build the carcass panels

Because there is no face frame, this entertainment center gains its structural strength from the plywood sides, shelves, and dividers, which are edged with solid pine nosing.

1 Cut the fixed shelves (X). Rout a $\frac{3}{4} \times \frac{3}{8}$"-deep dado across the top center of the top fixed shelf, where the divider (J) will fit.

2 Rout a $\frac{3}{4} \times \frac{3}{8}$"-deep dado across the bottom center of the bottom fixed shelf, where the divider (Z) will fit.

3 Cut nosing pieces (W). Lay out and cut slots for #0 biscuits spaced 4" apart for joining the nosing to the shelves. Join the shelves and nosing pieces with glue and biscuits, so the ends of the nosing are $\frac{3}{8}$" from the ends of the shelf, and clamp them together until the glue dries.

4 Cut a hole for a heat vent in the back center of each shelf, starting 1" from the back. The exact size of the cutouts will depend on the size of your heat vents.

5 Cut the top divider (J) and nosing (K). Attach the nosing to the divider with glue and biscuits spaced 4" apart.

6 Cut $1\frac{3}{8} \times 4$"-wide notches in the top and bottom rear corners of the divider, to provide space around

CUTTING LIST

Key	Qty.	Description & Size
A	2	**Upper door panel,** pine $\frac{3}{4} \times 16\frac{11}{16} \times 35\frac{3}{4}$"
B	2	**Lower door panel,** pine $\frac{3}{4} \times 16\frac{11}{16} \times 20\frac{3}{8}$"
C	8	**Door rail,** pine $\frac{3}{4} \times 2\frac{1}{2} \times 20\frac{15}{16}$"
D	3	**Upper door stile,** pine $\frac{3}{4} \times 2\frac{1}{2} \times 40$"
E	3	**Lower door stile,** pine $\frac{3}{4} \times 2\frac{1}{2} \times 24\frac{5}{8}$"
F	1	**Lower center stile,** pine $\frac{3}{4} \times 3 \times 24\frac{5}{8}$"
G	1	**Upper center stile,** pine $\frac{3}{4} \times 3 \times 40$"
H	8	**Shelf nosing,** pine $\frac{3}{4} \times 2\frac{3}{4} \times 19\frac{3}{4}$"
I	8	**Shelf,** plywood $\frac{3}{4} \times 20\frac{1}{2} \times 19\frac{3}{4}$"
J	1	**Upper divider,** plywood $\frac{3}{4} \times 21 \times 14\frac{7}{8}$"
K	1	**Upper divider nosing,** pine $\frac{3}{4} \times 2\frac{3}{4} \times 14\frac{7}{8}$"
L	1	**Base top nosing,** pine $\frac{3}{4} \times \frac{3}{4} \times 42$"
M	1	**Base top,** plywood $\frac{3}{4} \times 23 \times 42$"
N	1	**Bottom nosing,** pine $\frac{3}{4} \times 1 \times 40\frac{1}{2}$"
O	1	**Cabinet bottom,** plywood $\frac{3}{4} \times 22\frac{3}{4} \times 40\frac{1}{2}$"
P	2	**Side,** plywood $\frac{3}{4} \times 23\frac{1}{4} \times 67\frac{5}{8}$"
Q	1	**Top,** plywood $\frac{3}{4} \times 25\frac{5}{8} \times 45\frac{1}{4}$"
R	1	**Back,** plywood $\frac{1}{4} \times 41\frac{1}{4} \times 66\frac{5}{8}$"
S	1	**Stretcher,** pine $\frac{3}{4} \times 2\frac{7}{8} \times 40\frac{1}{2}$"
T	4	**Support block,** pine $\frac{3}{4} \times 1\frac{3}{4} \times 2\frac{1}{2}$"
U	1	**Crown molding,** pine $\frac{3}{4} \times 2\frac{5}{16} \times 48\frac{1}{8}$"
V	2	**Crown molding,** pine $\frac{3}{4} \times 2\frac{5}{16} \times 27\frac{1}{16}$"
W	2	**Fixed shelf nosing,** pine $\frac{3}{4} \times 1\frac{1}{2} \times 40\frac{1}{2}$"
X	2	**Fixed shelf,** plywood $\frac{3}{4} \times 23 \times 41\frac{1}{4}$"
Y	1	**Nosing,** pine $\frac{3}{4} \times 2\frac{3}{4} \times 25$"
Z	1	**Lower divider,** plywood $\frac{3}{4} \times 21 \times 25$"
AA	2	**Side trim,** pine $\frac{7}{16} \times 4\frac{1}{4} \times 25\frac{1}{4}$"
BB	1	**Front trim,** pine $\frac{7}{16} \times 4\frac{1}{4} \times 42\frac{7}{8}$"
CC	1	**Front base,** pine $1\frac{1}{2} \times 3\frac{1}{2} \times 42$"
DD	3	**Base supports,** pine $1\frac{1}{2} \times 3\frac{1}{2} \times 21\frac{1}{2}$"
EE	2	**Side nosing,** pine $\frac{3}{4} \times 1 \times 67\frac{5}{8}$"

Note: All plywood is pine.

Misc.: glue, #8 × 1¼" flathead wood screws, finish nails (8d, 4d), four 1⅜ × 2" magnetic touch latches, ⅝" wire brads, #0 biscuits, shelf supports, three heat vents, wire organizer, eight butt hinges (2 × 1⅜"), wooden grommet.

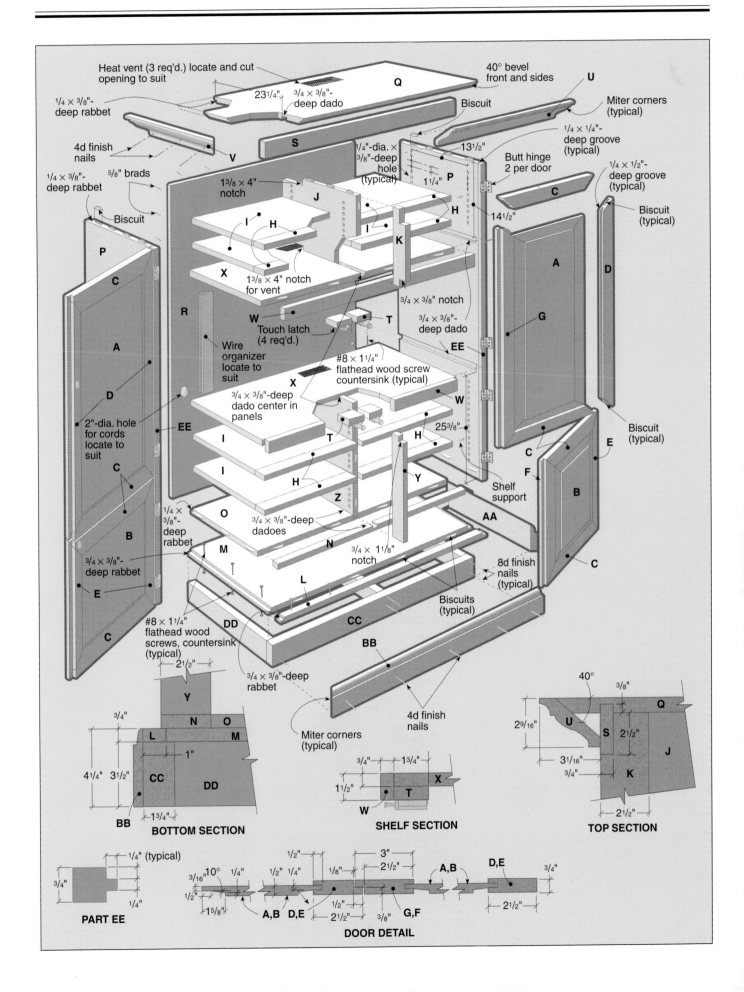

Heat vent (3 req'd.) locate and cut opening to suit

40° bevel front and sides

$1/4 \times 3/8"$- deep rabbet

$3/4 \times 3/8"$- deep dado

23 1/4"

Q

Biscuit

Miter corners (typical)

U

$1/4 \times 1/4"$- deep groove (typical)

4d finish nails

S

$1/4"$-dia. $\times$ 3/8"-deep hole (typical)

13 1/2"

Butt hinge 2 per door

V

1 1/4"

P

$1/4 \times 3/8"$- deep rabbet

$5/8"$ brads

$1 3/8 \times 4"$ notch

H

14 1/2"

C

$1/4 \times 1/2"$- deep groove (typical)

Biscuit

J

H

Biscuit (typical)

P

I

H

I

D

C

K

A

A

X

$1 3/8 \times 4"$ notch for vent

$3/4 \times 3/8"$ notch

G

R

$3/4 \times 3/8"$- deep dado

Wire organizer locate to suit

W

Touch latch (4 req'd.)

T

EE

D

#8 $\times$ 1 1/4" flathead wood screw countersink (typical)

W

2"-dia. hole for cords locate to suit

EE

X

$3/4 \times 3/8"$-deep dado center in panels

25 3/8"

E

I

T

H

C

C

I

H

Y

F

B

Shelf support

C

O

Z

$3/4 \times 3/8"$-deep dadoes

$1/4 \times 3/8"$- deep rabbet

M

N

AA

$3/4 \times 1 1/8"$ notch

C

$3/4 \times 3/8"$- deep rabbet

L

8d finish nails (typical)

E

#8 $\times$ 1 1/4" flathead wood screws, countersink (typical)

DD

$3/4 \times 3/8"$-deep rabbet

Biscuits (typical)

C

CC

Miter corners (typical)

BB

4d finish nails

BOTTOM SECTION

2 1/2"

Y

3/4"

N

O

L

1"

M

4 1/4"

3 1/2"

CC

DD

BB

1 3/4"

SHELF SECTION

3/4"

1 3/4"

X

1 1/2"

T

W

40°

3/8"

U

S

Q

2 9/16"

2 1/2"

J

3 1/16"

3/4"

K

2 1/2"

TOP SECTION

1/4" (typical)

3/4"

1/4"

PART EE

3/16"

10°

1/4"

1/2"

1/4"

3"

2 1/2"

1/8"

A,B

D,E

3/4"

1/2"

1 5/8"

A,B

D,E

1/2"

2 1/2"

G,F

3/8"

2 1/2"

DOOR DETAIL

the heat vents. Cut a ¾ × 2½"-high notch in the top front corner to fit around the stretcher, and a ¾ × ⅜"-high notch in the bottom front corner of the nosing to fit around the shelf nosing.

7 Cut the bottom divider (Z) and nosing (Y). Attach the nosing to the divider with glue and biscuits spaced 4" apart.

8 Cut a 1⅜ × 4"-wide notch in the top rear corner of the divider to provide space around the heat vents. Cut a ¾ × 1⅛"-high notch in the top front corner to fit around the shelf nosing.

9 Cut the cabinet bottom (O) and nosing (N). Attach the nosing to the bottom with glue and biscuits spaced 4" apart.

10 Rout a ¼ × ⅜"-deep rabbet along the back top edge of the bottom panel, where the back (R) will fit.

11 Rout a ¾ × ⅜"-deep dado across the center of the cabinet bottom, where the divider (Z) will fit.

12 Cut the top (Q) to size, beveling the sides and front to 40°. Rout a ¾ × ⅜"-deep groove across the bottom face of the top. The back edge of the groove should be 23¼" from the back edge of the top panel. Rout a ¼ × ⅜"-deep rabbet along the inside back edge where the back panel (R) will fit.

13 Cut the sides (P). Rout two ¾ × ⅜"-deep dadoes on the inside face of each side panel, where the fixed shelves will fit. The top edge of the top dado should be 14½" from the top of the side panel; the bottom edge of the bottom dado should be 25⅜" from the bottom of the side panel.

14 Rout a centered ¼ × ¼" groove along the front edge of both side panels, where the side nosing will fit. Rout a ¼ × ⅜"-deep rabbet along the inside back edge of each panel, where the back panel (R) will fit.

15 Cut the side nosing pieces (EE). Form ¼" tongues on one edge of each nosing piece by cutting ¼ × ¼" rabbets on both sides, using a router table.

16 Join the side nosing pieces to the sides with glue and clamp the pieces together until the glue dries.

17 Cut the stretcher (S) and back (R).

Assemble the carcass

1 Remove dried glue from all glued-up pieces. Sand the top, shelves, bottom, sides, and dividers to finished smoothness.

2 Cut three 10 × 6" rectangular scraps of ¾" plywood as an aid for holding the panels perpendicular.

3 Cut biscuit slots for joining cabinet bottom (O) and stretcher (S) to the sides (P). Bottom panel will be installed centered at ¾" above the bottom edge of the sides. Glue #0 biscuits into the slots in the side panels.

4 Lay a side panel on sawhorses, with the inside surface facing up. Glue the fixed shelves and the cabinet bottom in place, and brace them upright by clamping the plywood scraps alongside each piece.

5 Glue the stretcher (S) in place, then glue the remaining side panel over the upright pieces. Check to make sure the carcass is square, then let the glue dry completely.

6 Lay out and cut biscuit slots in the top edges of the side panels

and top divider, and in the top (Q). Glue the top divider into the top fixed shelf, propping it up with a scrap piece of plywood. Attach the top with glue and #0 biscuits.

7 Nail the back in place inside the rabbets using wire brads (do not glue the back).

Build & attach the base

The base of the entertainment center will be covered by a 4¼" trim molding. If you cannot find a supplier for this trim, you can make it yourself by routing an ogee profile on 4¼" pine stock.

1 Cut the base top (M) and the base top nosing (L). Lay out and cut biscuit slots every 4", then attach the nosing to the base top with glue and #0 biscuits. Clamp the pieces together until the glue dries.

2 Cut ¾ × ⅜"-deep rabbets along the top side edges of the glued-up base, where the sides (P) will fit.

3 Cut the 2 × 4 base supports (DD) and the base front (CC). Attach the base top to the base supports and front with glue and countersunk #8 × 1¼" flathead wood screws. Reinforce the base corners with 8d finish nails.

4 Lay the cabinet carcass on its back, and attach the base to the carcass with glue and #8 × 1¼" flathead wood screws driven through the base top and into the cabinet bottom.

5 Cut the trim pieces (AA, BB), miter-cutting the ends at 45°. Attach the trim with glue and 4d finish nails, lock-nailing the corners.

Build the doors

The panel doors are framed with mitered rails and stiles. The center stiles on the right side doors are slightly wider, because the rabbeted edges of these stiles will extend behind the adjoining doors. The raised panels are made from glued-up ¾" pine.

1 Cut the door rails (C) and stiles (D, E, F, G), miter-cutting the ends at 45°. On the center stiles (G, F), the miter cuts should be set in ½" from the edge, leaving a flattened tip on each end (see *Diagram*).

2 Using a router table, rout a centered ¼ × ½"-deep groove along the inside edge of each rail and stile, where the raised panels will fit.

3 Lay out and cut slots for #0 biscuits in the mitered ends of the rails and stiles. Test-fit the door frames and set them aside.

4 Cut the upper and lower door panels (A, B). On one side of each panel, make ⅛"-deep shoulder cuts for the bevels along all four edges, 1¾" from the edges.

5 To complete the bevels, set your tablesaw blade at a 10° angle and 1⅝" depth. Set the tablesaw fence ³⁄₁₆" from the edge of the blade. Complete the bevel cuts on all four edges of each panel, holding the panel upright against the

fence as you feed it across the blade.

6 Using a dado-blade set, rabbet the last ½" of the beveled edges of the panels, forming ³⁄₁₆"-thick tongues that will fit into the grooves in the rails and stiles.

7 Sand the rails, stiles, and panels to finished smoothness. Assemble the door rails and stiles around the panels with glue and #0 biscuits (do not glue the panels). Clamp the pieces together until the glue dries.

8 On the back side of the left upper and lower doors, cut ½ × ⅜"-deep rabbets along edge of the inside stile. On the front side of the right doors, cut matching ½ × ⅜"-deep rabbets. These overlapping rabbets will help align the doors when closed.

Make the adjustable shelves

1 Cut the shelves (I) from ¾" plywood. Cut the shelf nosing (H) from pine.

2 Lay out and cut biscuit slots in the nosing and the front edge of the shelves, spaced 4" apart. Attach the nosing pieces to the shelves with glue and #0 biscuits.

3 When glue is dry, slightly round over the nosing with sandpaper.

4 Lay out and drill ¼ × ⅜"-deep holes in the sides and dividers for the shelf pins that will hold the

adjustable shelves (see *Diagram*). A scrap of Peg-Board® makes a good template for aligning the holes accurately. On the dividers, offset the holes on each side so you don't drill completely through the dividers.

Finish the project

1 Cut the support blocks (T) for the touch latches. Attach the blocks behind the nosing pieces for the fixed shelves, using countersunk #8 × 1¼" screws.

2 Cut the crown molding pieces (U, V), miter-cutting the ends that will form the corners. Attach the crown molding to the cabinet with 4d finish nails, lock-nailing the corners.

3 Set all finish nails, and fill the holes with putty. Sand when dry.

4 Finish the cabinet carcass, the doors, and shelves to your taste (we used rustic oak penetrating oil).

5 Install the heat vents in the cutouts in the fixed shelves and cabinet top, as directed by the manufacturer.

6 You may wish to install plastic wire organizer tracks along the backs of the shelves depending on the types of electronic components you use. Attach them inside the cabinet with wire nails or with heavy-duty double-stick tape.

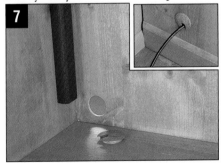

7 Cut a 2" exit hole for the wiring in the side or back, as needed, and trim the hole with a wooden grommet finished to match.

8 Mount the doors to the sides with butt hinges attached 2" from the top and bottom of each door.

9 Install magnetic touch latches on the spacers and the metal strike plates on the corresponding locations on the doors, following manufacturer's directions.

Country Cabinet

Make this country cabinet from pine and stencil it for added country flavor.

Primarily functional in origin, country furniture represents the handiwork of rural American farmers and woodcrafters of the eighteenth century who made their own furniture. The ornate furniture of the day, modeled after European styles and found in the cities, was beyond the means of the average family. Instead, many people made furniture themselves, omitting ornamentation that required extra cost, materials, and time to make.

Country furniture was made from inexpensive, readily available local woods. Pine was one of the woods most commonly used. Still inexpensive and readily available, pine is a good choice for this cabinet.

Most country furniture was finished with durable opaque paint or a thin wash. However, we finished this country cabinet with a light walnut oil stain, then added a hand-painted stencil, using acrylic paint. You can make this cabinet as rustic as you'd like by

choosing your own finish.

Building the carcass

Edge-glue ¾"-thick pine to make the top, sides, and shelves. Stock for the glue-up should be approximately 1" longer and wider than the final dimensions shown. Reverse the grain when gluing to minimize warping.

1 Cut and edge-glue enough ¾"-thick, 47¼"-long pine to make the sides (A). Clamp and let dry.

2 Cut and edge-glue enough

CUTTING LIST

Key	Qty.	Description & Size
A	2	**Side,** ¾ × 17¼ × 46¼"
B	1	**Top,** ¾ × 20 × 34"
C	2	**Shelf,** ¾ × 17 × 29¼"
D	1	**Apron,** ¾ × 5 × 30"
E	1	**Back,** ¼ × 29¼ × 39½"
F	1	**Drawer support,** 2 × 2⅝ × 17"
G	1	**Back stiffener,** ¾ × 1 × 28½"
H	2	**Stile,** ¾ × 3 × 41¼"
I	3	**Rail,** ¾ × 3 × 24"
J	2	**Drawer front and back,** ¾ × 4½ × 23⅞"
K	2	**Drawer side,** ¾ × 4½ × 17"
L	1	**Drawer false front,** ¾ × 5½ × 25"
M	1	**Drawer bottom,** ¼ × 16¼ × 23⅜"
N	2	**Door,** ¾ × 12 7/16 × 28⅝"
O	4	**Door stiffener,** ¾ × 2 × 11"
P	2	**Corner block,** ¾ × 5 15/16 × 5 15/16" (45°)

Note: All wood is pine, except for the back E and drawer bottom M, which are finish pine plywood, and drawer support F, which is maple.

Misc.: Glue, #0 biscuits, ¾" wood knobs, flathead wood screws (#6 × 1¼", #8 × 1¼", #8 × 2½", #10 × 2"), 1" wire nails, ⅜ × 1½"-long dowels, flush overlay hinges, magnetic catches.

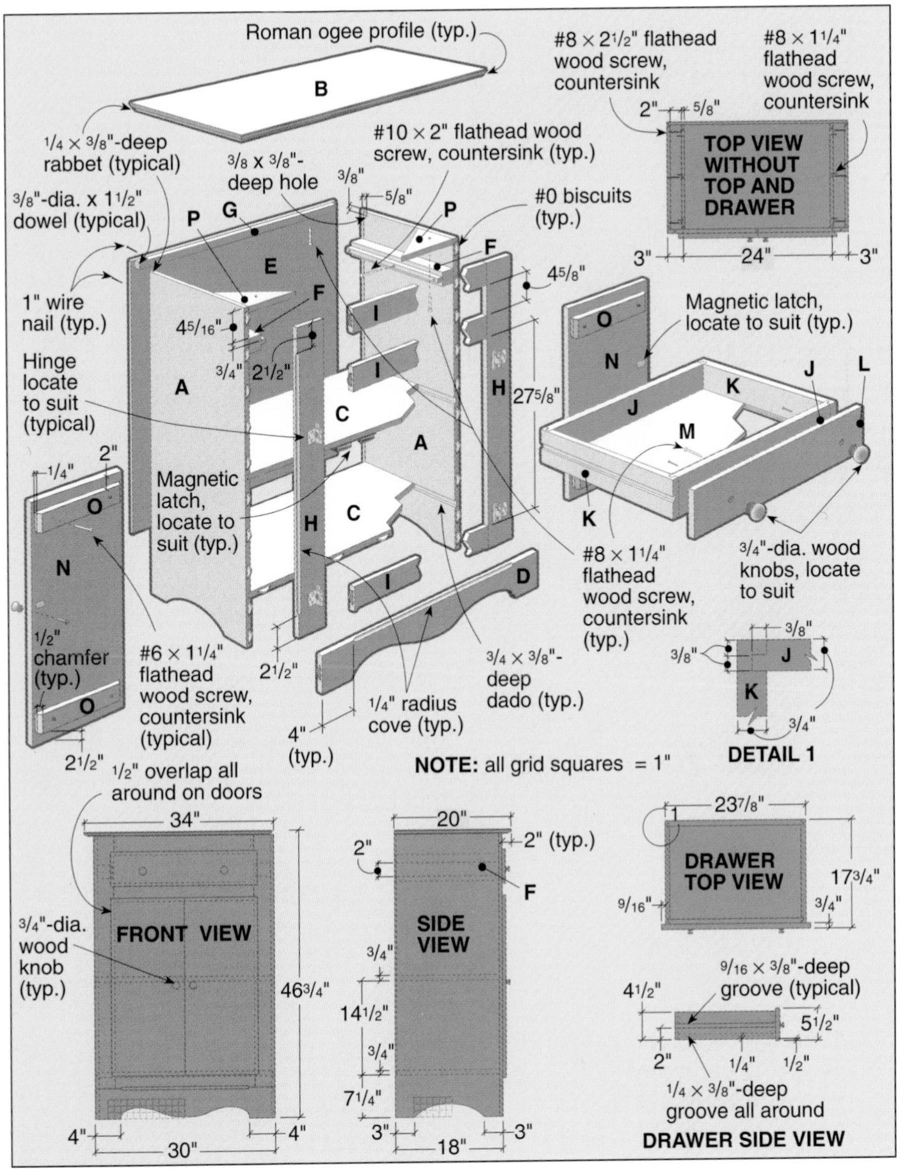

¾"-thick, 35"-long pine to make the top (B). Clamp and let dry.

3 Cut and edge-glue enough ¾"-thick, 30¼"-long pine to make the shelves (C). Clamp and let dry.

4 Cut the apron (D) from ¾"-thick pine.

5 Cut the back (E) from ¼"-thick finish pine plywood.

6 Joint one side edge of the top, sides, and shelves. Then mark, ripcut, and crosscut the pieces to their finished sizes.

7 Cut a ¼ × ⅜"-deep rabbet on the back inside edges of the sides and top to hold the back. Use a tablesaw and dado-blade set.

8 Measure and mark the dado locations on the sides for the two shelves. The bottom edges of the dadoes are located 7¼" and 21¾" from the bottom, respectively (see *Diagram*, cabinet side view).

BUYER'S TIP

When buying pine for country furniture, don't be too concerned with avoiding knots. You can search through the most economical grade of pine, #2 common, to find enough clear pine to make your project knot-free. Or you can use pine with visible knots to lend character and visual interest to the finish. Again, choosing your lumber from #2 common can give you plenty of knots and is much less expensive than buying true "knotty pine." Be sure to lay out the project so knots do not interfere with joinery or hardware.

WOODWORKER'S TIP

When edge-gluing stock and assembling face frames, keep a metal straightedge handy. Glue and clamp the assembly as needed. Be sure to alternate clamps on the top and bottom of the glue-up. When the clamps have been tightened, check the face with the metal straightedge to make sure the glue-up is flat. If the top is bowed up, release pressure on bottom clamps. Do the opposite to correct downward bowing. Check diagonally across face-frame joints.

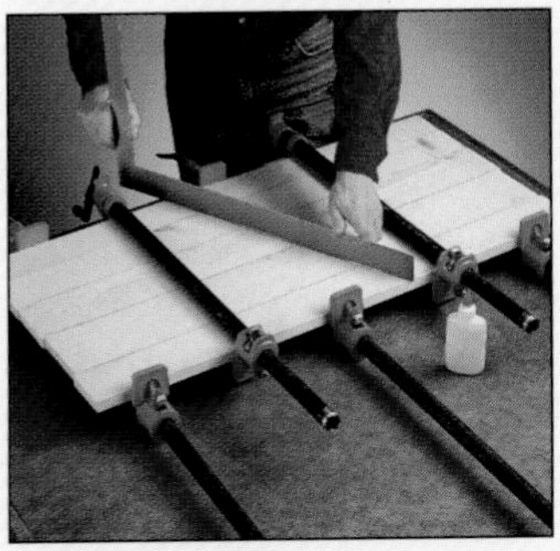

9 Cut ¾ × ⅜"-deep dadoes on the sides.

10 Transfer the curved cut-out profile to the bottom of the apron (see *Diagram*, front view, for pattern information).
11 Transfer the curved cut-out profile to the bottom of the side pieces (see *Diagram*, side view, for pattern information).
12 Cut out the curved patterns on the apron and side pieces using a bandsaw.
13 Sand the inside edge of the pattern curves on the apron and sides to finished smoothness.
14 Rout a 22"-long, ¼"-radius stopped cove on the front top edge of the apron, stopped 4" from each end (see *Diagram*, exploded view).
15 Cut the decorative profile into the bottom edge of the front and sides of the top, using a router and a Roman ogee bit.
16 Sand the top, sides, apron, and shelves to 220-grit smoothness.
17 Create stock for the drawer supports (F) from leftover hardwood (we used maple). Cut to length.
18 On your router table, cut a ⁷⁄₁₆ × ¾"-deep rabbet on the top and bottom of one 2" side of each sup-

port to produce a ½ × ⁷⁄₁₆"-deep tongue to fit the groove in the drawer sides. Round over the edges of the tongue to prevent splintering, using sandpaper.
19 Measure and mark the locations on the sides for the drawer supports so the top edges of the supports are 4⁵⁄₁₆" from the top.
20 Drill four shank holes counterbored ½" deep for #10 × 2" wood screws through the drawer support. Locate two of the holes in the rabbeted strip under the drawer slide tongue and two above the drawer slide tongue.
21 Clamp the drawer support to the side and mark its location. Then drill ½"-deep pilot holes in the side through the shank holes in the drawer support.
22 Unclamp the drawer support, apply glue to it, and realign it on the side, using the alignment marks. Clamp in place using bar clamps.

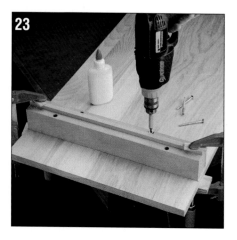

23 Drive #10 × 2" wood screws through the drawer support into the side. Keep clamped until dry.
24 Cut the back stiffener (G) from ¾" stock. Drill ⅜ × 1¼"-deep holes in the ends for dowel joints (see *Diagram*).
25 Drill ⅜ × ⅜"-deep holes in the sides for dowel joints, centered ⅝" from the back edge and ⅜" from the top edge so back stiffener will be flush with the back and top.
26 Attach the back stiffener to the upper corners of the sides with glue and ⅜ × 1½" dowels. Brace the sides for assembly by placing the shelves temporarily in the

dadoes in the sides.
27 Remove the shelves one at a time, apply glue, and install the shelves permanently in the dadoes in the sides.
28 Attach the back to the sides using 1" wire nails, squaring the sides as you go. Do not use glue.

Building the face frame

1 Cut the stiles (H) and rails (I) from ¾"-thick pine.
2 Rout a 36¼"-long, ¼"-radius stopped cove on the front outside corner of the stiles. Stop the cove 2½" from each end (see *Diagram*, exploded view).
3 Measure and mark slots for #0 biscuits in the stiles and rails (see *Diagram*, exploded view). Align the middle rail so there is 27⅞" between the middle and lower rails. Cut the slots using a biscuit joiner.
4 Dry-fit the face frame and biscuits to check the assembly fit.

5 Assemble the stiles and rails to form the face frame, using glue and #0 biscuits. Clamp the pieces using bar clamps. Set aside to dry.
6 Measure and mark slot locations for #0 biscuits in the sides, stiles, bottom shelf, bottom rail, and apron where they join. Space the biscuits so their centers are 6-8" apart. Then cut the slots using a biscuit joiner.
7 Dry-fit the assembly to check the fit.
8 Attach the apron to the sides using glue and #0 biscuits.
9 Attach the face frame to the sides and bottom shelf, using glue and #0 biscuits. Set aside to dry.

Making the drawer

1 Cut the drawer front and back (J), drawer sides (K), and drawer false front (L) from ¾"-thick pine.
2 Cut the drawer bottom (M) from ¼"-thick pine.
3 Cut a ¼ × ⅜"-deep groove on the insides of the drawer front, drawer back, and drawer sides, ¼" from the bottom of each piece, to hold the drawer bottom. Use a tablesaw and dado-blade set.
4 Cut a 9⁄16 × ⅜"-deep groove on the outside of the drawer sides 2" up from the bottom to slide over the drawer support.
5 Cut a ⅜ × ⅜"-deep rabbet on the outside ends of the drawer front and back.
6 Cut ⅜ × ⅜"-deep dadoes ⅜" from the ends on the insides of the drawer sides.
7 Sand the drawer parts to finished smoothness.
8 Glue and assemble the drawer front, back, and sides around the bottom. Do not glue the bottom. Clamp the assembled drawer, check for square, and let dry.
9 Measure and mark pilot holes on the front of the drawer false front for the pull knobs. Locate the holes to suit your design sense, but center them vertically on the drawer false front for stability. Drill the countersunk pilot holes using a drill press.

10 With the drawer in the cabinet, center and clamp the drawer false front over the drawer front. Then drive #6 × 1¼" screws at the pull knob locations to attach temporarily the drawer false front to the drawer.
11 Remove the drawer from the opening and place it facedown, resting on the drawer false front. Use a pencil to outline the position of the drawer front on the back of the drawer false front.
12 Drill countersunk shank holes for #8 × 1¼" flathead wood screws in the back of the drawer front and pilot holes inside the shank holes in the back of the drawer false front while the drawer false front is still temporarily attached.
13 Unscrew the drawer false front. Reattach it permanently to the drawer front, screwing through the pilot and shank holes in the drawer front into the drawer false front. Use glue and #8 × 1¼" flathead wood screws. Make sure the outline of the drawer front on the back of the drawer false front is aligned exactly with the drawer front.
14 Extend the holes for the pull knobs through the drawer front.
15 Attach the pull knobs to the drawer with the pull knob screws.

Making and fitting the doors

1 Edge-glue enough ¾"-thick pine for the doors (N). Stock for the glue-up should be 1" longer and wider than the final dimensions shown. Clamp and let dry.
2 Joint one edge of each door. Then mark, ripcut, and crosscut the doors to their finished size.
3 Cut the door stiffeners (O) from ¾"-thick pine. Cut a 15° chamfer ½" deep on the ends using a tablesaw. Leave ¼" unchamfered on each end (see *Diagram*).
4 Remove excess glue from the doors. Sand the doors to finished smoothness.
5 Measure and mark the inside faces of the doors with the locations of the door stiffeners. Place all of the stiffeners ¾" from the sides. Locate the top stiffeners 2" from the top of the doors and the bottom stiffeners 2½" from the bottom of the doors.
6 Drill four countersunk shank holes through each door stiffener for #6 × 1¼" wood screws.
7 Drill four pilot holes ⅜" deep in the doors for #6 × 1¼" wood screws. Drill the pilot holes through the shank holes in the door stiffeners.
8 Fasten the stiffeners to the door with glue and screws.
9 Mark the flush overlay hinge locations on the doors and stiles. Make sure the doors overlap the stiles and rails by ½", and leave a maximum gap of ⅛" between doors.
10 Drill pilot holes for hinges on the doors and stiles using a self-centering bit. Then install hinges.
11 Measure, mark, and drill shank holes for the pull knobs on the doors. Center the holes vertically 1" from edges. Then attach knobs.
12 Measure and mark the insides of the doors and center shelf for magnetic catches. The plates on the doors must align with the magnets on the bottom of the center shelf when installed.

Finishing up

1 Cut two corner blocks (P) from one piece of squared ¾ × 6 × 6" pine by cutting across the piece diagonally.
2 Drill a 5⁄64"-diameter shank hole for #8 × 1¼" wood screws in the center of each block to fasten the top. Drill 5⁄64" pocket screw holes in each corner to fasten the blocks to the face frame and sides.
3 Drill four evenly spaced countersunk shank holes for #8 × 1¼" wood screws in the back stiffener for attaching the top.
4 Center the top over the cabinet. Check the overhang on the front and sides.
5 Clamp the top to carcass. Drive screws through the corner blocks and stiffener to attach the top to the carcass.
6 Finish and seal the cabinet as desired.
7 Stencil the cabinet.
8 Apply beeswax to the drawer supports before using the drawers.

Maple Dresser

Fine materials and solid joinery make this dresser stand out.

Honey-colored maple and beveled edge detailing give this dresser an appealing look. The drawer pulls, made of contrasting walnut, add a unique contemporary touch.

Make the dust panels

We used basic frame-and-panel construction to make the dust panels. Although the dresser has only three dust panels, we built a fourth frame without a panel, to which the top is fastened.

1 Cut the panel stiles (H) and rails (G) for the three dust panels and the frame supporting the top.
2 Cut a ¼ × ⅜"-deep groove centered on the inside edge of three sets of the panel stiles and rails, where the dust panels will fit.
3 Cut ¼ × ⅜"-long tenons at the ends of all of the rails, to fit in the grooves in the stiles.
4 Cut the three lauan dust panels (I). Finish-sand the panels.

5 Glue and clamp the three dust panels. Do not apply glue to the panel edges. Glue and clamp the fourth frame for the top as well, then check for square, let dry.
6 Drill ³⁄₁₆" countersunk holes through the top frame (see *Diagram*). These holes will be used to

attach the top, so the countersinks should be located on the bottom of the frame.

Make the carcass

1 Cut the sides (B) out of ¾" maple plywood. Score the cutting lines with a utility knife before sawing to prevent chipping the veneer.
2 Cut ⅜ × ¼"-deep rabbets along the back edge of the sides to hold the back. Sand the sides to finished smoothness.
3 Lay out and cut biscuit slots for #10 biscuits in the ends of the dust panels and top frame and the dresser sides. Slots should be spaced 4" apart.
4 Lay one side piece on a flat surface with the biscuit slots facing up. Cut four 2 × 6 × 12" blocks from scrap wood to brace the frames while you're attaching them to the side (see *Diagram*, side view, for correct location.)

5 Attach the top frame to the side using glue and biscuits. Clamp a block to the frame to hold it upright. Repeat the procedure to at-

tach the remaining dust panels to the side, clamping on opposite sides for each consecutive block.
6 Attach the other side to the dust panels and top frame, using glue and biscuits. Clamp the carcass, check for square, and let glue dry.

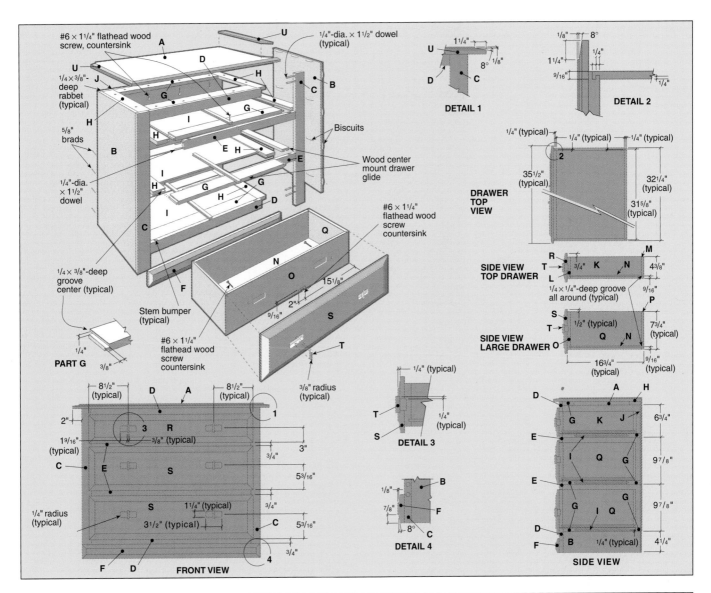

7 Cut the face frame stiles (C), top and bottom rails (D), and cross rails (E). Dry-assemble the face frame so the top edge of the rails are flush with the top edge of the dust panels. Mark the location of the rails on the stiles. Drill two evenly spaced $\frac{3}{8} \times \frac{7}{8}$"-deep holes in the stiles for each rail, and use dowel points to mark the matching holes on the rails. Drill $\frac{3}{8} \times \frac{7}{8}$"-deep holes in the rail ends.

8 Glue and assemble the face frame with $\frac{3}{8} \times 1\frac{1}{2}$" dowels. Clamp and check for square. Let the glue dry.

9 Attach the face frame to the carcass so the edges are flush, using biscuit joints. Check for square and let the glue dry.

10 Drill $\frac{1}{4}$" holes in the top of the cross rails and bottom rail, $\frac{3}{8}$"

CUTTING LIST

Key	Qty.	Description & Size
A	1	**Top,** maple plywood $\frac{3}{4} \times 15\frac{3}{4} \times 35\frac{1}{2}$"
B	2	**Sides,** maple plywood $\frac{3}{4} \times 17\frac{1}{4} \times 31\frac{1}{2}$"
C	2	**Face frame stiles,** maple $\frac{3}{4} \times 3 \times 31\frac{1}{2}$"
D	2	**Top & bottom rails,** maple $\frac{3}{4} \times 2 \times 32\frac{1}{2}$"
E	2	**Cross rails,** maple $\frac{3}{4} \times 1\frac{3}{4} \times 32\frac{1}{2}$"
F	1	**Toe plate,** maple $\frac{3}{4} \times 3\frac{1}{2} \times 38\frac{1}{2}$"
G	8	**Panel rails,** poplar $\frac{3}{4} \times 3 \times 31\frac{3}{4}$"
H	8	**Panel stiles,** poplar $\frac{3}{4} \times 3 \times 17$"
I	3	**Dust panels,** lauan plywood $\frac{1}{4} \times 11\frac{11}{16} \times 31\frac{11}{16}$"
J	1	**Back,** lauan plywood $\frac{1}{4} \times 27\frac{1}{4} \times 37\frac{11}{16}$"
K	2	**Top drawer sides,** maple $\frac{1}{2} \times 4\frac{3}{8} \times 16\frac{1}{2}$"
L	1	**Top drawer front,** maple $\frac{3}{4} \times 4\frac{3}{8} \times 32\frac{1}{4}$"
M	1	**Top drawer back,** maple $\frac{1}{2} \times 4\frac{3}{8} \times 31\frac{3}{4}$"
N	3	**Drawer bottom,** maple plywood $\frac{1}{4} \times 15\frac{1}{8} \times 31\frac{5}{8}$"
O	2	**Large drawer front,** maple $\frac{3}{4} \times 7\frac{3}{4} \times 32\frac{1}{4}$"
P	2	**Large drawer back,** maple $\frac{1}{2} \times 7\frac{3}{4} \times 31\frac{3}{4}$"
Q	4	**Large drawer sides,** maple $\frac{1}{2} \times 7\frac{3}{4} \times 16\frac{1}{2}$"
R	1	**Top drawer false front,** maple $\frac{3}{4} \times 6 \times 35\frac{1}{2}$"
S	2	**Large drawer false fronts,** maple $\frac{3}{4} \times 9\frac{3}{16} \times 35\frac{1}{2}$"
T	6	**Drawer pulls,** walnut $\frac{3}{8} \times \frac{1}{2} \times 1\frac{3}{4}$"
U	1	**Edging,** maple $\frac{3}{4} \times 3\frac{1}{2} \times 8$'

Misc.: glue, #10 biscuits, $\frac{3}{16}$"-dia. stem bumpers, $2 \times \frac{3}{4}$"-high center-mount drawer glide, $\frac{5}{8}$" brads, flathead screws (#6 × 1", #6 × 1$\frac{1}{4}$"), $\frac{3}{8} \times 1\frac{1}{2}$" dowels.

from the front and side edges, for the stem bumpers (plastic caps that support the drawer sides).

Shape the beveled edges

The drawer false fronts, top edging, and the toe plate all have raised-panel shaping, so you'll save time if you prepare these parts all at once. You can use the same steps to prepare all of them, but note that the edging (U) is shaped on only one edge.

1 Cut the toe plate (F), upper drawer false front (R), lower drawer false fronts (S), and edging (U) out of ¾" solid maple.

2 For the edging, cut a 3½" × 8' strip of ¾" thick solid maple. Cut off one 4' piece for the front and two 2' pieces for the sides.

3 To shape the false fronts, outline the raised area on each piece, then set the piece facedown on your tablesaw and make ⅛"-deep definition cuts along the outline.

4 Set your saw blade to an 8° angle, with the blade height at 1¼", and the fence ⁷⁄₁₆" from the blade, then make the beveled cuts with the workpiece set upright against the tablesaw fence. Readjust the blade height as needed (see *Diagram*).

5 Bevel one side of each edging piece, following *steps 2 and 3.*

6 Finish-sand all of the shaped pieces, using 180-grit, then 220-grit sandpaper.

Making the drawers

The drawers are made using five-piece construction, with

drawer corner joints at the front (see photo below), and interlocking dadoes and rabbets at the back (see *Diagram*).

Drawer corner joints are formed with interlocking dadoes. On one of the dadoes, one shoulder is trimmed shorter than the other.

1 Cut the top drawer sides, front and back (K, L, M), and the larger drawer fronts, backs, and sides (O, P, Q).

2 To prepare each front piece for the corner joint, install a ¼"-wide dado blade. Set the drawer front on end against the fence, and cut a ¼ × ⁹⁄₁₆"-deep dado, centered on the edge. Make the same cut in the other end of the front.

3 Trim the shoulders of the dado on the inside face to ¼" in length.

4 Cut a ¼ × ⁹⁄₃₂"-deep dado on the inside face at the front and back ends of each side piece, ¼" in from the ends. The extra depth will leave room for glue when the sides and front are joined.

5 Cut a ¼ × ¼"-deep rabbet at each end of the drawer back, to form tongues that will fit into the dadoed sides.

6 Cut a ¼ × ¼"-deep groove in the sides, back, and front, ⁹⁄₁₆" above the bottom edge, to hold the bottom panel.

7 Cut the drawer bottoms (N) from ¼" plywood; finish-sand all drawer parts.

8 Glue and clamp each drawer's front, back, and sides around the bottom (don't glue the bottom). Check each drawer for square and let the glue dry.

9 Cut both pieces (the runner and

guide) of the center drawer glides to 16¾" long.

10 Flip each drawer upside down and use a ¾" chisel to cut a 2 × ⁹⁄₁₆"-deep notch in the center of the drawer back and front, to hold the drawer guide.

11 Fit the guide in the notches and attach with wood glue and #6 × 1¼" screws driven into the notches.

Complete the drawers

The drawer pulls fit in recesses cut into both the false fronts and the drawer fronts behind them. To cut the recess through both parts at once, you'll need to align and attach the false front to the drawer before cutting the recess.

Spacer strips, made out of scrap wood, make it easier to line up the false fronts on the dresser. Start at the top and work your way down, so any spacing discrepancies will fall at the bottom.

We made a template for cutting the recesses, and then used a router with a bushing guide to cut the actual recesses in the fronts. You'll have to make the opening in your template slightly oversized to compensate for the space taken up by the bushing guide. To determine how much, install the bushing guide and bit in your router, and measure the distance from the edge of the router bit to the outside of the bushing guide. Make the opening in your template larger by this amount.

1 Attach the front of the drawer guide runner to the center of the front dust panel rails using a #6 × 1¼" screw. Rest the back end, unattached, on the back of the dust panel frame.

2 Carefully lift the drawer into the opening, sliding it over the runner. Line up the front of the drawer until it is flush with the cabinet face frame by pivoting the back end of the guide runner side-to-side. Once it's positioned, glue the back end of the drawer runner in place and secure with a #6 × 1¼" screw.

3 Let the glue dry, then from behind the dresser, clamp the drawer to the dust panel frame underneath to keep it from slipping back when you attach the false fronts.

4 Mark the location for the drawer pull recesses on the false fronts (see *Diagram*).

5 To make it easier to line up the false fronts, make two straight-edge spacer strips (1¼" × ¾" wide, and at least 12" long) out of scrap wood.

6 Align the 1¼" spacer so the top edge is flush with the top of the face frame. Clamp it in place.

7 Position the false front for the top drawer against the 1¼" spacer and adjust it so there is 1½" space on each side. Drive #6 × 1¼" screws at the drawer pull locations to attach the false front to the drawer temporarily. Repeat for the other drawers, using the ¾" spacer strip.

8 To complete each drawer, remove it from the opening and stand each one so the false front is facedown. Use a pencil to outline the position of the drawers onto the false fronts.

9 Unscrew the false front from the drawer, then attach it to the drawer with glue and 1¼" screws driven 2" in from the side edges, making sure it is lined up with the outline. Let the glue dry.

10 Make a template for cutting the recesses in the false fronts by cutting a 35½"-wide piece of ½" scrap plywood. Mark the location of the recesses (see *Diagram*).

11 Use a jigsaw to cut out the recess shapes, making sure to cut

the openings slightly oversized to allow for the space that will be taken up by the bushing guides.

12 Position the jig over the false front. Use a router with a straight bit and bushing guide to cut the 1¼ × 3½" recesses. Make several passes, extending the bit ¼" each time, to cut the full 1¼" depth of the recesses for the drawer pulls.

13 Use a ¼" chisel to cut a ⅜ × ¼ × ⅜"-deep notch centered in the top and bottom edge of each recess.

14 Finish-sand the drawer fronts.

Make the drawer pulls

For maximum strength, prepare the drawer pulls with the wood grain running vertically.

1 Cut six 1¾ × ⅜"-wide pieces of ½" walnut. Finish-sand the pulls, rounding over the front edges.

2 Apply glue to the ends of each pull and attach to a drawer false front in the notches in the recess. Clamp in place until the glue dries. Remove excess glue.

Making the top

The top is made out of maple plywood with beveled maple edging. The edging is attached to the front and sides of the top with biscuit joints and is mitered at the front corners—the edging is cut off straight at the back.

1 Cut the plywood top (A).

2 Miter-cut the ends of the edging that meet at the front corners of the top. Lay out and cut slots for biscuits at the miter joints.

3 Clamp the edging to the plywood, so the tops are flush. Mark positions for the biscuit joints about every 4" on the edging and plywood. Unclamp the edging, and cut the biscuit slots.

4 Glue and clamp the edging pieces to each other and to the top using glue and biscuits. Take extra care to make sure the mitered ends are tightly bonded.

5 Let the glue dry, then finish-sand the surfaces, taking care to avoid sanding through the veneer.

Add the back, top & toe plate

1 Cut the back (J) from ¼" lauan plywood. Finish-sand the back.

2 Fasten the back in place with ⅝" brads.

3 Center the top on the carcass, so the back edges are flush and the overhang is equal on both sides. Clamp in place and drive screws from underneath, through the support frame into the top.

4 Drill three equally spaced ⅛" holes through the bottom rail of the dresser.

5 Apply a coat of glue to the back of the toe plate, then attach it so it's flush with the bottom and sides of the carcass. Drive #6 × 1" wood screws through the back side of the stiles and bottom rail into the toe plate.

Finish the dresser

We used a clear water-based polyurethane finish to protect and show off the natural wood tones. Take extra care to apply the finish evenly, following the grain, to avoid being left with a blotchy or uneven surface.

1 Finish-sand the dresser, using 220- to 320-grit sandpaper.

2 Apply the polyurethane to all surfaces, both inside and out. Do not dab it in the corners—instead, place a foam brush in the corner and carefully drag it out in each direction. Let the finish dry thoroughly before continuing.

3 Sand the surface lightly, with 400-grit paper, and carefully wipe it clean.

4 Repeat steps 2 and 3, applying at least three coats of finish. After finishing, install the stem bumpers in the holes at each side.

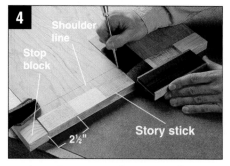

Hope Chest

A special place for cherished possessions, a hope chest is the perfect coming-of-age gift.

Hope chest: The name itself is rich with images of fond anticipation and the passing of blessings from one generation to another. For such a treasured item, a simple box or trunk just won't do. A hope chest should be beautiful and built to last a lifetime, and our design is both. And because it was built by a loved one, this hope chest will be even more special.

The hope chest shown here is built as two sections: a spacious, cedar-lined trunk for storing fine linens; and a base with three drawers that serves as a pedestal for the upper trunk. A divider panel with protruding walnut trim separates the two sections, while

highlighting the walnut lid.

Because all the visible surfaces of our hope chest are wide panels of glued-up hardwood, carefully choosing and gluing-up the walnut and cherry stock is crucial to the success of the project. Allow at least a week to make and dry the panels before you cut the parts. Make panels slightly larger than the finished sizes of the parts.

Building the trunk

1 Cut the sides (C) and the front and back (B) to finished size from glued-up cherry panels, using a jointer and tablesaw to make sure the panels are square.

2 Use a marking gauge to draw lines along the side edges on both faces of the front, back, and side pieces, ¾" from the edges on each workpiece. These lines (called shoulder lines) will mark the depth of the box joints.

3 Cut a 1½" × 15" strip of scrap wood to use as a story stick. Mark a box joint layout onto the story stick—fingers and notches should

be 2½" high. Shade in every other section with a pencil.

4 Set the workpiece on your bench, and butt a stop block

against the top or bottom edge. Secure the stop block and the workpiece to your workbench, then butt one end of the story stick against the stop block. Use a try square to extend joint lines onto the workpieces from the story stick and mark the lines with an awl. Begin with a finger at the top edge of the front and back, and start with a notch at the tops of the sides.

5 Use a Japanese dovetail saw (dozuki) to cut along the short

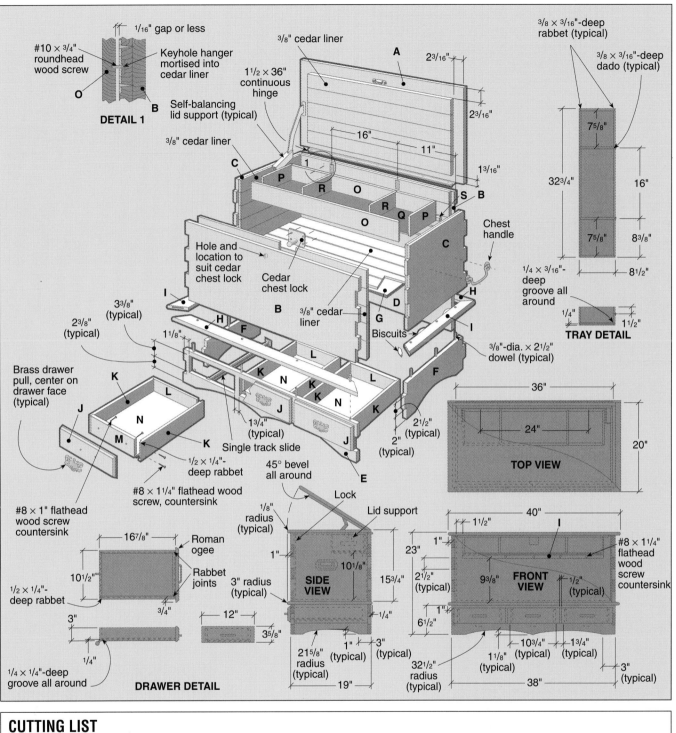

CUTTING LIST

Key	Qty.	Description & Size
A	1	**Lid,** walnut ¾ × 20 × 40"
B	2	**Trunk front, back,** cherry ¾ × 15 × 38"
C	2	**Trunk side,** cherry ¾ × 15 × 19"
D	1	**Base back,** walnut ¾ × 6½ × 38"
E	1	**Base front,** walnut ¾ × 6½ × 38"
F	2	**Base side,** walnut ¾ × 6½ × 19"
G	1	**Divider,** plywood ¾ × 14¼ × 34"
H	2	**Divider frame front, back,** walnut ¾ × 3 × 40"
I	2	**Divider frame side,** walnut ¾ × 3 × 20¼"
J	3	**Drawer false front,** walnut ¾ × 3⅝ × 12"
K	6	**Drawer side,** basswood ½ × 3 × 16⅜"
L	3	**Drawer back,** basswood ½ × 3 × 10"
M	3	**Drawer front,** basswood ½ × 3 × 10"
N	3	**Drawer bottom,** birch plywood ¼ × 10 × 16⅜"
O	2	**Tray front, back,** cherry ⅜ × 4 × 32¾"
P	2	**Tray side,** cherry ⅜ × 4 × 8⅛"
Q	1	**Tray bottom,** cherry plywood ¼ × 8⅛ × 32⅜"
R	2	**Tray divider,** cherry ⅜ × 3½ × 8⅛"
S	1	**Tray support,** cherry ¾ × ¾ × 32¾"

Misc.: Glue, flathead wood screws (#8 × 1", #8 × 1¼"), #10 × ¾" roundhead screws, two self-balancing lid supports, 1½ × 36" brass continuous hinge, one pair keyhole hangers, two chest handles, three single track drawer slides, chest lock, three brass drawer pulls, ⅜ × 3½" aromatic cedar (75 lin. ft.), ¾" brads, ⅜" dowels, #0 biscuits.

layout lines from the edge to the shoulder line. Finish the cut with the saw blade perpendicular to the workpiece, to ensure that the corners of the box joints are square.

6 To remove material for the box joint notches, set each workpiece upright and clamp a wide scrap block on one side, with the tops flush, to form a surface for supporting a router. Make sure the clamps won't interfere with the path of your router.

7 Mount a ¾" mortising bit in your router, set to ¾" depth, then rout the sides of the notches, cutting into the scrap block so the cut isn't rounded at the end. Rout away the material between the side cuts.

8 Dry-test the box joints, then apply glue to the fingers and notches, and reassemble the joints. Clamp with bar clamps, checking for square.

9 Let the glue dry, remove any excess glue, and finish-sand the trunk.

Build the drawer section

The outside dimensions of the lower base section must match those of the upper trunk exactly, for the pieces to fit together perfectly.

1 Cut the back (D), front (E), and sides (F) from ¾"-thick walnut.

2 On the bottom edge of the front (E), lay out two 32½"-radius curves with a bar compass (see *Diagram*). The curves should begin 3" in from each end and extend up 1" from the bottom edge. Cut out the curves with a bandsaw, then smooth the edges with a drum sander.

3 Lay out the 10¾ × 3⅜" drawer openings on the front. Openings should be 2⅜" from the bottom and 1⅛" from the sides, with a 1¾"-wide strip of uncut wood between drawer openings.

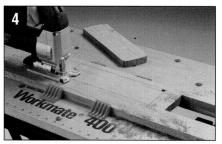

4 Cut out the drawer openings with a sabersaw and a fine-tooth blade. Smooth the cut edges with a file or sanding block.

5 Lay out and cut 21⅝"-radius curves (see *Diagram*) in the sides (F), and smooth the cut edges with a drum sander.

6 Lay out and cut box joints in the front, back, and sides of the base section. The front and back pieces should start with 2" fingers on the top; sides should start with 2" notches (see *Diagram*). Otherwise, use the same techniques as for the upper chest (*steps 2 to 10, Building the trunk*).

7 Glue and clamp the base section together, making sure it is square.

8 Let the glue dry, then remove excess glue and sand the base section to finished smoothness.

Join the trunk & base

The trunk and base sections are joined with a plywood divider panel that's framed with 3"-wide walnut trim. Dowels are inserted through the divider and anchored in the trunk and base sections to hold the sections of the hope chest together.

1 Cut the divider (G) from ¾"-thick plywood. Cut the front and back divider frame pieces (H) from ¾"-thick walnut. Miter-cut the ends of the frame pieces at 45° angles to fit around the divider.

2 Cut slots for #0 biscuits in the edges of the divider and the divider frame pieces, spaced every 4". Also cut biscuit slots in the mitered ends of the divider frame pieces.

3 Join each frame piece to the divider and to the adjoining frame piece with glue and biscuits, and clamp. Let the glue dry.

4 Remove all of the excess glue, then round over the edges of the frame pieces slightly.

5 Set the framed divider panel between the trunk and the base section, so the divider overhangs by 1" on the sides and front. Outline the edges of the trunk and the base section on the divider.

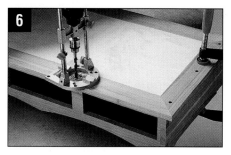

6 Remove the trunk. Install a ⅜" bit in your portable drill, then attach a portable drill guide set for a right angle. Set the bit stop on the drill guide to 1⅞" drilling depth, then drill a ⅜"-diameter dowel hole ⅜" inside the marked outline, through the divider frame and into the base section. Locate one hole over each "stile" in the front piece, and drill three holes in each side and three in the back (see *Diagram*).

7 To drill dowel holes in the trunk, turn the trunk upside down, place the divider on it with the outline lined up with the edge. Extend each dowel hole about 1" into the edges of the trunk.

8 Apply glue to the top edges of the base section, then set the divider onto it, so the dowel holes align. Apply glue to 2½ × ⅜"-diameter dowels and drive them fully into the dowel holes.

9 Apply glue to the bottom edges of the upper chest, then lower the chest onto the dowels. Force the pieces tightly together and clamp them until the glue dries. Remove excess glue.

Building the drawers

1 Cut the drawer fronts (M), backs (L), and sides (K), from ½" basswood, and the bottoms (N) from ¼"-thick birch plywood.
2 Cut ¼ × ¼" grooves in the sides, fronts, and backs, ¼" up from the bottom edges, to hold the drawer bottoms.
3 Cut ½ × ¼"-deep rabbets on the front and back edges of the sides, where the drawer fronts and backs will fit.
4 Make each drawer by gluing the front, back, and sides around the bottom panel (don't glue the bottom panel in place). Check to make sure the drawers are square, then reinforce the joints with countersunk #8 × 1¼" wood screws.
5 Cut the false fronts (J) from ¾" walnut. Shape the edges of the false fronts with a router and Roman ogee bit.
6 Complete each drawer by centering the false front over the drawer front, and attaching it with glue and countersunk #8 × 1" wood screws driven from inside the drawer.

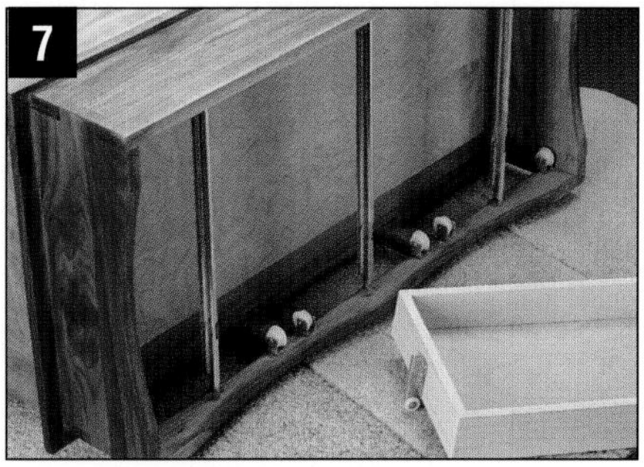

7 Fasten the rollers for the drawer glides to the bottom of each drawer, following manufacturer's directions. Fasten the tracks for the glides to the front and back of the base section. Install the drawers and test the fit.

Building the lift-out tray

1 Cut the front and back (O) for the tray from ⅜"-thick cherry. Cut ⅜ × 3/16"-deep rabbets on each end, where the sides will fit.
2 Cut ⅜ × 3/16"-deep dadoes, 7⅝" from each end of the front and back piece, where the dividers will fit. Cut ¼ × 3/16"-deep grooves, ¼" up from the bottom edges, where the tray bottom will fit.
3 Cut the tray sides (P) from ⅜" cherry. Cut ¼" × 3/16"-grooves, ¼" from the bottom edges, where the tray bottom will fit.
4 Cut the tray dividers (R) from ⅜"-thick cherry and the bottom (Q) from ¼"-thick cherry plywood.
5 Glue and clamp the back, front, and sides around the bottom and dividers. (Don't glue the bottom in place.) Check to make sure the tray is square, then let the glue dry.
6 Install #10 × ¾" roundhead screws in the back of the tray, 1½" below the top, centered on the back edges of the dividers. Let the screws extend ¼" (they'll be inserted into the keyhole hangers to hang the tray).

Building the lid

1 Cut the lid (A) to finished shape, then round over the sides and front of the top slightly, using a block plane, then sandpaper.
2 Position the brass piano hinge along the back, underside edge of the top, and outline it on the wood.

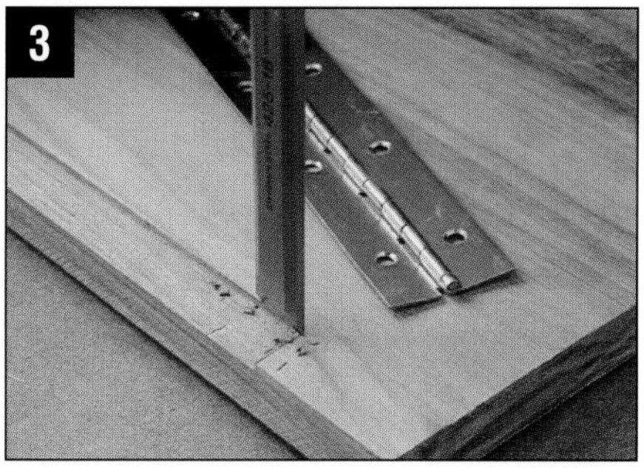

3 Use a router and ¾" mortising bit to create the mortise for the hinge. Either use a straightedge to guide your portable router, or rout the mortise on your router table. Clean out the corners of the mortise with a chisel.
4 Position the hinge in the mortise, and tape it it place. Use a self-centering (vix) bit to drill pilot holes for the mounting screws, then attach the hinge.
5 Position the lid on the trunk, so it overhangs by 1" on the front and sides. Mark the location of the hinge onto the back edge of the trunk.
6 Remove the trunk, then repeat *steps 3 to 4,* above, to rout a mortise on the top edge of the back piece to hold the piano hinge. Remove the hinge from the top and lay it in the mortise on the chest to drill pilot holes with a self-centering bit. Don't install the hinge permanently until the hope chest has been finished.

Finishing the hope chest

1 Coat the chest, the drawers, and the top with natural-tone penetrating oil, inside and out.
2 Let the oil dry overnight, then polish the surfaces with paste wax for a hand-rubbed look.
3 Line the interior of the chest with ⅜"-thick aromatic cedar attached with ⅞" brads (see *Diagram*). Note: Aromatic cedar can be purchased most economically at lumber and building centers, where it's sold by the board foot. If you're unable to find raw aromatic cedar stock you can usually purchase precut cedar closet panels, which are more expensive.
4 Lay out and cut mortises for two keyhole fasteners in the back of the chest, to hold the roundhead screws installed in the back of the tray. The keyhole fasteners should be positioned 1½" from the top edge. Install the keyhole fasteners in the mortises.

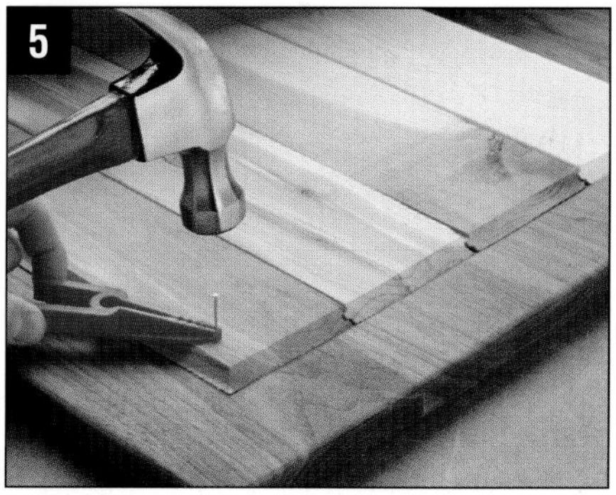

5 Cover the bottom surface of the top panel with aromatic cedar. The cedar should be inset 2 3/16" on the sides and front, and 1 3/16" at the back. Bevel the exposed edges of the lining at 45°.
6 Attach the lid to the trunk, and add a lid support on each side.
7 Lay out and cut a mortise for the lid lock, then install the lock.
8 Install the drawer pulls and the chest handles.

Curio Cabinet

Mirrors and light make this curio cabinet a lovely showplace for your treasures.

Curio cabinets have a way of becoming the focal point of any room they occupy. A well-designed curio cabinet will display your collectibles without overpowering them. The long lines and mirrored back of this oak curio cabinet focus special attention on your treasures by allowing them to be viewed from all sides.

Like many woodworking projects, this cabinet is made with frame-and-panel construction. Unlike most projects using this construction technique, however, the panels are glass. This cabinet has six framed glass panels: Four of them are joined together to make the basic cabinet framework, and the other two become the cabinet doors. Add a top, a mirrored back, molding, and lighting, and the curio cabinet is ready for your collectibles.

Choose wood that's straight and even-grained for your cabinet. The finer the grain, the better, because strong grain patterns will draw attention to the wood, not the contents of the cabinet.

Building the side frames

The side frames hold the glass panels and help form the structural framework of our curio cabinet. As a working material, glass gives little room for error because it can't be bent or trimmed easily. Make sure the frames that hold the glass panels are square.

1 Cut four cabinet stiles (A), four side rails (E), and two middle rails (F) to make the side frames. Sand out the saw marks.

2 On each pair of stiles, mark the

locations of the top, middle, and bottom rails (see *Diagram*). Lay out and drill holes for ⅜ × 1¼" dowels at these joints. The dowel holes need to stay at least ½" away from the top and bottom edges of the rails, so the dowels are not accidentally cut when you make the rabbet grooves for the glass.

3 Dry-fit the frames, then glue and clamp them together with pipe clamps. Check that they're square, then let the glue dry.

4 Unclamp the side frames and remove any excess glue. Make a

⅜ × ⅜" rabbet cut for the glass around the inside edges of the panel openings, using a router and a ⅜" piloted rabbet bit. Square off the rabbet cuts with a sharp wood chisel.

WOODWORKER'S TIP

Use a guide stick the same length as the stiles as a template for drilling holes for shelf pins. Drill holes in the guide stick, making sure they're at the proper intervals.

CUTTING LIST

Key	Qty.	Description & Size
A	8	**Cabinet stile**, ³/₄ × 2 × 72"
B	4	**Cabinet rail**, ³/₄ × 4 × 20"
C	4	**Door stile**, ³/₄ × 1¹/₂ × 64"
D	6	**Door rail**, ³/₄ × 1¹/₂ × 10¹¹/₁₆"
E	4	**Side rail**, ³/₄ × 4 × 10¹/₂"
F	2	**Middle rail**, ³/₄ × 2 × 10¹/₂"
G	2	**Top, bottom**, ³/₄ × 14¹/₂ × 22¹/₂"
H	4	**Door glass**, ¹/₈ × 8⁵/₁₆ × 30³/₈"
I	4	**Side glass**, ¹/₈ × 11¹/₈ × 31¹/₈"
J	4	**Shelf glass**, ¹/₄ × 14³/₈ × 22³/₈"
K	1	**Back**, ¹/₄ × 21³/₈ × 64³/₈"
L	1	**Mirror**, ¹/₄ × 20⁵/₈ × 63⁵/₈"
M	2	**Face cleats**, ³/₄ × ³/₄ × 21"
N	2	**Side cleats**, ³/₄ × ³/₄ × 14¹/₂"
O	1	**Door cleat**, ³/₄ × 2¹/₄ × 62³/₄"

Note: All wood is oak, except the back (K), which is ¼" A/C plywood.

Misc.: Glue, finish nails (4d, 6d), ½" wire brads, #6 × 1¼" brass wood screws, ⅜ × 1¼" dowels, masking tape, 16 × 20" oak veneer, 7' of Colonial base molding (3¼"), 7' of 45° crown molding, 7' oak 1 × 4, (6) 1½" straight-pin hinges, (2 sets) bullet catches, right-hand glass door lock, curio cabinet light, (16) ¼" shelf pins, ¼" oak strips (70'), glazier's points.

5 On the side frames, drill ¼ × ⅜"-deep holes for ¼" shelf pins, beginning 1' from the bottom and ending 1' from the top. This will give you several options for customizing your shelf space.
6 Sand the side frames with 120-grit sandpaper.

Making the front & rear frames

The frames in our curio cabinet provide most of the structural strength. The front frame also anchors the glass cabinet doors, and the rear frame is fitted with a large mirrored panel and a ¼" plywood back. The recess formed by rabbet cuts in the rear frame is designed to give the glass room for expansion and contraction.
1 Cut four cabinet stiles (A) and four cabinet rails (B), and arrange them into pairs.
2 On each pair of stiles, mark the locations of the top and bottom rails (see *Diagram*). Lay out and drill holes for ⅜ × 1¼" dowels at these joints, following the procedure used in *step 2* of the *Building the side frames* section. Dry-fit the

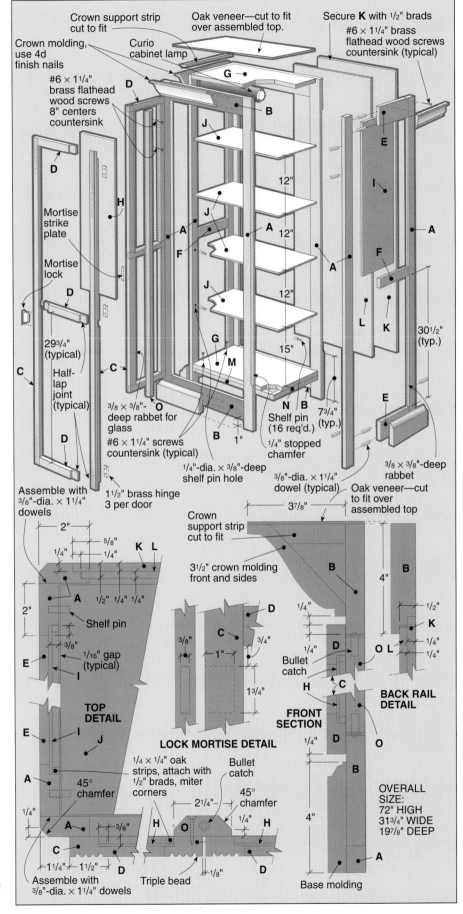

front and rear frames to make sure the dowels line up, then glue and assemble the frames. Square up the frames, then clamp them together to dry. After drying, unclamp the frames and remove any excess glue.

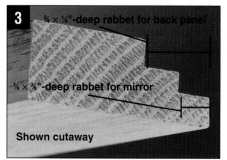

3
¾ × ¼"-deep rabbet for back panel

¼ × ⅜"-deep rabbet for mirror

Shown cutaway

3 Make a ¾ × ¼"-deep rabbet cut on the inside of the back of the rear frame, to hold the plywood back (K). Also make a ¼ × ⅜"-deep rabbet cut on the bottom edge of the first rabbet, to hold the mirror. Square off the corners of the cuts with a sharp wood chisel.
4 Cut the back (K) and test-fit it in the frame, then remove the back and set it aside.

Assembling the cabinet framework

Join the side frames to the back and front frames with dowels to form the cabinet framework.
1 Lay out and drill mating ⅜ × ¾"-deep holes in the cabinet stiles every 4" for dowel joints between the side frames and the front and rear frames. Dry-fit the frames to test the fit, then glue and clamp the frame pieces with pipe clamps. Let the glue dry.

2

Side rail

Back rail

2 On the insides of the frames, scribe a line around the inside of the bottom rails, ¾" down from the tops of the rails.

3 Cut the ¾ × ¾" oak cleats (M, N) that support the cabinet bottom. Attach the side cleats (N) to the side frames, so the tops are just even with the scribed lines, using three countersunk #6 × 1¼" flathead wood screws per cleat. Also attach the long cleats (M) to the front and rear frames so the tops are even with the scribed marks.
4 Cut the bottom and top panels for the cabinet(G).
5 Fasten the bottom to the cleats with three #6 × 1¼" wood screws per side, driven through counterbored pilot holes. Plug the counterbores with oak plugs and sand smooth. Finish-sand the bottom.
6 Attach the top by screwing through the tops of the frames and into the edges of the top panel with countersunk #6 × 1¼" wood screws.
7 Finish-sand the frames, slightly rounding all the corners.

Building the doors

The cabinet doors are made by building two frames using half-lap construction. For perfectly square frames, cut the stiles and rails 1" oversized, leaving ½" extra wood on each end. Assemble the frames first, then remove the extra wood by cutting, sanding, or planing.
1 Measure and cut the door rails (D) and door stiles (C) 1" oversize, then mount a molding head cutter in your tablesaw and cut a triple-bead groove down the center of each stile.
2 On the backs of the stiles and the fronts of the rails, make a 2 × ⅜"-deep rabbet-type cut to form the overlapping half-lap joints. Make sure the cuts are flat.
3 Dry-fit the door frames to check the fit of the half-lap joints. Apply glue to both parts of each joint and clamp them together with handscrews. Be sure they're square, then let the glue dry.
4 Unclamp the doors after drying, and remove any excess glue. Make a ⅜ × ⅜" rabbet cut around the insides of the frames to hold the glass and oak retainer strips. Square off the corners of the cut with a wood chisel.

5 At the half-lap joints, trim the excess wood from the oversized rail and stile joints.
6 Cut a ¾ × 2¼ × 62¾" piece of oak for the door cleat (O). (When attached to the left door frame, the cleat covers the gap where the door frames meet, stiffening the frames.) Cut 45° chamfers in the edges of the cleat so it can't be seen through the door glass. Attach the cleat to the back of the left door frame, using glue and countersunk #6 × 1¼" wood screws driven at 8" intervals. The cleat should be positioned so it's centered behind the ⅛" gap where the doors meet, and the ends are ⅝" from the top and the bottom.
7 On the outer stiles of both door frames, lay out and make mortise cuts for the hinges. Start one cut 3" from the top, one 29" down from the top, and one 3" from the bottoms of the stiles.
8 Install the hinges (we'll remove them later for finishing), and mark the hinge locations on the cabinet corner posts. Mortise the posts, then mount the doors. Check to make sure the doors have the proper ⅛" clearance at the tops, bottoms, and meeting point.
9 Remove the hinges, then finish-sand the door frames, using 220-grit sandpaper.

Trimming & finishing

Give your cabinet a crowning touch with crown and base molding. Because of its angled top, you'll need to square off the crown molding stock with a crown support strip that will fill the gaps between the top of the crown molding and the cabinet. The base molding is miter-cut and attached directly to the cabinet with finish nails.
1 Set a 7'-long piece of 45° crown molding upside down against the rip fence of your tablesaw, so the edge that contacts the cabinet is against the fence. Measure the distance from the fence to the inside edge of the molding along the tablesaw surface to determine the setback distance and the proper size for the crown support strip.

2 Cut a piece of 1 × 4" oak to 7' in length to use for the crown support strip. Bevel-rip one edge of the strip at 45°. Make a straight rip cut along the other edge of the strip, so the width at the wider side is equal to the setback distance measured in *step 1*.

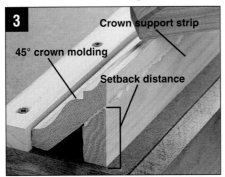

Crown support strip
45° crown molding
Setback distance

3 Glue the crown support strip to the crown molding, flush with the top, then clamp the assembly against a flat surface to dry.

4 Miter-cut the crown molding assembly to fit around the front and the sides of the cabinet, flush with the top. Fasten the assembly in place by driving 4d finish nails up through the base of the crown molding at a slight angle.

5 Cut a piece of oak veneer to cover the entire trimmed-out top of the cabinet. Glue the veneer down, then set a weight on top of the veneer until the glue dries.

6 Slightly round the bottom edges of the legs and base molding with sandpaper, to prevent chipping. Miter-cut and attach the base molding with 4d finish nails.

7 Shape the outside edges of the cabinet stiles with a router and ¼" chamfer bit. Start 4" above the base molding and end 4" below the crown molding.

8 Set all nail holes with a nail set, then fill with putty. Finish-sand the moldings, then vacuum the dust from the cabinet.

9 Stain and finish the cabinet. A natural Danish oil is ideal for finishing oak.

Adding the hardware

1 Install the light you've purchased for the inside top of the curio cabinet, following the manufacturer's instructions.

Grommet

2 Cut an exit hole for the lighting wire in the side of the cabinet, then insert a matching grommet into the exit hole.

3 Lay out and drill holes for the bullet catches in the top and bottom ends of the door cleat (O), and in matching positions on the top and bottom cabinet panels. Install the bullet catches, following the manufacturer's directions.

4 Install the lock (see *Diagram*), following the manufacturer's instructions. Wait until after you've installed the glass panels and the mirror to add any doorknobs.

Installing the glass

Handling glass requires extra care and safety precautions. Always wear safety glasses and sturdy work gloves.

1 Cut the glass panels, then install the panels one at a time. Beginning with the side frames, center each panel in its recess so there is a ⅛" gap at the top, and a ¹⁄₁₆" gap on each side. Tape the panel to the middle rail to hold it in place temporarily.

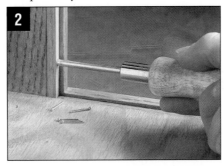

2 Cut a strip of ¼ × ¼" oak to fit one side of the frame. Drill pilot holes every 8" in the strip, then position and attach it, using ½" wire brads driven through the pilot holes with a brad pusher.

3 Cut an oak strip to fit along the bottom of the panel and fasten it in place. Be careful not to push the glass panel too tightly against the frame.

4 Cut and install the other oak strips using the same procedure. Secure the rest of the glass panels in the side frames with oak strips.

5 Carefully lay the cabinet face-down on a flat, smooth surface. Cut the mirror (L) to size, then carefully center it in the deeper rabbeted recess of the back frame. You may want to get a helper for this step. Make sure the mirror is fitted snugly into the backs of the rabbets. To ensure the mirror stays in place until the back is installed don't move the cabinet.

6 Place the ¼" plywood back (K) into the shallower rabbeted recess of the back frame, and fasten it in place with ½" wire brads driven every 8" into the back edges of the back frame.

7 Set the doors on a flat, padded surface. Install the glass in the doors using oak strips. Rehang the doors on the cabinet front.

8 Attach doorknobs or any other external hardware. Move the cabinet to its permanent location, keeping the cabinet upright and square—a sudden twist can break glass panels. Cut the glass shelves and smooth the edges with emory paper. Install the shelf pins and then install the shelves.

WOODWORKER'S TIP

Tape an "X" across each piece of glass with masking tape to prevent the glass from shattering into tiny shards if it breaks, and to make it easier to see.

Barrister's Bookcase

You don't have to be a lawyer to love the Old World charm of this solid oak bookcase.

Some bookcases are designed simply to be a convenient spot to stash your old books and magazines, and some, like this barrister's bookcase, are much more. With its solid oak construction and stately design, our bookcase is a true showpiece that can be handed down in your family for generations to come.

The fixed shelves and solid oak construction combine to make this barrister's bookcase one of the sturdiest pieces of fine furniture you'll find.

Making the side panels

The solid oak raised panels are one of the keys to the appeal of our barrister's bookcase. Made from glued-up ¾" oak, the panels are shaped with a tablesaw.

1 Cut the front stiles (A), rear stiles (B), and the side rails (C, D, E). Install a dado-blade set in your tablesaw, and cut a ¼ × ⅜"-deep groove, centered in the inside edge of each frame piece, to hold the raised panels (F). The middle side rails (D) will have ¼ × ⅜"-deep grooves in both the top and the bottom edges.

2 Mount a router in your router table and use it to cut ⅜ × ¼"-deep rabbets in both sides of the rail ends, forming ¼ × ⅜"-high tenons.

3 Cut ¼ × ¼" rabbets on the inside back edges of the rear stiles (B) to hold the back panel (N).

4 Cut the raised panels (F) to finished size from ¾" oak stock, making sure they are square.

5 On your tablesaw, make a ⅛"-deep cut, 1¾" in from all four edges of each panel, to form the inside shoulders of the shaped edges.

CUTTING LIST

Key	Qty.	Description & Size	Key	Qty.	Description & Size
A	2	**Front stile,** ¾ × 2 × 58 7/16"	J	3	**Shelf,** 1 1/16 × 14⅛ × 34"
B	2	**Rear stile,** ¾ × 2 × 58 7/16"	K	1	**Top panel,** ¾ × 14⅛ × 34"
C	2	**Side rail** (top), ¾ × 5⅜ × 10¾"	L	6	**Panel liner,** ½ × 12½ × 12⅛"
D	4	**Side rail** (middle), ¾ × 2 × 10¾"	M	1	**Cover,** ¾ × 17 × 40"
E	2	**Side rail** (bottom), ¾ × 8 × 10¾"	N	1	**Back panel,** ¼ × 33⅛ × 58¼"
F	6	**Raised panel,** ¾ × 10⅝ × 14 5/16"	O	6	**Door rail,** ¾ × 2¼ × 32¼"
G	3	**Rail,** ¾ × 4 × 32½"	P	6	**Door stile,** ¾ × 2¼ × 12 3/16"
H	1	**Front rail** (bottom), ¾ × 6⅝ × 32½"	Q	3	**Glass panel,** ⅛ × 10 13/16 × 28½"
I	3	**Follower strip,** cut to fit hinges			

Note: All wood is oak, except parts L and N, which are oak plywood.

Misc.: Glue, ⅝" brads, 1" wire nails, 4d and 6d finish nails, ⅜ × 1½" dowels, 7 linear ft. 3½" oak crown molding, 7 linear ft. base molding, 24 linear ft. ¼ × ¼" oak strips, 12" flipper hinges (3 sets), ¾" brass doorknobs (6), oak filler crayon, wood putty.

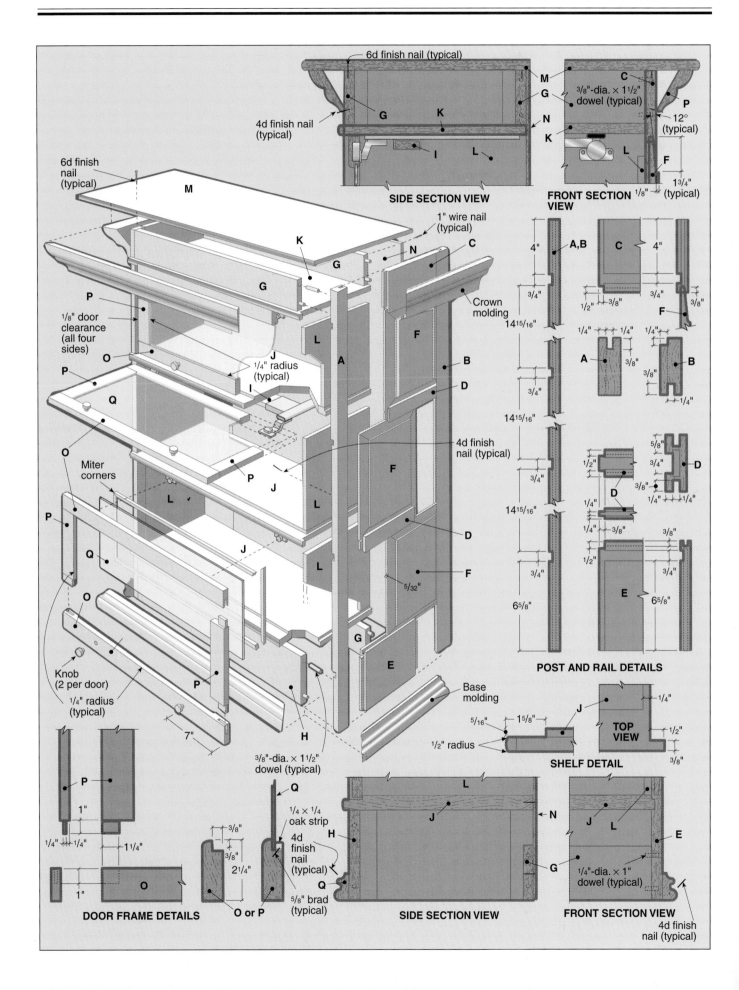

6d finish nail (typical)

M

G

K

I

L

SIDE SECTION VIEW

M

G

N

K

C

³/₈"-dia. × 1¹/₂" dowel (typical)

P

12° (typical)

L

F

¹/₈"

1³/₄" (typical)

FRONT SECTION VIEW

6d finish nail (typical)

4d finish nail (typical)

M

K

G

G

P

¹/₈" door clearance (all four sides)

O

J

¹/₄" radius (typical)

I

P

Q

O

Miter corners

P

Q

O

Knob (2 per door)

¹/₄" radius (typical)

7"

H

³/₈"-dia. × 1¹/₂" dowel (typical)

1" wire nail (typical)

N

C

G

Crown molding

L

F

A

B

D

F

4d finish nail (typical)

L

D

L

F

G

E

Base molding

5/32"

A,B

4"

³/₄"

14¹⁵/₁₆"

³/₄"

14¹⁵/₁₆"

³/₄"

14¹⁵/₁₆"

³/₄"

6⁵/₈"

C

4"

³/₄"

¹/₂"

³/₈"

³/₈"

F

¹/₄"

¹/₄"

A

³/₈"

¹/₄"

³/₈"

B

³/₈"

¹/₄"

⁵/₈"

¹/₂"

³/₄"

³/₈"

D

³/₈"

¹/₄"

¹/₄"

D

¹/₄"

³/₈"

¹/₂"

³/₄"

³/₈"

³/₄"

E

6⁵/₈"

POST AND RAIL DETAILS

¹/₄"

J

TOP VIEW

¹/₂"

³/₈"

⁵/₁₆"

1⁵/₈"

¹/₂" radius

SHELF DETAIL

P

1"

¹/₄"

¹/₄"

1¹/₄"

O

1"

DOOR FRAME DETAILS

³/₈"

³/₈"

2¹/₄"

O or P

Q

¹/₄ × ¹/₄ oak strip

4d finish nail (typical)

⁵/₈" brad (typical)

L

J

H

Q

G

N

SIDE SECTION VIEW

J

L

E

G

¹/₄"-dia. × 1" dowel (typical)

FRONT SECTION VIEW

4d finish nail (typical)

6 Set your tablesaw blade at a 12° angle, then make relief cuts on all four edges of each panel face. The tops of the cuts should meet with the cuts made in *step 5*, forming ⅛"-high top shoulders. The edges of the panels should be ⁵⁄₃₂" thick after the relief cut is made.

7 Set your tablesaw blade height at ⁷⁄₁₆", and set the fence ⁷⁄₃₂" from the blade. With the back face of each panel against the fence, trim around all four edges, creating ⁷⁄₃₂ × ⁷⁄₁₆"-high tongues that fit into the rail and stile grooves.

8 Sand the rails, stiles, and panels with 120- then 220-grit sandpaper. If you plan to stain the panels, do it now, because it will be more difficult to stain the panels once they are inserted into the frames.

9 Dry-fit the rails, stiles, and panels, and mark the locations of the rails onto the stiles.

10 Clamp one of the stiles to your workbench, with the groove facing up. Glue one end of a top rail into the groove, flush with the top edge of the stile. Slide the top panel into the grooves in the stile and the rail. Glue the middle rails into the stile, being careful not to get any glue on the edges of the panel.

11 Insert the middle and bottom panels, then glue the bottom rail and the other stile into position. Lay the frame-and-panel assembly flat on your worksurface, square it up, and clamp with bar clamps.

12 Repeat *steps 10 to 11* for the other side panel.

Making the carcass

Because they are fixed in place, the shelves in our bookcase take on much of the structural duty of holding the carcass together.

1 Cut the lower rear rail and the two top rails (G), and the bottom front rail (H).

2 Lay out and drill holes for ⅜ × 1½" dowels that will attach all four rails to the side panels. Use two dowels at each joint, being careful not to drill more than halfway through the thickness of any parts to be joined.

3 Cut the shelves (J) from 1¹⁄₁₆"-thick stock, and cut the top panel (K) from ¾"-thick stock.

4 Cut ¾ × ⁵⁄₁₆"-deep rabbets on both top ends of all the shelves.

5 On the top, front edge of each shelf and the top panel, cut a 1⅝ × ⁵⁄₁₆"-deep rabbet for the door setback, using a dado-blade set.

6 Install a ½" roundover bit in your router table, then round over the bottom front edges of the shelves and top panel. Make the round-over in the top front edge of the top panel, then raise your router bit ⁵⁄₁₆" (to compensate for the setback in the shelves) and round over the top edges of the shelves.

7 Using a handsaw, make a ½"-deep cut into the ends of each shelf and the top panel, ⅜" in from the front edges. Then, starting at the rear of each shelf, trim ½" from each end with your tablesaw (leaving a ¼"-wide tongue on the ends of the shelves). Stop the cut about 1" before you reach the handsaw cut. Finish the trim cut with the handsaw, making a ½ × ⅜"-deep lip at each front corner.

8 Sand the shelves with 120- then 220-grit sandpaper.

9 Scrape any excess glue from the side panels, then rout four ¾ × ¼"-deep dadoes on the inside face of each side panel (see *Diagram*) to hold the shelves and the top panel. Note: All dadoes should be routed into rails in the side panels.

10 Lay one of the side panels face-down on a covered surface. Attach the rails with dowels and glue.

11 Glue the shelves and top panel into the side panel, making sure the overhangs fit neatly over the front stiles.

12 Glue the other side panel in place. Make sure the carcass is square, then clamp it with padded bar clamps. Let the glue dry.

13 Cut panel liners (L) from ½" oak plywood. Apply oak veneer tape to the front and top edges, and trim off any excess tape. Sand the panel liners with 120- then 220-grit sandpaper.

14 Set the panel liners on the shelves, against the inside faces of the side panels. Arrange the liners so they are flush with the inside shoulder of the 1½" setback in the shelves, then attach them to the side panels with 4d finish nails (three per side).

15 Cut the cover (M) from glued-up ¾" oak stock. Round over the front and side edges of the cover to match the profile of the shelf edges, then attach it by driving 6d finish nails down into the top edges of the rails, spaced at 6" intervals.

16 Measure the dimensions of the front and sides of the carcass. Miter-cut two side trim pieces and one front trim piece from 3½" crown molding to fit around the top of the bookcase carcass (see *Diagram*).

17 Trim the top of the carcass with the miter-cut pieces of crown molding. Fasten the molding in place with 4d finish nails driven through pilot holes into the top and bottom of the crown molding at 6" intervals, then lock-nail the joints. Fill any gaps in the joints with wood putty.

18 In the same manner as with the crown molding, trim the base of the cabinet with miter-cut pieces of base molding. Fasten the base molding with 4d finish nails driven at 6" intervals, then lock-nail the joints. Fill any gaps in the joints with wood putty.

19 Set all nail heads with a nail set, then fill each hole with wood putty. Let the putty dry, then sand smooth with 120-grit sandpaper. Finish-sand the carcass and trim with 220-grit sandpaper, wipe clean, then apply oil or stain to the entire carcass. We used dark oak tinted tung oil, and we also applied several coats of water-based polyurethane to the bookcase for protection.

Make & hang the doors

The doors for our bookcase are made from oak frames with glass panels that protect the contents from dust. The doors are attached with pivoting "flipper"-type hinges so they can be tucked safely out of the way when open.

Contrary to standard frame-and-panel construction, the rails of our door frames run the full width of the frame, holding the tenons cut into the stiles. This provides a more solid surface for anchoring the hinges. The tenons we used (called "stub" tenons) are also a little unusual, because the outside edges are flush with the stiles on one side only, creating an L-shape. This prevents the mortise-and-tenon joint from being cut when the recesses for the glass panels are routed.

1 Cut the door rails (O) and the door stiles (P).

2 Cut a 1 × ¼"-deep rabbet on the top and bottom of each stile end to form tenons. Cut a 1" notch from the inside of each tenon, creating a ¼ × 1 × 1¼" stub tenon.

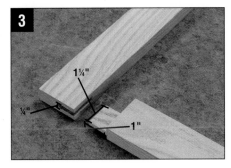

3 Cut a ¼ × 1 × 1¼"-deep mortise in the center of each rail end to hold the stub tenons of the stiles. To make the cuts, we used a mortising attachment mounted in our drill press, but you can also cut the mortises by removing waste material with a ³⁄₁₆" twist bit, then squaring off the sides with a chisel.

4 Test-fit then assemble the frames, gluing the mortise-and-tenon joints together. Clamp with bar clamps, check for square, and let the glue dry.

5 Scrape away excess glue, and rout a ⅜ × ⅜" rabbet on the rear, inside edges of the frames to hold the glass panels (Q). Square off the corners of the rabbets with a wood chisel.

6 Rip strips of oak stock to ¼" square, then miter-cut the strips to make retainer strips for securing the glass panels. Sand the strips and the frames to finished smoothness, then finish the frames and strips to match the carcass. Set the strips aside until the glass panels are installed.

7 Cut the follower strips (I) for the flipper door hardware, sand them smooth, and apply oil or stain. Attach one follower strip between each pair of glides (see manufacturer's directions).

8 Mount the tracks for the flipper hinges onto the undersides of the top panel and the shelves (excluding the bottom shelf), according to the manufacturer's directions.

9 Attach the top rails of the door frames to the hinge-and-follower assemblies, and adjust the position of the hinges as needed.

10 Once you have the door frames mounted, mark their position and remove them. Cut ⅛"-thick glass panels (Q) to fit.

11 Carefully set the glass panels into the recesses at the back of each door frame, then set the ¼ × ¼" mitered retainer strips on all four edges of each glass panel.

12 Drill ¹⁄₃₂"-diameter pilot holes every 4", then secure the glass panels in place by driving ⅝" wire brads through the pilot holes with a brad pusher. Fill the holes with an oak filler crayon.

13 Reattach the doors to the flipper hinges.

Finish the cabinet

1 Cut and finish-sand the back panel (N), then finish to match the rest of the bookcase. Insert the panel into the rabbeted recess in the back of the carcass, and secure in place with 1" wire nails driven every 6". Do not glue.

2 Attach the brass doorknobs to the door frames (see *Diagram*).

Armoire

Store your clothes in style.

A beautiful piece of furniture, the armoire provides a practical, satisfying storage space for your clothes.

Making the carcass

1 Cut sides, (A), top/bottom (B), partition (C), and supports (E) from ¾"-thick oak plywood.

2 Cut a ¼ × ⅜"-wide rabbet along back inside edges of the sides to hold the back (F).

3 Cut back from ¼"-thick oak plywood. Sand to finished smoothness.

4 Draw a line 1" from each end of two of the top/bottom panels. Draw lines on inner faces. Then cut slots for #20 biscuits centered ⅜" inside the lines.

5 Cut slots for #20 biscuits centered on the top and bottom edges of the supports.

6 Sand supports and top/bottoms to finished smoothness.

7 Fasten top/bottoms to supports with glue and biscuits to form lower cabinet. Clamp, check for square, and allow to dry.

8 Cut slots for #20 biscuits centered ⅜" from top and bottom edges, and 9⅛" up from bottom edge on inside face of each side.

9 Cut corresponding slots in top/bottom pieces for biscuit joints with the sides.

10 Cut slots for #20 biscuits centered 11½" from side of the top of the lower cabinet and underside of the top of the main cabinet to join with the partition.

11 Cut slots for #20 biscuits centered in top and bottom of partition that match slots cut in lower cabinet and main cabinet parts.

12 Cut nosing (D) for partition from ¾"-thick oak.

13 Cut slots in nosing and partition to join with #20 biscuits. Attach nosing to partition with biscuits and glue. Clamp and let dry.

14 Sand partition, nosing, top/bottom, and sides to smoothness.

15 Stand lower cabinet on its front face. Fasten partition to lower cab-

inet with glue and biscuits.

16 Attach top to the partition with glue and biscuits. Biscuits and glue will hold the pieces without clamping for several minutes.

17 Fasten sides to top/bottom pieces with glue and biscuits. Clamp sides around tops/bottoms with bar clamps.

18 Fasten back to sides, partition, and top/bottom pieces with #6 × ¾" wood screws, squaring as you go. Adjust clamps as necessary.

Making the frames

1 Cut face stiles (G), top rail (H), face rail (I), and bottom rail (J) from ¾"-thick oak.

2 Use a beam compass to mark a

48⅜"-radius arc on the bottom of the top rail. Cut the arc on a bandsaw and sand with a drum sander.

3 Sand stiles and rails until smooth.

4 Measure and mark locations of rails on the edges of stiles.

5 Cut slots for #0 biscuits centered on the edge at the joint locations in the stiles and on ends of rails.

6 Attach stiles to rails with glue and biscuits. Check for square and flatness. Clamp and allow to dry.

7 Remove excess glue with a chisel. Dry-fit face frame to cabinet carcass.

8 Mark locations on carcass and face frame for biscuit joints.

9 Cut slots in face frame and carcass. Attach frame to carcass with glue and #20 biscuits.

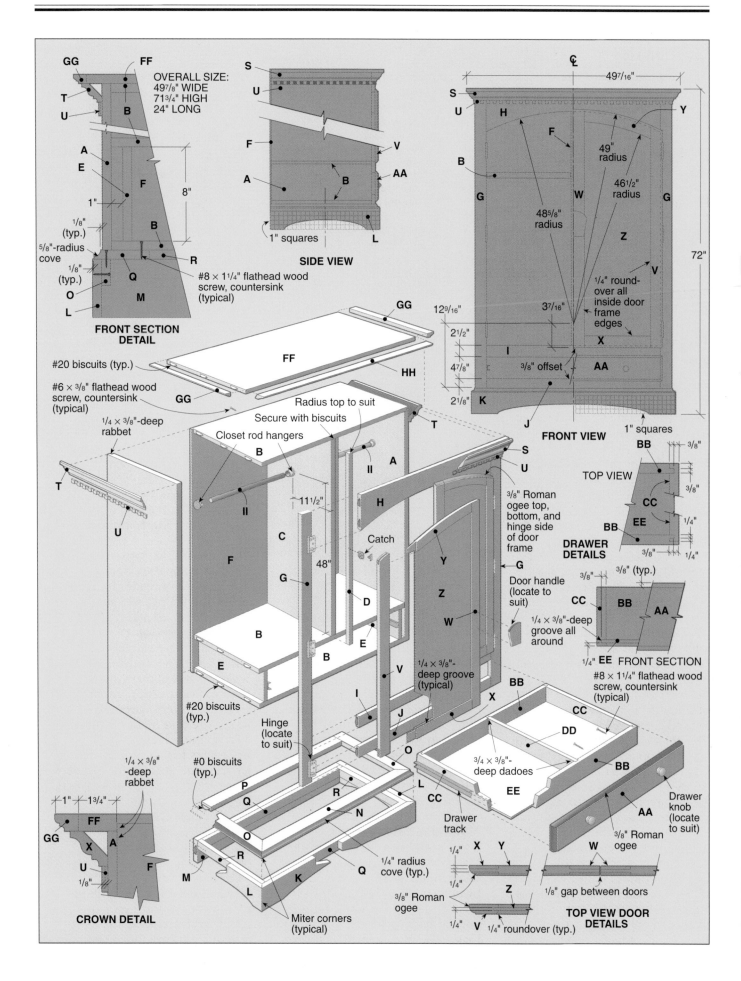

GG FF

OVERALL SIZE:
49⁷/₈" WIDE
71³/₄" HIGH
24" LONG

T
U
B

A
E
F

1"

1/8"
(typ.)

5/8"-radius
cove

1/8"
(typ.)

O
L

Q
M

B

R

#8 × 1¹/₄" flathead wood
screw, countersink
(typical)

FRONT SECTION DETAIL

S
U

F

A

B

V

AA

1" squares

L

SIDE VIEW

C̶L

49⁷/₁₆"

S
U

H
F

B

G

W

49"
radius

46¹/₂"
radius

48⁵/₈"
radius

Z

Y

G

V

1/4" round-
over all
inside door
frame
edges

72"

12⁹/₁₆"

2¹/₂"

4⁷/₈"

2¹/₈"

I

X

K

3/8" offset

J

AA

FRONT VIEW

1" squares

GG

FF

HH

GG

#20 biscuits (typ.)

#6 × ³/₈" flathead wood
screw, countersink
(typical)

1/4 × 3/8"-deep
rabbet

T

U

Closet rod hangers

Radius top to suit

Secure with biscuits

B

II

A

T

S

U

H

Catch

G

D

E

F

C

48"

11¹/₂"

II

B

E

B

E

#20 biscuits
(typ.)

1/4 × 3/8"-deep
rabbet

1" 1³/₄"

FF

GG

X

A

U

F

1/8"

CROWN DETAIL

#0 biscuits
(typ.)

P

Q

O

R

M

R

L

K

Q

N

Hinge
(locate
to suit)

Miter corners
(typical)

3/8" Roman
ogee

1/4" radius
cove (typ.)

Door handle
(locate to
suit)

1/4 × 3/8"-deep
groove all
around

3/8" Roman
ogee top,
bottom, and
hinge side
of door
frame

Y

Z

W

G

V

I

J

X

1/4 × 3/8"-
deep groove
(typical)

O

L

CC

Drawer
track

BB

CC

DD

BB

EE

3/4 × 3/8"-
deep dadoes

AA

Drawer
knob
(locate
to suit)

3/8" Roman
ogee

TOP VIEW

BB

CC

EE

BB

3/8"

3/8"

1/4"

DRAWER DETAILS

3/8" (typ.)

3/8"

CC

BB

AA

EE **FRONT SECTION**

1/4"

#8 × 1¹/₄" flathead wood
screw, countersink
(typical)

X

Y

Z

V

W

1/4"

1/4"

1/4"

1/4"

3/8" Roman
ogee

1/4" roundover (typ.)

1/8" gap between doors

TOP VIEW DOOR DETAILS

CUTTING LIST

Key	Qty.	Description & Size	Key	Qty.	Description & Size	Key	Qty.	Description & Size
A	2	**Side,** ¾ × 23¼ × 66½"	M	1	**Base back,** ¾ × 4¾ × 45½"	Y	2	**Upper rail,** ¾ × 7¼ × 20⁷⁄₁₆"
B	3	**Top/bottom,** ¾ × 23 × 43¾"	N	1	**Plinth front,** ¾ × 4 × 46¾"	Z	2	**Panel,** ¼ × 16³⁄₁₆ × 48³⁄₁₆"
C	1	**Partition,** ¾ × 23 × 56¼"	O	2	**Plinth side,** ¾ × 4 × 24¾"	AA	1	**False front,** ¾ × 5⅝ × 41"
D	1	**Nosing,** ¾ × ¾ × 51¹¹⁄₁₆"	P	1	**Plinth back,** ¾ × 4 × 38¾"	BB	1	**Front/back,** ¾ × 4⅝ × 39¼"
E	2	**Support,** ¾ × 8 × 23"	Q	2	**Long cleat,** ¾ × 2½ × 44"	CC	2	**Drawer side,** ¾ × 4⅝ × 23"
F	1	**Back,** ¼ × 44½ × 66½"	R	2	**Short cleat,** ¾ × 2½ × 23⅜"	DD	1	**Divider,** ¾ × 4⅛ × 22¾"
G	2	**Face stile,** ¾ × 2½ × 66½"	S	1	**Front crown,** ⁹⁄₁₆ × 2⅛ × 49½" *	EE	1	**Drawer bottom,** ¼ × 22½ × 38½"
H	1	**Top rail,** ¾ × 9⅝ × 40¼"	T	2	**Side crown,** ⁹⁄₁₆ × 2⅛ × 25⅜" *	FF	1	**Cap,** ¾ × 25⁵⁄₁₆ × 47⅞"
I	1	**Face rail,** ¾ × 2½ × 40¼"	U	1	**Dentil,** ¼ × ¾ × 120"	GG	2	**Side nosing,** ¾ × 1 × 26⁵⁄₁₆"
J	1	**Bottom rail,** ¾ × 2⅛ × 40¼"	V	2	**Outer stile,** ¾ × 2½ × 49¹⁄₁₆"	HH	1	**Front nosing,** ¾ × 1× 49⅞"
K	1	**Base front,** ¾ × 4¾ × 47"	W	2	**Inner stile,** ¾ × 2½ × 52⁷⁄₁₆"	II	2	**Closet rod,** 1¼"-dia. × 21¼"
L	2	**Base side,** ¾ × 4¾ × 24⅞"	X	2	**Lower rail,** ¾ × 2½ × 20⁷⁄₁₆"			

Note: All wood is oak except Side (A), Top/bottom (B), Partition (C), Support (E), Back (F), Panel (Z), Bottom (EE), and Cap (FF), which are oak plywood, and Closet rod (II), which is pine.

Misc.: Glue; #6 x 1¼", ⅜" flathead wood screws; #0, 20 biscuits; spring overlay hinges, door/drawer pulls, closet rod hangers, #2, 4, 8 finish nails; drawer slides, 22". * Approximate measurements, pieces must be custom-cut.

10 Clamp face frame to carcass with pipe clamps and allow to dry.

Making the doors

1 Cut outer stiles (V), inner stiles (W), upper rails (Y), and lower rails (X) to length and width from ¾"-thick oak.
2 Use a beam compass to mark a 49"-radius arc on top of upper rails, starting at the top of one corner.
3 Cut a 2½ × ¼"-deep rabbet on both faces of each end of upper and lower rails to leave a ¼"-thick tenon at each end.
4 Mark a 46½"-radius arc on the bottom of each upper rail running from the same end as the 49" arc and ending at the tenon shoulder on the opposite end. The arcs form rails that are 2½" wide.
5 Cut the arcs using a bandsaw. Note: bottoms of the tenons are cut perpendicular to shoulders so they do not follow the arc.
6 Sand on a stationary sander.
7 Cut a ¼ × 2½"-deep mortise centered in top and bottom edges of each end of inner and outer stiles.
8 Dry-fit stiles and rails.
9 Mark radius of upper rail across the ends of the stiles. Radius-cut the ends with a bandsaw.
10 Round over the inside edge of the outer face of each stile and rail with a ¼"-radius roundover bit.
11 Use a router to cut a ¼ × ⅜"-deep groove on inside edge of stiles and rails to hold panels.
12 Cut panels (Z) to length and width from ¼"-thick oak plywood.

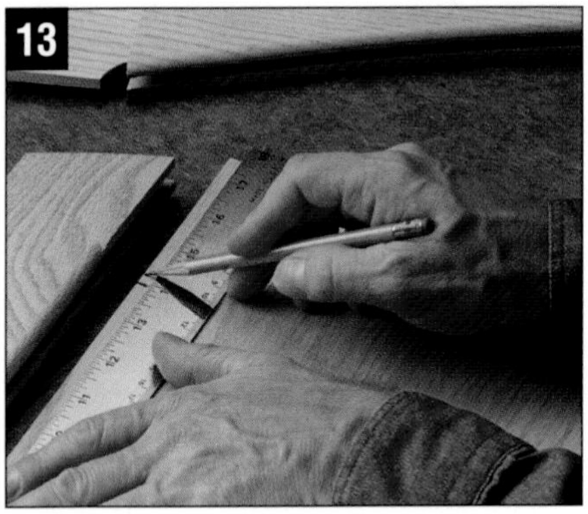

13 Slide each panel into corresponding door frame with upper rail removed. Clamp stiles to lower rail. Square the frame. Mark locations of upper rail mortises on the edges of the plywood. Remove panel from frame. Mark a point ¼" above mortise marks; then use top rail as a template to draw curve on panel. Cut curve on a bandsaw.
14 Sand rails, stiles, and panels to finished smoothness.
15 Apply glue to mortises and tenons. Assemble doors; then clamp and let dry.

Making the base

1 Cut base front (K), base back (M), side (L), long cleat (Q) and short cleat (R) to length and width from ¾"-thick oak.
2 Miter-cut both ends of base front and one end of each base side to make 45° miter joints in the front.
3 Transfer grid design from *Diagram* to base front and sides. Cut shapes on a bandsaw.
4 Sand top and bottom edges to finished smoothness.
5 Cut slots for #0 biscuits in the ends of long cleats and sides of the short cleats to join with biscuits.
6 Apply glue to the joints. Clamp short cleats to long cleats. Let dry.
7 Clamp base front, sides, and back to cleat frame. Drill countersink, shank, and pilot holes for #6 flathead wood screws through cleats into base.
8 Attach base back and front to the cleat frame with glue and #8 × 1¼" wood screws. Be sure mitered corners of front line up perfectly with the corners of the frame.
9 Attach sides to frame with glue and #8 × 1¼" wood screws. Start with mitered corners, then work back to ends. Clamp and let dry.

10 Reinforce corners by driving #4 finish nails through joints from each direction at the miters to cross-nail joints, and by nailing

the sides to back. Set nails and fill holes with wood putty.
11 Sand base to smoothness.
12 Cut plinth front (N), plinth side (O), and plinth back (P) from ¾"-thick oak.
13 Rout a ⅝"-radius cove in front edge of base front and base sides.
14 Miter-cut both ends of top and front end of each side.
15 Cut slots for #0 biscuits in miters and at ends of the sides for biscuit joints.
16 Assemble plinth with biscuits and glue. Clamp, check for square, and let dry.
17 Sand plinth to smoothness.
18 Attach plinth to base by cutting slots in top edges of the base and bottom of the plinth for biscuit joints. Allow a ⅛" reveal at the front and sides of plinth. Apply glue. Clamp and let dry.

Assembling the cabinet

1 Lay carcass on its back on a flat worktable.
2 Center plinth/base against bottom of the carcass. Back of carcass will be flush with back of the plinth/base. Allow plinth to extend ¾" past carcass on sides and front.
3 Drill countersink, shank, and pilot holes for #8 flathead wood screws through the plinth into the bottom of the carcass.
4 Drive #8 × 1¼" screws through holes to fasten base to the carcass.

Making the molding

1 Cut or plane stock to ¾ × ¾" thick for side nosing (GG) and front nosing (HH).
2 Rout a classical profile along one edge of the front and side nosing.
3 Cut the cap (FF) from ¾"-thick oak plywood.
4 Miter-cut the front and side nosing to length and attach to the cap with biscuits and glue. Cross-nail the miters.
5 Sand the cap with nosing to finished smoothness.
6 Center the cap over the cabinet and attach with # 6 finish nails.
7 Cut or plane stock to ¾ × ¼" thick for dentil molding (U). Three 48"-long pieces will provide all the dentil needed.
8 Set up a tablesaw to cut ¾ × ¾" dadoes on the face of the dentil. Leave a ¾"-wide space between each dado.
9 Sand dentil strips to finished smoothness.
10 Miter-cut 2¼" crown molding to length to fit the cabinet front and sides.
11 Place the front crown molding against the cap and cabinet so the beveled edges are flat against both cap and cabinet. Fasten the front crown with #4 finish nails driven into cap and the cabinet every 4".

12 Miter-cut dentil strips to fit across cabinet front with mitered corners. Center the front strip so miters occur in dentil blocks equally on both ends. Attach the dentil strips to the cabinet so the top is tight against the bottom of the crown. Fasten the dentil with #4 finish nails. Repeat this procedure with side crown and dentil.

Making the drawers

1 Cut false front (AA), drawer front/back (BB), drawer side (CC), and divider (DD).
2 Cut ¼ × ¼" grooves starting ¼" from the bottom of inside of each drawer side and front, running the length of each piece.
3 Cut a ¼ × ¾"-deep dado centered in each end of all drawer fronts and backs for drawer corner joints. Place each front and back on tablesaw with inside face down. Make a ⅜ × ⅜" rabbet cut to form a ¼ × ⅜" tenon.
4 Cut ¼ × ⅜"-deep dadoes ¼" from the inside ends of each drawer side for corner joints.
5 Cut a ¼ × ⅜"-deep dado centered on inside of each front/back to hold divider.
6 Cut drawer bottom (EE) from ¼"-thick oak plywood.
7 Sand drawer parts to smoothness.
8 Assemble drawer around drawer bottom, using glue. Clamp, check for square, and let dry.
9 Attach the divider to the front/back with glue. Do not glue the divider to the drawer bottom.
10 Install the drawer glides using manufacturer's instructions. Test-fit the pieces.
11 Rout a ⅜" Roman ogee profile around drawer false front.
12 Drill evenly spaced ⅛"-diameter holes through false front at drawer pull locations.
13 Place the false front against the drawer in the cabinet. Align the false front to overlay the stiles and rails by ⅜". Secure false front to the drawer temporarily by driving #6 × 1¼" screws through the false front into the drawer at the pull locations.
14 Remove drawer and false front. Extend holes for fastening the pulls by drilling through drawer front using the holes in the false front as a guide.
15 Drill countersink and shank holes for #6 × 1¼" screws in drawer front.
16 Apply glue to front and false front, then use the drawer pull bolts to align the two pieces. Fasten the front to the false front with #6 × 1¼" screws.
17 Finish the armoire as desired.

Attaching the hardware

1 Install the hinges on the doors.
2 Drill the holes for screws to mount hinges to frame using a vix bit. Attach hinges with screws.
3 Drill holes in door stiles for pulls. Install custom door pulls.
4 Install magnetic catches on doors and partition.
5 Cut closet rods (II) from 1¼"-diameter material.
6 Install the closet rod with hangers centered on the sides and partition 12" from the top.

INDEX OF TIPS

METRIC CONVERSIONS

U.S. Units to Metric Equivalents

To convert from	Multiply by	To get
Inches	25.4	Millimeters (mm)
Inches	2.54	Centimeters (cm)
Feet	30.48	Centimeters (cm)
Feet	0.3048	Meters (m)

Metric Units to U.S. Equivalents

To convert from	Multiply by	To get
Millimeters	0.0394	Inches
Centimeters	0.3937	Inches
Centimeters	0.0328	Feet
Meters	3.2808	Feet